Words of VALEDICTION *and* REMEMBRANCE

Canadian Epitaphs of the Second World War

Eric McGeer

Vanwell Publishing Limited
St. Catharines, Ontario

Vanwell Publishing acknowledges the financial support of the Government of Canada through the Book Publishing Industry Development Program for our publishing activities.

Design and layout: Carol Matsuyama
Cover design: Renée Giguère
Front cover photo: Reichswald War Cemetery (Steve Douglas)

Vanwell Publishing Limited
1 Northrup Crescent
P.O. Box 2131
St. Catharines, Ontario L2R 7S2
sales@vanwell.com
tel: 905-937-3100
fax: 905-937-1760

Printed in Canada

Library and Archives Canada Cataloguing in Publication
McGeer, Eric, 1955–
Valediction and remembrance : Canadian epitaphs of the Second World War / Eric McGeer.
Includes bibliographical references and index.
ISBN 978-1-55125-095-3
1. Epitaphs—Canada. 2. Soldier's monuments—Canada. 3.
Epitaphs—Europe. 4. Soldiers' monuments—Europe. 5. World War, 1939–1945—Monuments—Europe. 6. World War, 1939–1945—Registers of dead—Canada. I. Title.
D763.I82O77   2007   940.54'654   C2007-905560-5

Table of Contents

Stone-cutters fighting time with marble, you foredefeated
Challengers of oblivion
Eat cynical earnings, knowing rock splits, records fall down,
The square-limbed Roman letters
Scale in the thaws, wear in the rain. The poet as well
Builds his monument mockingly;
For man will be blotted out, the blithe earth die, the brave sun
Die blind, his heart blackening:
Yet stones have stood for a thousand years,
And pained thoughts found
The honey peace in old poems.

Robinson Jeffers, *To the Stone-Cutters* (1925)

Introduction and Acknowledgments

WE WHO WATCHED THAT LIFE SO BRIGHT & BRIEF
MARK THIS MARBLE WITH OUR LOVE & GRIEF.
Warrant Officer II David Lachlan Bain, RCAF, 30.3.43 (age 27)
[ESBJERG (FOURFELT) CEMETERY, DENMARK]

OUR DEAR NORBERT. ABOVE HIS LOWLY GRAVE WE WRITE
THESE SIMPLE WORDS "HE DIED TO SAVE."
Private Norbert MacIntyre, NNSH, 23.3.45 (age 25)
[GROESBEEK CANADIAN WAR CEMETERY, THE NETHERLANDS]

WITH THOUGHTS AND TEARS WE MARK THIS GRAVE WHERE LIES OUR SON.
Flying Officer Donald Stuart Maxwell Bowes, RCAF, 31.3.45 (age 21)
[BECKLINGEN WAR CEMETERY, GERMANY]

THE IDEA OF WRITING THIS BOOK developed out of a trip to Normandy in 1998 to fulfill a longstanding desire to see the D-Day beaches and the battlefields where Canada's soldiers, including a number of veterans I had met over the years, fought so bravely during the summer of 1944. No doubt I am neither the first nor the last Canadian to find a visit to Normandy a profoundly moving experience, one that took me far beyond the histories of the campaign in my understanding of the terrain, the nature of the fighting, and the cost of the Allied victory. While walking through the Canadian war cemetery at Bény-sur-Mer, I came upon a headstone bearing a personal inscription in Greek which from my background in Classics I recognised as a quotation from the *Iliad*. The lines made an ennobling farewell to a young man fallen on a foreign battlefield in the service of his country; but like the isolated strains in Finnish, Hungarian, Icelandic, and Hebrew sounding among the larger chorus in English and French, they would surely be lost on all but a very few visitors. One thought led to another as I read the words of parting engraved on the headstones, drawn from Scripture, hymns, literature, popular songs of the day, or composed by next of kin who had obviously thought carefully about their valedictions. It struck me that in their abundance and diversity these individual expressions of sorrow and consolation, touching, heartfelt, and permanent, spoke more poignantly than any memorial for the burden of loss borne by thousands of parents, wives, and children for the rest of their lives. This impression grew as I visited the other Canadian war cemeteries and came upon simple yet trenchant reminders of the particularity of each loss:

HE WAS ONLY ONE IN A MILLION, BUT HE WAS MINE. EVER REMEMBERED BY MOTHER.
Rifleman Donald Melford Darby, RRR, 28.9.44 (age 21) [CALAIS]

JOHNNY, WHY DID YOU GO AWAY? NEVER FORGOTTEN. MOTHER
Private John Albert Vandenbrooks, RHLI, 30.9.44 (age 18) [SCHOONSELHOF]

THAT GRIEF IS COMMON DOES NOT MAKE ONE'S OWN LESS BITTER.
Private Murray Smith, RC, 20.10.44 (age 21) [ADEGEM]

HIS HOMELAND WEEPS FOR SACRIFICE SO COSTLY.
HIS MOTHER WEEPS THAT HE RETURNS NO MORE.
Private Thomas Herbert Harrington, CH, 1.11.44 (age 19) [BERGEN-OP-ZOOM]

A book listing and discussing Canadian epitaphs from the Second World War seemed worthwhile on several grounds. It would put before interested readers a meaningful testimonial to the efforts and sacrifice of an earlier generation, not only the soldiers, sailors, and airmen who lost their lives on active service, but the families back in Canada who coped each day with the possibility of losing those they loved and then had to face the terrible reality that their worst fears had come to pass. Such a collection would also gather into one place inscriptions from many war cemeteries, some of which, like Bény-sur-Mer, are well known and much visited, whereas others, such as Ravenna or Kiel, attract scant attention despite the number of Canadian headstones they contain. And even though the epitaphs have lost none of their force and clarity, they speak with the voice of a different time and thus require some explanation of their sources and context.

The following considerations have guided the composition of this work. It became clear early on that it was neither practical nor desirable to list every inscription, much as each epitaph of a fallen serviceman deserves recording, since they run into the thousands, are often formulaic or commonplace (*Gone but not forgotten, Rest in peace*), and in many cases record details of limited interest (*Son of . . . born in . . .*). I have taken epitaphs from as many cemeteries as I could reach in northwest Europe and Italy, and with the generous (and gratefully acknowledged) assistance of Steve Douglas, founder of the Maple Leaf Legacy Project, consulted hundreds of photos, but there are Canadian war graves scattered throughout southeast Asia, India, North Africa and other distant lands that are simply too far-flung to reach. Readers will notice that despite their vital contribution to the war effort few members of the Royal Canadian Navy or the Merchant Navy are represented in the collection of epitaphs, since most sailors were lost or buried at sea and so have no known grave.

To offer a representative sample of the epitaphs, and to elaborate on their significance to contemporary readers now two generations removed from the war, I have in all but one chapter begun by citing epitaphs found in a particular military cemetery and extracting a theme or subject for discussion, usually with reference to epitaphs from other cemeteries and, where comparison is instructive, from the First World War.

The book consists of two parts. The first and longer part opens with an introductory essay on the Bény-sur-Mer Canadian War Cemetery which reflects on the epitaphs in their setting and their place in the national memory of the war. From there the focus shifts to the Dieppe Canadian War Cemetery and the response of the epitaphs to a tragedy that has never ceased to haunt Canadian memory. Two chapters then examine the influence of Great War commemoration and the longer tradition of gravestone inscriptions dating from Antiquity in shaping the diction, content, and consolatory themes of the epitaphs. The next chapter deals with the exceptional body of inscriptions on the graves of airmen which allude to the experience of aerial warfare and the pride of the RCAF crews who fought "in the burning sky." This leads to a chapter on the professions of loyalty—to country, faith, family, to unit and comrades—that suggest the motives or commitment that lay behind the serviceman's decision to enlist and to do his duty. The first part ends with a selection of inscriptions allowing the words of the families to speak for themselves, placing before the reader an uninterrupted sequence of valedictions recording not only the sacrifice of so many young lives but also, and just as movingly, the fortitude and dignity of the bereaved.

Where the first part concentrates on the traditions and themes within the English Canadian epitaphs of the Second World War, following lines of inquiry opened by Jonathan Vance's magisterial *Death So Noble*, the second part singles out three groups of inscriptions which should modify our understanding of the attitudes towards the war among Canada's French and ethnic populations. The contribution of French Canadians to the national war effort has been obscured amidst the controversies over conscription and Quebec's place in Canada; however, the epitaphs of French Canadian servicemen offer valuable, overlooked evidence for the beliefs and principles that they or their families felt worth defending. Similarly, the inscriptions in foreign languages supply important evidence for the reaction to the conflict among Canada's many ethnic minorities. Nearly twenty years ago a conference convened to discuss the minorities in wartime Canada concluded, in perversely Canadian fashion, that "Canada's war . . . was not their war," yet the epitaphs supply compelling testimony to the contrary, that the members of various ethnic groups did in fact feel that it was "their war," both out of loyalty to their adoptive country and to their ancestral lands. The revisiting of French and ethnic Canadian attitudes paves the way for a chapter presenting the epitaphs of Jewish servicemen which underline the loyalty to Canada shown by a religious minority whose rate of enlistment was the highest of any ethnic group, as well as the readiness of young Jewish men and women to rally to the defence of their people. The record of their sacrifice and commemoration gives them an honoured place in the history of Jewish resistance to the evils of Nazism.

The final chapter returns to Normandy, to the largest Canadian cemetery of the Second World War at Bretteville-sur-Laize. Just as the first chapter was inspired by an inscription drawn from Homer, the last comes to rest on lines from Virgil's *Aeneid* engraved on a number of Canadian headstones. As the Second World War passes from living into historical memory, the Virgilian echoes enhance the timelessness of the war cemeteries and the enduring claim of the epitaphs on the sympathies of succeeding generations who may see in this record of human suffering and courage analogies with their own time.

My main purpose in writing this book has been to inspire Canadians travelling abroad to visit the war cemeteries where their forebears lie at rest and to look with renewed interest at the story that the monuments and epitaphs combine to tell. It also aims to fill a gap. The remarkable history of the Imperial War Graves Commission (the Commonwealth War Graves Commission since 1960), which began with Fabian Ware's singlehanded efforts to register the graves of the fallen and evolved into a world-wide organisation overseeing the commemoration of 1.7 million servicemen in accordance with the precepts established by its founders in 1917, has been well described, notably in Philip Longworth's *The Unending Vigil* and Mark Quinlan's *Remembrance*. So have the war cemeteries and memorials honouring the Canadian dead of two World Wars in Herbert Fairlie Wood and John Swettenham's *Silent Witnesses*, G. Kingsley Ward and T.A. Edwin Gibson's *Courage Remembered*, and Robert Shipley's *To Mark Our Place*. Although the provision made by the Commission's founders to allow relatives of the fallen to contribute a short valedictory inscription is duly mentioned in studies of the forms and rituals of remembrance, to my knowledge only one book, John Laffin's collection of Australian epitaphs of the Great War, *We Will Remember Them*, has addressed the thousands of individual farewells, from every layer of society, that constitute a record unique in history. While the focus here is on Canadian epitaphs, I have occasionally introduced British, Australian, or South African examples for sake of comparison and to draw the reader's attention to equally rich, and largely untapped, bodies of evidence for the response of fellow Commonwealth populations to the immeasurable personal tragedies of the wars.

A word on my approach to the epitaphs. "When a stranger has walked round a country church-yard and glanced his eye over so many brief chronicles, as the tomb-stones usually contain, of faithful wives, tender husbands, dutiful children, and good men of all classes, he will be tempted to exclaim . . . 'Where are all the bad people buried?'" Thus William Wordsworth in his *Essays Upon Epitaphs*, acknowledging the tendency in funerary inscriptions to idealise the departed and to make more of them in death than they were in life. *We loved him in life too little, we love him in death too well*, warns a Canadian epitaph from the First World War; and in reading the epitaphs of either war we should be careful not to accept every one at face value. Not all soldiers were paragons of virtue, ready to lay down their lives for lofty principles in calm assurance of earthly renown or heavenly reward. Some, of course, would hardly qualify as model citizens, and from the blank spaces on the headstones we may infer that certain of them were no great loss to anyone. The language of the epitaphs can also be flowery, sentimental, imitative, or prone to cliché. Many were modelled on generic types used by funeral homes or on condolence cards. These precautions, however, are offset by two considerations worth bearing in mind. First, no matter what they or their motives were, these young men were volunteers who died in the service of their country and lost the chance to fulfill the promise of their lives or to make something more of themselves. Their epitaphs warrant a respectful, if not uncritical, reading. Second, even if the recurrence of certain phrases tends to dull the reader's appreciation, when such a phrase appears on the graves of two brothers, an only son, or a dimly remembered father, it reminds us that most people are at a loss for words in the face of overwhelming sorrow. Understandably, they rely on formulaic expressions hallowed by usage and custom. In the circumstances, it is all the more impressive that so many next of kin did contribute inscriptions deeply affecting in their directness and emotional honesty. With this in mind, I have tried to sift through the epitaphs to indicate their general range while concentrating on examples memorable for their effect or illustrative of particular trends.

The inscriptions on the headstones were engraved in a specially designed font. While tacitly correcting the odd spelling mistake or supplying punctuation, I have presented the inscriptions above the details of the serviceman's name, rank, unit or force, date of death, age (where noted), and, where relevant, decorations. Square brackets enclose the name of the war cemetery where the serviceman is buried; where no cemetery is noted, the reader may assume that the epitaph comes from the one chosen as the setting of the chapter. Canadian regiments and units have been cited in abbreviated form (e.g., SHC for Seaforth Highlanders of Canada), while British or other foreign regiments are cited in full to help distinguish them from Canadian examples. A list of all abbreviations will be found in the appendix. The Canadian Virtual War Memorial (http://www.vac-acc.gc.ca/remembers) has proven to be a most useful tool in verifying the information concerning each casualty. The site is ever expanding as relatives of the fallen contribute memorabilia, and readers may wish to check for photos or documents pertaining to a particular serviceman. The Commonwealth War Graves Commission also has an informative website (http://www.cwgc. org) containing a register of all Commonwealth casualties and military cemeteries as well as several sections describing the Commission's tasks, historical exhibits, and publications. The staff of the Commission responded promptly and helpfully to all my inquiries, and I am pleased to take the opportunity to record my gratitude for their assistance, and my deep admiration for the work they do.

The inscriptions in French and over a dozen foreign languages are given in the original and in translation. For their help with these epitaphs, I offer my thanks to Professor Borje Vahamaki of the University of Toronto (Finnish), Ms. Andrea Kovacs of Victoria College (Hungarian), Professor Libby Garshowitz of the University of Toronto (Hebrew), Ms. Janice Chan of Celta (Gaelic), and Dr. Kristin Johansdottir of the University of Manitoba (Icelandic). Mr. Bernard Mikofsky helped with several valedictions in Czech and Ukrainian which required some reconstruction, and I thank him for confirming the translations of all inscriptions from Slavic languages. Translations from other languages are mine, as are any errors they may contain.

I am equally grateful to the many people who have helped me along the way. My thanks go first to Mr. Ben Kooter and Ms. Angela Dobler of Vanwell Publishing for accepting this work for publication and for graciously extending the deadline for submission when our beloved daughter Sarah arrived, appropriately enough, on November 11, 2006. All Canadians with an interest in their country's military past are indebted to Vanwell for its support of authors writing in this field. For their many thoughtful comments and suggestions concerning the religious aspects of the epitaphs I thank Canon Milton Barry of Grace Church on the Hill, and Rabbi Baruch Frydman-Kohl of Beth Tzedec Congregation. An American friend and colleague, John Nesbitt, read several chapters and offered pertinent advice from an outside perspective. Mme Hélène Vallée of the Canadian Jewish Congress kindly sent photocopies of two booklets containing valuable information on Jewish Canadian servicemen. Finally, I wish to record my gratitude to Carol Matsuyama for artfully laying out an unusual manuscript, and to my friend Matt Symes for making a number of photos usable for publication.

It is my good fortune to teach at St. Clement's School among a staff I respect and admire for their knowledge and dedication. The school's principal, Ms. Patricia Parisi, allowed generous leave time so that I could complete this and other projects; my colleague Dr. Catherine Danter put her expertise in architectural history at my disposal on many occasions; and my fellow history teachers, David McClellan and Glenn Domina, read and commented on a number of chapters. A former student, Candace Mak, deserves special thanks for transcribing the Canadian epitaphs in the Sai Wan War Cemetery in Hong Kong. Her willingness to go well out of her way on someone else's behalf exemplifies the finest traditions of our school, whose students, with their high level of character and ability, make teaching the most rewarding profession imaginable. I remember with particular fondness the students in my Latin classes who graduated in 2002 and 2003, an interesting, lively, and promising group of young women whom I have missed very much ever since they set off for university.

To my dear wife Sylvia, I am most grateful of all. She has accompanied me to all manner of remote places, open to all the elements, as we roamed here, there and elsewhere in search of some very elusive destinations. Her constant interest and encouragement have made all the difference. Were this book not intended primarily as a tribute to the fallen, I would gladly dedicate it to her for all she has done.

THEIR STORY LIVES ON, WOVEN INTO THE STUFF OF OTHER MEN'S LIVES.
Captain Elmes Patrick Trevelyan Green, PPCLI, 1.5.44 (age 30) [NAPLES]

Aan onze Canadeesche bevrijders—"To our Canadian liberators"—reads the inscription on a monument placed at the back of the Canadian war cemetery at Bergen-op-Zoom. Having travelled and lived in the Netherlands, I have met many people who lived through the five years of German occupation and who remembered the arrival of Canadian soldiers in their towns and villages as an awakening from a long nightmare. The intense joy and relief of liberation felt by the Dutch in 1945 were shared in the other countries released by the Allied armies from the grip of a barbaric regime. The words *"for freedom," "for liberty," "for democracy"* found in so many inscriptions can sometimes lose their force through repetition; but to the people who have suffered occupation, these terms have a depth of meaning that those who have never lost their freedom will never know. The reputation that Canada enjoys in the world is more than half owing to the men and women who "laid the world away and gave up the years to be" to restore freedom and the hope of a world made new. To them, and to those Canadians continuing in their example today, this epitaph makes the most fitting dedication:

**TO THE EVER GLORIOUS MEMORY OF THE ONE WHO DIED AND
TO THE UNDYING HONOUR OF THOSE WHO SERVED.**
Sergeant Joseph William Lapp, 48th HC, 3.10.43 (age 31) [BARI]

CHAPTER ONE

Words of Valediction and Remembrance
Bény-sur-Mer Canadian War Cemetery, Normandy

THE WAR IS OVER. SLEEP ON, DEAR SON.
Rifleman Lant Freeman, RWR, *8.6.44 (age 22)*

The Bény-sur-Mer Canadian War Cemetery lies at the top of a gently rising hill overlooking the landing zones assigned to the 3rd Canadian Infantry Division and its supporting units on June 6, 1944. To the north, the towns of Courseulles-sur Mer, Bernières-sur-Mer, and St. Aubin-sur-Mer, the latter two distinguished by mediaeval church spires profiled against the contrasting blue of the English Channel and the sky, punctuate the stretch of Normandy coastline codenamed Juno Beach. In the rolling farmland around the cemetery, church spires also mark the first places liberated as the Canadians pushed inland: Graye-sur-Mer, Banville, and Ste Croix-sur-Mer along an arc to the northwest, Reviers and Amblie to the southwest; Tailleville due east, and the village of Bény-sur-Mer itself, to the southeast.

These towns and villages have stood for centuries, but if their names strike a chord today, it is for a few hours of savage fighting that passed over them one spring morning six decades ago. Yet as one traces the path of the Canadian army in the course of the Normandy campaign, the past comes beckoning at every step. The settlements and rivers which Canadian soldiers passed bear names transformed into French from Celtic, Latin, and Norse origins. The Maple Leaf route through Caen to Falaise and on to Elbeuf and Rouen retraces the path of the armies led by Edward III and Henry V during the Hundred Years War. During the 1430s, Sir John Fastolf, one of the historical figures subsumed into Shakespeare's Falstaff, was Lord Lieutenant of Caen, the gateway to Normandy which Canadians would pay a heavy price to wrest from German hands. The *route nationale* 158 which formed the axis of the Canadian advance to Falaise follows a road first laid out by the Romans; and the castle at Falaise looming over the scenes of the gruelling final stages of the battle of Normandy rests on the site of an earlier castle where William the Conqueror was born. *Nos a Gulielmo victi victoris patriam liberavimus*—"we who were conquered by William have liberated the land of the Conqueror"—declares the inscription over the memorial to the missing at the British war cemetery at Bayeux, no more than a few minutes' walk from the museum where the Bayeux Tapestry depicts the story of the Duke of Normandy's invasion of England in 1066.

A sequence of scenes in the Tapestry eerily prefigures the reverse invasion staged nine centuries later. The preparation of William's fleet, the loading of provisions and equipment, and the disembarkation in England anticipate the construction of the landing craft and specialised transport for the Allied armada and the effort necessary to keep the armies supplied once they had secured a lodgement on the Normandy coast. Troubling parallels appear in other scenes. A woman and her child look on as William's soldiers set fire to a house in a scene calling to mind the gutted churches in Caen, left unrestored in memory of the old city's destruction by Allied bombs in 1944, or a grave in the churchyard at Soulangy of three French children killed in the bombardments which preceded the attacks on Falaise. The Tapestry's graphic depiction of the carnage at Hastings hints at sights which veterans of Normandy prefer to forget—the crumpled bodies of the dead, the burnt tanks and vehicles, crashed aircraft, the awful detritus of modern warfare.

As the summer of 1944 fades from living memory into history, memorials preserving the record of Canada's part in the Normandy battles have come to stand among the monuments of other ages. A plaque honouring servicemen from Ontario is affixed to the 12th-century Chapelle St-Georges within the ducal chateau at Caen. Cairns in village squares commemorate Canadian soldiers and regiments, and local signs inscribed *Rue de Colonel Charles Petch, Avenue des Glengarriens, Impasse des Regina Rifles* mark roads and laneways. Interspersed among these testaments of heroism and gratitude are others recalling dark episodes: the murder of Canadian prisoners of war at the Abbaye Ardenne and the Chateau d'Audrieu, the decimation of the Black Watch at Verrières Ridge, and the fate of the British Columbia and Algonquin regiments on a lonely hill near the hamlet of Estrées-la-Campagne.

The presence of Canadian memorials in Normandy, a crossroads in the history of France and England, also evokes the unique character of the Canadian army that fought there. Alone of the nations engaged in the Normandy campaign, Canada was the heir to the traditions of two founding countries, and within her army's ranks were men mindful of their ancestral ties. The language and faith of the predominantly Norman settlers who peopled New France endure in the valedictory words chosen by the parents of Private Leo Joseph Quevillon, a French Canadian from Timmins who died on July 31, 1944, at age 21: *Nous l'avons donné à Dieu pour le salut de France. Son père et sa mère. Canada (We gave him to God for the salvation of France. His father and mother. Canada).* Similar professions of fidelity to their heritage are found on the headstones of many Canadian soldiers of French descent, just as the first words of Lance Corporal William Gordon Thompson's epitaph, *For Canada, King and Empire,* proclaim the shared allegiance of English-Canadian soldiers to their own and to their mother country.

Set within a landscape where the echoes of the past resound, the Bény-sur-Mer war cemetery draws the visitor from the present back into the Norman summer of 1944. The entrance way leads through a corridor of maple trees to the Stone of Remembrance, placed between two flanking towers. Beyond this imposing threshold, the symmetrical lines ordering the layout of the cemetery reinforce the impression of military precision and dignity. In the centre stands the Cross of Sacrifice, at the intersection of two aisles which divide the cemetery into quarters. The headstones of the fallen are deployed in sixteen sections, perfectly aligned along a frontal or a diagonal perspective, and face the beholder like an army drawn up on parade. The colours of the flowers and shrubs planted along each row relieve the uniform white of the headstones, and the trees planted between sections cast shadows in the sunlight. Shrouded from the sight and sounds of the outside world by the trees clustered around its precincts, the cemetery conveys a sense of isolation and permanence, of a place complete in itself. There are times when silence reigns, broken only by the singing of birds or the sighing of the wind.

PEACE, MY SON, MY PEACE I LEAVE WITH YOU.
GOD IS THE MESSENGER OF LOVE BETWEEN THEE AND ME.
Private Robert Cameron Milburn, NS(NB)R, 8.6.44 (age 19)

"AND JESUS SAID, PEACE BE UNTO YOU." THE STARS WILL SHINE DOWN ON YOU, SON.
Sergeant William George Murray QORC, 9.7.44 (age 24)

THINE IS A PERFECT REST, SECURE AND DEEP.
Flight Sergeant Joseph Pearson Duns, RCAF, 7.6.44 (age 19)

MAY THE DOVE OF PEACE FOREVER HOVER OVER OUR LOVED ONE WHO GAVE HIS ALL.
Flight Lieutenant Paul Gilbert Johnson DFC, RCAF, 18.7.44 (age 24)

"THAT THEY MAY REST FROM THEIR LABOURS: AND THEIR WORKS DO FOLLOW THEM."
REV. XIV. 13
Lieutenant Bruce Herbert McRoberts, QORC, 25.7.44 (age 30)

BLESSED SLEEP AFTER THE BATTLE.
Private Fred Vincent Bigelow, NNSH, 8.7.44 (age 19)

All but five of the 2,048 servicemen buried here are Canadian. In row upon row, the recurrence of maple leaves carved into the headstones commands the eye. Below this national emblem, a sequence of details identifies each soldier: enlistment number (for privates and non-commissioned officers), rank, name, regiment, date of death, and, in most cases, age. The headstone contained space for a cross to be engraved below this register, but if the soldier had indicated no religious affiliation, or if the family so wished, the religious symbol was omitted. Families also had the option to choose or to compose a personal inscription, not to exceed 66 characters, to serve as a last farewell. This was inscribed in the lower register of the headstone, beneath the cross.

The headstones have their own stories to tell. Each one retrieves the name of a soldier from the anonymous casualty figures cited in the accounts of the Normandy battles—359 Canadians killed on D-Day, 658 in the first week of fighting to establish the bridgehead, 262 in the attack on Caen on July 8, and so on. In many cases the combination of a soldier's date of death with his regiment points to the action in which he lost his life. The collation of June 6 with the Queen's Own Rifles of Canada places Private Robert Graham Burnett among the men killed in the costly assault at Bernières-sur-Mer. The date June 7 and the regiment North Nova Scotia Highlanders put Private Lambert Avery Fleet among the 84 soldiers killed in the vicious first encounter with the 12th SS Panzer in the hamlet of Authie. On June 8, a harrowing day in the history of the Royal Winnipeg Rifles, 19-year old Corporal James Lierris Kyle was one of the soldiers taken prisoner in the village of Putot-en-Bessin and subsequently murdered by his captors at the Chateau d'Audrieu. Private Frank Keleher was one of the North Shores from New Brunswick who died in the attacks on Carpiquet airport on July 4. These and other convergences of dates and regiments—the First Hussars and the Queen's Own Rifles on June 11 at Le Mesnil-Patry, the Highland Light Infantry of Canada on July 8 at Buron—chart the progression of the fighting, measured not in lines on a map or in objectives gained, but in the aggregate of individual lives lost.

The headstones reveal different degrees of loss. Some note the death of an only son, in one instance of an only child, whereas others bear witness to the compounded tragedy suffered by a distressingly high number of families. No less than twelve pairs of brothers lie buried in the Bény-sur-Mer cemetery, a total of double bereavement unmatched in any other Commonwealth cemetery of the Second World War. Six families had to cope with the loss of two sons on the same day in the same action. The Westlake family of Toronto lost one son on June 7, and two more just four days later. The tally does not end here. Five soldiers in Bény-sur-Mer have a brother buried in one of the other Normandy cemeteries; eight have brothers at rest in Italy, Belgium, or Holland. One family, the Wagners of Teeterville, Ontario, has a son buried in Bény-sur-Mer, a second on the road to Falaise in the Bretteville-sur-Laize Canadian war cemetery, and a third in the Groesbeek Canadian war cemetery in Holland. Another family, the Lanteignes of Caraquet, New Brunswick, lost three sons between June 12 and September 15, 1944; one is buried in Bény-sur-Mer, the second in Bretteville-sur-Laize, and the third in the Coriano Ridge war cemetery in Italy. Yet a third family, the Kimmels of Milner, British Columbia, lost two sons ten days apart in Normandy and a third in Italy six months later.

Nineteen headstones bear a maple leaf and a cross, and the simple inscription, *A soldier of the Second World War, A Canadian regiment, Known unto God*, reprising the formula composed by Rudyard Kipling for the myriads of unidentified dead of the 1914–1918 war. Sadder even than these are the headstones recording the lonely details of a name, regiment, and date of death, but no age, no cross or inscription, as though the soldier had no attachments, nothing to embrace his memory, no one to mourn his passing.

Then there are the Jewish soldiers whose places are marked by a Star of David. Two of them, Private Joseph Gertel of the North Nova Scotia Highlanders and Rifleman Israel Freedman of the Royal Winnipeg Rifles, rest beneath headstones which carry inscriptions in Hebrew:

HERE LIES JOSEPH MORDECHAI, SCION OF LEVI, THE SON OF ISRAEL AND MIRIAM GERTEL, WHO FELL IN BATTLE IN FRANCE ON THE SEVENTEENTH DAY OF TAMMUZ 5704.

OUR BELOVED SON ISRAEL FREEDMAN WHO FELL ON THE BATTLEFIELD FOR THE HONOUR OF HIS PEOPLE AND HIS GOVERNMENT.

Engraved within the Star of David are five letters forming an acronym based on the passage in I Samuel 25: 29: *"serura bisror hahayyim . . . may his soul be bound up in the bonds of eternal life."* In their own way, these graves symbolise what the Third Reich had set out to destroy, not only a race of human beings, but a whole way of life, a religion with its ancient language and traditions. In a letter of condolence to Rifleman Freedman's mother, a fellow soldier wrote, "Izzy, like other Jewish boys, had something more to fight for, a greater cause . . . a duty not only to King and Country but to the Jewish people the world over." Equally ennobling are the words on the headstone of another young Jewish soldier, Bombardier George Meltz of the Royal Canadian

Artillery, who died on July 8, 1944 at age 25, fighting in defence of his country and his people: *Deeply mourned by wife and family. He died so Jewry shall suffer no more.*

A PRIVATE IN THE ARMY, HE GAVE NO LESS THAN THE HIGHEST ABOVE HIM, HIS LIFE.
Private Jean Baptiste Lanteigne, RC, 12.6.44 (age 31)

TONY WAS A FORWARD OBSERVATION OFFICER—THE UNSUNG HEROES OF THE WAR.
Captain Anthony Larratt Smith, RCA, 27.7.44 (age 36)

IN LOVING MEMORY OF A DEAR FATHER AND HUSBAND.
BRAVE WORDS OF A BRAVE MAN, "TAKE THE OTHERS. I'M DONE FOR."
Sapper Thomas Kelly Anderson, CRCE, 22.6.44 (age 44)

IN LOVING MEMORY OF A SOLDIER BRAVE WHO ON 'D' DAY HIS LIFE HE GAVE.
Rifleman Ronald Anthony James Cutler, RRR, 6.6.44 (age 26)

HIS WAS THE STEADY COURAGE NEVER LACKED BY SINGLENESS OF HEART.
Captain Byron Eric Fowler, SDGH, 18.7.44 (age 28)

"DIED IN THE LINE OF DUTY." WHAT FINER EPITAPH COULD A SOLDIER WISH
IN SO SIMPLE A PARAGRAPH.
Major Charles Christie Hill, QOCHC, 9.6.44 (age 32)

IN THOUGHT, FAITH. IN DEED, COURAGE. IN LIFE, SERVICE. IN DEATH, VICTORY.
Lance Corporal Clare Davidson Kines, RWR, 8.6.44 (age 29)

AND NOW ABIDETH FAITH, HOPE, LOVE, THESE THREE:
BUT THE GREATEST OF THESE IS LOVE.
Reverend William Alfred Seaman, CCS, 21.7.44

Where histories of the Normandy campaign concentrate on the conduct of the battles and the decisions of the commanders, it is in the record of the headstones where the burden of the fighting can be measured. It fell upon the soldiers in the rifle companies, the tank crews, the artillerymen, the sappers and engineers, signallers, stretcher bearers, the pilots, even the regimental padres, two of whom lie buried in Bény-sur-Mer. These were the men who "dragged the war forward an inch at a time" as they captured this village, secured that crossing, or occupied a crucial piece of ground. The achievement of these objectives depended on the courage and skill, elevated at times to heroism and self-sacrifice, of ordinary young men whose names are known to no one but the families who bore the blow of their loss:

TO THE WORLD HE WAS JUST ANOTHER ONE. TO US, HE WAS OUR DARLING SON.
Private Lawrence Burton Perkins, SDGH, 7.6.44 (age 26)

THOUGH ALL THE WORLD FORGETS, LOVINGLY REMEMBERED
BY MOTHER, DAD AND SISTER MARY.
Private Lorne High, HLIC, 8.7.44 (age 22)

A WONDERFUL SON, BROTHER, HUSBAND AND FATHER.
Corporal Hugh Archibald Munroe, RRR, 6.6.44 (age 24)

Variations of the three epitaphs above appear on many headstones, but in every case they retain a particularity reminding us that the death of each soldier took a young man from the service of his country, and ended a part of many other lives:

A TRUE CANADIAN. A BRAVE SOLDIER. A BELOVED SON AND BROTHER.
Corporal Alfred Thomas Morton, ESR, 30.7.44 (age 24)

A GOOD SON, A LOVING BROTHER, AND A LOYAL SOLDIER. REST IN PEACE.
Private Arthur High Annett, CH, 31.7.44 (age 34)

IN LOVING MEMORY OF A GOOD SOLDIER AND A DEAR SON. EVER REMEMBERED.
Private Kenneth Neil Joseph Rozak, CHO, 9.6.44 (age 18)

REMEMBRANCE OF A DEAR HUSBAND AND SON. A FINE SOLDIER AND A TRUE GENTLEMAN.
Lance Corporal Ernest Archibald Gentles Bell, SDGH, 8.7.44 (age 34)

LIFE WILL NEVER BE THE SAME NOW THAT WE HAVE LOST YOU. EVER LOVINGLY REMEMBERED, WIFE, SON, MOM AND SISTER.
Rifleman Sidney Stephen Ryan, QORC, 6.6.44 (age 27)

IL LAISSE DANS LE DEUIL SON PÈRE ET SA MÈRE M. ET MME ARSÈNE OUELLET, DEUX FRÈRES ET SIX SŒURS.
(He leaves in mourning his father and mother, Mr. and Mrs. Arsene Ouellet, two brothers and six sisters.)
Corporal Lionel Ouellet, RC, 6.6.44

IN LIFE HE LOVED AND WAS LOVED BY ALL. THAT THOSE HE LOVED MIGHT LIVE, HE GLADLY DIED. PAULINE AND DAUGHTER YVONNE
Private Walter John Zator, RRC, 14.7.44 (age 20)

SOMETIME WE'LL UNDERSTAND. ALWAYS REMEMBERED BY WIFE AND FOUR CHILDREN.
Sergeant Murray Louis Burns, RCA, 5.8.44 (age 31)

I HAVE ONLY YOUR MEMORY, DEAR HUSBAND, TO REMEMBER MY WHOLE LIFE THROUGH.
Rifleman George Alexander, RWR, 16.7.44 (age 21)

A BEAUTIFUL FUTURE PLANNED, ONLY TO END IN A DREAM. DEAR, MY THOUGHTS ARE EVER OF YOU AND WHAT MIGHT HAVE BEEN.
Trooper Robert Lawrence Morton, 17th DY, 26.7.44 (age 24)

DEARLY BELOVED HUSBAND OF SYLVIA DINARI AND FOND FATHER OF BRUCE ALLAN.
Sapper Jack Allan French, CRCE, 7.7.44 (age 29)

LONELY, DREARY ARE THE DAYS SINCE ONE WE LOVE WENT AWAY. LOVINGLY REMEMBERED BY HIS GRANDMOTHER.
Private Raymond McEwen, NNSH, 8.7.44 (age 36)

HE WAS OURS AND WE REMEMBER. FATHER, MOTHER, SISTERS AND BROTHERS.
Trooper George Nugent McKinlay, FGH, 11.6.44 (age 30)

SADLY MISSED AND EVER REMEMBERED BY MOM, DAD, JOAN, CALVIN, BETTY AND PALS TOMMY AND MATT.
Corporal Herbert Smith, LWR, 3.8.44 (age 21)

A TRUE FRIEND, A SON MOST DEAR, A LOVING BROTHER LIETH HERE. GREAT IS OUR LOSS.
Corporal Stanley Smith, CSR, 10.6.44 (age 34)

REMEMBERED ALWAYS IN DEATH AS IN LIFE. AL., MUM, DAD, FAMILY AND YOUR PRINCESS.
Corporal Wesley Collins, RWR, 5.7.44 (age 24)

DEARLY BELOVED SON OF ROSS AND ELSIE JOHNSON AND BROTHER TO CLAIRE.
Flying Officer Ross Eveleigh Johnson, RCAF, 15.7.44 (age 21)

JOHNNY. "SOLDIER REST, THY WARFARE O'ER."
MOTHER, SHEILA, MARTIN, ELLEN AND MICHAEL MOURN. R.I.P.
Sergeant John Joseph O'Connell, CSR, 1.7.44 (age 26)

FATHER, WE LOVE YOU. ERLING AND FAMILY, HAROLD AND ERNIE.
Lance Corporal Sverre Lea, CPC, 12.6.44 (age 35)

SADLY MISSED BY FRIENDS.
Lance Corporal Nicholas Prady, TSR, 25.7.44 (age 24)

EVER REMEMBERED BY HIS PARENTS, SISTERS AND BROTHERS AND ALL IN CANADA.
Corporal Alexander Rutherford, RCASC, 8.6.44 (age 23)

HE DIED TO SAVE US ALL. IN OUR HEARTS HE'LL ALWAYS BE.
NEVER FORGOTTEN BY HIS WIFE AND FIVE CHILDREN.
Private Soloman Kline, CSR, 8.7.44 (age 38)

DEAR DAD AND HUSBAND, WE LOVE YOU NOW AS WE LOVED YOU THEN.
OLGA, DENISE AND VINIA
Regimental Sergeant Major Edward Rhodes, HLIC, 22.6.44 (age 37)

BELOVED HUSBAND OF BETH MONTGOMERY. FATHER OF ANN, PEGGY,
GERALDINE AND JACK.
Sergeant Gerald William Leveridge, NNSH, 12.8.44 (age 32)

NEVER FORGOTTEN BY LOVING WIFE MARGARET AND DAUGHTERS ANNE AND SHIRLEY.
Private Henry Coltman, HLIC, 7.7.44

EVER REMEMBERED BY HIS WIFE JOYCE, SON GEORGIE,
GRANNY BERRY, MUM AND DAD SEABROOK.
Private George Frederick Leonzio, LSR, 4.8.44 (age 23)

IN LOVING MEMORY OF EWALT, A DEAR HUSBAND AND DADDY. EVERY DAY IN SILENCE
WE REMEMBER. SADLY MISSED BY HIS LOVING WIFE AND DAUGHTER CONNIE.
Private Ewalt Brandt, CSR, 10.6.44 (age 27)

GRAND MERCI À NOTRE HÉROS. MAMAN S'ENNUIE, FERNAND. NOUS TE PLEURONS.
(In deep thanks to our hero. Mama misses you, Fernand. We weep for you.)
Private Fernand Jean Louis Hains, RC, 6.6.44 (age 28)

"LEST WE FORGET" AS A FAMILY. JACK WAS THE BEST OF US, BRAVE, UNSELFISH AND TRUE.
Rifleman Jack Silas Jacobs, QORC, 11.6.44 (age 20)

HE MADE OTHERS BETTER BY HIS GOODNESS. NEVER AFRAID OF GIVING HIS BEST.
Captain Vincent Elmer Stark, HLIC, 8.7.44 (age 29)

EVER REMEMBERED BY MUM, DAD, BIRNIE, GLORIA, JOYCE AND MARR.
Private George Crawford Hadden, CSR, 10.6.44 (age 19)
Rifleman James William Dunbar Hadden, RRR, 19.7.44 (age 20)

One by one the headstones present inscriptions arresting in their dignity and simplicity, conveying in a few words the impact of a young soldier's death on his family and a depth of sorrow moving even to strangers over sixty years later. From the parents of Emerson Robert James, a private with the North Shore Regiment killed on D-Day, at age 18: *We have suffered since we lost you. Life will never be the same.* The words of parting, chosen or adapted from a list, or composed by the families themselves, reveal the terms on which they accepted the finality of their loss, its meaning, and the consolation by which they sought to allay their grief. Their responses emerge in many forms, as endearments, prayers, pledges of eternal love and longing, tribute to the soldier's character and courage, or gratitude for his sacrifice. Silence, too, was a choice. The absence of an inscription suggests that for some the loss was too painful, perhaps even too embittering, for words. Others may have preferred to bestow the respectfulness implicit in silence upon the soldier's grave.

Those who elected to bid farewell drew upon valedictory themes that were many and varied. Some dwelt on the prospects and hopes denied by death at so young an age, whereas others found comfort in the acceptance of God's will or in the hope of a reunion in a life to come. The prevailing theme, however, is the affirmation of an imperishable bond of remembrance:

LE DERNIER CADEAU DE L'AMOUR——SOUVENIR.
(Love's last gift, remembrance.)
Private Arthur Bouchard, RC, 6.6.44 (age 28)

SLEEP WELL. WE SHALL REMEMBER THROUGH ALL TIME.
Rifleman Ward Walsh, RRR, 24.7.44

WE'VE KNOWN SO MUCH OF HAPPINESS, ONE GIFT OF GOD THAT DEATH CANNOT DESTROY.
Flying Officer Leonard Ralph Allman, RCAF, 6.6.44 (age 24)

"REMEMBRANCE." TO HAVE KNOWN AND LOVED HIM IS OUR REWARD.
Sapper Alfred James Leslie Martin, CRCE, 6.6.44 (age 35)

FOR IMMORTAL REMEMBRANCE, IN VALOUR YOU HAVE LAID YOUR LIFE FOR FREEDOM.
Rifleman Mikie Wintoniw, RWR, 6.6.44 (age 26)

OUR DARLING.
Sergeant Robert James Lidstone, HLIC, 8.7.44 (age 23)

MOTHER'S HERO.
Lance Corporal James Albert Johnston, RRR, 8.7.44 (age 27)

GOD WILL TAKE CARE OF YOU, ROLAND DEAR. WE WILL ALL MEET AGAIN.
Private Roland Eugene Sothe, RCAMC, 16.8.44 (age 23)

SOIS ASSURÉ DE NOTRE IMMORTEL SOUVENIR. TA MÈRE, TON PÈRE, TA SŒUR.
(Rest assured of our everlasting remembrance. Your mother, father, and sister)
Private Roland Albert Giguère, SDGH, 18.7.44 (age 23)

TO ONE WHO DIED BEFORE HE HAD A CHANCE TO LIVE.
Sergeant Stanley George Machnee, RCA, 15.7.44 (age 28)

HE ALSO GAVE.
Trooper David Maurice Legassick, 1st Hussars, 11.6.44 (age 19)

DEAR BUD, NOTHING CAN TAKE AWAY THE LOVE OUR HEARTS HOLD DEAR. "OUR LOYAL SON."
Corporal Albert George Mercer, CH, 19.7.44 (age 21)

GRACE FOR ALL.
Rifleman Edward Heinrichs, RWR, 5.7.44 (age 19)

SEIGNEUR, RENDEZ-LUI EN BONHEUR CE QU'IL DONNA EN TENDRESSE ET DÉVOUEMENT.
(Lord, grant to him in happiness what he gave in gentleness and devotion.)
Lieutenant Raymond James Lapierre, RC, 6.6.44 (age 27)

NOUS NOUS SOUVENONS ET NOUS PRIONS.
(We remember and we pray.)
Private Georges Godin, RC, 18.7.44 (age 27)

DUTIFUL, HAPPY AND GENEROUS.
Lieutenant Robert Eliot Austin, BWC, 21.7.44 (age 23)

HE LOVED HONOUR MORE THAN HE FEARED DEATH. SLEEP ON, DEAR BUDDY, IN PEACE.
Corporal Horace John Smith, RHLI, 26.7.44 (age 20)

"JIMMY" ALWAYS IN MY HEART.
Rifleman James Brisbane Morgan, RWR, 16.6.44 (age 34)

TWO LITTLE WORDS NOT HARD TO WRITE, I WILL REMEMBER THEM ALL MY LIFE, "MY SON."
Gunner William Stanley Daye, RCA, 13.7.44 (age 38)

WHEN DUTY CALLED, HE ANSWERED.
Trooper Kenneth Middleton Hutchinson, FGH, 4.7.44 (age 22)

LOVE LIKE A BRIDGE SPANS THE SPACES THAT DIVIDE. PARTED, YET IN DREAMS
WE WALK TOGETHER SIDE BY SIDE.
Corporal Roger Joseph Firman, RWR, 8.6.44 (age 21)

WE WILL ALWAYS REMEMBER OUR BOY.
Private John Erickson, NNSH, 8.7.44 (age 19)

DEAR SON, MAY WE WHO REMAIN BE WORTHY OF YOUR GREAT SACRIFICE.
Rifleman Russel Kenneth Adamson, QORC, 6.6.44 (age 19)

LOVED, REMEMBERED, LONGED FOR ALWAYS.
Private John Stewart, HLIC, 8.7.44 (age 29)

SOME DAY I WILL JOIN YOU IN THE GREAT BEYOND UNKNOWN.
THEN MY SORROW WILL BE O'ER, I WILL NOT BE ALONE.
Rifleman Raymond Morse Nelson, RRR, 12.6.44

OUR SON AND BROTHER, NEVER A FATHER TO BE. SACRIFICIAL CHILD.
Private Romeo Neault, NNSH, 8.7.44 (age 23)

UPON THE ALTAR OF THE WORLD HE STOOD, RETURNED LIFE, LOVE, FAME AND MANHOOD.
Major John Vernon Love, RRR, 6.6.44 (age 25)

DUTY WELL DONE, MATE. THERE WAS, THERE IS, NO GENTLER, STRONGER, MANLIER MAN.
Sergeant William James McLean, FGH, 6.7.44 (age 24)

GOD ALONE UNDERSTANDS.
Captain Robert Gibson Shinnan, RRR, 9.6.44

In a far corner of the cemetery lies a soldier whose inscription evokes an age-old heroic ideal and imparts a timeless example of the suffering wrought by war. On the headstone of John Logan, a 27-year old Lieutenant in the Sherbrooke Fusiliers who died of wounds on August 12, 1944, are these words in Greek:

ΕΙΣ ΟΙΩΝΟΣ ΑΡΙΣΤΟΣ

ΑΜΥΝΕΣΘΑΙ ΠΕΡΙ ΠΑΤΡΗΣ

Lieutenant Logan's epitaph was chosen by his father, Harry Tremaine Logan, for many years professor of classics at the University of British Columbia, and a veteran of the First World War. The lines come from book 12 of the *Iliad* and are spoken by the Trojan hero Hector. In the midst of battle, the Trojans have beheld an omen sent by the gods and are deliberating whether it counsels advance or retreat until Hector settles the issue by declaring, "one omen is best, to fight for your country." These words are in themselves a fitting tribute to a young soldier who gave his life for his country; but the association with Hector confers a singular dignity upon his memory. Of all the warriors portrayed in the *Iliad*, Hector enlists the deepest sympathy, for his valour in battle, his sense of duty to his people, and for his refusal to retire from the fighting even though he has done his share and more. In a famous scene, his wife pleads with him to withdraw from the battle. You are my whole world, she tells him, as she recounts the loss of her father, her mother, and her brothers. But Hector cannot. He knows that in the end he is fated to die and that his city must fall, yet he strives with all his might to put off the day when Troy will be razed, his father and family put to the sword, his wife led off into slavery. Hector embodies courage, in very human terms: he is no stranger to rashness or to fear, but his unwillingness to forsake his comrades or to dishonour himself in the eyes of others impel him to face what must be faced, even on the verge of death. And after death in battle has torn him from his family, it is left to his father to recover the body and to provide for his son the proper rituals of mourning and burial.

The *Iliad* is universal in its portrayal of men in battle, not only for its depiction of the savagery and emotional turbulence of the battlefield, but above all for its vision of the pitiless nature of war, revealed by the misery that it visits indiscriminately upon young and old, men and women, parents and children, even the uninvolved and the undeserving. The poem is uncompromising in its exposure of the transience and the expendability of human lives. Scores of young warriors are singled out for a brief recitation of their homes and parents, their qualities and distinctions, at the very moment when their lives come to an end. They are cut down before they have the chance to realise their hopes or to make their reputations, and their names survive only because they died in a famous war:

> Then Telamonian Aias struck the son of Anthemion, Simoeisios, a strong young man not married. His mother had given birth to him by the banks of the Simoeis, coming down from Ida where she had gone with her parents to watch over their flocks: and so they called him Simoeisios. But he could not repay his dear parents for the care of his rearing, but his life was cut short, brought down by the spear at the hands of great-hearted Aias. . .

Then Diomedes, master of the war-cry, killed Axylos, son of Teuthras.
He lived in well-founded Arisbe, a man rich in substance, and hospitable
to all men—his house was by the road, and he would entertain all who
passed. But none of them faced Diomedes for him then, and saved him from
a miserable death, but he took the life from both of them, Axylos and his
lieutenant Kalesios, his charioteer on that day. . .

Thirty centuries later, brief notices epitomise young men who came from the far-flung corners of a distant land to fight and die in their thousands in the greatest war the world has ever known:

DIED OF WOUNDS AT CAEN. BORN AT MARGAREE, NOVA SCOTIA. "REST IN PEACE."
Private John Charles McFarlane, CSR, 9.7.44 (age 19)

NOT JUST TODAY BUT EVERY DAY IN SILENCE WE REMEMBER. SON OF KATE & MICHAEL
KOCHAN, THORHILD, ALBERTA, CANADA.
Private James Kochan, CH, 26.7.44 (age 25)

ONLY SON OF ROY AND FLORENCE SQUIRE OF GLENCOE, ONTARIO, CANADA.
Private Howard Squire, ESR, 29.7.44 (age 19)

HERE RESTS THE ONLY SON OF WILLIAM AND CORA SAMSON, ALBERTVILLE, SASKATCHEWAN.
Rifleman Alfred Samson, RWR, 4.7.44 (age 32)

BORN AT EGMONT BAY, P.E.I., APRIL 12TH 1924. SON OF MARGARET AND
PROSPER GALLANT. R.I.P.
Private Joseph Frank Gallant, NNSH, 8.7.44 (age 20)

BELOVED AND ONLY SON OF RORY S. AND MARGARET MACKINNON. A ROMAN CATHOLIC.
R.I.P.
Lieutenant Donald Columba MacKinnon, NNSH, 8.7.44 (age 26)

FILS DE FEU ARTHUR BARRETTE ET DE DIANA LAFOREST.
NÉ À CHICOUTIMI, QUÉBEC, CANADA.
(Son of the late Arthur Barrette and Diana Laforest.
Born in Chicoutimi, Quebec, Canada.)
Sergeant Paul Barrette, CRCE, 6.6.44 (age 33)

DEAREST YOUNGEST SON OF ROBERT AND MARY, BROTHER OF JOHN AND BOB.
TORONTO, ONTARIO.
Lieutenant Murray Joseph Fitzpatrick, SFR, 8.7.44 (age 24)

"YOU WILL NEVER BE FORGOTTEN." MOTHER, DAD, DAVID & ELIZABETH.
GORDON INDIAN RESERVE, PUNNICHY, SASKATCHEWAN.
Private Kenneth Wilfred Pratt, RWR, 7.6.44 (age 20)

OF WEYMOUTH, NOVA SCOTIA. HAROLD, A LOVING SON, GONE BUT NOT FORGOTTEN.
MAY HE REST IN PEACE.
Private Harold Alexander MacGowan, CSR, 15.7.44 (age 28)

FIFTH SON OF FRED AND EDNA PRIMEAU, CHATHAM, ONTARIO.
Private Joseph Primeau, RRC, 19.7.44 (age 21)

ICI REPOSE LE FILS DE EDOUARD FONTAINE ET DE MARIA DÉSORMEAU, MONTRÉAL.
(Here lies the son of Edouard Fontaine and Maria Desormeau, Montreal.)
Private Henri Joseph Edouard Fontaine, RC, 6.6.44 (age 19)

BELOVED SON OF PHILOMENE ROUSSEL, EDMUNSTON, N.B., CANADA.
Private Adrien Leo Roussel, RC, 6.6.44 (age 23)

BORN IN THAMESVILLE, ONTARIO. SON OF DAN CULNAN AND ANN SCHNEKENBURGER.
Private John Windline Culnan, QORC, 11.6.44 (age 21)

BELOVED SON OF ALEX AND PARASKA KINDRACHUK OF HAFFORD, SASKATCHEWAN.
Private George Kindrachuk, RRR, 9.6.44 (age 25)

BELOVED SON OF STEPHEN AND MATILDA BELLEFONTAINE,
WEST CHEZZETCOOK, NOVA SCOTIA. R.I.P.
Private Oswald Joseph Bellefontaine, NNSH, 7.6.44 (age 24)

A ROMAN CATHOLIC. BELOVED SON OF DAN AND CATHERINE RODGERS,
STE ANNE, MANITOBA.
Rifleman Henry Rodgers, RWR, 8.6.44 (age 22)

BORN IN NORTH VANCOUVER, B.C., 1922. ENLISTED IN CANADIAN SCOTTISH 1940.
Private Norman Ross Fairweather, SDGH, 7.6.44 (age 21)

HE HAS GONE ACROSS THE RIVER WHERE THE SHORES ARE EVERGREEN. EVER REMEMBERED
BY MOTHER AND THE REST OF THE FAMILY, RIDING PARK, MANITOBA, CANADA.
Gunner Chester Hebner, RCA, 11.7.44 (age 29)

NÉ À ST. THÉRÈSE, N.B., CANADA. MORT POUR L'HONNEUR. R.I.P.
(Born in St. Thérèse, N.B., Canada. Died for honour's sake. R.I.P.)
Private Arthur Roy, RC, 8.6.44 (age 25)

NOUS DE VAL ALAIN, LOTBINIÈRE, P.Q., CANADA, ADMIRONS SA MORT
POUR DIEU ET LA PATRIE.
*(We of Val Alain, Lotbinière, P.Q., Canada, admire his death
for God and his native land)*
Private Joseph Raoul Roch Bédard, RCASC, 18.7.44

GRADUATE ROYAL MILITARY COLLEGE, CANADA. MOTTO—TRUTH, DUTY, VALOUR.
Major Gavin Fraser Rainnie, RCA, 6.6.44 (age 36)

"*From little towns we came, by little towns we lie. . .*" For every volunteer from Toronto, Montreal, or Vancouver, there are half a dozen others from mining towns, parishes, counties, fishing villages, and farming communities whose names are engraved on the headstones of Canadian soldiers buried thousands of miles from their homes in St. Félix-de-Kingsey, Indian River, Yorkton, Easton's Corners, Owen Sound, New Waterford, Jonquière, Fassett, Stoughton, Cordova Mines, Matane, Arnprior, Cap-aux-Meules, Chatham, Windthorst, Pickering, St. Thomas, Camperville. These placenames recall a day and age when a larger part of Canada's population lived in small towns and rural settlements, when the still semi-industrialised country relied for its prosperity on the production of grain and raw materials, and when popular sentiments and attitudes were shaped by influences no longer current:

HE SAW A WIDER VISION, THE EMPIRE AND ITS NEED,
AND CAME WITH SWIFT DECISION TO DO THE UTMOST DEED.
Private Donald Rhyburn Morrison, NNSH, 5.7.44 (age 21)

DUTY NOBLY DONE FOR KING AND COUNTRY.
Rifleman Frank Holmes, QORC, 6.6.44

"BE PREPARED." "TO DO MY DUTY TO GOD AND MY KING."
Lieutenant Fleming Ladd Irving, 1st Hussars, 6.6.44 (age 21)

BEHOLD, I WILL CAUSE BREATH TO ENTER INTO YOU AND YE SHALL LIVE. EZEKIEL XXXVII. 5
Craftsman John Loewen, CRCEME, 4.8.44 (age 24)

"BLESSED ARE THE PEACEMAKERS FOR THEY SHALL BE CALLED THE CHILDREN OF GOD."
Rifleman Thomas Edward Forrester, RWR, 4.7.44 (age 21)

AND JESUS INCREASED IN WISDOM AND STATURE, AND IN FAVOUR
WITH GOD AND MAN. ST. LUKE II. 52
Trooper Ernest Ross Lumsden, FGH, 5.7.44 (age 19)

HE HUMBLED HIMSELF AND BECAME OBEDIENT UNTO DEATH. PHILIPPIANS II. 8
Corporal Richard Selwyn Lewis, CRCE, 16.8.44 (age 31)

SO HE PASSED OVER AND ALL THE TRUMPETS SOUNDED FOR HIM ON THE OTHER SIDE.
Lance Corporal John Ernest Walker NS(NB)R, 6.6.44 (age 24)

VOUS TOUS QUI PASSEZ DITES AU CIEL POUR MOI UNE AVE. MON JÉSUS, MISÉRICORDE.
(All you who pass by, say a 'Hail Mary' to heaven for me. Jesus, have mercy)
Private Louis Philippe Lauzier, RC, 4.7.44 (age 26)

ALL WE HAVE OF FREEDOM, ALL WE USE OR KNOW,
THIS OUR FATHERS BOUGHT FOR US, LONG AND LONG AGO. KIPLING
Sergeant David James Byers, RRC, 20.7.44

I WILL KEEP ALIGHT THE TORCH OF COURAGE YOUR DYING HAND PASSED ON TO ME.
Lance Sergeant William Stewart, CRCE, 7.6.44 (age 43)

WHO COULD DIE A BETTER DEATH, FOR HE GAVE HIS LIFE FOR ONE AND ALL. MOTHER
Private William Sylvester Bousfield, CSR, 8.7.44 (age 27)

The Canada from which these soldiers came was in many respects a different country from the one in which we live today. Two generations ago Canada was a dominion that saw its security and welfare in connection with those of Great Britain and the British Empire. The names in the Bény-sur-Mer cemetery echo a time when the population was half British and a third French in origin; but alongside the Smiths, MacDonalds and Tremblays lie comrades with names like Chermishnuk, Ruggerio, Husak, Weitzel, Wladyka, Andrijouski, Cohen, Moenaert, Gavrilo, Sigurdson, Poniedzielski, Radocy, Kachor, Toivonen, Nokusis, van de Veen, Schumilas, Capraru, Tedavič, and Tolstad which herald the evolution of Canada into a land home to people of all races and religions. The frequency of epitaphs drawn from Scripture or hymns reflects the beliefs of a generation more religious, or at least more church-going, than our own, one that turned for spiritual solace to the King James Bible, the Book of Common Prayer, or to *The Pilgrim's Progress*. In their turn, many French epitaphs profess the

Catholicism of an older, ultramontane Quebec now changed out of all recognition in the wake of the Quiet Revolution. It was a generation of English Canadians schooled in the poems of Kipling and Tennyson exalting duty, patriotism, and sacrifice, ideals reinforced by the war poems of Rupert Brooke and John McCrae, the memoirs of Canon Scott, and the public monuments and annual ceremonies commemorating the Glorious Dead of the Great War. It was a country whose people read different books and newspapers, watched different films, turned on the radio for information and entertainment, and whose expectations and values during the first half of the twentieth century were tempered by the experience of two world wars and a prolonged economic depression, trials from which Canadians born after 1945 have been spared.

SLEEP, MY SON, ON FRENCH SOIL. MAY THE SOIL BE LIGHT UPON YOU.
Sergeant Wesley Williams Miskow, RWR, 6.6.44 (age 23)

A DISTANT LAND IS HONORED WITH THE GLORY OF HIS CLAY.
HIS SPIRIT IS IN CANADA, HIS SOUL WITH GOD TODAY.
Rifleman Alfred Martin Peterson, RWR, 8.6.44 (age 31)

WE COULD NOT HOLD YOUR HAND, WE DID NOT SEE YOU DIE.
WE ONLY KNOW YOU PASSED AWAY AND COULD NOT SAY GOODBYE.
Private Charles Elmer Kenneth Carmichael, QORC, 18.7.44 (age 22)

DE BIEN LOIN PAR L'OCÉAN TA MÈRE PRIE POUR TOI.
(From far away across the ocean your mother prays for you.)
Corporal Antoine Gionet, NS(NB)R, 6.6.44 (age 25)

NOT IN HIS NATIVE LAND, BUT UNDER FOREIGN SKIES,
FAR FROM THOSE WHO LOVE HIM, IN A SOLDIER'S GRAVE HE LIES.
Rifleman William Thomas, RWR, 8.6.44 (age 36)

IF IN A FAR OFF COUNTRY YOU MUST LIE, YOUR IMAGE IN OUR HEARTS WILL NEVER DIE.
Rifleman Norman Blue, RWR, 5.7.44 (age 18)

PEACEFULLY SLEEPING, DEAR SON AND BROTHER, WITH YOUR DEAR COMRADES
IN A FAR AND DISTANT LAND.
Private Charles Sweeney, SDGH, 18.7.44

HE SLEEPS IN A FOREIGN LAND IN A GRAVE WE NEVER SEE.
MAY GOD GUIDE SOME KIND HAND TO LAY A FLOWER FOR ME. MOTHER
Private Thomas Leo Laton, RCASC, 9.8.44 (age 28)

Canada in 1939 was a country of nine provinces and 11,500,000 people which put over a million men and women in uniform, and lost over 42,000 in six years of war. Military cemeteries around the world index the human cost of Canada's effort on land, at sea, and in the air. Beginning with Bény-sur-Mer, a series of Canadian War Cemeteries marks the route of the victory campaign from the landing beaches to the Rhineland. But where the Commonwealth cemeteries from Normandy to Holland attract a steady stream of visitors, others lie in the recesses of the war where Canadian servicemen gave their lives in actions overshadowed by the D-Day landings and the victory campaign in northwestern Europe. One Canadian soldier who died on June 6, 1944 was 37-year old Private Arthur Cloutier of the Royal Canadian Army Service

Falaise Castle, ancestral seat of the Dukes of Normandy and birthplace of William the Conqueror.

Statue of William the Conqueror in the main square at Falaise.

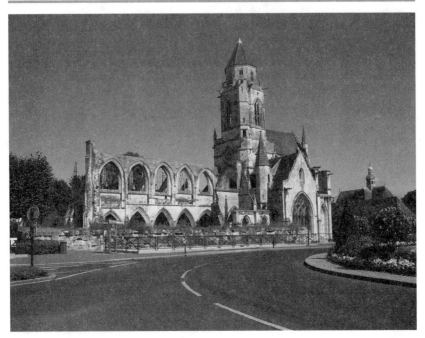

The ruins of Vieux St-Etienne, Caen.

The Memorial to the Missing at Bayeux.

Grave of three French children at Soulangy churchyard, killed "by gunfire and bombardments while evacuating, all three on August 12, 1944."

In the empty fields south of Caen, a monument commemorating the battle fought by the British Columbia Regiment and the Algonquin Regiment on Pt. 140.

Plaque honouring the capture of Pt. 195 by the Argyll and Sutherland Highlanders of Canada.

The burial ground at Bény-sur-Mer.

". . . a debt not only to King and Country but to the Jewish people the world over."
The grave of Rifleman Israel Freedman of the Royal Winnipeg Rifles.

Corps: *Pense à moi sur cette terre, comme je penserai à toi au ciel* (*Think of me on this earth, just as I will think of you in heaven*) reads the inscription on his headstone, to be found not in Normandy but in Minturno War Cemetery, an impressive but seldom visited monument of the Italian campaign and one of thirty-eight sites where Canadian servicemen lie buried in Italy.

Few today remember that July 10, 1943 was in fact Canada's first D-Day, when the First Division landed near the Sicilian town of Pachino and commenced the long climb from Sicily up through the Italian peninsula. Beneath the ruins of a Norman castle atop the hill town of Agira, against the backdrop of Mount Etna, begins a Canadian *via dolorosa* that winds through Ortona, Cassino, Rome, Montecchio, on to Ravenna and beyond, recording the sad legacy of a lesser known chapter of Canada's military past. Contrasting with the long, grinding campaigns are the isolated tragedies commemorated at the Sai Wan War Cemetery in Hong Kong, and at the Canadian War Cemetery at Dieppe, while the scale of Canada's participation in the air war can be measured by the wide scattering of cemeteries where Canadian airmen are buried, from England to Germany, from North Africa to India, and even in southeast Asia, as far away as Japan.

HERE IN SILENCE HIS MEMORY SPEAKS FOR FREEDOM.
Private Willard James MacArthur, NBR, 17.8.44 (age 27)

HE RESTETH NOT ALONE. GOD BLESS OUR DEAR BOY. MOTHER AND DAD.
Private Gordon Joseph McBride, RRR, 6.6.44

Tranquil, unchanging, the silent cities of the war dead preserve the memory of Canada's contribution to victory in the Second World War. They represent a significant part of Canada's past and meaning as a country that we do not see in our own land. They were constructed in accordance with the precepts and examples established by the Imperial War Graves Commission after the First World War and maintained for the war dead of the Commonwealth after the Second. Within the pattern of official and collective commemoration, however, there exists a stark, heartrending record of individual response to the tragedy of the war, expressed and preserved in thousands of personal inscriptions. They, too, are part of the national memory of the Second World War, at its most basic level. What follows is the result of an effort to collect these expressions of loss and consolation and to present a sample of them as evidence of the lasting cost of the war to untold Canadian families: *You said goodbye, we did not know it was forever*—where did bereaved families turn for words of comfort, or tribute to the fallen, and how might these words have reconciled them to the loss of a son, brother, husband, or father whose grave they would in all likelihood never see?

BORN FEBRUARY, 1919. FRANK, BELOVED SON OF MIKE AND KATRINA OSTER, SHORNCLIFFE, MANITOBA, CANADA.
Rifleman Frank Oster, RWR, 8.6.44 (age 25)

BELOVED SON OF HARRY & SOPHIA SHINETON. BORN AT HIGHLEY, ENGLAND, 1921. R.I.P.
Corporal William Shineton, FGH, 4.7.44

BORN 17TH JULY, 1922, IN WILLOWBROOK, SASKATCHEWAN, CANADA.
Sapper Howard Stolar, CRCE, 6.6.44 (age 21)

FILS BIEN AIMÉ DE ROSE A. JEAN. NÉ 5 DÉCEMBRE, 1922, MONTRÉAL.
Private Joseph Maurice Jean, RC, 4.7.44 (age 21)

The valedictions enshrine the memory of the young Canadians who, in kinder circumstances, might still be alive today, looking back gratefully on full, useful lives, enriched by family and friendship. Instead, along with tens of thousands of young men from the other Allied nations, they lost their lives in the struggle to turn back the worst threat to human life and decency ever to arise, and for this they are owed an abiding debt of remembrance. The epitaphs, and the ages, of these Canadian soldiers at rest in Bény-sur-Mer present the most compelling reason for this book:

HE WENT FREELY TO FIGHT BESIDE OTHER FREE MEN FOR THE FREEDOM OF US ALL.
Trooper Hugh Hjalmar Michael Lismore, 1st Hussars, 6.6.44 (age 21)

OUR DEAR SON GAVE AS OTHERS WHO ARE GONE,
AND FOR US LIBERTY WON WITH OUR ALLIED SONS AS ONE.
Rifleman Norman Walker, RRR, 8.7.44 (age 20)

WHO DIED THAT FREEDOM SHALL NOT PERISH FROM THE EARTH. "AT REST."
Rifleman William Willis, QORC, 5.7.44 (age 19)

FROM HIS NATIVE SOIL WITH OTHERS TO GIVE HIS ALL, LIKE OTHERS,
THAT LIBERTY MIGHT BE A HERITAGE FOR OTHERS.
Private Arthur James Fraiser, HLIC, 8.7.44 (age 21)

HE DIED SO YOUNG THAT WE MAY LIVE IN FREEDOM. WELL DONE, SON.
Rifleman George Robert Coe, RRR, 9.7.44 (age 19)

LET US NOT FORGET. HE DIED THAT OTHERS MIGHT LIVE IN PEACE, FREE FROM FEAR.
Private Howard Welch, NS(NB)R, 4.7.44 (age 19)

THE EARTH IS A BETTER PLACE BECAUSE OF HIM. "REST IN PEACE."
Private Cyril McQuillan, CHO, 11.7.44 (age 20)

R.I.P. SON OF CANADA, YOU GAVE YOUR LIFE FOR OUR DELIVERANCE.
MAY YOU BE BLESSED IN HEAVEN.
Lance Corporal Elmer Grenville Swan, RCCS, 6.6.44 (age 23)

FREE MEN EVERYWHERE SHOULD REMEMBER THEM. ON VOUS AIME.
Major Frederick Edward Hodge, RWR, 8.6.44 (age 25)

HE GAVE HIS LIFE FOR US. WHAT HAST THOU GIVEN FOR HIM.
Private James Robert Mullis, CHO, 21.7.44 (age 20)

FURTHER READING:

Longworth, Philip. *The Unending Vigil. The History of the Commonwealth War Graves Commission.* London: Constable, 1967. Reprinted by Pen & Sword Books, Barnsley, South Yorkshire, 2003.

Quinlan, Mark. *Remembrance.* Hertford: Authors OnLine Ltd., 2005.

Wood, Herbert Fairlie, and Swettenham, John. *Silent Witnesses.* (Canadian War Museum Historical Publications, Number 10). Toronto: Hakkert, 1974.

CHAPTER TWO

"From Canada's shore to a Dieppe beach. . ."
Dieppe Canadian War Cemetery,
Hautôt-sur-Mer, France

THIS WAS HIS HONOR, FOR WHAT HE BELIEVED HE FOUGHT . . . EVEN UNTO DEATH.
Sergeant Morris Greenberg, RRC, 19.8.42 (age 24)

The view over Dieppe from the German gun emplacements on the western headland takes in at a glance the odds against the Canadians who scrambled ashore on the morning of August 19, 1942. Immediately below lies White Beach where the Royal Hamilton Light Infantry landed in front of the famous casino, long since demolished and replaced by a municipal swimming pool. From here the beach and esplanade follow the curve of the shoreline towards the jetty extending from the town's eastern headland, where the chapel of Notre Dame de Bon Secours presides over the harbour entrance. These were the landmarks branded into the memory of the Essex Scottish who survived the ordeal on Red Beach. If you look along the coastline further to the east, you can make out the opening in the chalk cliffs at Puys where the Royal Regiment of Canada was massacred on Blue Beach. If you turn to face west, the broad aperture of the Scie Valley at Pourville marks the area designated as Green Beach where the South Saskatchewans and Cameron Highlanders shared the meagre scraps of success doled out on that ungenerous day. Any Canadian visitor surveying the main beach from the heights above will find it hard not to transform the minute figures of the strollers and sunbathers below into the khaki-clad targets that spilled out of the landing craft under the guns of the German defenders ranged along the cliffs.

A walk along the shoreline reverses the perspective and drives home the plight of the soldiers sent into the assault. Men and tanks struggled to gain purchase on the shingled incline of the beach, while the expanse of open ground they had to cross stirs awareness of the attackers' exposure to fire from three sides sweeping the approaches to the town. The regimental monuments placed along the esplanade pay tribute to the men who fought as well as they could in circumstances so heavily weighted against them. Among the soldiers who grimly persevered in their tasks while their comrades dropped around them were the men and officers of the Fusiliers Mont-Royal. The Fusiliers were not part of the first assault, having been detailed for use as a floating reserve. They were ordered to land in the mistaken belief that parties of the Essex Scottish had gained their objectives in the town; instead, the Fusiliers came off the boats into the midst of a disaster. "All the tracer bullets that criss-crossed and whistled by made our heads spin; it was a little like finding yourself on a giant road where the cars were rushing past from every direction at all speeds," was Sergeant Lucien Dumais's description of the chaotic scene on the beach. For most, the Dieppe raid was a matter of clinging to what little cover they could find. Incredibly, a number of Fusiliers still managed to get across the esplanade and into the town before making their way back to the boats and evacuation to England.

The memorial to the Fusiliers Mont-Royal at Dieppe was dedicated in 1962 on the twentieth anniversary of the raid. It is the only one put up by the regiment to commemorate its role in two world wars. A list of the Fusiliers' battles in France and Flanders is inscribed on one side. On the other stand these words, translated from the French: *To the memory of those who set out from Canada and shed their blood on the earth of France while fighting under the banner of a French Canadian regiment.* It is appropriate that Dieppe was the place chosen for the memorial, and the name most prominently displayed among the battle honours, for the connections between the port and French Canada reach back into the 16th century. Fishing fleets from Dieppe had ventured across the Atlantic for decades before three commercial expeditions set sail for Canada between 1599 and 1601. Lasting links were forged in the early years of the 17th century when Aymar de Chastes, the governor of Dieppe, was appointed viceroy of New France. Louis Hébert, one of many *Dieppois* who came with Champlain to Quebec, established the first family in the new colony. Jesuit missionaries set out for New France from Dieppe in 1610, followed in 1639 by the teaching order of the Ursulines and the nursing sisters of the Augustines. Their mother convent in Dieppe lent her *Sœurs Hospitalières* to care for the wounded and dying Canadians brought to the Hôtel Dieu in the aftermath of the raid.

Of the 584 Fusiliers who went into battle at Dieppe, 125 made it back to England to fight another day. Most of the men lost at Dieppe were prisoners of war, but the final reckoning yielded a total of 119 dead. One was a soldier from Montreal, the regiment's home:

REPOSE EN PAIX, MON GARS.
QUE CETTE TERRE DE FRANCE TE SOIT LÉGÈRE.
(Rest in peace, my boy.
May this earth of France be light upon you.)
Private Joseph Eugène Jacques Marceau, FMR, *19.8.42 (age 22)*

Private Marceau's epitaph hearkens back to the old Roman formula, *sit terra tibi levis* ("may the earth lie light upon you"), aptly recast by his father to acknowledge a young French Canadian's sacrifice on behalf of his ancestral land. Nearby lie his comrades, almost all of them from Montreal, whose families bade them farewell in these ways:

O LIBERTÉ, AYEZ PITIÉ DE CEUX QUI S'AIMAIENT. DONNEZ-MOI L'ESPÉRANCE ET LA PAIX.
(O liberty, have mercy on those who loved each other. Grant me hope and peace.)
Private Louis Boily, FMR, *19.8.42 (age 31)*

TON SOUVENIR RESTE GRAVÉ DANS NOTRE CŒUR AVEC L'ESPOIR
DE SE REJOINDRE UN JOUR.
(Your memory remains engraved in our heart with the hope
of meeting you again one day.)
Lance Sergeant Jean Paul Beauvais, FMR, 19.8.42 (age 23)

CET ENFANT VOULAIT CHANTER L'AMOUR ET LA GRANDEUR D'UN GESTE. IL A TOUT DIT.
(This child wished to sing of love and the greatness of a deed. He has said all.)
Lieutenant Pierre André Trudel, FMR, 19.8.42 (age 22)

ADIEU, MÈRE CHÉRIE, QUE MES YEUX N'ONT PU REVOIR.
(Farewell, beloved mother, whom my eyes could not behold again.)
Private René Filion, FMR, 19.8.42 (age 33)

PUISSE TON SACRIFICE PORTER SES FRUITS.
(May your sacrifice bear its fruits.)
Private Maurice Dallaire, FMR, 19.8.42 (age 25)

PRIEZ POUR QUE MON SACRIFICE ET CELUI DE MES COMPAGNONS N'AIT PAS ÉTÉ VAIN.
(Pray that my sacrifice and that of my comrades was not in vain.)
Private Armilias Chevalier, FMR, 19.8.42 (age 26)

MORT EN HÉROS POUR LA PATRIE, LAISSANT UNE FEMME ADORÉE ET
UNE PETITE FILLE CHARMANTE. QUE DIEU LUI BÉNISSE.
(Died as a hero for his country, leaving an adored wife and a
delightful little daughter. May God bless him.)
Lance Sergeant Maurice Lapointe, FMR, 19.8.42 (age 31)

IN MEMORY OF OUR SON WHOM WE LOVE SO MUCH. GOD KEEP HIM. MOTHER AND FATHER.
Corporal Joseph Desroches, FMR, 19.8.42 (age 23)

MON FILS BIEN-AIMÉ ROGER. ON SE RÉUNIT TOUS DANS NOS PRIÈRES.
PÈRE, MÈRE, FRÈRE ET SŒUR
(My beloved son Roger. We are all reunited in our prayers.
Father, mother, brother and sister)
Private Roger Dubuc, FMR, 19.8.42 (age 23)

Dieppe was a propaganda gift to the Germans which they gratefully exploited, recording the carnage on the beaches in newsreels and photos, and playing up their victory as a decisive blow to Allied hopes of returning to the continent. When it came to the task of collecting and burying the dead, however, the victors accorded full respect to the fallen. They requisitioned French labourers to transport the bodies to the communal cemetery at Janval, on the outskirts of Dieppe. Shortly afterwards, an order came from the German headquarters at Rouen that the bodies should be transferred to the military plot near Bois des Vertus which the British had used during their sojourn on the continent in 1940. Here, with full military honours, the Canadians were reburied, laid out back to back in long double rows conforming with German practice. When the architects and gardeners of the War Graves Commission resumed the task of transforming the wartime burial grounds into permanent military cemeteries, they retained the unusual arrangement of the graves at Dieppe as they remade the site in the image of the cemeteries constructed after the Great War. The ground was levelled and capped by a lawn, trees and flowers planted, and a formal entrance built of stone. The precinct was enclosed by a hedge border to create the peaceful, contemplative aspect of an English garden. The result is a solemn place of remembrance that maintains the dignity of human grief, collective and individual. The Cross of Sacrifice, the Stone of Remembrance, and the uniform headstones uphold the principle of equal commemoration owed to soldiers of all ranks. The personal details incised on each headstone fulfill the Commission's intention to recognise each of the fallen who, with the exception of a very few, were not soldiers by profession but citizens drawn to the service of their country.

For symbolic reasons the Dieppe Canadian War Cemetery was the first of the Second World War cemeteries to be built in northwestern Europe, with the work reaching completion in 1949. It is one of twenty-two Commonwealth war cemeteries in Normandy bearing the dates 1939–1945, yet the feeling of the Great War burial grounds tarries at Dieppe. The grave of Captain Roy Dillon, of the Fusiliers Mont-Royal, kindles one memory of service in two wars. Dillon, a graduate of Loyola College, had seen action in 1918. He was one of the four thousand Great War veterans who presented themselves for overseas service in 1939, and was still young enough, at age thirty-nine, to be accepted. Blinded and mortally wounded in the landing, he continued to call out encouragement to his men as his life slowly seeped away. His headstone bears no epitaph, but the valedictory words contributed by the family of Squadron Sergeant Major Alexander Howden Tough, of the Calgary Regiment, outline a similar record of service:

HE DID HIS DUTY—1918 & 1942.
REMEMBERED BY HIS LOVING WIFE VALERIE, PETER & GILLIAN.

The burial grounds of the Second World War tend to be collection cemeteries, where the servicemen killed in the course of campaigns lasting several weeks or months were gathered. By contrast, three out of four burials at Dieppe resulted from one day's fighting, giving the cemetery a unity of time, place, and action reminiscent of the battlefield cemeteries clustered along the Western Front. The high proportion of unidentified burials in Dieppe, uncommon in a Second World War cemetery, is another trait of the war to end all wars; but it is the repetition of a single date, *19th August 1942*, echoing the *1st July 1916* carved into thousands of headstones along the old front line on the Somme, that juxtaposes the tragedies that befell successive generations in Great Britain and the Commonwealth:

ONE OF THE LEEDS PALS. "IN THEE, O LORD, DO I HOPE."
Serjeant Matthew Hudson Mossop, West Yorkshire Regiment, 1.7.16 (age 26)
[SERRE ROAD NO. 1]

BELOVED SON OF HARRY AND MABEL SMITH. 5 WALNUT STREET S., HAMILTON, CANADA.
Lance Corporal Gerald Hamilton Smith, RHLI, 19.8.42 (age 26)

GONE BUT NOT FORGOTTEN BY HIS WIFE MYRTLE,
1154 ALBERT ROAD, WINDSOR, ONTARIO, CANADA.
Private Henry Knapp, ESR, 19.8.42 (age 26)

The decimation of the Pals battalions, made up of the volunteers who flocked to the colours in 1914 from the same towns, districts, workplaces, associations, and schools, lies at the core of the painful memory in Great Britain of the first day on the

Somme. Similarly for Canadians, if on a lesser scale, the Dieppe raid was a national tragedy felt most acutely in the places whose young men had enlisted in locally based regiments. The undeniable benefit of shared background in inculcating regimental pride and discipline was offset by the potential cost to communities and families when these regiments went into battle. The appalling losses suffered by the Royal Regiment of Canada cast ripples of grief through Toronto, home to the regiment and to these soldiers:

BREATHE ON ME, BREATH OF GOD.
Private John Allister Mason, RRC, 19.8.42 (age 26)
[HYMN, BREATHE ON ME, BREATH OF GOD, BY EDWIN HATCH, 1835–1889]

CHRIST DIED THAT I, ARTHUR WOODBURY, MAY LIVE.
Private Arthur Clifford Woodbury, RRC, 19.8.42 (age 21)

THE STEPS OF A GOOD MAN ARE ORDERED BY THE LORD.
Private Thomas McIvor, RRC, 19.8.42 (age 43) [PSALM 37: 23]

THOSE WHO LOVE GOD CAN NEVER SEE EACH OTHER FOR THE LAST TIME.
Private Norman McLean, RRC, 19.8.42 (age 21)

LET HIS NAME BE NUMBERED WITH THE SAINTS.
Private James Henry Speed, RRC, 19.8.42 (age 37)

EACH DAY, EACH HOUR, A STEP FORWARD, A DANGER PASSED, A VICTORY WON.
Private Donald Barrington Taylor, RRC, 19.8.42 (age 26)

HE WILL ALWAYS LIVE FOR THOSE WHO LOVED HIM. REMEMBERING, WE WILL LOOK UP.
Lieutenant John Duckenfield Pearce, RRC, 19.8.42 (age 32)

CHERISHED IN THE HEARTS OF THOSE HE LEFT BEHIND.
SADLY MISSED BY UNCLE BILL, AUNT CONNIE AND FAMILY.
Private Edward George Smith, RRC, 19.8.42 (age 23)

HIS MEMORY IS WRITTEN IN LETTERS OF LOVE IN THE HEARTS OF THOSE HE LEFT AT HOME.
Sergeant Ewart Peaks, RRC, 19.8.42 (age 34)

MEMORY BRINGS YOU BACK ONCE MORE TO THE TIME WE WERE TOGETHER,
TO THE HAPPY DAYS OF YORE.
Private George Charles Adams, RRC, 19.8.42

JIM, OUR DEAR SON AND BROTHER. YOUR MEMORY HALLOWED IN THE LAND YOU LOVED.
Private James Robert White, RRC, 19.8.42 (age 22)

"HE WAS A VERRAY PARFIT GENTIL KNIGHT"
Lieutenant John Alexander Foster, RRC, 19.8.42 (age 23)
[CHAUCER, CANTERBURY TALES, PROLOGUE]

FOR BRITANNIA, ALL SHE STANDS FOR, AND OUR LITTLE CHILDREN, HE GAVE HIS LIFE.
Private Edward William Adams, RRC, 19.8.42 (age 25)

ALWAYS IN OUR HEARTS.
Private Mason Lewis Williamson, RRC, 19.8.42 (age 28)

AND WHILE HE LIES IN PEACEFUL SLEEP HIS MEMORY WE SHALL ALWAYS KEEP.
Private Thomas Edward Williamson, RRC, 19.8.42 (age 29)

The ranks of the Royal Hamilton Light Infantry were filled by men from the regiment's home town, as well as by recruits from neighbouring villages and farming communities. Thorold, Dundas, Brantford, and Dunnville were among the towns whose young men fell at Dieppe. One family in the hamlet of Simcoe lost two sons; a third was taken prisoner. The family of another Simcoe soldier killed in the raid was to lose a second son two years later in Italy:

PEACE, PERFECT PEACE.
Private Arthur Oliver Barber, RHLI, 19.8.42 (age 29)
Private Wesley David Barber, RHLI, 19.8.42 (age 32)

GREATER LOVE HATH NO MAN THAN THIS. "TILL WE MEET AGAIN"
Private Lloyd Martin Anderson, RHLI, 19.8.42 (age 26)
Trooper Joseph Allan Anderson, GGHG, 26.9.44 (age 21) [CESENA]

O DEATH, WHERE IS THY STING? O GRAVE, WHERE IS THY VICTORY? LOVING MOTHER.
Private Frank O'Neill, RHLI, 19.8.42 (age 22) [I CORINTHIANS 15: 55]

JESUS, TENDER SHEPHERD, HEAR ME, BLESS THY LITTLE ONE TONIGHT.
Private James Mulholland, RHLI, 19.8.42 (age 25)
[HYMN, JESUS, TENDER SHEPHERD, HEAR ME, BY CHARLOTTE ARLINGTON PYE BARNARD, 1834–1869]

**THE FIGHT FOR RIGHT HE HAS WON. THE KING OF KINGS HAS SPOKEN,
"THOU FAITHFUL ONE, WELL DONE."**
Private Edward Richard Walters, RHLI, 19.8.42 (age 20)

HE GAVE HIS LIFE FOR VICTORY AND NOW MAY HE REST IN PEACE.
Private Raymond William Taylor, RHLI, 19.8.42 (age 22)

OUR BILL. R.I.P.
Private William George Owen, RHLI, 19.8.42 (age 20)

A LOVING SON AND A TRUE SOLDIER.
Corporal Murray Herbert Henderson, RHLI, 19.8.42 (age 20)

KEEP ALIVE THEIR PRIDE, REMEMBER HOW THEY LIVED, REMEMBER WHY THEY DIED.
Private Gordon William Gurden, RHLI, 19.8.42 (age 22)

**BELOVED SON, WE ARE SAD BUT GRATEFUL THAT WITH MANY OTHERS
YOU DIED TO SAVE OUR EMPIRE.**
Private Michael Walter Mack, RHLI, 19.8.42 (age 27)

**"FOR GOD AND THE KING" HIS MOTTO WAS. HE SERVED THEM WELL.
WE MOURN HIS LOSS.**
Private Warren Harvey Tuck, RHLI, 19.8.42 (age 19)

"SOLDIER REST, THY WARFARE O'ER, SLEEP THE SLEEP THAT KNOWS NOT BREAKING."
Private Andrew John McConnell, RHLI, 19.8.42 (age 25)
[SIR WALTER SCOTT, THE LADY OF THE LAKE]

SOLDIERS DON'T DIE, THEY ARE JUST TRANSFERRED.
Private James Allan Paterson, RHLI, 19.8.42 (age 25)

The Essex Scottish completes the roll of the Ontario regiments that fought at

Dieppe. The volunteers from Windsor and the adjacent townships who furnished its manpower were descendants of Scots, English, and Irish settlers, but the Essex also drew recruits from the French settlements scattered throughout the region:

CHERISH WELL HIS GREAT SACRIFICE AND THAT OF THOSE WHO LOVE AND MISS HIM.
Lance Corporal Leo Joseph Trombley, ESR, 19.8.42 (age 22)

WE THINK OF HIM IN SILENCE, HIS NAME WE OFTEN RECALL.
ALL THAT'S LEFT TO ANSWER IS HIS PICTURE ON THE WALL.
Private Clayton Kenneth Collison, ESR, 19.8.42 (age 21)

A GALLANT SON WHO DIED THAT OTHERS MIGHT LIVE IN PEACE AND FREEDOM.
Corporal Elmore Regis Donnelly, ESR, 19.8.42 (age 27)

"LO, I AM WITH YOU ALWAYS." VI. AND JEANNE.
HE DIED THAT I MIGHT SERVE HUMANITY. MOTHER
Private William Wallace Black, ESR, 19.8.42 (age 25) [MATTHEW 28: 20]

"THE FATHER HATH NOT LEFT ME ALONE; FOR I DO ALWAYS THE THINGS THAT PLEASE HIM."
Private Douglas Charles Rinker, ESR, 19.8.42 (age 22) [JOHN 8: 29]

DEAR SON RUSSELL LEE. LOVINGLY REMEMBERED BY MOM AND DAD,
BROTHERS RAYMOND AND DON.
Private Russell Lee O'Connor, ESR, 19.8.42 (age 18)

OUR DEAR SON WILFRED DANIEL. EVER LOVINGLY REMEMBERED BY MOM AND DAD,
BROTHERS RAYMOND AND DON.
Private Wilfred Daniel O'Connor, ESR, 19.8.42 (age 20)

Added to the mix were Canadians of more recent vintage. One of them was a young soldier born in Budapest whose family commended his service to his adopted country in his mother tongue:

SZÜLETETT MAGYAR DE HÜ KANADAI LEGDRÀGÀBBAT ADA IFJÙ ÉLETÉT HAZÀJÀÉRT.
(Born a Hungarian, but as a faithful Canadian gave his country
the most precious thing, his young life.)
Lance Corporal Alexander Taylor, ESR, 19.8.42 (age 20)

The family of a young Jewish soldier had come to Windsor from Poland in 1935. Samuel Berger signed up in June 1940, went overseas in 1941, and was killed in his first engagement. His parents chose the last line of a poem entitled *Death Comes a Knocking*, written by the American Jerome B. Bell in 1940, to honour the memory of their son:

SUCH SOULS FOREVER LIVE IN THE BOUNDLESS MEASURE OF THE LOVE THEY GIVE.
Private Samuel Berger, ESR, 19.8.42 (age 22)

This poetic quotation came to the minds of a bereaved wife and family:

"OUT OF THE HEART, A RAPTURE, THEN A PAIN; OUT OF THE DEAD, COLD ASHES, LIFE AGAIN"
JOHN BANNISTER TODD
Private Newton Anderson Barnard, ESR, 19.8.42

Private Barnard's epitaph contains a small mistake, as the author in question was the American poet and Catholic priest John Banister Tabb (1845–1909). While families in search of literary quotations to serve as epitaphs turned to Shakespeare, Tennyson, Housman, or other eminent names in English literature, tracing the quotations on headstones leads to dozens of authors whose names and works, like Tabb's poem *Evolution*, are forgotten today. The miscellany of authors from whom quotations were selected, and the relative permanence or transience of their reputations, are shown in these inscriptions found in the Dieppe war cemetery and frequently quoted elsewhere. The first is taken from Shelley's poem *Adonais*, the encomium to his friend John Keats. The second is from *There is No Death*, by John Luckey McCreery (1835–1906), a poet popular in his own lifetime but unheard of nowadays:

HE HATH AWAKENED FROM THE DREAM OF LIFE.
Lieutenant James Chaney Palms (of U.S.A.*),* ESR, *19.8.42 (age 27)*

THERE IS NO DEATH. THE STARS GO DOWN TO RISE UPON SOME OTHER SHORE.
Gunner Morris Robert Vick, RCA, *19.8.42 (age 26)*

Another oft-quoted verse appears on the headstone of a soldier from Toronto:

WARM SUNSHINE, SHINE KINDLY HERE; WARM WIND, BLOW SOFTLY HERE;
SOFT GREEN SOD, LIE LIGHT; BRAVE HEART, GOOD NIGHT.
Private Cyril Lloyd Sproule, RRC, *19.8.42 (age 33)*

This tender appeal to the elements of nature to shelter the grave of a loved one comes from the final stanza of an otherwise unmemorable poem, *Annette*, by Robert Richardson. The poem and its author would have languished in obscurity had not Mark Twain adapted the last lines for the gravestone of his daughter Susy upon her death in 1896. These lines then found their way into many anthologies, principally because they were attributed to Twain himself, and so entered the repertoire of funerary verse.

A quotation popular during the war which has since slipped over the horizon appears on the headstone of a soldier from Winnipeg, the town where his regiment, the Queen's Own Cameron Highlanders, was based:

"GIVE ME A LIGHT THAT I MAY TREAD SAFELY INTO THE UNKNOWN."
Private John Burton Tully, QOCHC, *19.8.42*

The line is taken from a poem entitled *God Knows*, written by Minnie Louise Haskins and privately published in 1908. The poem was a favourite of Queen Elizabeth, later the Queen Mother, who suggested it to King George VI for use in his Christmas broadcast of December 1939, at a time when Britain and the Commonwealth were anxiously contemplating the trials to come. So apposite did his listeners find these prayerful words that they were widely reprinted on cards and included in the second edition of the *Oxford Dictionary of Quotations*.

THEY SHALL BE CHANGED BUT THOU ART THE SAME. PS. CII.27
Lieutenant Llewellyn Clark Bell, RHLI, *19.8.42 (age 31)*

"IN THE WAY OF RIGHTEOUSNESS IS LIFE: AND IN THE PATH THEREOF THERE IS NO DEATH."
Signalman Wallace John Browne, RCCS, *19.8.42 (age 27)* [PROVERBS 12: 28]

"COME YE BOUGHT, BUT NOT WITH GOLD, WELCOME TO THE SACRED FOLD."
WITH LOVE, MAM.
Sapper Glyn Jones, CRCE, 19.8.42 (age 22)

FROM TIRED JOY AND GRIEF AFAR AND NEARER THEE, FATHER, WHERE THINE OWN
CHILDREN ARE, I LOVE TO BE.
Sergeant Charles Hadfield Teather, RHLI, 19.8.42 (age 37)

"IN FULL AND GLAD SURRENDER I GIVE MYSELF TO THEE, THINE UTTERLY AND ONLY AND
EVERMORE TO BE."
Lieutenant Percy Owen Lee, ESR, 19.8.42 (age 23)

The King James Bible had not yet ceded its place to the revised versions which have now supplanted it in the English-speaking world. Its archaic, lofty cadences ring forth in hundreds of consolatory passages drawn from Scripture. The words of John 15: 13 ("Greater love hath no man. . .") and II Timothy 4: 7 ("I have fought the good fight. . .") made appropriate epitaphs for soldiers fallen in defence of their country and stand out as the two passages most often used for inscriptions. The Beatitudes inspired many families seeking spiritual comfort, as did the Psalms; but recourse to a remarkably wide range of quotations, from every book of the Bible, is a feature distinguishing Protestant from Catholic burials. So, too, is the fashioning of epitaphs from hymns and religious verse. Selections from such well known hymns as *Rock of Ages* or *Abide With Me* predominate, but again the repertoire is strikingly plentiful. Many of the hymns quarried for epitaphs were written during the second half of the 19th century, when legions of versifiers rose to the defence of religious belief against the assaults launched by the disciples of Darwin, Marx, and Nietzsche. The words of hymns and religious poems composed in this era would have come readily to the parents of English Canadian soldiers, members of a generation born in the last years of Queen Victoria's reign and well versed in the hymnbooks of the Church of England and the Protestant denominations.

The words of a hymn introduce a selection of epitaphs inscribed on the headstones of soldiers from western Canada. These men came from Prairie towns and farmsteads to join the Camerons, the South Saskatchewans, and the Calgary Regiment:

WHEN THE MORN AWAKENS, THEN MAY I ARISE, PURE AND SINLESS IN THY HOLY EYES.
Corporal Eldon Thornton Hatch, QOCHC, 19.8.42 (age 28)
[HYMN, *NOW THE DAY IS OVER*, BY SABINE BARING-GOULD, 1825–1878]

HE IS IN THE HANDS OF GOD. A PROUD FAMILY REMEMBERS WITH LOVE AND GRATITUDE.
Sergeant Lewis Robley Graham, QOCHC, 19.8.42 (age 35)

BELOVED ON EARTH, REGRETTED GONE, REMEMBERED IN THE GRAVE.
Private Alan Charles Hancock, QOCHC, 19.8.42 (age 37)

HE WAS ONLY ONE OF MANY, BUT HE WAS OURS. SEE YOU IN THE MORNING, ROB.
Private Robert Edward Stewart, QOCHC, 19.8.42 (age 22)

GOOD SON AND BROTHER, TRUE FRIEND, A LOVING, VALIANT YOUTH. THANKS BE TO GOD.
Lieutenant Leonard George Kempton, SSR, 19.8.42 (age 21)

REMEMBERED FOREVER BY ALL THOSE WHO HOLD YOU DEAR TO THEIR HEARTS.
WIFE AND FAMILY
Private Donald Tyman, SSR, 19.8.42 (age 24)

GONE BUT NOT FORGOTTEN, SOLDIER BRAVE.
Private Gordon Danforth, SSR, 19.8.42 (age 27)

TRUTH, DUTY, VALOR: FEAR NAUGHT. REST IN PEACE, DEAR ONE.
MOTHER, DAD AND FAMILY
Captain Douglas Gordon Purdy, CR, 19.8.42 (age 22)

Four times as many Canadians died at Vimy Ridge as at Dieppe, yet the former is enshrined in national memory as a catalyst in Canada's emergence as a nation while the latter remains a byword for military failure and a waste of lives. The casualty figures crowned the disappointment of the Dieppe raid. Chafing at the long period of inactivity in England, the Canadians had been eager to go into action, only to see nearly three thousand soldiers of the 2nd Division expend their years of training and preparation in a few hours. Just one of the commanders who led their regiments ashore returned to England. The commander of the Camerons was killed almost as soon as he set foot on French soil:

"WE'LL ALWAYS WALK BESIDE YOU. . ." MOTHER, GUY AND PEG.
Lieutenant Colonel Alfred Capel Gostling, QOCHC, 19.8.42 (age 39)

It would be two years before the 2nd Canadian Infantry Division, remanned and refitted, entered the lists once again, this time in the battles south of Caen during the summer of 1944. The victory in Normandy, which opened the way to the liberation of the Channel ports and a triumphant return by the Canadians to Dieppe in early September 1944, came at a high price to the regiments returning to the continent to avenge their defeat of two years before. The toll exacted from one family is posted on a headstone at Dieppe recording two names and two dates of death:

BELOVED ONLY SONS OF GEORGE ALLAN AND MARY ALMA INGRAM, TORONTO, CANADA.
Private Kenneth James Ingram, RRC, 19.8.42 (age 20)
Sergeant Robert Dalton Ingram, RRC, 13.8.44 (age 23)

Almost every Canadian war cemetery contains one or more pairs of brothers, or a note beside a name in the register stating that a brother also fell. Occasionally, however, an inscription communicates the saddening image of a family already afflicted by loss at home forced to absorb the added blow of a death on active service:

GONE HOME TO LITTLE PAULINE. MAY THEY REST IN PEACE. EVER REMEMBERED.
MARGE & SON JIM.
Private Richard Podger, ESR, 19.8.42 (age 26)

Not all the Canadians killed at Dieppe are buried there. The wounded brought back to England who died afterwards were buried in the Canadian section at Brookwood cemetery, near London, while a small plot in the British cemetery at Rouen houses their comrades left behind who succumbed to their wounds. For weeks after the raid, bodies of the dead washed ashore and were interred in local churchyards. After the war, the diaspora of Dieppe burials was regathered among the dead of two wars at Boulogne and Dunkirk, and among their countrymen in the Canadian war cemeteries at Calais, Adegem, and Holten. These epitaphs commemorate soldiers laid to rest far from the place where they died in battle:

MORT SI JEUNE POUR QUE NOUS VIVIONS LIBRES!
(He died so young that we may live in freedom!)
Lieutenant André Marcel Raoul Joseph Vennat, FMR, 19.8.42 *(age 32)* [BROOKWOOD]

SON EXEMPLE, NOTRE SOUVENIR. SA FEMME EVA DUMAINE, SA FILLE MARIE JEANNE.
(His example, our remembrance. His wife Eva Dumaine,
and his daughter Marie Jeanne)
Private Jean Louis Dumaine, FMR, 19.8.42 *(age 35)* [ROUEN]

IN LOVING MEMORY OF OUR DEAR SON. DIED OF WOUNDS. MAY HIS SOUL REST IN PEACE.
Private Lawrence Austin McConville, RHLI, 19.8.42 *(age 19)* [BROOKWOOD]

THOSE LEFT BEHIND ARE VERY DEAR BUT NONE REPLACES YOU.
Private Fred Fletcher, RHLI, 21.8.42 *(age 21)* [BROOKWOOD]

CROWNS FOR THE VALIANT, O WHAT THEIR JOY AND THEIR GLORY MUST BE IN HEAVEN.
Private Arthur Jones, RHLI, 8.9.42 *(age 35)* [ROUEN]
[HYMN, *O WHAT THEIR JOY*, ATTRIBUTED TO PETER ABELARD, 1079–1142]

ENEMIES NONE DID THEY BUT KNOW HIM. SO GREATLY LOVED. HE HAD NO RIGHT TO DIE.
Private John Bryan Cronin, RHLI, 19.8.42 *(age 26)* [CALAIS]

"MY SON, KEEP THY FATHER'S COMMANDMENT AND FORGET NOT THE LAW OF THY MOTHER"
Private Austin Joseph Rhynard, RHLI, 19.8.42 *(age 21)* [CALAIS] [PROVERBS 6: 20]

HE HAD A CHEERY SMILE, A PLEASANT WAY, HE WAS SO KIND.
Private Roy Liege Clausen, RHLI, 26.8.42 *(age 28)* [HOLTEN]

"THY GRACE IS SUFFICIENT FOR ME."
Private Thomas Stainton, ESR, 19.8.42 *(age 26)* [ROUEN]
[HYMN, *I LIVE BUT IN THEE*, BY FANNY CROSBY, 1820–1915]

A FOREST RANGER. SERVED IN TWO WORLD WARS.
SHOWED US HOW TO LIVE AND HOW TO DIE.
Private George Thomas Underdahl, SSR, 19.8.42 *(age 46)* [BROOKWOOD]

QUE TON ÂME SOIT SANCTIFIÉ POUR LE SACRIFICE QUE TU NOUS A RENDU. TA MÈRE
(May your soul be blessed for the sacrifice on our behalf. Your mother)
Private Alphonse Gaudias Bélanger, QOCHC, 19.8.42 *(age 22)* [ROUEN]

FAR FROM CANADA BUT EVER REMEMBERED BY FATHER, MOTHER, SISTERS AND BROTHERS.
Private Andrew Joseph Laing, QOCHC, 19.8.42 *(age 23)* [ADEGEM]

The loss of a son, husband, or father on active service confronted families with death on its harshest terms: a rupture untimely, violent, and faraway, denying the chance to say goodbye. From its inception the War Graves Commission had held firm to its decision, against considerable public outcry, that the bodies of the fallen would not be repatriated but would remain in the lands where they had been buried. As a result, most Canadian families, as well as those in the Dominions beyond the seas, had to resign themselves to the realisation that they might never visit the grave where a loved one lay at rest. The invitation to contribute a personal inscription will have offered one of the few ways for the bereaved to assuage the multiple pains of their loss. These Dieppe epitaphs dwell on the themes of separation, of a parting without farewell, and the wish to preserve some connection with the departed:

HE SLEEPS BESIDE HIS COMRADES, HIS GRAVE I MAY NEVER SEE.
MAY SOME KIND HAND LAY A FLOWER FOR ME.
Private Roland Dewar Bryan, RRC, 19.8.42 (age 22)

HE LITTLE THOUGHT HE WOULD NO MORE RETURN; WE ONLY KNOW HE PASSED AWAY
AND COULD NOT SAY GOOD-BYE.
Private Robert Davidson Murphy, ESR, 19.8.42 (age 37)

FAR FROM NATIVE LAND AND LOVED ONES HE NOBLY PAID THE SUPREME SACRIFICE.
Private William Baines Murcell, RRC, 19.8.42 (age 29)

WHEN DAYS ARE DARK AND FRIENDS ARE FEW, DEAR GEORGE, I LONG FOR YOU.
HIS LOVING WIFE AND SON.
Private George Page Bloomfield, RRC, 19.8.42 (age 26)

ABSENT, UNSEEN BUT ALWAYS NEAR.
Lance Corporal Francis Herbert Smith, RHLI, 19.8.42 (age 26)

HE AND THEY GAVE THEIR YOUNG LIVES THAT WE MAY LIVE. HE IS EVER WITH US IN SPIRIT.
Private Bertram Howard Capnerhurst, ESR, 19.8.42 (age 18)

Even though the full account of the planning and conduct of the operation did not emerge until after the war, it was plain enough to the Canadian public from the casualty lists in the newspapers and the memorial services held across the country that Dieppe had been a sanguinary affair. The justification of the raid as a trial run for an eventual invasion only emphasized what a hazardous undertaking Operation Jubilee had been. And yet, despite the strong criticisms directed at the planners, one looks in vain for any hint of protest or cynicism on the headstones of the soldiers killed at Dieppe. No doubt there were families angered by the heedlessness that had squandered so many lives, who felt that the headstone of a fallen son or husband was not the place to air their views. Had they wished to do so, however, the War Graves Commission was prepared to accept inscriptions voicing anger or resentment. Inscriptions were subject to review, but this was on the grounds of length and propriety, not of opinion. The purpose was to discourage epitaphs expressing unseemly sentiments in war cemeteries designed to bestow lasting dignity upon the fallen. How widely expression of feelings might range, however, is evident from these examples of First World War epitaphs showing that next of kin could and did supply epitaphs in which they did not disguise feelings of acrimony at their loss:

HE DID HIS DUTY. MY HEART KNOWETH ITS OWN BITTERNESS. MOTHER
Private Reuben Turton Haley, Duke of Wellington's Regiment, 15.8.18 (age 30)
[PUCHEVILLERS]

A BURSTING BUD ON A SLENDER STEM, BROKEN AND WASTED, OUR BOY.
Private Thomas Leonard Michael Quinlan, Royal Warwickshire Regiment, 9.4.15
(age 19) [RATION FARM]

ANOTHER LIFE LOST, HEARTS BROKEN, FOR WHAT.
Private William Lincoln Rae, 20th Battalion Australian Infantry, 8.8.18 (age 24)
[VILLERS-BRETONNEUX]

The beach at Puys where the Royal Regiment of Canada was virtually wiped out on August 19, 1942.

The esplanade at Dieppe, with the chapel of Notre Dame de Bon Secours visible on the headland opposite.

Monument to the Essex Scottish Regiment on Red Beach.

Plaque at Puys dedicated to the men of the Royal Regiment of Canada killed on Blue Beach.

A view over the main beach revealing the perspective of the defenders.

The shingled beach over which tanks and infantry struggled to advance.

The monument to the Fusiliers Mont-Royal.

Double rows of headstones at Dieppe Canadian War Cemetery.

The entrance to the cemetery.

A row of Dieppe burials at Boulogne Eastern Cemetery.

(top) *"If death be the price of victory..."*

(bottom) *A rare call for vengeance in the Hebrew inscription on the headstone of Sergeant Samuel Moses Hurwitz.*

Others rejected the consolation that the soldier's death in battle had been redeemed by victory, or the notion that the war had been a means to achieving worthy ends:

IF DEATH BE THE PRICE OF VICTORY, O GOD FORBID ALL WARS.

Private John Thomas Wray, Lancashire Fusiliers, 10.3.16 (age 36) [AUTHUILLE]

GOD SPEED THE DAY WHEN WAR SHALL BE NO MORE AND EVERY HEART FEEL GLAD.

Airman 2nd Class Albert Edmund Manton, RAF, 20.2.19 [TERLINCTHUN]

BORN AT KOBE, JAPAN, 9TH OCTOBER 1890. SACRIFICED TO
THE FALLACY THAT WAR CAN END WAR.

2nd Lieutenant Arthur Conway Young, Royal Irish Fusiliers, 16.8.17 (age 26) [TYNE COT]

THEY THAT TAKE THE SWORD SHALL PERISH WITH THE SWORD. MATTHEW 26: 52

Private Eugene Thomas Smith, 2nd CMR, 10.8.18 (age 31) [BOUCHOIR]

MANY DIED AND THERE WAS MUCH GLORY.

Sergeant William John Clegg, CAMC, 1.10.18 [BRAMSHOTT CHURCHYARD]

The discovery of the circumstances of his son's death led one father to insist on an inscription proclaiming the icy truth of his son's fate, with a rejoinder restoring honour to his memory:

SHOT AT DAWN. ONE OF THE FIRST TO ENLIST. A WORTHY SON OF HIS FATHER.

Private Albert Ingham, Manchester Regiment, 1.12.16 (age 24) [BAILLEULMONT]

Discordant sentiments are exceptional, however, and are even more difficult to find among the epitaphs of the Second World War. A simple *Waarom?* (*Why?*) on a South African headstone in Ravenna War Cemetery questions fate rather than the war itself, and it would seem that to the peoples of the Allied nations the nature of the enemy and his works left little doubt that the war had to be fought and won. Still, there were some, like the families of these British and Canadian servicemen, who decried the unfairness and wastefulness of it all:

"TO SAVE THE WORLD" THE OLD MAY CRY, BUT TO DO SO THE YOUNG MUST DIE.

Sergeant Frederick Harold Cowley, Royal Artillery, 3.10.43 (age 35) [SANGRO RIVER]

BELOVED, YOU WERE TOO YOUNG TO PAY THE DEBT.
YOU ARE NOT DEAD TO US BUT SLEEPING.

Driver Ernest Charles Treadwell, Royal Engineers, 26.5.44 (age 20) [CASSINO]

SLEEP WELL, DOUGGIE. YOUR WIFE, SON AND PARENTS KNOW THE PRICE WAS TOO HIGH.

Flight Sergeant Douglas William Webb, RAF, 9.2.45 (age 29) [ESBJERG]

"O THAT I MIGHT IN DYING SO ENLIGHTEN MAN! AND BY THIS SUFFERING SHOW
TO HIM HIS FOLLY."

Flying Officer Leonard Dennis Harvey Jenner, RAF, 8.6.45 (age 24) [PADUA]

MANKIND'S FOLLY, ANOTHER SACRIFICE.

Private Gordon Alexander Pease, CH, 9.9.44 (age 24) [BAYEUX]

"MAN'S INHUMANITY TO MAN MAKES COUNTLESS THOUSANDS MOURN."

Corporal Benjamin Morrison, BWC, 24.7.44 (age 23) [BRETTEVILLE-SUR-LAIZE]
Private Wilbur Allan Prough, RHLI, 18.10.44 (age 19) [SCHOONSELHOF]

[ROBERT BURNS, MAN WAS MADE TO MOURN]

Latent in the epitaph of a sixteen-year-old Canadian soldier buried at Ortona is the parents' bitterness that their son had been just another bit of cannon fodder to the recruiters, the faceless "they" who allowed a boy well under military age to sign up for overseas service. Similar resentment that "they" had squandered the love and care invested in a child infuses the epitaph of another young soldier buried in Holland. Parallelism and studied understatement give both epitaphs greater impact:

HE SIGNED HIS NAME FOR VICTORY AND AFTER A TIME THEY PUT IT ON A CROSS.
Private Gordon Ott, HPER, 30.1.44 (age 16) [MORO RIVER]

I HAD RAISED HIM TO MANHOOD AND THEY LAID HIM TO REST.
Private Thomas Clinton Beers, NS(NB)R, 27.2.45 (age 24) [GROESBEEK]

Conspicuous by their rarity, even after the full revelation of the crimes committed by the Nazis, are cries of hostility or demands for vengeance. This call for divine retribution, composed in Hebrew and thus concealed from all but a few, is inscribed on the headstone of a Jewish Canadian soldier buried in Holland:

HERE LIES THE HONOURED SAMUEL MOSHE,
THE SON OF CHAIM ABRAHAM HALEVI HURWITZ. MAY GOD AVENGE HIS DEATH.
FROM MONTREAL, CANADA. THE NINTH DAY OF KISLEV 5705.
Sergeant Samuel Moses Hurwitz, CGG, 17.4.45 (age 26) [BERGEN-OP-ZOOM]

Infrequent as they are, these inscriptions display the breadth of tone and content permitted. In the case of Canadian epitaphs, the number of languages and the various scripts in which epitaphs appear further indicate the lengths to which the War Graves Commission went to accommodate the requests of next of kin. But if trawling through the epitaphs from both world wars yields only isolated cases of dissent from the prevailing themes of sacrifice, duty, or patriotism, comparison between the two also reveals a difference at the other end of the scale. Few epitaphs from the Second World War rise to these levels of Great War idealism:

HIS LAST WORDS ON LEAVING HOME, FAREWELL, I WILL DO MY BEST.
2nd Lieutenant Alan Williamson Kent, Northumberland Fusiliers, 27.4.15
[VLAMERTINGHE]

IF I FALL, I SHALL HAVE DONE SOMETHING WITH MY LIFE WORTH DOING.
Private George Lawrence Holmden, 5th BCI, 19.8.15 (age 20)
[BERKS CEMETERY EXTENSION]

BE ASHAMED TO DIE UNTIL YOU HAVE GAINED SOME VICTORY FOR HUMANITY.
Lance Corporal George Edward Pike, RNR, 1.7.16 (age 33) ['Y' RAVINE]

FOR SONS AS YET UNBORN WILL READ HOW BRITISH SONS MET BRITAIN'S NEED.
Private Oswald Rowland, Royal Fusiliers, 17.2.17 (age 21) [REGINA TRENCH]

HE WENT OUT A GALLANT GENTLEMAN.
Captain Francis Ritson, Dorsetshire Regiment, 17.6.17 (age 26) [TORREKEN FARM]

I AM GOING. MY COUNTRY NEEDS ME.
Private Edward Ephraim Panabaker, PPCLI, 31.10.17 (age 19) [NINE ELMS BRITISH]

Examples of these declarations, elegies to the generation winnowed by the Great War and scarcely comprehensible today, could easily be multiplied. They speak with the voice of a bygone day and age, issuing from the far side of the historical chasm gouged between 1914 and 1918. And yet, contrary to received opinion, by no means did the slaughter in the trenches extinguish the general belief that the sacrifice had been necessary and meaningful, least of all in Canada. During the war, and after, even as disillusionment set in during the late 1920s, Canada produced no Owen, Graves, or Sassoon of her own to denounce *pro patria mori* as "the old lie". The perception of the Great War in Canada, and the ways in which it shaped the response to the losses of the Second World War, are subjects for another chapter. There is a body of inscriptions unique to Dieppe, however, which can be explained only with reference to the epitaphic precedents of the First World War:

LIBERTY AND FREEDOM HAD TO BE WON BY THE WILLING SACRIFICE OF LIFE.
Private William Stanley Mills, 5th CMR, *26.3.16 (age 24)* [MAPLE COPSE]

KILLED LEADING AN ATTACK AT REGINA TRENCH. LOYAL À MORT.
Lieutenant Willoughby Chatterton, 3rd BCI, *8.10.16 (age 26)* [ADANAC]

HE FELL AT THE SOMME. IT IS IMMORTAL HONOR.
Private James Edward Stickels, RCR, *9.10.16 (age 18)* [CONTAY]

MORT À VIMY À L'AGE DE 30 ANS EN COMBATTANT POUR LA GRANDE CAUSE.
(Died at Vimy at the age of 30 fighting for the great cause.)
Private Arthur Goyette, 22nd (FC)B, *11.4.17* [BRUAY]

PRINCIPAL, PUBLIC SCHOOLS, ARMSTRONG, B.C. VIMY RIDGE. O VALIANT HEART.
Private Thomas Rankine, 46th BCI, *18.4.17* [BRUAY]

KILLED NEAR PASSCHENDAELE.
Private Edward Francis Montagu Beldam, 2nd CMR, *30.10.17 (age 28)* [TYNE COT]

KILLED IN ACTION AT CAMBRAI. I SHALL GO TO HIM, BUT HE SHALL NOT RETURN.
Private William Campbell Bartling, 52nd BCI, *1.10.18 (age 30)* [CANADA CEMETERY]

To English Canadians and, lest we forget, to some French Canadians, the First World War assumed mythic status in the country's history, thanks to the performance of the Canadian Expeditionary Force whose exploits had won the admiration of the major Allies and become a source of national pride that endures to this day. The gallant stand at Ypres, the triumph of Vimy Ridge and the Hundred Days, and the tenacity shown by Canadian soldiers at Courcelette and Passchendaele had given a fledgling dominion of the British Empire a distinguished place on the international stage. The wish to unite a soldier's name with the battles that had enhanced the country's reputation was part of a broader desire to make of the fallen an elect—the Glorious Dead—whose valour and sacrifice gave them primacy of honour in the national memory:

HE IS NOT DEAD WHOSE MEMORY STILL IS LIVING WITHIN A NATION'S HEART.
WIFE & LITTLE SON
Major Norman Campbell Pilcher, 5th CMR, *19.5.16* [POPERINGHE NEW]

ALL THESE WERE THE GLORY OF THEIR TIME.
Lieutenant Lionel Hyman Eliot, 75th BCI, *9.4.17 (age 29)* [CANADIAN CEMETERY NO. 2]

WHEN THE DRUM ROLLS LET YOUR MOOD BE WORTHY OF OUR DEATHS.
Company Sergeant Major William Phillips, 87th BCI, *9.4.17 (age 27)*
[CANADIAN CEMETERY NO. 2]

DORS, JEAN PAUL, DANS UN DOUX SOMMEIL. LA CROIX GARDERA TA DEMEURE.
(Sleep, Jean Paul, in gentle repose. The Cross will stand over your resting place.)
Private Jean Paul Grignon MM, 75th BCI, *9.8.18 (age 26)* [CAIX]

THEIR GRAVES ARE ALTARS. HONOR AND PRAISE BUT MOURN THEM NOT.
Major Ralph Russell James Brown, 44th BCI, *31.10.17 (age 42)* [NINE ELMS BRITISH]

IN YEARS TO COME WHEN TIME IS OLDEN, CANADA'S DREAM SHALL BE OF THEM.
Gunner Donald Lachlan McKinnon, CFA, *13.9.17 (age 25)* [AUBIGNY]

Just as the bereaved of the Great War preferred to remember the Somme and Passchendaele as testaments of heroism rather than as ghastly hecatombs, so too did families a generation later see Dieppe as a synonym for courage and a pledge of faith in eventual victory. It had been a military catastrophe, but we should not forget that the raid had also been a statement of the Allies' intent to liberate the countries occupied by the Nazis and that the Canadians had been picked to deliver the message. The Fusiliers Mont-Royal could claim to be the first French Canadian regiment to have struck a blow for the liberty of France, a consoling honour which inspired the families of these soldiers to salute them as the heroes of Dieppe:

DIED FROM WOUNDS INFLICTED AT DIEPPE RAID. HE DID HIS DUTY TO THE END.
Private Maurice Malo, FMR, *3.9.42 (age 21)* [BROOKWOOD]

REPOSE EN PAIX CHER FRÈRE BIEN-AIMÉ, TOI TOMBÉ À LA PLUS NOBLE DES CAUSES.
(Rest in peace dearly beloved brother, you who fell in the noblest of causes.)
Sergeant Donat Beaudoin, FMR, *19.8.42 (age 29)* [BOULOGNE]

FILS DE M. ET MME OMER ST-GERMAIN. MORT AU CHAMP D'HONNEUR À DIEPPE.
(Son of Mr. and Mrs. Omer St. Germain. Died on the field of honour at Dieppe.)
Private Jean Paul St. Germain, FMR, *19.8.42 (age 25)*

EN L'HONNEUR DE PHIL. HÉROS DE DIEPPE S'EST SACRIFIÉ POUR NOUS.
(In honour of Philippe. The hero of Dieppe sacrificed himself for us.)
Corporal Philippe Le Bel, FMR, *19.8.42 (age 26)*

A LA DOUCE MÉMOIRE DE BRAVE SOLDAT. HÉROS DE DIEPPE.
(In fond memory of a brave soldier. A hero of Dieppe.)
Private Louis Philippe Grenier, FMR, *19.8.42 (age 24)*

WE WILL ALWAYS REMEMBER THE HEROES OF DIEPPE. WE PRAY FOR YOU. R.I.P.
Sergeant Joseph Maurice Alphonse Lapointe, FMR, *19.8.42 (age 22)*

The Norman port could not evoke similar ties of ancestry and history in English Canadians. They drew instead from their own traditions, from the uplifting hymns and verses inherited from the First World War, and from the conviction that a son or husband's death at Dieppe had not been for nothing, but was part of a symbolic turning point in the war, the first step towards victory and the restoration of freedom:

A VALIANT HEART WHO TO YOUR GLORY CAME.
Lieutenant William George Rogers Wedd, RRC, 19.8.42 (age 27)

AT THE GOING DOWN OF THE SUN AND IN THE MORNING WE WILL REMEMBER THEM.
Private Andrew Redpath Hendry, RRC, 19.8.42 (age 33)

GOD BLESS OUR DEAR BROTHER AND SON WHO BRAVELY FOUGHT FOR US. EVER
REMEMBERED BY FAMILY.
Private Bert Dalton Doonan, RRC, 19.8.42 (age 23) [MERS-LES-BAINS]

A WHISPER RAN THROUGH ALL THE EARTH, "DIEPPE IS LIBERTY'S REBIRTH."
Captain Norman Andrew Thomson Young, QOCHC, 19.8.42 (age 41)

OUR ONLY SON AND BROTHER. REST IN THE ARMS OF JESUS. THE BATTLE OF DIEPPE IS WON.
Private John Lendzioszek, RHLI, 19.8.42 (age 23) [BROOKWOOD]

YOUTH AND STRENGTH TO GIVE, FROM CANADA'S SHORE TO A DIEPPE BEACH TO DIE,
THAT WE MIGHT LIVE.
Private Hamilton Russell Stewart, SSR, 19.8.42 (age 34)

The Dieppe raid remains the most controversial and intensively scrutinised military operation in Canadian history, perhaps overly so. The criticisms and justifications offered in hindsight are of no avail against the finality of the past and cannot undo the fate of the men who went ashore that day. For all the controversy generated by Operation Jubilee, the responses of the families who felt its impact for the rest of their lives rarely enter the story. Years after the raid, when the volatile, wrenching emotions of grief had subsided, and enough time had gone by to put their loss in some perspective, the parents, wives, and children composed their farewells. There can be few Canadian visitors to Dieppe who are not stricken to silence at the sight of the cliffs, the beaches, and all that they imply. The words of the families supply the rest.

FURTHER READING:

Couture, Claude-Paul. *Opération « Jubilee ». Dieppe 19 août 1942.* Paris : Editions France-Empire, 1969.

Dumais, Lucien. *Un canadien à Dieppe.* Paris: Editions France-Empire, 1968.

Edmondson, John S., and Edmondson, Douglas. "Memories and reflections on the Dieppe Raid of 19 August 1942," *Canadian Military History* 13/4 (2004), 47–61.

Greenhous, Brereton. *Dieppe, Dieppe.* Montreal: Art Global, 1992.

Mordal, Jacques. *Les canadiens à Dieppe.* Paris: Presses de la cité, 1962.

Richard, Béatrice. *La mémoire de Dieppe. Radioscopie d'une mythe.* Montreal: VLB Editeur, 2002.

Robertson, Terence. *Dieppe. The Shame and the Glory.* Toronto: McClelland and Stewart, 1962.

Roland, Charles G. "On the beach and in the bag: The fate of Dieppe casualties left behind," *Canadian Military History* 9/4 (2000), 6–25.

Whitaker, Denis. *Dieppe: Tragedy to Triumph.* Toronto: McGraw-Hill Ryerson, 1992.

Sylvia McGeer

CHAPTER THREE

Echoes of the Great War
Calais Canadian War Cemetery, France

"TO YOU FROM FAILING HANDS WE THROW THE TORCH, BE YOURS TO HOLD IT HIGH."
Pilot Officer Perry Clinton Foster, RCAF, 18.6.42 (age 24)

The swift British and American advance that followed the defeat of the German armies in Normandy raised hopes that the war in the west might be over before the end of 1944. Within days of the final battles around Falaise, two capitals, Paris and Brussels, had been liberated. Like the streams released from a burst dam the Allied spearheads raced for the German border as the high command debated where best to aim the fatal thrust into the vitals of the Reich. The tantalising choices before the Allies in September 1944 and the bold attempt by the airborne forces to leapfrog onto the Rhine and Maas bridges in eastern Holland relegated the much less dramatic operations of First Canadian Army to the fringes of the war. When the bulk of the German forces withdrew to defensive positions blocking the approaches to their homeland, Hitler gave orders that large garrisons be left in the fortresses along the Channel coast to deny the Allies the harbours necessary for their lines of supply and to protect the coastal guns and launch sites of the V-1 rockets. While the British and Americans clutched at the prospect of a war-winning drive into Germany, it fell to the Canadians to capture the Channel ports and gun batteries in "a strange drama of mediaeval siege mingled with modern warfare." Given thankless tasks, begrudged the means to carry them out efficiently, and then scolded for their tardiness, the Canadians sweeping up the long left flank styled themselves for the rest of the war as "the Cinderella army."

NOT DEAD BUT LIVING IN DEEDS. SUCH LIVES INSPIRE.
Lieutenant Howard John Wilson, RCAMC, 14.9.44 (age 26)

BRAVE SOLDIER; LOYAL COMRADE; CHRISTIAN GENTLEMAN; LOVED BY ALL.
Lieutenant William Ernest Tranton, NS(NB)R, 17.9.44 (age 23)

He was a cheerful little soldier.
Private Donald Grant Houlston, NS(NB)R, 17.9.44 (age 19)

**I am the real vine's shoot but my Father in Heaven is the vine's dresser.
St. John XV. 1**
Private Leroy Charles Nichols, SDGH, 19.9.44 (age 22)

Killed in action. Just a boy. Endowed with everything but sacrificed all.
Rifleman Donald Wellesley Stewart, RRR, 25.9.44 (age 19)

"Until the day dawn, and the day-star arise in your hearts."
Captain Chad Noel Humphrys, NS(NB)R, 26.9.44 (age 26) [II Peter 1: 19]

"One who never turned his back but marched breast forward." Browning
Lieutenant Gordon Dunlap Campbell, NNSH, 29.9.44 (age 28)

The soldiers of the Cinderella army who died in the battles to clear the Channel coast predominate among the 594 Canadian servicemen interred on a hill midway between Boulogne and Calais. A long grass pathway leads up to the burial ground laid out on a levelled terrace. Thick stands of evergreens planted along the borders shelter the site from the winds that a generation earlier had compelled the builders of the Great War cemeteries in the Pas-de-Calais to lay the headstones flat. Most of the Canadian headstones date from September 1944, but a quorum of Dieppe casualties and the two hundred pilots and sailors of mixed nationalities at rest beside them bear witness to the sparring across the Channel during the long interval between Dunkirk and D-Day. The view to the west takes in the promontory of Cap Gris Nez where the Highland Light Infantry of Canada and the North Nova Scotia Highlanders silenced the coastal guns that since 1940 had lobbed shells across the Dover Straits; and beyond, the white cliffs of the English coast glimmer through the mist over the Channel. Surveyed from a cemetery of the Second World War, the narrow gap separating island and continent brings a sense of awe mingled with relief. A moat twenty-two miles wide was all that stood between survival and defeat in 1940, yet it made enough of a barrier to preserve Britain and with her the frail hope that the Nazi triumphs need not prove permanent.

The Canadians helping to undo the results of 1940 set forth from Normandy along the Channel coast, crossing the Somme River near Abbeville at the end of August 1944. Here they entered a corner of France well trodden by their fathers during the Great War. For four years Picardy and the Pas-de-Calais had hosted the armies of Great Britain and the Dominions as they poured across from England to disembark at Boulogne or Calais and begin the march up to the front lines. The return to the battlefields where "Byng's Boys" had made the country's name was marked by a ceremony at Vimy Ridge honouring the soldiers of the Canadian Corps and reminding their successors of the high reputation it was theirs to uphold.

He took up the torch and held it high.
Sergeant Thomas Edward Dell, LWR, 10.9.44 (age 22)

**Now by crosses row on row you linger where the poppies grow.
Not dead but just away.**
Private John Cote, HLIC, 19.9.44 (age 21)

One of the Channel towns liberated by the Canadians was Wimereux, which fell to the North Shore Regiment in an attack designed to limit damage to the town and casualties to the inhabitants. Soldiers aware of the town's Canadian connection would have been relieved to learn that their precautions had spared the communal cemetery where Lieutenant Colonel John McCrae had been laid to rest. A flat headstone, often speckled with poppies left by visitors, marks his place. A plaque dedicated by the government of Ontario now commemorates the site, and lines from *In Flanders Fields* are inscribed on the cemetery wall; but it is sad to realise from the absence of a personal inscription on the grave that whatever the joys of McCrae's life, marriage and children were not among them. The appeal of his poem, however, is apparent from the number of headstones, of both wars and all English-speaking countries, which quote its verses. The first stanza transformed the poppy into a universal symbol of remembrance and regeneration; the second dwelt on the joys of life lost to the dead; and the final stanza, with its passing of the torch and injunction not to break faith with those who lay in Flanders fields, spoke with new relevance in 1939 to a generation called upon to take up the quarrel with the foe their fathers had faced, and to the survivors who affirmed their pact with those they mourned by pledging to finish the work left undone:

"TO HOLD IT HIGH." THE MOTTO OF HIS SQUADRON.

Flying Officer Arthur Allen Styles Flemington, RCAF, 29.4.43 (age 31) [BROOKWOOD]

THE TORCH YOUR FAILING HANDS PASSED ON IS OURS TO HOLD AND CARRY ON.

Lieutenant John Lawrence Morgan, RCR, 17.5.44 (age 28) [CASSINO]

"IF YE BREAK FAITH WITH US WHO DIE WE SHALL NOT SLEEP. . ."

Lieutenant Vaughan Stuart Allan, PPCLI, 15.12.44 (age 22) [RAVENNA]

WE SHALL NOT BREAK FAITH.

Pilot Officer Donald Hanna, RCAF, 21.2.45 (age 22) [REICHSWALD FOREST]

LET YOUR REST BE SWEET AND DEEP. WE WILL KEEP FAITH WITH YOU WHO LIE ASLEEP.

Flight Lieutenant Hedley Charles Cormick Goodyear, RCAF, 23.4.44 (age 25)
[HANOVER]

GOD GRANT THE CAUSE FOR WHICH THEY DIED SHALL NOT FAIL THROUGH ME.

Corporal Gordon Thygesen, NNSH, 7.6.44 (age 33) [BÉNY-SUR-MER]

HIS TASK IS FINISHED, OURS JUST BEGUN, TO BRING PEACE. WE SHALL NOT FAIL HIM.

Private Clive Austin Mills, ASHC, 24.10.44 (age 19) [BERGEN-OP-ZOOM]

WE THE TASK INHERIT, THE UNFINISHED TASK FOR WHICH THEIR LIVES WERE SPENT.

Lieutenant Donald Charles MacKenzie MC, RWR, 22.4.45 (age 30) [HOLTEN]

OUR SLEEPING SONS IN MUTE APPEAL STIR SILENTLY LEST THOU FORGET
FOR THEE WE DIED.

Pilot Officer Joseph Lawrie Outerson, RCAF, 25.4.45 (age 20) [SAGE]

The spectre of the Great War hovers over every Canadian cemetery of the Second World War, but the ties with 1914–1918 seem strongest at Calais where the rhetoric of commemoration reveals itself as more than fine words. The line from Lawrence Binyon's *For the Fallen* (1914), recited at Remembrance Day ceremonies from their inception in the 1920s, had a weightier meaning for Mrs. Marjorie Stephenson, a widow of the First World War and a bereaved mother of the Second:

AT THE GOING DOWN OF THE SUN AND IN THE MORNING WE WILL REMEMBER THEM.
Captain John Norman Stephenson, NNSH, 7.9.44 (age 29)

The plural "them," an abstraction to us, was all too literal to the people twice afflicted by loss. The register book records that Captain Stephenson's father and namesake, Private John Stephenson, was killed in France in November 1917. He has no known grave and is one of the 8,000 Canadians listed among the missing on the panels of the Menin Gate in Ieper. The inscription on his son's grave is by no means the only one in which the valediction to a soldier who fell in the Second World War spoke for another lost without a trace in the First.

The grave of a Royal Winnipeg officer killed in the outworks of fortress Calais bears the phrase from Ecclesiasticus 44: 14 which had inspired Rudyard Kipling's choice of the inscription to be used in all the war cemeteries:

THEIR BODIES ARE BURIED IN PEACE BUT THEIR NAME LIVETH FOR EVERMORE.
Major Frederick Scott Allen, RWR, 27.9.44 (age 25)

"It was necessary to find words of praise and honour which should be both simple and well known, comprehensive and of the same value in all tongues, and standing, as far as might be, outside the flux of men and things," wrote Kipling in his capacity as literary advisor to the Imperial War Graves Commission when he submitted "Their name liveth for evermore" as the collective tribute to be engraved on the Stone of Remembrance. So deep was his solicitude for the reputation of the fallen (one of them being his son, listed as missing after the battle of Loos in 1915) that he, the most famous author of his time, felt that it did not "beseem any man to use his own words in this matter" but to choose a passage from a venerable authority. Kipling had previously compiled a list of quotations from Ecclesiasticus which he sent to next of kin requesting personal inscriptions; but his selection of this particular passage was made with an eye to the future. He foresaw a time when the cause the soldiers had fought for would be "lost, stultified, jeered down and variously defiled . . . but the memory of all that crowd of demi-gods will stand." He also counted on the readers' familiarity with the source. Chapter 14 of Ecclesiasticus (the title given to the apocryphal Wisdom of Sirach, the work of a Jewish sage who lived in the second century B.C.) opens with a eulogy of the kings and heroes of ancient Israel whose names enjoy lasting renown and inspire succeeding generations, then turns to the anonymous many who have vanished from memory. "Yet these also were godly people," forgotten in name but remembered for their qualities and achievements. Their reward lies in the blessings of a secure lineage and a reputation enduring "days without number," passed on when all their people and descendants convene in remembrance.

SO FAIR, SO YOUNG, THE SONG OF YOUTH HAD SCARCE BEGUN.
Pilot Officer Walter Donald Huff, RCAF, 16.6.44 (age 19)

**REMEMBRANCE IS A GOLDEN CHAIN, FOR YOU WERE OUR SON, MAC,
AND WE REMEMBER.**
Pilot Officer George Edward Sinclair, RCAF, 12.5.44 (age 20)

**TWO HEARTS LOVED YOU ALWAYS AND WILL LOVE YOU IN DEATH THE SAME.
MOM AND DAD**
Sergeant George William Easton, RCA, 7.9.44 (age 22)

OUR ONLY CHILD. TO CLASP HIS HAND AND HEAR HIS VOICE THAT MEANT SO MUCH TO HIS MUM & DAD.
Private Frederick Richard Langley, BWC, 12.9.44 (age 23)

THERE IS SOMEONE WHO MISSES YOU SADLY BUT TRIES TO BE BRAVE AND CONTENT.
Bombardier James Charles Gray, RCA, 7.1.45 (age 24)

A BRIGHTER HARBOUR BECKONED WHERE PEACE AND LOVE PREVAIL.
Corporal John Wilfred Linder, RRR, 25.9.44 (age 23)

GOD SAW HIS FOOTSTEPS FALTER, GENTLY CLOSED HIS EYES AND WHISPERED, PEACE BE THINE.
Gunner George Thomas Lockett, RCA, 7.9.44 (age 28)

WHEN YOUR LIFE WAS BRIGHTEST YOU WERE TAKEN FROM A WORLD OF SORROW TO ETERNAL REST.
Rifleman David Raymond Swedberg, QORC, 30.9.44 (age 21)

OUR DARLING IS SHELTERED BY THE ROCK OF AGES, ANCHORED ON GOD'S GOLDEN SHORE.
Private Joseph Gerald Fisher, RCAMC, 6.9.44 (age 24)

MINE TILL THE DAY BREAK AND JESUS COMES TO GIVE PEACE TO THE WORLD. MOTHER
Private Humphrey Holloway, HLIC, 19.9.44 (age 21)

WE THINK YOU ARE ONE WITH THE CLOUDS AND THE SUN, THE VALLEYS UNDEFILED.
Private Ralph Glenwood Anderson, TSR, 18.9.44 (age 19)
[ROBERT SERVICE, THE ATAVIST, IN RHYMES OF A ROLLING STONE, 1912]

"GOOD NIGHT, SWEET PRINCE, AND FLIGHTS OF ANGELS SING THEE TO THY REST."
Sergeant Maurice Edward Clark, RRR, 6.9.44 (age 32)

LOVE IS IMMORTAL, AND MAKES ALL THINGS IMMORTAL.
Flight Lieutenant Kenneth Richard Walley, RCAF, 20.10.44 (age 28)
[WILLIAM SAROYAN, THE HUMAN COMEDY, 1943]

HE FOLLOWED AFTER THINGS OF THE SPIRIT.
Private Donald Richard Carey Smith, CH, 8.9.44 (age 35)

"LOOKING UNTO JESUS, THE AUTHOR AND FINISHER OF OUR FAITH." HEBREWS XII. 2
Sergeant John Muir, RCA, 24.9.44 (age 29)

"I HAVE REDEEMED THEE, I HAVE CALLED THEE BY NAME; THOU ART MINE." IS. XLIII. 1
Rifleman Zeigfried Heppler, RWR, 2.9.44 (age 23)

"GREATER LOVE HATH NO MAN THAN THIS." ST. JOHN XV. 13. PER ARDUA TENDIMUS ALTE.
(Through trials we strive for the high road.)
Lieutenant Gordon Benjamin Anstey Bate, 12th MD, 30.8.44 (age 30)

PRO DEO, PRO PATRIA. IN GOD'S WILL WAS HE STRONG. HIS MEMORY LIVETH FOR EVER.
Private Raymond Gordon Hill, NNSH, 17.9.44 (age 19)

YOUR UNSELFISH LIFE, IT HAS NOT DIED. GOOD NIGHT, BRAVE HEART, GOOD NIGHT.
Private Douglas John Picken, NNSH, 17.9.44 (age 20)

"THE WORTHY DIE THAT LESSER SOULS MAY LIVE." OUR BELOVED SON,
HUSBAND AND DAD.
Lieutenant Caleb Evert Sutherland, NNSH, *17.9.44 (age 30)*

HAPPY IN LIFE HE BRAVELY DIED FOR FREEDOM. LOVINGLY REMEMBERED BY FAMILY.
Private Joseph Owen Lloyd, BWC, *13.9.44 (age 21)*

"I HAVE LOVED THEE WITH AN EVERLASTING LOVE." JEREMIAH XXXI. 3
Trooper Robert Austin Acres, 12th MD, *5.9.44 (age 24)*

A BRAVE CANADIAN SOLDIER. ALL THE CITIZENS OF OUR FREE,
GOD-GIVEN LAND, REMEMBER THEM.
Lance Corporal Alex Feschuk, CH, *9.9.44 (age 23)*

The foregoing epitaphs from Calais encompass the response to the second culling of the young in a span of three decades. Expressions of regret and inexorable sorrow alternate with others showing the sources of consolation to which families turned. They point to the places where comfort was to be found, in Scripture and religious belief, in the affirmation of the principles for which Canada had fought, the examples of loyalty and courage the fallen represented, and in the conviction that the sacrifice of life had been meaningful. In all of these valedictions, refrains of the Great War sound once again, for the response of the previous generation to the tragedy of 1914–1918 set a pattern for the commemoration of the war dead and the consolation of the mourners that was to be repeated in the years after the Second World War. To recognise the influence of First World War precedents on the epitaphs composed for the fallen of the Second, we must step back to the years after the Armistice.

Victory, but the price was dear—the six words on the headstone of Private Richard Vidal, killed in September of 1918 during the advance of the Hundred Days, the Canadian Corps' crowning achievement of the Great War, encapsulate the reactions among Canadians to a conflict which had taken over 60,000 of their countrymen from their midst. Pride in the contribution of Canada's soldiers to the Allied triumph was tempered by the grief at the death toll, terrible and benumbing, wholly unforeseen in 1914, that demanded commemoration capable of giving meaning and redemption to loss on such a scale and, above all, solace to the mourners. The memory of the Great War that evolved in Canada in the years after the war, so thoughtfully explored by Jonathan Vance, responded to the need for consolation by defining the religious, patriotic, or moral principles for which Canadian soldiers had given their lives, and by exalting their sacrifice in a just war waged in defence of humanity and Christian civilisation against a barbarous aggressor. The larger significance of the war, the reasons for the expenditure of so many young lives, and the rewards of victory found symbolic representation from one end of the country to the other. Local monuments of every kind, memorials, church windows, war art, statues, and plaques sanctified the triumphs and sacrifice of Canada's soldiers and provided a focal point for the annual rituals of remembrance that hallowed the memory of the fallen.

ONE OF CANADA'S BEST. NOW OUR MUCH LOVED DEAD.
Private John Wilson Aikens, 18th BCI, *15.9.16 (age 24)* [CONTAY]

OUR DEAD ARE NEVER DEAD TO US UNTIL WE HAVE FORGOTTEN THEM.
Private John Cameron Robertson, 14th BCI, *3.6.16 (age 29)* [HOOGE CRATER]

ONLY THOSE WHO HAVE LOST LOVED ONES KNOW THE BITTERNESS OF "GONE."
FROM HIS LOVING MOTHER.
Sapper Herbert William Procter, CE, 28.10.17 [NINE ELMS BRITISH]

If ubiquitous public monuments and yearly ceremonies assigned meaning and purpose to the war, the lingering effects were felt in countless homes where the bereaved mourned their losses and in the convalescent hospitals where men eked out what little remained of their lives: *92nd Batt. In loving memory of Pte. John Finn. Gassed in the Somme-1918. Died Sept. 18 1919. Age 24 years. 32nd Batt. In loving memory of Pte. Hugh Quinn. Wounded 1917. Died Davisville Hosp. July 24 1920. Aged 36 years*—these and many other notices on the grass-covered tablets in Toronto's Prospect Cemetery speak for the maimed and gassed who clung to life long enough to die in their own country and for the veterans, worn out in body or spirit, who expired in their forties or fifties, just as much casualties of the war as their comrades at rest in France or Flanders. Now that the Great War has all but slipped from living recall, the burdens borne by the survivors and the intensity of their sorrow have become remote to us. Before turning to the themes and rhetoric of consolation developed in response to the First World War and carried over to the Second, we must remind ourselves of the plight of the parents, wives, and children which the memorials and rituals were meant to assuage. For many it was pointless to speak of consolation. No words, no matter how reassuring or ennobling, could alleviate the pain of their loss:

SON OF MY HEART, LIVE FOR EVER. THERE IS NO DEATH FOR YOU AND ME.
Private Hal Sutton, 5th BCI, 22.5.15 (age 18) [HINGES]

FORGIVE, O LORD, A MOTHER'S WISH THAT DEATH HAD SPARED HER SON.
Sergeant Thomas Armstrong, 28th BCI, 31.1.16 (age 25) [KEMMEL CHATEAU]

THE ONLY CHILD OF AGED PARENTS.
Private Vernon Keith Merchant, 58th BCI, 6.6.16 (age 16) [RAILWAY DUGOUTS]

LONGING TO SEE HIM, TO HEAR HIM SAY MOTHER.
Private Stanley Aylett, 16th BCI, 4.9.16 (age 28) [COURCELETTE]

THE BRAVE LIES FAR FROM HOME, HIS PARENTS' HEARTS MELTING WITH PAIN.
Private Clifford Doucet, RCR, 11.4.17 (age 21) [BARLIN]

HE WOULD GIVE HIS DINNER TO A HUNGRY DOG AND GO WITHOUT HIMSELF.
Gunner Charles Douglas Moore, CAAB, 19.9.17 (age 30) [PETIT-VIMY]

THE SHELL THAT STILLED HIS TRUE BRAVE HEART BROKE MINE. MOTHER
Corporal James Edward Noble, 25th BCI, 13.6.18 (age 21) [WAILLY ORCHARD]

DEATH IS NOT A BARRIER TO LOVE, DADDY. KAYE
Private Peter William Lapointe MM, 2nd BCI, 17.8.18 (age 34) [ST. SEVER]

SIX BROTHERS IN ALL ANSWERED THE CALL. ONE CRIPPLED, THREE KILLED.
Private Robert Scott Chalmers, 5th BCI, 1.9.18 (age 37) [UPTON WOOD]

The personal inscriptions remain an underappreciated source for the study of Canada's memory of the Great War. In their wide range they preserve the reactions of the bereaved, varying from praise of the fallen for their heroic sacrifice, their devotion to duty, to lamentation at their untimely, undeserved deaths. Very few, as noted in the previous chapter, give way to bitterness or adverse commentary on the war. *For King and country, thus he fell, a tyrant's arrogance to quell*, on the grave of Private Harrison Allen, and A *nation spoke to a nation*, the first line of Rudyard Kipling's paean to Canada's imperial loyalties, *Our Lady of the Snows*, chosen by the family of Lieutenant John Lant Youngs for his grave near Vimy Ridge, are rare instances of triumphalism. More illustrative of general trends is the tribute to Private Stephen Henry Taylor, *Faithful husband, loyal citizen, brave soldier, true salvationist*, or the one to Private Isaac William Jones, *Honour the memory of Canada's bravest and best*, that enshrined the virtues of the fallen and commended them to posterity as the embodiment of the country at its finest. Private Leslie White, killed at Vimy Ridge, was but one of the country's soldiers who had emerged in purest form from the crucible of battle: *Gold proved by fire. God proved him and found him worthy for Himself.*

FOUR YEARS HAVE PASSED AND STILL I MISS HIM.
HOW I MISS HIM NONE CAN TELL. MOTHER
Private George Hall, 60th BCI, 3.4.17 (age 25) [ECOIVRES]

SPLENDID YOU PASSED . . . INTO THE LIGHT THAT NEVERMORE SHALL FADE.
Private Robert Edmond Barry Denny, 16th BCI, 22.5.15 (age 24) [BETHUNE TOWN]

LORD GOD OF HOSTS, BE WITH US YET, LEST WE FORGET, LEST WE FORGET.
Private Robert John McLean Campbell, 43rd BCI, 28.10.17 (age 30) [NINE ELMS BRITISH]

The laborious process of confirming the identity of over a million war dead (nearly half of them listed among the missing) and contacting the next-of-kin in the distant dominions of the British Empire meant that most inscriptions were submitted years after the war, when the passage of time had dulled the initial impact of loss and put the war in a certain context. By the early 1920s formal commemorative pieces, chief among them Binyon's *For the Fallen*, John Arkwright's *O Valiant Hearts*, and Kipling's *Recessional*, had pervaded public consciousness as models of the solemn, uplifting language proper to memorials and headstones. The use of high diction, given to idealism and depictions of glorious death in war, tends today to invite reproof for cloaking the horrors of the Great War in language irreconcilable with the horrors of the conflict. No doubt its euphemisms sheltered the bereaved from the awful deaths died in the trenches and gave the war a significance which we no longer accept. Yet two points deserve emphasis.

To Canadians, as to the peoples of the British Empire, the victory of 1918 represented the triumph of one value system over another. The collapse of Tsarist Russia and the entry of democratic America in 1917 transformed the Allied cause into a crusade to create a better world, founded on the principles set out in President Wilson's Fourteen Points, that would abide by a just and stable peace. The defeat of autocracy and militarism, and the moral obligation imposed by the war's appalling cost to uphold the ideals of freedom, democracy, justice, and concord among nations, would ensure that such a catastrophe could never happen again. The consoling belief that a loved one had selflessly given his life in a divinely sanctioned cause for a new world order made its way onto many a headstone:

YOUNG MEN, YE HAVE OVERCOME THE WICKED ONE. I JOHN 2. 13
Private William Gilbert Raymond McGreer, 47th BCI, 11.8.18 (age 21) [CÉRISY-GAILLY]

NO THOUGHT OF SELF OR EARTHLY WEALTH BUT GAVE ALL FOR HOME AND LIBERTY.
Private Frederick Charles Whitcutt, 31st BCI, 15.11.15 (age 35) [KEMMEL CHATEAU]

HE DIED SO THAT LIFE MIGHT BE A SWEETER THING TO ALL. HE LIVETH.
Private William Sime, 28th BCI, 29.9.16 (age 35) [ADANAC]

ALL OUR BEAUTY AND PEACE AND JOY WE OWE TO LADS LIKE YOU.
Private George Richard Emmitt, 75th BCI, 9.4.17 (age 20)
[GIVENCHY ROAD CANADIAN]

RIGHT IS STRONGER THAN MIGHT.
Private Albert Edward Boustead, 15th BCI, 17.4.17 (age 32) [BRUAY]

TO ALL THOSE WHOSE NOBLE FEALTY GAVE LIFE ITSELF TO SET LIFE FREE, THY PRAISE.
Lieutenant William Kitchener Kift, 116th BCI, 29.4.17 [ETAPLES]

HE DIED THAT WE MIGHT LIVE AND LOVE AND SERVE.
Private Walter Martin, 1st BCI, 3.5.17 (age 21) [ORCHARD DUMP]

I COULDN'T DIE IN A BETTER CAUSE (FROM HIS OWN LIPS).
Lance Corporal Clayton Robertson Selkirk, 5th CMR, 23.6.17 (age 21) [PETIT-VIMY]

YET REMEMBER THIS, GOD AND OUR GOOD CAUSE FIGHT UPON OUR SIDE.
Private Sydney James Turner, 2nd BCI, 23.7.17 (age 28) [FOSSE NO. 10]

HE LOVED CHIVALRY, TRUTH AND HONOUR, FREEDOM AND COURTESY.
Private Oliver Bilton, 24th BCI, 15.8.17 (age 27) [LOOS]

HE ALLURED TO A BETTER WORLD AND LED THE WAY.
Company Sergeant Major Arthur Hamilton Dunlop, 4th CMR, 27.10.17 (age 30)
[NINE ELMS BRITISH]

WE GRUDGE NOT OUR LIFE IF IT GIVE LARGER LIFE TO THEM THAT LIVE.
Captain Alexander MacGregor, 28th BCI, 9.8.18 (age 31) [ROSIÈRES]

SLEEP, DEAR SON. HONOUR, JUSTICE, DUTY, ALL SURVIVE BY YOUR MORTAL FALL.
Lieutenant Mackay Mackay, PPCLI, 27.8.18 (age 28) [LIGNY-ST. FLOCHEL]

THE BLOOD OF HEROES IS THE SEED OF FREEDOM.
Private Ivor Powell, 87th BCI, 4.9.18 (age 39) [DURY MILL]

Families contributing epitaphs to be engraved on headstones in war cemeteries to be maintained in perpetuity were mindful that the words honouring soldiers fallen for such ideals should be appropriate to their setting. Archaism and diction one or two removes from common speech seemed the medium of expression necessary to accord lasting and universal meaning to the death of a loved one, especially if the inscription took the form of a prayer, invocation, or declaration of principle, as so many do. When the vernacular proved inadequate to the occasion, Latin served to elevate the tone and import of an inscription above the temporal. Although the epitaphs of the Great War may as a result sound stilted to our ears, they impress sympathetic readers by their forbearance and dignity in the face of unprecedented catastrophe. The people who contributed these inscriptions were the first to realise what kind of war industrialised countries and technically advanced armies could fight, and they saw in this terrible experience a warning to the future. It is deeply moving to read in the farewells they bade to their loved ones the hope that out of their suffering some lasting good might emerge:

BREAK, DAY OF GOD, SWEET DAY OF PEACE, AND BID THE SHOUT OF WARRIORS CEASE.
Sergeant Wellesley Seymour Taylor, 14th BCI, 1.5.16 (age 24) [CHESTER FARM]

AD DIRIGENDOS PEDES NOSTROS IN VIAM PACIS.
(To guide our footsteps on the path of peace.)
Private Joseph Michaud, 22nd (FC)B, 15.7.16 (age 26) [ELZENWALLE BRASSERIE]

THE WORK OF RIGHTEOUSNESS SHALL BE PEACE.
Private Campbell MacAskill, RCR, 9.4.17 (age 22) [LA CHAUDIÈRE]

HE GAVE HIS LIFE TO END ALL WARS BETWEEN NATIONS.
Private Malcolm McLean, 50th BCI, 2.10.17 (age 24) [VILLERS STATION]

MAKE FIRM, O GOD, THE PEACE OUR DEAD HAVE WON.
Private James Adams Sullivan, CAMC, 8.12.17 (age 19) [ORPINGTON CHURCHYARD]

Visitors to the British war cemeteries will often notice German burials, marked by a distinct headstone, sometimes grouped in a separate section but just as often interspersed among the graves of their former enemies. This was a gesture of reconciliation on the part of the Imperial War Graves Commission's supervisors who regarded their work as the promotion of a hope cherished in the years after the Armistice. The graves of the fallen, of all countries, constituted the most potent argument in favour of peace, while the belief that the Great War was to be the "war to end all wars" offered consolation to the bereaved that the sacrifice of a son or husband, brother or father, had been, like that of Christ, "a ransom for many." *The blood of Christ, God's Son, cleanseth us from all sin*, paraphrases I John 1: 7 on the headstone of Private Ernest Spark McClelland, killed in April 1916 and buried in Chester Farm cemetery near Ypres. It is one of the Scriptural passages linking the suffering and sacrifice of Christ to the travails of the "soldiers of Christ" whose death in battle transformed them into saviours not only of their country but of mankind. As Vance has shown, after the Somme or Passchendaele the established churches which had endorsed the war were at a loss to explain the carnage in terms of historical theology as the working of God's providence. Redemption through sacrifice, however, achieved by soldiers shedding their blood in emulation of Christ, gave meaning to their deaths which had contributed to victory (in itself proof of the righteousness of the Allied cause) and the prospect of a world purged of iniquity. When the families of Lance Corporal Colin Ramsay Broughton (*One of Christ's faithful warriors*), Private John Earl Reid (*A volunteer for Jesus*), and Private Leslie Ernest Unthank (*A Christian hero*) ranked their sons among the elect who had "died that others might live," they found solace in a conviction widely shared among Canadians that the battlefields of France and Flanders were, in the words of Arkwright's hymn, "a lesser Calvary":

HE GAVE HIS PURE SOUL UNTO HIS CAPTAIN CHRIST.
Lieutenant Guy Melfort Drummond, 13th BCI, 22.4.15 (age 27) [TYNE COT]

THOU THEREFORE ENDURE HARDNESS, AS A GOOD SOLDIER OF JESUS CHRIST.
Private Cyril George Michael Brimble, 27th BCI, 16.10.15 (AGE 27)
[LOCRE CHURCHYARD] [II TIMOTHY 2: 3]

HE DIED FOR OTHERS. EVEN SO DID CHRIST.
Lieutenant Thomas Hart MacKinlay, 29th BCI, *26.10.16* (AGE 28)
[BOULOGNE EASTERN]

I WILL GO WITHOUT A MURMUR AND HIS FOOTSTEPS FOLLOW STILL.
Gunner Oscar George Plewis, CFA, *31.3.18 (age 22)* [BELLACOURT]

LIKE CHRIST HE THOUGHT OF OTHERS.
Private Alexander Armstrong, 19th BCI, *26.4.18 (age 33)* [BAC-DU-SUD]

JESUS DIED FOR ME. I'M NOT AFRAID TO DIE FOR HIM.
Private Alexander Falconer McDonald, CMGC, *9.9.18 (age 21)* [TERLINCTHUN]

IT IS FINISHED.
Driver Alex Henderson, CFA, *15.11.18* [ETAPLES] [JOHN 19: 30]

Other hopes and beliefs expressed in the epitaphs were deeply rooted in Christian teachings concerning death and its meaning, which had undergone a significant shift in the later nineteenth century. *Presbyterian in faith . . . Church of England . . . Of the Roman Catholic faith and virtuous*—these proclamations of denominational affiliation highlight the central place of religion in the lives of Canadians born in the 1880s and 1890s to parents born about the time of Confederation. The spiritually minded inhabitants of Victorian Canada grew up in an era when advances in science and medicine, improved living conditions and longer lifespans, and changing views on the relation between the Creator and humankind altered attitudes towards death and consolation. In the first half of the nineteenth century clergymen had fulminated on the terrors of death and the eternal punishment of the wicked to impress mourners with the urgency of repentance and strict adherence to the laws of a wrathful God. Over the second half of the century, however, the Anglican and Protestant churches adopted a gentler approach aimed at comforting the griefstricken by emphasizing the bliss of the faithful departed. Funeral sermons, devotional tracts, hymns, and religious verses now portrayed death as a passage to a better world, a release from the turmoil of this dark world of sin, and the gateway to life eternal in a heavenly abode where loved ones would be reunited. Lines from contemporary religious verse—"*Not dead but gone before,*" "*Peace, perfect peace,*" "*Safe in the arms of Jesus*"—sound themes common among epitaphs presenting the tranquil image of death and the afterlife:

HE LIVETH STILL, OUR SOLDIER BOY, IN THAT FAR LAND OF PEACE AND JOY.
Sergeant William Victor Tranter, 1st BCI, *10.6.15 (age 21)* [WIMEREUX]

YOU WILL WAIT, DEAR JAMES, FOR OUR COMING IN GOD'S BLESSED HOME.
Private James Anthony St. Dennis, 21st BCI, *20.10.15 (age 20)* [RIDGE WOOD]

LIFE BEGINS.
Private Charles McKillop, 1st BCI, *18.3.16* [DRANOUTRE]

THERE IS NO DEATH. WHAT SEEMS SO IS TRANSITION TO A HIGHER LIFE.
Private Leonard Endicott, 2nd BCI, *25.4.16 (age 26)* [WOODS CEMETERY]

HE BEAT US HOME—A LITTLE BIT.
Driver Walter George Ross, CFA, *9.7.16 (age 18)* [ELZENWALLE BRASSERIE]

SAFE FROM THE WORLD'S TEMPTATIONS.
Private Archibald Hugh Linton, 46th BCI, 16.1.17 (age 20) [VILLERS STATION]

SORROW VANISHED, LABOUR ENDED, JORDAN PASSED.
Private Lionel Tom Hunt, 31st BCI, 23.4.17 (age 24) [ECOIVRES]

TRANSPLANTED BY HIS FATHER'S CARE TO FAIRER WORLDS ABOVE.
Private Fred Gordon McNeil, 46th BCI, 1.5.17 (age 20) [VILLERS STATION]

DEATH LIKE A NARROW SEA DIVIDES THAT HAPPY LAND FROM OURS.
Private Archibald Baxter, 220th BCI, 31.5.17 (age 18) [SHORNCLIFFE]

WE SHALL MEET IN THE LIFE OF LOVE ETERNAL THROUGH LIGHT, O GOD, TO THEE.
Private Robert Edward Atkinson, 31st BCI, 6.11.17 (age 39) [DOCHY FARM]

AMONG THOSE OTHER LIVING WHOM WE CALL DEAD.
Sergeant Thomas Harold Carling Bissett, 47th BCI, 1.11.18 (age 33) [AULNOY]

Implicit in these inscriptions, typical of many more, is a denial of death which the romanticised vision of heaven and the afterlife came to be. As palliating as this vision may have been in the years before 1914, its hold on mourners during and after the war will have been all the stronger. *"But who shall return us our children?"* keened Rudyard Kipling in a poem giving voice to the suffering he knew as a bereaved father, capturing in a single plaintive line the despair of a once confident, optimistic generation that had, for the first time in history, expected its children to live on in a world of ever increasing progress and bounty. The spiritualist movement that flourished in Great Britain during the 1920s attests the desperation of those who could not bring themselves to accept the finality of their loss and the termination of their hopes. Less radical, but just as urgent, was the belief that the dead were in a better place, in the care of a merciful, compassionate God, and assured of the reward of salvation in recompense for their torments and achingly early deaths in the service of humanity. The oft-chosen words from Revelation 2: 10, "Be thou faithful unto death and I shall give thee a crown of life," held out the promise to the worthy of life everlasting. For those seeking religious assurance there were other reminders from Scripture of God's covenant with his servants:

AND I WILL RESTORE TO YOU THE YEARS THE LOCUSTS HAVE EATEN.
Corporal William Bowyer, 7th BCI, 23.7.15 (age 35) [BAILLEUL] [JOEL 2: 25]

AND THEIR SINS AND THEIR INIQUITIES WILL I REMEMBER NO MORE. HEB. 8. 12
Corporal Alfred Jones, 20th BCI, 24.7.16 (age 31) [RIDGE WOOD]

GOD HATH DELIVERED MY SOUL FROM THE PLACE OF HELL FOR HE SHALL RECEIVE ME. PS. 49. 15
Driver Charles Percival Maxted, CE, 3.8.16 (age 24) [LIJSSENTHOEK]

IF WE SUFFER, WE SHALL ALSO REIGN WITH HIM.
Sergeant David Ainslie Hunter, 102nd BCI, 9.4.17 (age 26) [GIVENCHY ROAD]
[II TIMOTHY 2: 12]

May our sacrifice be holy, may it not be in vain, the plea on the headstone of Private Walter Raye Adsit, speaks for the dead and the bereaved of the Great War. In the end, what consolation the families could find rested on the core belief that the sacrifice had not been in vain, for otherwise the horrendous loss of life became unbearably futile. For Canadians, as for the peoples of the British Empire, the debt to the fallen imposed more than gratitude or honoured remembrance. Incumbent on the survivors was the duty to safeguard the legacy which the dead had bequeathed:

JUSTICE OWES THEM THIS, THAT WHAT THEY DIED FOR BE NOT OVERTHROWN.
Private George Franklin Hargrave, 29th BCI, 15.1.19 (age 22) [BRUSSELS TOWN]

But if victory and all that it stood for redeemed the losses suffered by the Allied nations, defeat exacerbated the terrible cost of the war in the vanquished countries, whose dead would truly have died in vain unless the outcome of 1918 were reversed. It must have rekindled the pain of loss in the bereaved as they saw their hopes of peace and a better world crumble away during "the no man's years between the wars." Nevertheless, Hitler's determination to avenge Germany's two million war dead by unleashing a new war summoned up the blood of Canadians who were similarly determined not to let the victory achieved at such a price in lives be overturned. The Great War veterans who tried to re-enlist in 1939, or the fathers who sent their sons to the recruiting stations, were in no small measure keeping faith with those who lay in Flanders fields. Cognizance of the debt to their forebears of 1914–1918 is much underestimated among the factors that led Canadians to take up arms a second time.

A SOLDIER'S SON, AT REST.
Private Jerrold Mayhew, RRC, 29.6.43 (age 24) [BROOKWOOD]

Looming behind the headstones of the Second World War is the unfinished business of the First. "Bloody fools. We have them on the run. That means we shall have to do it all over again in another twenty-five years," was Andrew McNaughton's less than jubilant reaction to news of the ceasefire on November 11 1918. The commander of the Canadian Corps' artillery was not the only soldier to question the wisdom of the politicians in concluding an armistice when the enemy, though groggy, was still on his feet. When his gruff prediction came true in 1939, McNaughton took up where he left off in 1918, returning to uniform to play a leading role in the national war effort as the architect and emblem of the Canadian Army overseas. Both of his sons signed up for the task of upholding the verdict reached in 1918; one was lost on air operations over Germany:

HERE LET THE SLOW BELL TOLL; ON THE OTHER SIDE THE TRUMPETS SOUND FOR HIM.
Squadron Leader Ian George Armour McNaughton, RCAF, 23.6.42 (age 22) [SAGE]

The young Canadians who signed up for overseas service had been nurtured in the memory of the Great War. Some even bore names given by parents who wished to honour famous deeds and figures. Gunner John Vimy Mugford, buried at Bény-sur-Mer, was one of the Canadian children named after the country's iconic victory. So was Vimy Ridge Piercy, the wife whose words of parting appear on the headstone of her husband, Rifleman James Piercy, killed in Normandy and buried at Bretteville-sur-Laize. Less readily understood today is the esteem accorded the namesakes of Corporal Douglas Haig McIntee, buried at Groesbeek (*Remembered by his mother*), or Flight Sergeant Lloyd George Anderson (*Honoured among the nation's heroes*) at

Rheinberg. Both were sons of Great War veterans and both had brothers who also died on active service in World War II.

In 1920s Canada there was no shortage of family namesakes. Many a soldier who served in the Second World War bore the name of a relative killed in the First. One was Captain Stephen Bird, the son of Will Bird, a veteran and well-known memoirist of the Great War. Will Bird had gone overseas after his younger brother, Private Stephen Bird, was killed in 1915. In his book *Ghosts Have Warm Hands*, Bird relates the strange tale of how his dead brother returned to lead him away from a spot that was shortly afterwards blasted by shells. Years later, it was to be Bird's sad task to describe in his history of the North Nova Scotia Highlanders the circumstances of his son's death in action. The inscription he chose for the headstone, with its Great War overtones, nods at the brother and namesake lost in Flanders:

HE LIVED, FELT DAWN, SAW SUNSET GLOW,
LOVED AND WAS LOVED—HIS MEMORY REMAINS.
Captain Stephen Stanley Bird, NNSH, *8.7.44 (age 24)* [BÉNY-SUR-MER]

Another soldier bearing a name associated with the Great War lies in Normandy. Lieutenant Fred Fisher of the Canadian Grenadier Guards died on August 8, 1944, at age 23, not far from the site that became the Bretteville-sur-Laize Canadian War Cemetery. He was the nephew of Lance Corporal Fred Fisher, the first Canadian-born soldier to win the Victoria Cross and first of seventy Canadians to receive the Empire's highest decoration in the First World War. His gallant conduct gilded the saga of Second Ypres where the reputation of Canada's fighting men was born in the heroic stand against the Germans and the cloud of poison gas. Lance Corporal Fisher was killed in the same action and his body was never found. One of his two brothers who survived the war perpetuated the name by passing it on to a son whose inscription records his fidelity to those who had gone before:

HE FOLLOWED THE TRADITION OF HIS FAMILY AND HIS NAMESAKE,
FRED FISHER, V.C. 1914–1918.
Lieutenant Fred Fisher, CGG, *8.8.44 (age 23)* [BRETTEVILLE-SUR-LAIZE]

More than sixty years after the end of the Second World War, it can be startling to realise how closely the second conflict followed upon the first. The proximity of family tragedies appears most jarringly in two Canadian graves at Brookwood where Private Daniel Cocklin, one of the last Canadians claimed by the Great War, lies among the soldiers who died of wounds or disease in 1919. Two rows away, the first Canadian burials of the Second World War include his son, Private James Connaty Cocklin, who died on active service in December 1939. Elsewhere the headstones bind the two wars together in their impact on so many of the same people. Men old enough to serve in the first were still young enough to die in the second; an already grievous loss incurred in the first was compounded in the second; and boys left fatherless by the first left their children fatherless when they were killed in the second:

BORN PORT ALBERT, ONTARIO. SERVED 1914–1918, 1940–1944.
"FOUGHT A GOOD FIGHT."
Private Alexander MacKenzie, CSR, *9.6.44 (age 52)* [BRETTEVILLE-SUR-LAIZE]

HE WAS A GOOD SOLDIER AND SERVED HIS COUNTRY IN TWO WARS.
Corporal Clarence Frederick Spalding, CRCE, *26.6.44 (age 48)* [BROOKWOOD]

(top) *The entrance to Calais Canadian War Cemetery*
(Steve Douglas).

(bottom) *The headstone of Lieutenant-Colonel John McCrae at Wimereux*
(Steve Douglas).

The grave of a young British soldier at Ovillers, near the old front line of the Somme, inscribed with verses from "In Flanders Fields".

British and Canadian graves at Courcelette (Sylvia McGeer).

The Canadian memorial at Passchendaele.

Plaque in the veterans' section at Toronto's Prospect Cemetery.

The grave of Captain John Norman Stephenson at Calais.

Captain Stephenson's father commemorated on the Menin Gate at Ieper (Ypres).

The words of Laurence Binyon and John McCrae on two Canadian headstones of the Second World War at Ravenna War Cemetery.

HIS BROTHERS, JOSEPH EDGAR AND CHARLES RUDOLPH, WERE KILLED IN FRANCE 16.7.16 AND 27.8.18.
Reverend George Alexander Harris, 1st CPB *(CCS), 7.6.44 (age 34)* [RANVILLE]

REST, DEAR SON, FOR GOD AND KING YOU DID YOUR BEST, AS YOUR FATHER BEFORE YOU.
Private Ernest Vernon Mitchell, SSTCA, *29.5.44 (age 21)* [BEACH HEAD]

HE DIED, AS DID HIS FATHER, FOR KING AND COUNTRY.
Gunner Foster Farrow, RCA, *8.8.44 (age 29)* [BRETTEVILLE-SUR-LAIZE]

IN SPEM RESURRECTIONIS.
(In hope of the resurrection.)
Lieutenant Reginald Basil Hingston, 24th BCI, *8.8.18 (age 33)* [VILLERS-BRETONNEUX]

IN LOVING MEMORY.
Captain Basil William Hales Hingston, RCIC, *19.9.44 (age 29)*
[ARNHEM OOSTERBEEK]

LOVE AND REMEMBRANCE LAST FOR EVER. WIFE & 3 BOYS.
Private Samuel Melling, 20th BCI, *8.5.18* [BELLACOURT]

SUNSHINE PASSES, SHADOWS FALL, LOVE'S REMEMBRANCE OUTLASTS ALL. MARGARET & BABY DOREEN.
Private Gordon Melling, BWC, *13.10.44 (age 29)* [BERGEN-OP-ZOOM]

"Keep the same headstones, the same monuments . . . in a hundred years' time 1914 and 1939 will all be part of one war," was the recommendation of Sir Edwin Lutyens, one of the Imperial War Graves Commission's principal architects, to a committee convened in November 1939 to decide upon the commemoration for the dead of a new war which he, like most of his contemporaries, saw as the resumption of the contest adjourned *sine die* in 1918. His summation, "It is certainly the same sacrifice for the same cause," would have rung true for the peoples of Britain and the Commonwealth as they prepared for the second time in a generation to face an enemy driven by the same militaristic and expansionist impulses as in 1914. And so it was that the commemorative traditions of the Great War, in symbol and word, extended to those who died in its sequel. The same Cross of Sacrifice with its inset Crusader sword presides over the graves of soldiers fallen in a righteous cause; the same Stone of Remembrance suggests an altar transforming their deaths into sacrificial offerings; and the same rounded headstones in their tidy rows assert the equality of all ranks in death, the shared sorrow among those who mourned them, and the debt of remembrance owed to all alike. But for the dates inscribed on the portals, the burial grounds of the Second World War mirror those of the First, so seamlessly were the precepts that guided construction of the Great War cemeteries transmitted from the founders of the War Graves Commission to their successors.

"A VERRAY PARFIT GENTIL KNIGHT."
Major David Brian Robertson, RWR, *3.5.45 (age 24)* [HOLTEN]

IN PEACE AND HONOUR REST YOU HERE, MY SON. SHAKESPEARE
Pilot Officer Wilson Albert Reason, RCAF, *31.5.42 (age 24)* [REICHSWALD FOREST]

AND FLIGHTS OF ANGELS SING THEE TO THY REST. SHAKESPEARE
Corporal Charles Neale, LWR, 9.8.44 [BRETTEVILLE-SUR-LAIZE]
Flying Officer Colin Maxwell Hay DSO, RCAF, 6.3.45 (age 31) [BROOKWOOD]

"FOR HE TO-DAY THAT SHEDS HIS BLOOD WITH ME SHALL BE MY BROTHER."
KING HENRY V
Private Basil Nicholson, SDGH, 13.10.44 (age 18) [ADEGEM]

"WE FEW, WE HAPPY FEW, WE HAPPY BAND OF BROTHERS. . ."
Pilot Officer Kenneth Lorne Patience, RCAF, 28.5.44 (age 21) [HEVERLEE]

"THE VALIANT NEVER TASTE OF DEATH BUT ONCE."
Warrant Officer II George Albert Andrews, RCAF, 24.2.44 (age 21) [HARROGATE]

"AND THE ELEMENTS SO MIXED IN HIM THAT ALL THE WORLD MAY SHOUT, THIS WAS A MAN."
Signalman John Booton, RCCS, 19.11.40 (age 37) [BROOKWOOD]

LET ALL NATURE STAND UP AND SAY, THIS WAS A MAN. HIS NAME LIVETH FOR EVERMORE.
Rifleman Kenneth John Woodcock, RWR, 30.3.45 (age 24) [GROESBEEK]

SLEEP DWELL UPON THINE EYES, PEACE IN THY BREAST; WOULD I WERE SLEEP AND PEACE,
SO SWEET TO REST.
Trooper Frederick West, RCD, 4.9.44 (age 33) [GRADARA]

"HIS LOYALTY HE KEPT, HIS LOVE, HIS ZEAL." MILTON
Lieutenant Harry Percy Saunders, RCA, 16.2.45 (age 27) [GROESBEEK]

"NOTHING IS HERE FOR TEARS. . . NOTHING BUT WELL AND FAIR. . . IN A DEATH SO NOBLE."
Lieutenant Albert Edwyn Francis Wayte, RCIC, 20.9.44 (age 27)
[ARNHEM (OOSTERBEEK)]

"HOW CAN MAN DIE BETTER THAN FACING FEARFUL ODDS. . ." MACAULAY'S "HORATIUS"
Flight Sergeant William Elliott Brown, RCAF, 22.7.42 (age 20)
[EINDHOVEN (WOENSEL)]

"FOR THE ASHES OF HIS FATHERS AND THE TEMPLES OF HIS GODS."
Corporal Fraser Dewar, RCR, 1.1.44 (age 36) [MORO RIVER]

THE LOSS THAT BROUGHT US PAIN, THAT LOSS BUT MADE US LOVE THE MORE.
TENNYSON
Private Bernard Christopher O'Reilly, RCIC, 24.2.44 (age 22) [BROOKWOOD]

FIGHTING FOR HUMANITY HE FELL. GOD'S ANGELS SAW HIM AND THEY WEPT.
"GOD'S FINGER TOUCHED HIM AND HE SLEPT."
Private George Nelson Towart, RCR, 24.7.43 (age 18) [AGIRA]

IN MEMORY OF OUR DEAR SON DOUGLAS. "THE PATH OF DUTY WAS THE WAY TO GLORY."
Corporal Douglas Wade, BWC, 12.10.44 (age 24) [BERGEN-OP-ZOOM]

MY STRENGTH IS AS THE STRENGTH OF TEN BECAUSE MY HEART IS PURE.
Private Garfield Eugene Frost, BWC, 31.10.44 (age 20) [BERGEN-OP-ZOOM]

"YOURS IS THE EARTH AND EVERYTHING THAT'S IN IT." KIPLING'S "IF"
Lieutenant William Beverley Robinson, RCIC, 10.8.44 (age 23) [BÉNY-SUR-MER]

FROM LITTLE TOWNS WE CAME, BY LITTLE TOWNS WE SLEEP, LEAVING THAT WORLD WE WON FOR YOU TO KEEP.
Lieutenant George Rupert Jeffares, WR, 2.9.43 *(age 22)* [BROOKWOOD]

E'EN AS HE TROD THAT DAY TO GOD SO WALKED HE FROM HIS BIRTH, IN SIMPLENESS AND GENTLENESS, AND HONOUR AND CLEAN MIRTH.
Lance Corporal Douglas Sumner Orford, NNSH, 7.6.44 *(age 23)* [BÉNY-SUR-MER]

GLORY IS THE LEAST OF THINGS THAT FOLLOW THIS LAD HOME.
Lieutenant Richard Owen Buckland Williamson, 48th HC, 17.12.44 *(age 22)*
[RAVENNA]

"HE LEAVES A WHITE UNBROKEN GLORY, A GATHERED RADIANCE." RUPERT BROOKE
Lieutenant Russell Edward Ganong, CYR, 18.3.44 *(age 23)* [MORO RIVER]

"THESE LAID THE WORLD AWAY: POURED OUT THE RED SWEET WINE OF YOUTH."
Pilot Officer Ian MacCallum Hamilton, RCAF, 6.11.44 *(age 20)* [REICHSWALD FOREST]

HE SPILLED THE SWEET RED WINE OF LIFE THAT OTHERS MIGHT BE FREE.
Private Douglas Vincent Tobin, NNSH, 7.6.44 *(age 27)* [BÉNY-SUR-MER]

"AND IF THESE POOR LIMBS DIE, SAFEST OF ALL." RUPERT BROOKE
Major Robert Gordon Slater, BWC, 19.10.44 *(age 32)* [BERGEN-OP-ZOOM]

THINK ONLY THIS OF ME: THAT THERE'S SOME CORNER OF A FOREIGN FIELD THAT IS FOR EVER ENGLAND.
Lance Corporal William Lloyd Douglas, SHC, 11.12.43 *(age 21)* [MORO RIVER]

"IN THAT RICH EARTH A RICHER DUST CONCEALED."
Gunner Redvers Albert Adair, RCA, 31.8.44 *(age 24)* [MONTECCHIO]

THERE IS IN THIS EARTH A RICHER DUST CONCEALED, A DUST WHOM CANADA BORE.
Lance Bombardier Henry William Cowie, RCA, 18.10.44 *(age 21)* [ADEGEM]

"IF I SHOULD DIE ON FOREIGN SOIL BE THIS FOREVER CANADA."
Corporal Lester Harvey McConnell, SHC, 26.12.43 *(age 28)* [MORO RIVER]

The commemorative traditions inherited from the Great War included a canon of literary texts deemed appropriate for use on public monuments and individual headstones. The classics of English literature, Chaucer, Shakespeare, and Milton, supplied passages both ennobling and consoling, but the literary epitaphs show a general preference for the Victorian authors whose works would have been standard reading fare for Canadians educated in the literature of the Mother Country. Kipling's odes to the empire's soldiers or his edifying checklist of manly virtues, *If*, were learned by heart in school when memory work and recitation were staples of pedagogy. Macaulay's *Horatius at the Bridge* was another recital piece that came to the minds of families wishing to commend a soldier's heroic defence of kith and kin. The poetry of Rupert Brooke captured the spirit of willing sacrifice which lay at the core of the myth of the Great War in Canada, and his most famous line, making some corner of a foreign field forever England, was easily reworked to fit Canadian sensibilities.

Foremost among the poets taken to heart by the bereaved of both wars was Tennyson. His long elegy, *In memoriam A.H.H.*, composed in response to the death of his friend

Arthur Hallam, remained the most influential literary meditation on death and consolation well into the twentieth century. Except for *The Pilgrim's Progress* and the Bible, *In memoriam* inspired more epitaphs than any other text. Even a few examples of the lines taken from the poem reveal its wide currency:

"FORGIVE MY GRIEF FOR ONE REMOVED, THY CREATURE WHOM I FOUND SO FAIR."
Sergeant Robert Dunbar Robertson, 48th HC, 26.12.43 (age 37) [MORO RIVER]

GOD'S HAND TOUCHED HIM AND HE SLEPT. HIS NAME LIVETH FOR EVER.
REST IN PEACE.
Private Thomas Charles Flew, RCR, 4.9.44 (age 19) [ANCONA]

"THEY HAVE THEIR DAY AND CEASE TO BE; THEY ARE BUT BROKEN LIGHTS OF THEE."
Pilot Officer Arthur Clifford Pettifor, RCAF, 11.3.45 (age 29) [REICHSWALD FOREST]

"OH YET WE TRUST THAT SOMEHOW GOOD WILL BE THE FINAL GOAL OF ILL."
Lance Sergeant John Alexander Bullions, IRC, 28.4.45 [HOLTEN]

"AND FROM HIS ASHES MAY BE MADE THE VIOLET OF HIS NATIVE LAND."
Lieutenant Robert Whyte Patterson, PR, 20.12.44 (age 28) [VILLANOVA]

"FAR OFF THOU ART BUT EVER NIGH; WE HAVE THEE STILL AND WE REJOICE."
Lance Corporal Lawrence John Scott, RCR, 18.12.43 (age 19) [MORO RIVER]

"BUT TRUST THAT THOSE WE CALL THE DEAD ARE BREATHERS OF AN AMPLER DAY."
Warrant Officer II Daniel Harmer Noakes, RCA, 24.5.44 (age 30) [CASSINO]

The longing which the bereaved felt for the departed led many families to choose a line from another well-known poem, *Break, Break, Break*, in which Tennyson portrayed himself alone with his ineffable grief while the world carried on around him. The inscription below is one of many:

O FOR A TOUCH OF A VANISHED HAND AND THE SOUND OF A VOICE THAT IS STILL.
Private Palmer Clifford Knutson, RCASC, 17.8.45 (age 35) [HOLTEN]

"Sunset and evening star. . ." introduces a lyric which Tennyson asked to be placed at the end of all editions of his poetry. *Crossing the Bar*, written in his eightieth year, touched readers with its calm acceptance of death and for its evocation of "that Divine and Unseen Who is always guiding us." Relatives of airmen found the first and last lines particularly appropriate:

"SUNSET AND EVENING STAR AND ONE CLEAR CALL FOR ME!" MISSED BY ALL THE FAMILY.
Pilot Officer Sidney Albert Wilson, RCAF, 17.6.44 (age 29)
[AMERSFOORT (OUD LEUSDEN)]

I HOPE TO SEE MY PILOT FACE TO FACE WHEN I HAVE CROSSED THE BAR. TENNYSON
Flight Sergeant Leonard Thomas Olmstead, RCAF, 7.9.43 (age 25) [DURNBACH]

As Poet Laureate, Tennyson composed a number of poems marking state occasions or contemporary events. One such piece was *The Charge of the Light Brigade*, quoted on a headstone at Bretteville-sur-Laize. Another, frequently cited in epitaphs of both World Wars and pressed into service again upon the death of Winston Churchill in 1965, was his *Ode on the Death of the Duke of Wellington* (1852). The lengthy encomium contained these lines extolling in faithfully Victorian terms the Iron Duke's devotion to his country:

NOT ONCE OR TWICE IN OUR ROUGH ISLAND-STORY THE PATH OF DUTY
WAS THE WAY TO GLORY.
Flight Lieutenant Roy Russell Boulter, RCAF, 17.9.44 (age 23) [ARNHEM OOSTERBEEK]

This uplifting sentiment was part and parcel of many epitaphs, as in the two examples given here. The ode's concluding prayer also made an apt inscription:

THE PATH OF DUTY LED TO GLORY. HE DIED THAT OTHERS MAY LIVE. REST IN PEACE.
Private Philip Henry Gibson, IRC, 31.8.44 (age 32) [MONTECCHIO]

IN LOVING MEMORY OF A DEAR SON. THE PATH OF DUTY WAS HIS WAY TO GLORY.
Private Robert Walker, BWC, 1.4.45 (age 19) [GROESBEEK]

"GOD ACCEPT HIM, CHRIST RECEIVE HIM." TENNYSON
Lieutenant Arthur Percival Thompson, FGH, 28.9.44 (age 26) [BERGEN-OP-ZOOM]

Absent from anthologies of Great War poetry published since the 1960s are the scores of inscriptions and poems that promoted the ideal of "a death so noble" repudiated in the works of Sassoon, Owen, Graves, and others now regarded as the authentic voices of the war. Robert Service, of Klondike fame, is perhaps the only name that might ring a bell today among the poets whose tributes to the fallen of 1914–1918 fit equally well a generation later. Service's *Rhymes of a Red Cross Man*, published in 1916, inspired the first two epitaphs below; those that follow present a line from Herbert Asquith's *The Volunteer*, a moving reminder from William Wilfred Gibson's *Lament*, a line from Winifred Mary Letts's *The Spires of Oxford*, echoes of Tennyson in Owen Seaman's *I Saw the Morning Break*, and a call for remembrance from Robert Bridges, the Poet Laureate between 1913 and 1930:

WILL GLORY OF ENGLAND NEVER DIE SO LONG AS WE'VE LADS LIKE HIM.
ROBERT SERVICE
Major Henry William Hook, WG, 7.7.45 (age 45) [SAI WAN]

THE GLORY OF CANADA WILL NEVER DIE AS LONG AS WE HAVE LADS LIKE YOU.
Sergeant Francis William George Cosgrave, RCAF, 26.11.44 (age 32) [HARROGATE]

"HIS LANCE IS BROKEN; BUT HE LIES CONTENT WITH THAT HIGH HOUR IN WHICH
HE LIVED AND DIED."
Gunner Samuel Victor Martin, RCA, 24.5.44 (age 34) [CASSINO]

THEY WHO WENT UNGRUDGINGLY, SPENT THEIR LIVES FOR US, LOVED, TOO,
THE SUN AND THE RAIN.
Flight Lieutenant Ralph Edward Naylor, RCAF, 26.3.45 (age 28) [GROESBEEK]

HE GAVE HIS MERRY YOUTH AWAY FOR COUNTRY AND FOR GOD.
Captain Lewis Lovett Johnstone Sutherland, NNSH, 8.7.44 (age 23) [BÉNY-SUR-MER]

I SAW THE MORNING BREAK.
Lieutenant Steadman Bucknell Henderson, 8th PL (NB)H, 31.8.44 (age 25)
[MONTECCHIO]

"I SAW THE POWERS OF DARKNESS PUT TO FLIGHT, I SAW THE MORNING BREAK."
Warrant Officer I Carl George Baker, RCAF, 31.8.43 (age 21) [RHEINBERG]

OUT OF DEATH AND NIGHT SHALL RISE THE DAWN OF AMPLER LIFE.
Private Donald Whitman Cook, BWC, 13.10.44 (age 26) [BERGEN-OP-ZOOM]

REMEMBER THE LOVE OF THEM WHO CAME NOT HOME FROM THE WAR. ROBERT BRIDGES
Flying Officer Charles William Cecil Crowdy, RCAF, 25.4.44 (age 21) [SCHOONSELHOF]
Corporal Roderick Burton Haig, RCCS, 29.5.44 (age 25) [CASSINO]
Flight Lieutenant Paul Allen Cornell Maeder, RCAF, 18.12.44 (age 20) [BROOKWOOD]

Visitors to the Memorial Chamber enclosed within the Peace Tower in Ottawa will notice an inscription carved above the doorway. The same words also happen to stand on a headstone in the Canadian war cemetery in Villanova:

ALL'S WELL, FOR OVER THERE AMONG HIS PEERS A HAPPY WARRIOR SLEEPS.
Captain Frank Sydney Stebbens, RCA, 15.12.44 (age 38)

The author of this line, John Ceredigion Jones (1883–1947), was a Welsh immigrant to Canada who submitted a poem entitled *The Returning Man* to a Montreal newspaper in 1919. When in 1927 the architect of the Memorial Chamber, John Pearson, sought a parting benediction for the families of the fallen, he recalled the line but was unable to remember its provenance until a newspaper campaign attracted a letter from Jones verifying his authorship. Although a prolific versifier, Jones is as utterly unknown today as the poets who crafted these lines, typical of the memorialising poems that filled newspapers and weekly magazines during the 1920s:

THEY SHALL RETURN WITH LAUGHING FACES. SPIRITS LIKE THEIRS CAN NEVER DIE.
Lieutenant Lyman Cyrus Day-Smith, SHC, 16.12.44 (age 25) [RAVENNA]
[J. LEWIS MILLIGAN, *THEY SHALL RETURN*]

THEY ARE NOT DEAD, LIFE'S FLAG IS NEVER FURLED.
Pilot Officer William Alfred Sneath, RCAF, 23.6.43 (age 30) [HEVERLEE]
Private Nelson Ward Clark, SSR, 14.10.44 (age 29) [SCHOONSELHOF]
[EDWIN MARKHAM, *OUR DEAD OVERSEAS*]

A GOLD STAR ON GOD'S SERVICE FLAG.
Trooper Howard Wilson Neff, SAR, 5.3.45 (age 20) [GROESBEEK]
[EDGAR GUEST, *THE GOLD STAR*]

Not all the commemorative inscriptions were solemn or mournful. The cult of games and sportsmanship in Victorian England, and the cliché that the battle of Waterloo had been won on the playing fields of Eton, carried over into Great War epitaphs. *He played the game, He died as he lived, a sportsman,* and *His C.O.'s tribute, "Though a boy he played a man's game to the finish,"* are Canadian inscriptions from the First World War reflecting the patently English notion that the sturdy character bred by schoolboy athletics translated into gallant conduct on the battlefield. The exhortation in Sir Henry Newbolt's once famous *Vitaï Lampada*, "Play up! play up! and play the game!" makes us think of the footballs kicked off at the start of the Somme offensive and the decimation of the young officers from the Public Schools; but as distasteful as some modern critics have found the metaphor of sport as warfare, to say of a fallen soldier that he had played the game to the end was to make him the embodiment of the virtues most admired in his time:

JUST THIS LINE HE WISHED WE GRAVE, "HE PLAYED THE GAME."
Flying Officer Peter George Harvey MacGregor, RCAF, 23.4.44 (age 22)
[REICHSWALD FOREST]

YOU PLAYED THE GAME TO THE FRONT LINE, BALL AND BAT WITH YOU.
YOU WERE ON GOD'S SIDE.
Guardsman John Burchmans Maguire, GGFG, 14.4.45 (age 27) [HOLTEN]

IN WAR, AS IN PLAY, HE GAVE HIS ALL.
Pilot Officer John Carlos O'Connell, RCAF, 13.5.44 (age 22) [BRUSSELS TOWN]

Next of kin also turned to the hymns that had become fixtures in Remembrance Day ceremonies. The verse from *O Valiant Hearts* (sometimes known as *The Supreme Sacrifice*), played every November 11, can be cited nearly in full from Canadian headstones in Second World War cemeteries:

"SPLENDID YOU PASSED, THE GREAT SURRENDER MADE, INTO THE LIGHT. . ."
ARKWRIGHT
Pilot Officer Robert George Brock DFC, RCAF, 25.4.44 (age 25) [DURNBACH]

O VALIANT HEART, WHO TO YOUR GLORY CAME, THROUGH DUST OF CONFLICT.
Lieutenant George Wharton Dauphinée, RCD, 31.10.44 [GRADARA]

TRANQUIL YOU LIE, YOUR KNIGHTLY VIRTUE PROVED, YOUR MEMORY HALLOWED
IN THE LAND YOU LOVED.
Sergeant John James Murray, NNSH, 5.4.45 (age 28) [HOLTEN]

PROUDLY YOU GATHERED RANK ON RANK TO WAR, AS WHO HAD HEARD
GOD'S MESSAGE FROM AFAR.
Rifleman William Murray Feaviour, RWR, 8.6.44 (age 25) [BÉNY-SUR-MER]

ALL YOU HAD HOPED FOR, ALL YOU HAD, YOU GAVE TO SAVE MANKIND; YOURSELF YOU
SCORNED TO SAVE.
Private George Eric Donaldson, 48th HC, 24.1.44 (age 34) [BARI]

SPLENDID YOU PASSED, THE GREAT SURRENDER MADE, INTO THE LIGHT
THAT NEVER MORE SHALL FADE.
Private John Harold Simpson, ASHC, 20.4.45 (age 19) [HOLTEN]

It was more than familiarity or the fine words that moved so many of the bereaved of the Second World War to turn once more to the hymns and commemorative pieces of the Great War. As Vance has pointed out, one effect of Canada's Great War myth was to implant the notion of a just war firmly in the minds of Canadians. If few in the 1920s questioned the necessity of defeating the Kaiser's Germany and all it stood for, no one could doubt the justice of the Allied cause in fighting an enemy reanimated by a vicious ideology that called for the extinction of entire countries and races. The central themes of Great War commemoration, sacrifice and duty in a righteous cause, could only gain in relevance after a war in which the implications of victory or defeat were much graver than they had been a generation before. Arkwright's verse equating the sacrifice of the fallen with that of Christ resonated even more powerfully among the bereaved of the Second World War in light of the aims and atrocities of Nazi Germany:

O VALIANT HEART, ALL YOU HAD HOPED FOR, ALL YOU HAD YOU GAVE . . .
YOUR LESSER CALVARY.
Flight Lieutenant Douglas Earl Cawker, RCAF, 22.3.44 (age 24) [HANOVER]

LIKE HIS MASTER BEFORE HIM, IN SAVING OTHERS HIMSELF HE SCORNED TO SAVE.
Private James Kitchener Menzies, QOCHC, 27.10.44 (age 29)
[BERGEN-OP-ZOOM]

"THESE WERE HIS SERVANTS, IN HIS STEPS THEY TROD."
Lieutenant John Brenton Matthew, RCIC, 27.3.45 (age 24) [HOLTEN]

The nature of the Nazi regime cast the war as a confrontation between good and evil. It would be a mistake on our part today to overlook the religious dimensions of the conflict or to underestimate the power of spiritual consolation to the bereaved once the war was over. Nazism made no secret of its contempt for the teachings of Christianity, and the threat it posed to Judaeo-Christian civilisation was plain to see before the war. Even as a political movement it struck contemporary observers as a surrogate religion, tantamount to a rival faith with its ceremonies, symbols, and messianic fervour. The intimidating dynamism of the Nazi movement and the dreadful New Order it sought to impose prompted clergymen in the English-speaking world to reply with a passionate rehearsal of Christian principles opposing the brutality and moral nihilism of the enemy's ideology. It is tempting to ascribe the greater proportion of Scriptural quotations in Canadian epitaphs of the Second World War to the influence of the churches in marshalling the spiritual arguments against an enemy that to many was evil incarnate. Passages affirming God's support of a righteous cause underlay the moral foundation of the Allied war effort; the prophecies in chapter 21 of the book of Revelation envisioning a world purged of evil after Armageddon seemed particularly apt:

THOU HAST LIFTED ME ABOVE MY FOES: AND FROM THE MAN OF VIOLENCE SET ME FREE.
Sergeant John Percival Downing, CRCE, 6.6.44 (age 31) [BÉNY-SUR-MER] [PSALM 18: 48]

THE LORD IS MY LIGHT AND MY SALVATION: WHOM SHALL I FEAR? PSALM XXVII. 1
Sergeant Blake Bird Keyes, RCA, 4.8.44 (age 24) [BRETTEVILLE-SUR-LAIZE]

"THE FEAR OF THE LORD IS TO HATE EVIL."
Private Paul St. Clair Hiltz, WNSR, 13.12.43 (age 25) [MORO RIVER] [PROVERBS 8: 13]

FEAR NOT THEM WHICH KILL THE BODY BUT ARE NOT ABLE TO KILL THE SOUL.
ST. MATT. X. 28
Private Wilson Adison Costello, RCAMC, 24.7.44 (age 22) [BÉNY-SUR-MER]

"IF GOD BE FOR US, WHO CAN BE AGAINST US?" ROMANS VIII. 31. MOTHER
Rifleman Allan Francis Gray, QORC, 5.3.45 (age 19) [GROESBEEK]

"TAKE THE HELMET OF SALVATION AND THE SWORD OF THE SPIRIT WHICH IS
THE WORD OF GOD."
Private Robert James Taylor, IRC, 28.9.44 (age 19) [CESENA] [EPHESIANS 6: 17]

"THIS IS THE VICTORY THAT OVERCOMETH THE WORLD, EVEN OUR FAITH."
Private Roy Winfield Porter, CYR, *31.12.43 (age 27)* [MORO RIVER] [I JOHN 5: 4]

WE SHALL MEET AFTER ARMAGEDDON IN THE NEW WORLD TO LIVE FOR EVER IN PEACE.
Flight Sergeant Mason Argue Edwards, RCAF, *22.10.43 (age 19)* [HANOVER]

A BELOVED SON WHOM WE EXPECT TO MEET IN THE EARTH MADE NEW.
SEE REVELATION XXI. 1-27
Private Ralph Edmund Johnson, RCAMC, *14.8.44 (age 25)* [BRETTEVILLE-SUR-LAIZE]

THERE SHALL BE A NEW HEAVEN AND A NEW EARTH: THEN SHALL THERE BE NO MORE WAR.
Rifleman Douglas Walter Reid, QORC, *26.2.45 (age 20)* [GROESBEEK]
[CF. REVELATION 21: 1]

. . . HE THAT SAT UPON THE THRONE SAID, BEHOLD, I MAKE ALL THINGS NEW.
REVELATION XXI.5
Lieutenant John Armour Cambridge MC, WR, *15.4.45 (age 29)* [GROESBEEK]

"HE THAT OVERCOMETH SHALL INHERIT ALL THINGS AND I WILL BE HIS GOD
AND HE SHALL BE MY SON."
Private Harry Cochrane, HPER, *20.3.44 (age 37)* [MORO RIVER] [REVELATION 21: 7]

AND THEY SHALL BRING THE GLORY AND HONOUR OF THE NATIONS. REV. XXI. 26
Warrant Officer I John Harold Lemon, RCAF, *11.4.43 (age 22)* [DURNBACH]

The title of Dwight Eisenhower's war memoirs, *Crusade in Europe*, says everything about the moral clarity the war assumed for the members of the Allied coalition. The two British generals in overall command of the Canadians, Harold Alexander and Bernard Montgomery, were devoutly religious men who worked passages from the Bible and hymns they knew intimately into their addresses and exhortations to their soldiers. The final scene of *Mrs. Miniver*, the most popular motion picture of 1942, has the title character and her family, sitting in the bombed out shell of their church, listen to the vicar's exhortation that all must do their part in "a people's war" and then rise to sing "Onward Christian Soldiers" as fighter planes roar overhead. Not surprisingly, the consoling theme of the fallen soldier as the defender of Christian values and brave servant of Christ faithful unto death found many forms of expression:

A CRUSADER. BE THOU FAITHFUL UNTO DEATH AND I WILL GIVE THEE A CROWN OF LIFE.
Major George Paxton Cowan, RCA, *25.5.44 (age 39)* [CASSINO]

TILL CHRISTIAN LOVE AND BROTHERHOOD SHALL PREVAIL THROUGHOUT THE WORLD.
Trooper Enoch Owen, TRR, *21.7.44 (age 24)* [AREZZO]

HE CHALLENGED THOSE WHO WOULD DESTROY THE INNOCENT AND
THE WAY OF LIFE HE LOVED SO WELL.
Pilot Officer John Frederick Dowding, RCAF, *17.10.44 (age 17)* [HARROGATE]

"I AM FOR PEACE: BUT WHEN I SPEAK, THEY ARE FOR WAR." PSALM CXX. 7.
PEACE: PEACE BE WITH THEE.
Lance Corporal Francis Allen, CBH, *28.9.44 (age 30)* [CESENA]

HE'S GONE TO JOIN THAT GLORIOUS THRONG. HE GAVE HIS LIFE TO CONQUER WRONG.
Flight Sergeant Wallace Dorrance Anderson, RCAF, *7.9.43 (age 22)* [DURNBACH]

HE GAVE HIS LIFE TO TERMINATE EVIL THAT WE MIGHT LIVE.
Lance Corporal Russell Drue Fogarty, CYR, 13.9.44 *(age 27)* [CORIANO RIDGE]

AGAINST SIN AND EVIL YOU FOUGHT. A VICTORY WORTHY BUT DEARLY BOUGHT.
Private Alfred Thomas Sedgman, ASHC, 26.2.45 [GROESBEEK]

A SACRIFICE FOR THE SIN OF THE WORLD. A SACRIFICE WELL PLEASING TO GOD.
Private Martin Joseph Anderson, TSR, 23.10.44 *(age 23)* [BERGEN-OP-ZOOM]

TRUE HAPPINESS ON EARTH IS ENJOYED WHEN SACRIFICE LEADS TO HEAVEN.
Flying Officer Charles Theodore Storey, RCAF, 11.9.44 *(age 20)* [HARROGATE]

HE FEARED ONLY GOD SO HIS LIFE HE GAVE, THE WORLD FROM TYRANNY'S GREED TO SAVE.
Private William Paul Shea, QOCHC, 26.2.45 *(age 19)* [GROESBEEK]

A GALLANT YOUTH GAVE HIS LIFE THAT THY WAY MAY BE KNOWN UNTO ALL THE NATIONS.
Flight Lieutenant John Adair Woodward, RCAF, 27.9.44 *(age 24)* [BROOKWOOD]

MAY GOD'S HOLY FREEDOM NEVER FAIL. FOR THE CAUSE OUR BOY GAVE HIS ALL.
Trooper Paul Meredith Smee, BCD, 25.5.44 *(age 27)* [CASSINO]

"IN HIS STEPS."
Captain William Lisle Christie White, RRR, 9.7.44 *(age 28)* [BÉNY-SUR-MER]

"GOD SO LOVED THE WORLD THAT HE GAVE HIS ONLY BEGOTTEN SON." ST. JOHN III. 16
Private Wilfred Charles Cope, IRC, 5.12.44 *(age 22)* [RAVENNA]

CHRIST IN YOU, THE HOPE OF GLORY. COL. I. 27
Pilot Officer Roland Otis Nickerson, RCAF, 22.1.44 [BERLIN]

WITH HIS LIFE'S BLOOD HE PAID OUR DEBT. A BRAVE BOY, A NOBLE SON.
Private Ferdinand Leonard Nash, HPER, 19.7.43 *(age 20)* [AGIRA]

GLADLY WE FOLLOW OUR LEADER SO GRAND, THE WORLD WE MUST WIN FOR JESUS.
Private Kitchener Langille, NNSH, 25.3.45 *(age 28)* [GROESBEEK]

FOR GOD MUST WINNOW MEN LIKE WHEAT, THAT HE MAY SAVE A FEW.
Flying Officer Terrence Velleau McKee, RCAF, 17.1.45 *(age 24)* [BROOKWOOD]

WHEREVER MAN HAS FOUGHT FOR RIGHT, BESIDE HIM STANDS, COULD WE BUT SEE, ONE THAT WAS CRUCIFIED.
Private Walter James Carlington, RCAMC, 11.8.42 *(age 20)* [BROOKWOOD]

"THIS IS MY BELOVED SON IN WHOM I AM WELL PLEASED." ST. MATTHEW III.17
Flight Sergeant Davey William Newman, RCAF, 18.4.45 *(age 19)* [BROOKWOOD]

"FOR EVEN THE SON OF MAN CAME TO GIVE HIS LIFE, A RANSOM FOR MANY."
Lance Sergeant Charles William Barker, CRCE, 26.8.44 *(age 28)*
[BRETTEVILLE-SUR-LAIZE] [MATTHEW 20: 28]

"FATHER, IF THIS CUP MAY NOT PASS AWAY FROM ME EXCEPT I DRINK IT, THY WILL BE DONE." MATT 26: 42
Flying Officer John Burke Mahoney, RCAF, 21.1.44 *(age 27)* [HANOVER]

LORD, IF THOU WILT, MAKE US THINE OWN TO STAND BY THEE EVERMORE.
Gunner Henri Joseph Vincent, RCA, 4.12.43 *(age 41)* [MORO RIVER]

HE HATH FOUGHT TO REPROVE THE WORLD OF SIN, RIGHTEOUSNESS AND JUDGEMENT.
MAY HIS SOUL REST IN PEACE.
Sergeant Vincent Terrance MacDonald, CYR, *10.4.44 (age 22)* [MORO RIVER]
[JOHN 16: 8]

I HAVE FINISHED THE WORK WHICH THOU HAST GIVEN ME TO DO.
Pilot Officer Frank George Plecan, RCAF, *29.7.44 (age 26)* [HAMBURG] [JOHN 17: 4]

"FOR WHEN WE WERE YET WITHOUT STRENGTH, IN DUE TIME CHRIST DIED
FOR THE UNGODLY."
Private David Angelo Gooley, ASHC, *29.1.45* [GROESBEEK] [ROMANS 5: 6]

THE SKY DARKENED AND ONCE AGAIN THE SUN WENT DOWN WHILE IT WAS STILL DAY.
Sergeant John McKenzie Mitchell, QORC, *11.6.44 (age 24)* [BÉNY-SUR-MER]

DEAD AND DIVINE AND BROTHER OF ALL AND HERE AGAIN HE LIES.
Lance Corporal Nick Kozak, CH, *4.3.45 (age 26)* [GROESBEEK]
[WALT WHITMAN, *A SIGHT IN CAMP*]

A GOOD SOLDIER OF JESUS CHRIST PASSED TO HIGHER SERVICE.
Pilot Officer Grenville Gordon Stanley, RCAF, *2.3.43 (age 22)* [SCHOONSELHOF]

BELIEVING IN CHRIST AND IN FREEDOM HE VOLUNTEERED HIS LIFE. HE HATH PEACE.
Flight Sergeant William Edwin Gimby, RCAF, *18.8.43* (AGE 23) [KIEL]

ONWARD, CHRISTIAN SOLDIER, WITH THE CROSS OF JESUS GOING ON BEFORE.
Private William Arthur Knight, SHC, *21.1.44 (age 25)* [MORO RIVER]

ONLY ONE LIFE, 'TWILL SOON BE PAST, ONLY WHAT'S DONE FOR CHRIST WILL LAST.
Private John Riley, RHLI, *12.8.44 (age 22)* [BRETTEVILLE-SUR-LAIZE]

A SOLDIER OF THE CROSS WHO DID NOT LOSE THE BATTLE.
Private George Esser, QOCHC, *23.10.44 (age 20)* [BERGEN-OP-ZOOM]

HEREBY KNOW WE LOVE BECAUSE HE LAID DOWN HIS LIFE FOR US. I JOHN III. 16
Sergeant George Elliott French, 17th DY, *25.12.44 (age 31)* [BERGEN-OP-ZOOM]

HE FOLLOWED HIS LORD AND SAVIOUR WHO GAVE HIS LIFE TO SAVE MANKIND.
Corporal Gordon Scarth Wood, CSR, *21.4.45 (age 20)* [HOLTEN]

HE LIVED AND DIED A SOLDIER OF CHRIST AND HIS COUNTRY.
Private Adrian Joseph Phillips, RCASC, *8.12.45 (age 22)* [GROESBEEK]

"MY MARKS AND SCARS I CARRY WITH ME TO BE A WITNESS FOR ME THAT
I HAVE FOUGHT HIS BATTLES."
Corporal Sydney Guy Mosher, NS(NB)R, *24.4.45 (age 30)* [HOLTEN]
[THE PILGRIM'S PROGRESS]

THE GREAT COMMANDER HAS WRITTEN HIS NAME ON THE ROLL OF HIM WHO GAVE
HIS ONLY BEGOTTEN SON.
Private Roy James Muir, LER, *28.1.45 (age 23)* [RAVENNA]

SACRIFICE IS A LIFE-GIVING SEED OF DIVINE FRUITFULNESS, THE HIGHEST
FULFILMENT OF HUMAN LIVING.
Signalman Talbot Francis Papineau O'Neill, RCCS, *1.11.40 (age 19)* [BROOKWOOD]

CALAIS CANADIAN WAR CEMETERY

TO THE JUDGE OF RIGHT AND WRONG OUR PURPOSE AND OUR POWER,
OUR FAITH AND SACRIFICE BELONG.
Gunner Oakley Davis, RCA, 20.10.44 (age 35) [CORIANO RIDGE]

HE DIED FOR HIS FRIENDS. JESUS DIED AS A SUBSTITUTE FOR THE UNSAVED: IS HE YOURS?
Private John Wesley Atwood, RCR, 6.9.44 [CORIANO RIDGE]

The Canadian families who pledged their hopes that the sacrifices of the Great War had opened the way to a better world were looking at a very different postwar landscape than the one beheld by the bereaved a quarter of a century later. Gone were the old autocratic monarchies, relics of the Middle Ages, as were the rival empires and secret alliances that had triggered hostilities in 1914. It was not entirely unrealistic to believe that the war was a unique calamity never to be repeated now that the roots of conflict had been eradicated. Similar hopes that peace and stability would emerge from a dearly bought victory surfaced once again on Canadian headstones of the Second World War, but we should read them in the spirit of the post-1945 world. The second conflict had been far more consumptive of human life, most of Europe lay in ruins, and to the horrors of modern war had been added a systematic genocide and the obliteration of Hiroshima and Nagasaki. Even the victors shuddered at the means necessary to win the war, nor did peace seem likely to endure as Europe quickly divided into two armed camps. The Great War epitaphs heralding a better world owe something to the optimism of the pre-1914 era; the Second World War epitaphs speak to a world that could no longer count on surviving another major conflict.

OUR SACRIFICE WAS NOT IN HATE BUT RATHER IN HOPE OF UNIVERSAL PEACE.
Flying Officer Jack Lawrie McGill, RCAF, 24.3.44 (age 27) [BERLIN]

O GOD OF LOVE, O KING OF PEACE, MAKE WARS THROUGHOUT THE WORLD TO CEASE;
THE WRATH OF SINFUL MAN RESTRAIN; GIVE PEACE, O GOD, GIVE PEACE AGAIN.
Private Henry Edward Reynolds, NNSH, 7.6.44 (age 27) [BÉNY-SUR-MER]
[HYMN, O GOD OF LOVE, BY HENRY W. BAKER, 1861]

"SHOW US YOUR LIGHT, O GOD, THAT WE MAY FIGHT FOR PEACE WITH PEACE,
AND NOT WITH WAR."
Flying Officer Nicholas Peters, RCAF, 7.3.45 (age 30) [BECKLINGEN]

"IF WE LOVE ONE ANOTHER, GOD DWELLETH IN US, AND HIS LOVE IS PERFECTED IN US."
Flying Officer Gordon Hewlett Parker, RCAF, 28.4.44 (age 26) [HEVERLEE]
[I JOHN 4: 12]

HE HATH DONE WHAT HE COULD SO THAT WE MAY ALL LIVE IN PEACE, UNMOLESTED.
Private David Robert Hyde, RHLI, 8.3.45 (age 24) [GROESBEEK]

"MARK THE PERFECT MAN, AND BEHOLD THE UPRIGHT:
FOR THE END OF THAT MAN IS PEACE."
Lance Corporal Alvin Lloyd Lehman, IRC, 2.1.45 (age 21) [VILLANOVA] [PSALM 37: 37]

"A PEACE AND NATIONHOOD BOUGHT AT SUCH A PRICE WILL NOT SOON BE FORGOTTEN."
Warrant Officer I Robert Edgar Hall Cameron, RCAF, 25.4.44 (age 20) [BROOKWOOD]

HIS THE PRICE, FOR PEACE.
Pilot Officer Tracy Arthur Thomas Williams, RCAF, 24.8.43 (age 21) [BERLIN]

87

TO END WARS HE HAS GIVEN HIS LIFE.

Sergeant Jules Robert René Villeneuve, RCAF, 20.11.44 (age 22) [CHESTER (BLACON)]

HE GAVE HIS LIFE FOR A WARLESS WORLD AND FOR THE EMANCIPATION OF MANKIND.

Flying Officer George Alexander Mortimer, RCAF, 4.11.44 (age 21) [RHEINBERG]

GOD GIVE US THE PEACE FOR WHICH YOU FOUGHT. PROUDLY WE BEAR OUR DEEP LOSS.

Lieutenant Robert Murray Andrew, CH, 13.3.45 (age 31) [GROESBEEK]

THE LORD SHALL GIVE HIS PEOPLE THE BLESSING OF PEACE.

Corporal Joseph Frederick Stanley, 12th MD, 12.11.44 (age 31) [BERGEN-OP-ZOOM]
[PSALM 29: 11]

HE GAVE HIS LIFE THAT PEACE MIGHT BRING THE PROMISE OF A BETTER WORLD.

Private Wilfred Stanley Harrison, LSR, 12.9.44 (age 21) [ADEGEM]

I DIE IN HOPE THAT MY SON AND LOVED ONES MAY LIVE IN GODLY PEACE.

Private William Pervis Prellwitz, SSR, 26.10.44 (age 34) [BERGEN-OP-ZOOM]

HE HAS GIVEN HIS LIFE TO BRING BACK PEACE AND MAINTAIN OUR LIBERTIES. EVER REMEMBERED BY MOTHER.

Pilot Officer Joseph Louis Gaston Pelletier, RCAF, 5.3.45 (age 20) [HARROGATE]

WE SERVED AND PASSED ON THAT OUR LABOR MIGHT BRING YOU PEACE FOR EVERMORE.

Private Lloyd Norman Thompson, SHC, 17.9.44 (age 20) [CORIANO RIDGE]

MAY THE FUTURE WORLD BENEFIT THROUGH HIS EFFORTS AND SACRIFICE.

Trooper Austin William Brazier, SFR, 5.10.44 (age 20) [BERGEN-OP-ZOOM]

TOWARDS A BETTER WORLD.

Sergeant James Roy Addison Ruthven, RCAF, 29.12.43 (age 21) [BERLIN]

WHO GAVE HIS LIFE IN THE CAUSE OF HONOR, DECENCY AND A CHRISTIAN WAY OF LIFE.

Flying Officer William George Hunter, RCAF, 23.5.44 (age 29) [HARROGATE]

TO FASHION LIFE AS IN MY DREAMS I DIE. MAY VICTORY REMAIN SACRED.

Flying Officer Jerome Thomas Ellis Cumming-Bart, RCAF, 2.12.43 (age 25) [BERLIN]

THERE IS NOTHING MORE TO GIVE. MAY YOU ENJOY THE LIBERTY FOR WHICH HE DIED.

Private Warner Douglas Pinch, ESR, 19.2.45 (age 20) [GROESBEEK]

DEMOCRACY, THAT IS SO WELL WORTH DYING FOR MUST BE MADE WORTH LIVING FOR.

Flight Sergeant William Edgar Pilborough, RCAF, 8.6.42 (age 30) [HEVERLEE]

HE PASSED THIS WAY IN DEFENCE OF DEMOCRACY.

Pilot Officer Harold Edward Quinn, RCAF, 10.4.44 (age 23) [ESBJERG]

IN MEMORY OF OUR SON WHO GAVE HIS EARTHLY LIFE TO THE FREEDOM OF MANKIND.

Sergeant Charles Herbert Leslie Bell, RCAF, 10.9.42 (age 21) [VLISSINGEN NORTHERN]

MEN STILL DIE FOR FREEDOM, A TESTAMENT THAT LIFE IS GAINED BY DEATH IN HONOUR'S CAUSE.

Private Roy Wilmert Neilly, CH, 9.10.44 (age 19) [BERGEN-OP-ZOOM]

FAITHFUL UNTO DEATH FOR THE SURVIVAL OF FREEDOM.

Pilot Officer Alfred Brooks, RCAF, 27.1.44 (age 35) [BERLIN]

THAT YOU MAY LOOK TO THE FUTURE CONFIDENT, HOPEFUL, AND ABOVE ALL, FREE.
Flight Sergeant Merlin Lindsay John, RCAF, 23.12.43 (age 20) [HARROGATE]

THIS HERO YEARNED FOR LIFE AND DIED FOR PRECIOUS FREEDOM.
Sapper Ralph Joseph Collins, CRCE, 22.12.43 (age 28) [MORO RIVER]

CHERISHING THE MEMORY OF THE ONE WE LOVED WE FACE THE FUTURE WITH COURAGE.
Flying Officer Donald James McMillan, RCAF, 1.2.45 (age 23) [HARROGATE]

HE GAVE HIS ALL THAT WE MAY HAVE A BETTER WORLD TO LIVE IN. LONG LIVE HIS MEMORY.
Private Robert Edward Mohlman, PR, 28.8.44 (age 21) [MONTECCHIO]
Lance Corporal Douglas Earl Mohlman, HLIC, 17.9.44 (age 23) [CALAIS]

Research on war memorials and monuments has concentrated on the legacy of the Great War, with good reason. No truer measure could there be of that war's traumatic impact and the magnitude of the debt the survivors felt they owed to the fallen than the effort that went into the construction of thousands of memorials and war cemeteries. The Second World War, by contrast, did not inspire the same burst of creativity when the time came to memorialise the fallen, who in Britain and the Commonwealth were many fewer than in the First. Conformity with the patterns set after 1918 made sense on practical as well as aesthetic grounds. The bombed cities in Great Britain required rebuilding, political and social priorities had changed with the election of a Labour government, budgets were tight, and there was no reason to think that the monumental traditions of the Great War could be improved upon. Only for the air force memorials was any new form of commemoration necessary.

The personal inscriptions show the same continuity. This chapter has shown that English Canadian epitaphs, by and large, followed the examples of Great War rhetoric and aspirations. A last selection from Calais, however, points to the differences that set the Canadian epitaphs of the Second World War apart from the precedents of the First:

A CANADIAN SOLDIER WHO GAVE HIS LIFE FOR OUR COUNTRY. MAY GOD WATCH OVER HIM.
Rifleman Thomas Phillips, RRR, 15.9.44 (age 18)

IN LOVING MEMORY OF A DEAR SON AND BROTHER KILLED SERVING WITH THE REGINA RIFLES.
Corporal Thomas Richard Loader, RRR, 12.9.44 (age 22)

ST. JOHN'S, NEWFOUNDLAND AND NORTH SYDNEY, NOVA SCOTIA, CANADA.
Lieutenant Lawrence Bruce Thistle, RCAF, 13.6.44 (age 27)

BELOVED NEPHEW OF MR. AND MRS. DENNIS CYPRIEN, PINCHI, BRITISH COLUMBIA, CANADA.
Private Phillip Tyee, CH, 8.9.44 (age 20)

DE MONTRÉAL. GRAND DEVANT DIEU, GRAND DEVANT LES HOMMES,
GRAND POUR SA PATRIE. R.I.P.
*(From Montreal. Great before God, great before men,
great in the service of his country. R.I.P.)
Private Jean Poulet, RC, 17.9.44 (age 28)*

A YOUTH FOR EVER. HIS FLIGHT IS DONE. THROUGH LABOURS TO THE STARS HE WON.
Pilot Officer James Sydney Thomson, RCAF, 12.5.44 (age 20)

WILNO, ONTARIO, CANADA. ETERNAL REST GRANT UNTO HIM, O LORD.
PROSI O ZDROWAS MARYO.
(Ask for a 'Hail Mary'.)
Private Florian Frank Chippior, HLIC, 17.9.44 (age 23)

Some differences are minor, others telling. The epitaphs of the Second World War display a more consciously Canadian identity among the soldiers and airmen. Professions of allegiance to Britain, the norm in Great War epitaphs, give way to a primary loyalty to Canada felt by servicemen whose hometowns demonstrate the transition from a half British-born Canadian Expeditionary Force to a national army in which over four out of five were natives of Canada. The change in the army's organisation is evident from the reversion to the names of the old militia regiments which had been dropped when the CEF was organised into numbered battalions in 1914. The composition of the army had changed as well. Epitaphs in French reveal the much greater commitment of French Canadians to the national war effort; the occurrence of foreign languages in turn attests the presence and role of Canada's ethnic minorities. The distinctive RCAF badge, new to Second World War cemeteries, highlights the contribution of Canadian airmen and the casualty rates incurred in the air war. The inscriptions on the headstones of airmen introduce new motifs in the epitaphs that embrace the experience of aerial warfare, nascent in the Great War and brought to maturity in the Second World War. The continuity and changes in the commemorative traditions of the Great War will emerge in subsequent chapters, but the epitaphs of the Second World War also belong to a much longer history of sepulchral inscriptions, to which we now turn.

FURTHER READING:

Bourne, John. "The European and international consequences of the Armistice," in: *At the Eleventh Hour. Reflections, Hopes and Anxieties at the Closing of the Great War, 1918*. Ed. Hugh Cecil and Peter H. Liddle. Barnsley, South Yorkshire: Pen & Sword Books, 1998, pp. 315–326.

Cannadine, David. "War and death, grief and mourning in modern Britain," in: *Mirrors of Mortality. Studies in the Social History of Death*. Ed. Joachim Whaley. London: Europa Publications Limited, 1981, pp. 187–242.

Hoover, A.J. *God, Britain, and Hitler in World War II. The View of the British Clergy, 1939–1945*. Westport, Connecticut and London: Praeger, 1999.

Marshall, David. "'Death Abolished': Changing attitudes to Death and the Afterlife in nineteenth-century Canadian Protestantism," in: *Age of Transition. Readings in Canadian Social History, 1800–1900*. Ed. Norman Knowles. Toronto: Harcourt Brace & Company Canada, Ltd., 1998, pp. 370–387.

Shipley, Robert. *To Mark Our Place. A History of Canadian War Memorials*. Toronto: NC Press Limited, 1987.

Snape, Michael. *God and the British Soldier. Religion and the British Army in the First and Second World Wars.* London-New York: Routledge, 2005.

Young, Alan R. "'We throw the torch': Canadian memorials of the Great War and the mythology of heroic sacrifice," *Journal of Canadian Studies/Revue d'études canadiennes* 24/4 (1989–90), 5–28.

Vance, Jonathan. *Death So Noble. Memory, Meaning, and the First World War.* Vancouver: UBC Press, 1997.

_____. "Remembering Armageddon" in: *Canada and the First World War. Essays in Honour of Robert Craig Brown.* Ed. David Mackenzie. Toronto-Buffalo-London: University of Toronto Press, 2005, pp. 409–430.

Wilkinson, Alan. *The Church of England and the First World War.* London: SPCK, 1978.

Winter, J.M. *Sites of Memory, Sites of Mourning. The Great War in European Cultural History.* Cambridge: Cambridge University Press, 1995.

CHAPTER FOUR

"To you, dear son, we raise this token. . ."
Holten Canadian War Cemetery, The Netherlands

A THOUGHT TRUE AND TENDER TO SHOW I STILL REMEMBER.
REST IN PEACE. LOVING WIFE
Sapper John Culbertson, CRCE, 30.4.45 (age 33)

There are in every Canadian war cemetery headstones that condense the broader story of a campaign into its essentials and effects. At Holten Canadian War Cemetery in eastern Holland, the majority of the 1,355 Canadian graves solemnly chronicle the last full month of the war, when in April 1945 First Canadian Army completed the liberation of the eastern Netherlands and carried the victory campaign into the northern corner of Germany. Although this last campaign was not as fierce and costly as Normandy or the Rhineland, the rows of headstones at Holten speak for the obstinacy of an enemy devoid to the end of all rational considerations. Each day's advance confirmed the justice of the Allied cause as the Dutch joyfully welcomed the armies liberating them from the menace and hardships of a five-year occupation; but the erasure of young lives continued as the Germans persisted in a struggle by now utterly hopeless and pointless. Nearly 1,200 Canadian soldiers were killed in actions that seemed increasingly anti-climactic given that the Allied victory was only a matter of time. The daily casualty returns for April 1945 show that more than sixty Canadian soldiers were killed on two separate days, sixty-four on April 28 alone. Over fifty died on five different days, as did forty or more on seven other days. Amidst the scenes of gratitude and triumph that make the liberation of the Netherlands one of the proudest episodes in Canadian history stand these instances of the unremitting cruelty of the war:

INTO THE MOSAIC OF VICTORY ARE PLACED THESE PRECIOUS JEWELS, OUR SONS.
Lieutenant Robert Louis Richard, AR, 6.4.45 (age 23)

AMONG THE NOBLE HOST OF THOSE WHO PERISHED IN THE CAUSE OF RIGHT.
Rifleman Victor Alloway Rawlings, RRR, 9.4.45 (age 28)

FIVE BROTHERS IN ARMS, FOUR SURVIVE. LIFE'S WORK WELL DONE, NOW COMES REST.
Lance Corporal Frank Arthur Cherry MM, CSR, 10.4.45 (age 21)

MY DEAR ONLY SON JACK. HE WAS ALL THE WORLD TO ME. LOVINGLY REMEMBERED AND SADLY MISSED BY MOTHER.

Trooper John Raymond Bridges, SFR, 12.4.45 (age 21)

NÉ LE 13 AVRIL 1920, ST. GEORGES, MANITOBA, CANADA. TUÉ LE 13 AVRIL 1945, À ZUTPHEN, HOLLANDE.

(Born 13 April 1920, St. Georges, Manitoba, Canada. Killed 13 April 1945, in Zutphen, Holland.)
Gunner Omer Vincent, RCA, 13.4.45 (age 25)

WHOSOEVER READS HIS NAME SALUTES A MIGHTY COMPANY, ACKNOWLEDGING ALL WHO DIED THAT OTHERS MIGHT BE FREE.

Private William Arthur Stackhouse, LWR, 15.4.45 (age 22)

AMONG THE FIRST TO VOLUNTEER AND LAST TO DIE. BRAVE AND DEAR, SHIELD US HERE.

Gunner Joseph Patrick Egan, RCA, 19.4.45 (age 39)

HE FOUGHT WITH THOSE WHO BRAVELY FOUGHT AND IS BURIED WITH THE FALLEN DEAD.

Trooper Thomas Philip Birkett, BCR, 25.4.45 (age 26)

DEAR BRAVE LAD, TO GOD AND THY MOTHER I COMMEND THEE. DAD

Lieutenant Edwin Owen Copas, CH, 26.4.45 (age 23)

TU ES PARTI TROP TÔT. LA BATAILLE FINISSAIT. TA FILLE SERA MON RÉCONFORT.

(You left too soon. The battle was ending. Your daughter will be my comfort.)
Lieutenant Louis Philippe Coutlée, RM, 26.4.45 (age 26)

SLEEP PEACEFULLY, DEAR DADDY.

Corporal Walter Oscar Rintala, QORC, 26.4.45 (age 32)

Spasmodic resistance continued for five more days after Hitler's thousand-year Reich expired after little more than a decade, along with its founder, on April 30. As the war guttered out, another one hundred and fourteen Canadian soldiers were added to the list of fatalities, including twelve men killed on May 5, the day word went out that all offensive operations were to cease. It is troubling to realise that for these and other families the announcement of the war's end coincided with the arrival of telegrams conveying the hardly bearable news that they had been mere days or hours away from coming safely through:

NEITHER DEATH NOR LIFE SHALL BE ABLE TO SEPARATE US FROM THE LOVE OF GOD. ROMANS VIII. 38

Major Bramwell Ernest Churchill, RCA, 1.5.45 (age 40)

THERE ARE NO STARS BUT THOSE THAT SHINE ON THE ONES WHO STAYED BEHIND.

Lieutenant John Gourlay, IRC, 2.5.45 (age 32)

MY HEART IS FULL OF PAIN. IT WOULD BE HEAVEN, MY SON, TO HEAR YOUR VOICE AGAIN. MOTHER AND SISTER

Private William Thomas Morgan, RHLI, 3.5.45 (age 23)

HE IS NOT DEAD WHO GAVE HIS LIFE TO RID THE WORLD OF FEAR AND STRIFE.

Trooper Arthur Alfred Shepherd, 14th CH, 4.5.45 (age 21)

EARTH HAS NO SORROW THAT LOVE CANNOT HEAL.

Captain John Woodrow Colburn, RCASC, 5.5.45 (age 27)

A handful of epitaphs reveal the strength of feeling in the immediate aftermath of the war towards the enemy and the suffering they had inflicted on so many. Coming after the hard-fought assaults into the Reich in February and March, the final battles against a monstrous regime that had pulled everything down with it hardened the hearts of the soldiers who had seen their comrades die unnecessarily. The miseries imposed on the Dutch populace by the German occupiers and the encounter with the workings of Nazism even in its death throes added to the revulsion towards an enemy whose crimes against humanity stood fully exposed in 1945. Such was the disgust at the loathsome conduct of Nazi Germany that the Canadian commander, General Crerar, gave orders that the Canadian soldiers interred in enemy soil were to be brought back to Holland for permanent burial. With the exception of a single grave in the Reichswald Forest War Cemetery and a handful of Dieppe prisoners buried in Berlin, all Canadian soldiers who died in Germany were laid to rest at Groesbeek, within sight of the German frontier, or at Holten:

HIS LIFE HE GAVE IN GERMANY. OUR BRAVE AND LOVING SOLDIER SON. R.I.P.
Private James Kostey, RHLI, 8.3.45 (age 23) [GROESBEEK]

HONNEUR AU CANADIEN, PHILIPPE, DÉCÉDÉ EN ALLEMAGNE.
(Honour to the French Canadian, Philippe, who died in Germany.)
Private Philippe Bélanger, RM, 1.4.45 (age 32) [GROESBEEK]

IN MEMORY OF A CANADIAN SOLDIER KILLED ON ACTIVE SERVICE IN GERMANY.
MAY HIS SOUL REST IN PEACE.
Private Francis Wilber Spencer, SDGH, 28.4.45 (age 35)

IN LOVING MEMORY OF OUR DEAR SON JOSEPH, KILLED IN ACTION IN GERMANY. R.I.P.
Sapper Joseph Le Bano, CRCE, 21.6.45 (age 25)

The bitterness that prevailed in the years after the war has subsided. On the other hand, the inscriptions on Canadian headstones linking the fallen soldier to the land where he lies buried offer minute but durable testaments to the lasting bond of friendship between the Netherlands and Canada—a bond that was reaffirmed by the tumultuous reception given to returning veterans on the fiftieth and sixtieth anniversaries of the liberation. The thought that their sons lay at rest in a country forever grateful for their sacrifice seems to have been a source of comfort to the families of these soldiers:

HOLLANDSE HARTEN, BEWAKEN ONZE DAPPEREN. HEARTS OF HOLLAND,
GUARD OUR BRAVE.
Gunner Bruce Earl Douglas Kerr, RCA, 6.4.45 (age 22)

YOU LINGER WHERE THE TULIPS GROW, NOT DEAD BUT JUST AWAY.
Rifleman James Earl Aiken, QORC, 7.4.45 (age 19)

DEAR ONE, SLEEP WELL IN THIS BEAUTIFUL LAND FAR FROM HOME. MOTHER AND DAD
Trooper Robert Jeffery Lockhart, 14th CH, 27.4.45 (age 20)

Among the epitaphs at Holten that are rooted in a particular time and place are others echoing themes of loss and consolation that go back centuries in Western civilisation. The influence of Great War commemoration in shaping the response of the bereaved after the Second World War was the subject of the preceding chapter, but the messages of farewell belong to a much longer epitaphic tradition that began in Antiquity and continued well into the twentieth century. In form and content, prose or verse, in their simplicity and immediacy, or in their universalism, the epitaphs record the ways in which generations of human beings have confronted the inevitability of death, sought comfort from its pains, and compressed the memory and meaning of a life into a few words.

OUR DEAR BILL.
Private William Edward Bruyea, RCASC, 20.4.45 (age 21)

TONY. BORN 11 JUNE 1924. DIED OF WOUNDS. ALWAYS REMEMBERED.
Lance Corporal Anthony James Kucera, RWR, 27.4.45 (age 20)

YOUNGEST SON OF JAMES AND THE LATE MABEL TAYLOR, ACTON, ONTARIO, CANADA. REST IN PEACE.
Private George Taylor, LWR, 10.4.45 (age 21)

Many epitaphs present the same bare details, consisting of little more than the name and origins of the deceased, given in the earliest Greek inscriptions dating from the seventh century B.C. Yet even the most reticent inscriptions, confining themselves to date of birth, parentage, home town, or the enumeration of bereaved parents and siblings, allow the reader to imagine the ripples of grief running through a family or a small town at the news of a young man's death on active service. So do the nicknames and endearments (*Dear Johnny, Our Wibb, Aubrey darling, "Bobby," "Skeeter," "Wee Sandy," The champ, "Little Mons"*) or the inscriptions recording only the dates (*1918–1943, 1921–1945, June 25, 1919–July 25, 1943*) that drive home the brevity of these lives. If such inscriptions do not say a great deal about their subjects, it is because there was not a great deal to say about young men killed in their late teens or early twenties, before their lives had taken shape. Some were married, some had children, but for most of them enlistment for overseas service represented the first and only momentous decision of their lives.

The repetition of fixed formulae in ancient epitaphs (*"May the earth lie light upon you," "Do not grieve for me, dear parents," "Once I was not, then I was, now I am not, but I don't care"* being common Roman examples) anticipated modern habits. When choosing an epitaph, in ancient times as today, many people were content to select or adapt ready-made inscriptions, and the visitor to the war cemeteries will soon notice the recurrence of conventional forms. *"Gone but not forgotten"* and *"Rest in peace"* are ubiquitous examples of commonplace forms. *"One precious to our hearts has gone / The voice we loved is stilled / The place made vacant in our home / Can never more be filled"* and *"Father, in thy gracious keeping / Leave we now our dear son sleeping,"* two oft-found inscriptions, exemplify the stock verses pressed into service as epitaphs. This commemorative versecraft, most of it anonymous, reflects the change in attitudes, noted in the previous chapter, towards death and consolation during the latter part of the nineteenth century. It also signals the decline of the epitaph as a distinct epigraphic and literary genre. Generic epitaphs, a somewhat unfortunate by-product of a mass-communications era which has seen standardised greeting cards, birthday wishes, and messages of condolence displace the more engaging individualism of an earlier age, begin to appear in inscriptions from the First World War and become far more numerous in those from the Second. The gist of these farewells, still prevalent in

The damaged church at Rouvres, near a crucial bridge crossing used by Canadian tanks in the advance east of Falaise.

Street sign near Bény-sur-Mer.

The beach at Pourville, west of Dieppe, where the South Saskatchewan Regiment and the Queen's Own Cameron Highlanders of Canada landed on August 19, 1942.

British graves at Hunter's Cemetery, Beaumont Hamel, the Somme, July 1st, 1916.

A Great War burial ground (Nine Elms British War Cemetery, in West Flanders) including a German plot with distinct square-topped headstones.

The heather garden at Holten Canadian War Cemetery.

One of the first to volunteer, one of the last to die. A Canadian grave at Holten.

A fitting epitaph for an airman.

obituary notices and sympathy cards today, can be gleaned from the random selection from Holten. Unoriginal they may be, but the place where they are gives each one a worth and propriety of its own:

DEARER STILL AS THE YEARS DEPART HIS MEMORY LIVES WITHIN MY HEART. WIDOW
Private Howard John Linnell, QOCHC, 6.4.45 (age 22)

AS I LOVED YOU SO I MISS YOU. IN MY MEMORY YOU ARE NEAR AND REMEMBERED ALWAYS,
BRINGING MANY A SILENT TEAR.
Private William Maryglod, LSR, 25.4.45 (age 31)

A HAPPY HOME WE ONCE ENJOYED, HOW SWEET THE MEMORY STILL. DEATH HAS LEFT A
LONELINESS THE WORLD CAN NEVER FILL.
Lance Corporal William James Sullivan, AR, 7.4.45 (age 33)

SLEEP, GORDON DEAR. 'TWAS HARD TO BE PARTED THUS BUT GOD'S STRONG ARM
SUPPORTED US. R.I.P.
Private Gordon John Hopper, LWR, 16.4.45 (age 19)

PEACE, PERFECT PEACE. BY THRONGING DUTIES PRESS'D? TO DO THE WILL OF JESUS,
THIS IS REST.
Trooper Winston George Hooker, 12th MD, 7.4.45 (age 25)

The rituals of death naturally involve traditional formulae that are universal and particular at the same time. Standard texts, drawn from the burial services used in the various Christian denominations were often chosen as inscriptions, not least because they formed part of the rituals that the families had not had the chance to observe in a proper funeral. Passages from the books of Job and John—"*I am the resurrection and the life. . . ,*" "*I know that my Redeemer liveth. . . ,*" "*The Lord gave, and the Lord hath taken away. . .*"—have introduced the Order for the Burial of the Dead since the Book of Common Prayer defined Anglican worship in the sixteenth century. The assurances of St. Paul alluded to in the Collect of the burial service have been central to Christian consolation from the very beginnings of the church:

EVEN SO THEM ALSO WHICH SLEEP IN JESUS WILL GOD BRING WITH HIM. I THES. IV. 14
Sapper Andrew Lawrence Ford, CRCE, 7.4.45 (age 26)

The abbreviations A.M.D.G. (*Ad maiorem Dei gloriam*—"to the greater glory of God") and I.H.S. (*In hoc signo*—"in this sign," i.e. the Cross) identify the deceased as Roman Catholics. These inscriptions from Holten stand for many more taken from texts of Catholic prayers and services for the departed. The last one recalls the words attributed to St. Ambrose (on one headstone to St. Augustine), "We have loved him in life, let us not forget him in death," which are frequently quoted on the headstones of Roman Catholic servicemen:

MAY HIS SOUL AND THE SOULS OF ALL THE FAITHFUL DEPARTED REST IN PEACE. AMEN
Private John Theodore MacMillan, PR, 28.4.45 (age 19)

THEIR REWARD ALSO IS WITH THE LORD AND THE CARE OF THEM IS WITH THE MOST HIGH.
Rifleman Theodore Olenick, RWR, 21.4.45 (age 19)

"MAKE HIM TO BE NUMBERED WITH THY SAINTS IN GLORY EVERLASTING."
Lieutenant Keith William Mountford B.Sc., RCA, 20.4.45 (age 23)

LOVED IN LIFE AND LOVED IN DEATH. "BE MINDFUL, O LORD, OF THY SERVANT."
Private Frank Joseph Biernaski, SDGH, 28.4.45 (age 32)

One valediction popular during the Second World War might escape recognition today. *"Mizpah,"* a term appearing in the story of Jacob and Laban's covenant in Genesis 31: 44–55, served as a farewell in correspondence between servicemen and their families long separated by time and distance. Between loved ones parted by death it affirmed unbroken love and the promise of reunion, anchoring the human relationship within the larger relationship with God. Inscriptions consisting solely of this word are not uncommon; but its beauty and significance are revealed when the Biblical text is cited in full:

MIZPAH. THE LORD WATCH BETWEEN ME AND THEE WHEN WE ARE ABSENT ONE FROM ANOTHER.
Sergeant Edward Sombert, CPC, 5.8.45 (age 29)

A few inscriptions closely echo ancient prototypes and styles. It was a common convention in ancient tomb inscriptions to address passersby, usually to invite them to pause by the grave, to entreat their sympathy, and to wish them well on their own journey through life. *"Whoever wanders by. . . "* as one epitaph at Holten begins—the ubiquitous requests for prayers or for flowers to be laid at the grave that one finds on the headstones are but a variant of this tradition. Some ancient epitaphs, however, issued pointed reminders to readers to be mindful of their own mortality in a long *memento mori* tradition that lies behind the admonitions on these Second World War headstones. The first has many counterparts among ancient and Christian epitaphs up to the early nineteenth century, while the second cites a well-known line from the Roman poet Horace whose advice was not lost on soldiers whose concerns were very much of the present. The final pair retells the theme in Christian terms warning not only of death but of the judgement to come:

AS YOU ARE NOW, SO ONCE WAS I: AS I AM NOW, SO YOU SHALL BE; PREPARE FOR DEATH AND FOLLOW ME.
Private Melvin Clarence Collins, NBR, 12.4.45 (age 26)

CARPE DIEM, GEORGE, QUAM MINIMUM CREDULA POSTERO.
(Seize the day, George, entrust as little as you can to the morrow.)
Major Colin James Radcliffe, RRR, 28.7.45 (age 34) [GROESBEEK]

FAREWELL. "LOOK THY LAST ON ALL THINGS LOVELY, EVERY HOUR." WALTER DE LA MARE
Pilot Officer James Walter Gibbons, RCAF, 20.2.44 (age 32) [BERLIN]

MY LIFE IS RUN AND YOURS IS RUNNING. PREPARE, FOR THE JUDGEMENT DAY IS COMING.
Private Eric James Smith, PR, 5.2.44 (age 20) [MORO RIVER]

WATCH THEREFORE, FOR YE KNOW NOT WHAT HOUR YOUR LORD DOTH COME. MATTHEW XXIV. 42
Private Alfred Henry Yantz, RCR, 3.11.43 (age 28) [MORO RIVER]

Perhaps the best known classical epitaph is the one composed by Simonides for the Spartan dead at Thermopylae: *"Stranger, go tell the Spartans that here we lie in obedience to their orders."* The instruction to the reader to take back word of the fallen soldiers' last full measure of devotion resurfaces in these two epitaphs obviously indebted to the ancient model. The second example, derived from a First World War poem attributed to James Maxwell Edmonds (1875–1958) and frequently cited in personal inscriptions of the Second World War, has become known as the Kohima Epitaph from its use on the British memorial to the dead of the Burma campaign:

TELL ENGLAND, YE WHO PASS OUR MONUMENT, WE DIED FOR HER.
SO REST WE IN CONTENT.

Warrant Officer II Jack Athelston Hollinsworth, RCAF, *17.12.42 (age 34)* [AABENRAA]

WHEN YOU GO BACK, TELL THEM OF US AND SAY: FOR THEIR TOMORROW
WE GAVE OUR TODAY.

Company Sergeant Major Ernest Frank Clarke, LER, *23.5.44* [CASSINO]

Epitaphs in any day and age have always attempted to bestow praise or meaning upon the deceased—who or what they were, what they did, what qualities they possessed, what they stood for, what reputation they left on the earth. As one would expect, many turn into formulaic eulogies drawing from an inventory of stock epithets: soldiers are brave, husbands are tender and loving, sons are dutiful, and friends are loyal. "Say nothing but good about the dead" was an ancient proverb heeded as much today as in earlier times. Out of thousands of Canadian epitaphs from the Second World War only this one balances a standard tribute with an admission of difficulties the young man encountered in life:

YOUTH WAS A CHALLENGE, LIFE WAS A FIGHT. ALL OF HIS BEST HE GLADLY GAVE.

Pilot Officer Clement Hector Brown, RCAF, *12.9.44 (age 29)* [DURNBACH]

The very human tendency to idealise the departed can undermine the reader's confidence in the virtues the epitaphs assign to any given serviceman. The rhyming couplets and decorative sentiments in so many inscriptions reveal more about the projections of the bereaved than they do about their subjects, and here again the undifferentiated, ready-made eulogies generated by a mass communications industry have intruded among the more thoughtful, individually composed farewells. The following group from Holten begins with an assortment of standard tributes found in every war cemetery, providing a useful basis for comparison with epitaphs which in their biographical detail tell us something truly particular to the deceased:

A SOLDIER BRAVE AND TRUE WHO HAS GONE BEFORE LIVES IN OUR MEMORY EVERMORE.

Lance Corporal Howard Lewis Saunders, 14th CH, *12.4.45 (age 26)*

A COURAGEOUS SOLDIER LOYAL AND TRUE, ONE IN A MILLION, DEAR REX, THAT WAS YOU.

Lance Bombardier Rex Murray Hooker, RCA, *1.5.45 (age 24)*

DEVOTED SON, TRUE FRIEND, LOYAL PATRIOT. GAVE HIS LIFE FOR HUMANITY.

Lieutenant Clarence Foster Heald, RCIC, *31.3.45 (age 23)*

A MAN OF INTEGRITY.

Lieutenant Peter Brodie Hepburn, ASHC, *20.4.45 (age 32)*

MURRAY WAS A GOOD BOY.

Gunner Murray Charles McKay, RCA, *29.4.45 (age 29)*

A GOOD SCOUT.

Sergeant Thomas Kenneth Howatson, RCASC, *18.6.45 (age 25)*

If the artificial language of so many epitaphs tends to cloak the departed in a sentimental haze, the brief, unembellished notices work in counterpoint to remind us that there certainly were principled, conscientious, interesting young men recognised and remembered for what they were and what they had done. They emerge in the epitaphs which single out the qualities or attainments that put a distinct stamp on the serviceman. Participation in the Scouting movement was one testament to good character, adherence to a Christian way of life was another. Along with the epitaphs recording various talents or professions are others listing university degrees (sometimes included with the personal details on the upper register of the headstone) or, in one case, membership in a fraternity, a particular source of pride when a much smaller portion of the population went on to post-secondary education:

A KING'S SCOUT. HE GAVE HIS LIFE FOR LOVED ONES, HOME AND EMPIRE.
Private Lawrence Tales, RCR, 24.12.43 (age 21) [MORO RIVER]

A SCOUTMASTER. HE ENDEAVOURED TO DIRECT YOUTH INTO A MORE USEFUL LIFE.
Pilot Officer Glenn Thomas Douglas, RCAF, 21.7.44 (age 19) [ADEGEM]

A FIRST-CLASS SCOUT.
Sergeant Gerald Frederick Higgins, RCAF, 15.11.44 (age 21) [BROOKWOOD]

HE WAS A CHEERFUL CHRISTIAN BOY. LOVED CHILDREN AND ALL SMALL CREATURES.
Warrant Officer I Robert Emery Stewart, RCAF, 21.4.44 (age 23) [CHESTER (BLACON)]

LITTLE CHILDREN LOVED HIM.
Lance Bombardier Laurits Peter Jensen, RCA, 4.9.44 (age 42) [GRADARA]

HE HAD FOLLOWED THE PATH OF A CHRISTIAN.
Private John Bader, SSR, 28.8.44 (age 31) [BRETTEVILLE-SUR-LAIZE]

ALWAYS GUIDED BY HIS CONSCIENCE. TRULY A CHRISTIAN SOLDIER.
Corporal John Samuel Blackburne, SHC, 17.9.44 (age 29) [CORIANO RIDGE]

A DEEP THINKER AND FULLY CONSCIOUS OF HIS COUNTRY'S NEED. HE GAVE ALL FOR US.
Flying Officer Clarence Edgar Bell, RCAF, 13.10.42 (age 22) [BECKLINGEN]

THE FIRE WAS NEVER OUT WHILE ARTHUR WAS AROUND, THE FIGHT WAS NEVER LOST.
MOTHER AND FATHER
Fusilier Arthur Henry Wardrope, WG, 19.8.44 (age 19) [BROOKWOOD]

B.A. LL.B. NOTAIRE DES TROUPES CANADIENNES AUX QUARTIERS GÉNÉRAUX, LONDRES.
(B.A. LL.B. Solicitor of the Canadian troops at general headquarters, London.)
Corporal Joseph Rousseau Bastien, RM, 4.8.41 (age 47) [BROOKWOOD]

A NOBLE SON, MUCH BELOVED; A CLEVER WRITER. "PRESENT WITH THE LORD."
2 COR. V. 8
Bombardier Phillip Malcolm, RCA, 23.9.43 (age 24) [BARI]

DESSINATEUR, PAYSAGISTE, ET LINÉAIRE.
(Draughtsman, artist in landscapes and line drawings.)
Pilot Officer Joseph Jean Baptiste Benoit Huot, RCAF, 24.3.44 [BERLIN]

SOLDIER, ENGINEER, BELOVED SON. DEEP IN OUR HEARTS YOUR MEMORY NEVER FADES.
Lieutenant Warwick Edwin Walmsley Steeves, CRCE, 1.7.44 (age 26) [MINTURNO]

A SURGEON. HE SAVED OTHERS, HIMSELF HE COULD NOT SAVE.
Lieutenant Colonel Arthur Wesley Stanley Hay, RCAMC, 31.12.44 (age 42) [BROOKWOOD]

OF TEESWATER, ONTARIO. DOCTOR OF VETERINARY SCIENCE.
Captain James McLean McKague, RCA, 12.8.44 (age 27) [BRETTEVILLE-SUR-LAIZE]

"DICK" SON OF ALF. D. & "DAISY" STEWART OF OTTAWA, ONTARIO, CANADA.
QUEEN'S '43. HON.GRAD.COM.
Lieutenant Richard Norman Stewart, RCIC, 25.2.45 (age 24) [GROESBEEK]

B.SC. MANITOBA UNIVERSITY. "MURRAY." ONLY SON OF THOMAS AND HATTIE ROBERTS, WINNIPEG.
Flying Officer John Murray Roberts, RCAF, 27.7.44 (age 29) [BANNEVILLE]

"ALL HE HAD HOPED FOR, ALL HE HAD, HE GAVE." B.S.A. 1929 (TORONTO)
Sergeant Charles Edward Christie, PPCLI, 23.5.44 (age 41) [CASSINO]

BUZZ. EDMONTON. DELTA UPSILON. ALBERTA.
Rifleman George Joseph Reid, RWR, 21.2.45 (age 24) [GROESBEEK]

Biographical details on the headstones show the various walks of life from which Canada's volunteers came. In a manner reminiscent of the inscriptions on the tombs of Roman soldiers, the family of a fallen serviceman sometimes made the epitaph into a brief recitation of his military career:

ENLISTED IN CANADA, 1940. SERVED IN ENGLAND, SICILY, AND IN THE BATTLE OF ORTONA.
"HE DIED A HERO."
Corporal John William Herman, RCOC, 16.12.43 (age 22) [MORO RIVER]

SERVED IN CANADA, KISKA ISLAND, ENGLAND, FRANCE.
SON OF EDWARD MAILLET AND ROSANNA CORMIER.
Private Joseph Alcide Edmond Maillet, FMR, 8.8.44 (age 22) [BRETTEVILLE-SUR-LAIZE]

BORN IN ROGERSVILLE, NEW BRUNSWICK. ENLISTED IN KAPUSKASING, ONTARIO.
Corporal Fernand Joseph Hector Melanson, LWR, 2.11.44 (age 22) [BERGEN-OP-ZOOM]

MY SON SERVED 5 YEARS 7 MONTHS "WITHOUT FEAR OR FAVOUR." MOTHER
Lieutenant Francis Lewis Joseph Arnett, RCIC, 25.3.45 (age 29) [GROESBEEK]

BORN IN CANADA. REGIMENTED 27TH APRIL 1944. DIED IN ENGLAND. R.I.P.
Private Roger Faubert, RCIC, 10.4.45 (age 19) [BROOKWOOD]

CAME FROM CANADA TO JOIN THE R.A.F.
Aircraftman 1st Class John William Colley, RAF, 25.10.40 (age 20) [BROOKWOOD]

FALKLAND ISLANDS DEF. FORCE SEPTEMBER 1939. ONLY SON OF
GLADYS AND DUDLEY JOYCE.
Flying Officer David Dudley Plaister Joyce, RCAF, 2.6.42 (age 23) [REICHSWALD FOREST]

11.8.22 AVONLEA. 20.1.44 GERMANY. AIR GUNNER. 13 TRIPS. SLEEP WELL,
BRAVE HEART.
Sergeant Frank Gordon Sanderson, RCAF, 20.1.44 (age 21) [HAMBURG]

ROSEWARNE AVENUE, ST. VITAL, WINNIPEG. 78 SQDN. LINTON, 127 SQDN. LEEMING.
Squadron Leader Jack Montgomery Bissett DFC, RCAF, 31.3.44 (age 23) [RHEINBERG]

C/O, 401 SQDN. FROM "D" DAY NORMANDY THROUGH TO GERMANY.
"THY WILL BE DONE." R.I.P.
Squadron Leader William Thomas Klersy DSO, DFC & BAR, RCAF, *22.5.45 (age 22)*
[GROESBEEK]

The family information inscribed on these headstones suggests that a tradition of military service may well have led these airmen and soldiers to enlist. It is likely, too, that in some cases the young volunteers were taking up the torch passed by the generation that had fought in the Great War:

BELOVED ONLY SON OF LT. COL. AND MRS. G.D.K. KINNAIRD, EDMONTON, CANADA. "MIZPAH"
Warrant Officer II William Johnstone Kinnaird, RCAF, *1.4.43 (age 21)* [BAYEUX]

SON OF MAJOR ROBERT ROY, E.D. AND GRANDSON OF COLONEL A. ROY, M.V.O.
MONTREAL, CANADA.
Warrant Officer II Jean Robert Roy, RCAF, *15.4.43 (age 21)* [DURNBACH]

BELOVED SON OF MAJOR AND MRS. C.F. MOSS, SCARBORO' BLUFFS, ONTARIO.
"REST IN PEACE."
Private Charles Edward Moss, 48th HC, *23.5.44 (age 18)* [CASSINO]

JOHN, LOVED SON OF A WARRIOR. GOD TOOK THE BEST TO DWELL WITH HIM IN PARADISE.
HIS LOVING MOTHER
Sergeant John Christopher Smart, RCAF, *18.12.44 (age 18)* [BROOKWOOD]

The most significant fact of many a young serviceman's career was its ending. A terse *"Killed in action"* concludes a number of inscriptions, but some go a little further, using the inscription to record the details of place or circumstances which the families had received through official channels. It was the clearest statement of devotion to duty, although not all deaths on active service resulted from combat. Brookwood Cemetery, outside London, contains a large plot set aside for the Canadian soldiers and airmen who died in training or in accidents, of illness or wounds, or from enemy bombs (in the case of Captain Gall, a V-2 rocket), as some of these epitaphs relate:

KILLED ACCIDENTALLY. "SAFE IN THE ARMS OF JESUS."
Private William Boak, PPCLI, *20.7.42 (age 23)* [BROOKWOOD]

OUR DEAR SON AND BROTHER. KILLED ON FLYING OPERATIONS. ALWAYS LOVINGLY
REMEMBERED BY DAD, MOTHER AND PHYLLIS.
Sergeant Edward Alan Opie, RCAF, *13.9.43 (age 30)* [CHESTER (BLACON)]

IN LOVING MEMORY OF OUR BELOVED SON JOHN. KILLED IN ACTION OVER BELGIUM.
Flying Officer John Woollatt Burrows, RCAF, *28.4.44 (age 26)* [HEVERLEE]

KILLED BY ENEMY ACTION, GUARDS' CHAPEL, LONDON. ELDER SON OF D.M. & M. GALL.
HUSBAND OF MARION.
Captain John Douglas Gall, CGG, *18.6.44 (age 25)* [BROOKWOOD]

KILLED AT CANADIAN BATTLE SCHOOL, FINDON, SUSSEX, WHILE SERVING HIS COUNTRY.
Major Robert Plummer Lyon, 48th HC, *8.7.44 (age 35)* [BROOKWOOD]

IN LOVING MEMORY OF MY DEAR HUSBAND WHO WAS KILLED IN OOSTBURG, HOLLAND.
Lieutenant Ernest Edward Ottoway, QORC, *21.10.44 (age 32)* [ADEGEM]

OUR DEAR SON, KILLED IN MID-AIR. GREATLY MISSED BY MOM AND DAD. R.I.P.
Sergeant Ernest James Pridham, RCAF, 15.11.44 (age 18) [BROOKWOOD]

Where Canadian epitaphs most clearly fit into the long tradition of sepulchral inscriptions is in the themes of consolation which the Greeks and Romans deployed to alleviate the bitterness of loss. These themes were categorised in ancient treatises dealing with grief and were elaborated in letters of consolation and essays addressing the fear of death. Absorbed into the rhetoric of Christian consolation, even though they did not hold out the promise of life eternal offered by Christianity, they nevertheless exerted a strong influence on the response to death in the western world. Ancient epitaphs abound in lamentations that parallel the sorrows of parents centuries later coping with the untimely, violent, and faraway deaths of their sons. *"But he who lies here is too young,"* reads a Greek tomb inscription that voices the same protest as this Canadian example:

HE WAS ONLY A BOY.
Warrant Officer II John Robertson, RCAF, 31.8.43 (age 20) [SCHOONSELHOF]

"Let all the earth shed tears." Even in an age more accustomed to the arbitrariness of death the extinction of a young life and with it the chance to savour the joys of this existence struck the ancients as cruel and unfair. The death of children, an inversion of the natural order of things, was seen as particularly tragic and provoked from bereaved parents reactions as anguished as this Canadian father's lament for a fallen son:

"MY SON, MY SON! WOULD GOD I HAD DIED FOR THEE." II SAMUEL XVIII. 33
Flight Sergeant Harry Ernest Hansell, RCAF, 27.9.43 (age 19) [HANOVER]

Without a firm or widely accepted belief in an afterlife, the ancients drew what comfort they could from a repertoire of consolatory arguments familiar today: the afflicted must show patience and forbearance in their grief; they should look to famous examples of loss and grief; death puts an end to the troubles of life; the deceased enjoys a lasting reputation; the beauty of the gravesite makes a worthy, proper tribute; and the deceased has gained immortality. This last refers not to the immortality of the soul but to the everlasting renown of the deceased whose name and achievements will never fade from memory. Their virtuous conduct and heroic death have made them a source of pride to their families and an example to their people. *"Eternity shall speak of your spirit"*—this was the kind of praise reserved in Greek epitaphs for the citizens who went forth to fight for their city-states, and completely absent from Latin inscriptions upon the tombs of the professional soldiers who served in the Roman army. The inscriptions on the headstones of these Canadian citizen-soldiers follow in this assertion that exemplary virtue lives on even if we do not:

THIS MAN DIED AN EXAMPLE OF NOBLE COURAGE AND A MEMORIAL OF VIRTUE UNTO ALL HIS NATION.
Private Alphie Raymond Peltier, FMR, 26.2.45 (age 30) [GROESBEEK] [2 MACCABBEES 6: 31]

GOOD DEEDS ARE ETERNAL, THEY CANNOT DIE.
Flying Officer Percy Hornby Coates, RCAF, 4.9.43 (age 26) [BERLIN]

THOUGH THEY SLEEP, THEIR GLORY FADES NOT, THEIR DEEDS CAN NEVER DIE.
Flying Officer Wendell Stuart Curtis, RCAF, 7.11.44 (age 21) [REICHSWALD FOREST]

GONE BUT NOT FORGOTTEN. HIS COURAGEOUS DEEDS WILL LIVE FOREVER. DAD
Corporal Thomas Leonard Jenkins, 48th HC, *17.9.44 (age 24)* [CORIANO RIDGE]

THIS LAD'S LIFE WAS BUT A FEW DAYS BUT HIS NAME ENDURETH FOREVER.
Sergeant John Richard Martin, CGG. *1.11.44 (age 22)* [SCHOONSELHOF]

The argument that death put an end to the miseries of life seemed especially apt in the case of young soldiers released from the toils of war. The transition to a state of peace, or at least a respite from earthly cares, was accompanied by the belief that the deceased had passed to a better world:

FOR HIM, NO PAIN BUT DEATH WITH HONOUR, GOING LIKE A SOLDIER AND A MAN.
Private John Redmond Mahoney, NBR, *12.4.45 (age 30)*

MAY YOU AWAKEN, JACK, TO A NEW DAWN, FIRED WITH SUN, NOT WAR.
EVER IN OUR MEMORIES.
Trooper John Tovell Swain, RCAC, *9.4.45 (age 19)*

WAR SHALL HARM HIM NO MORE. MAY HIS SACRIFICE BE NOT IN VAIN. MOTHER AND DAD.
Flight Sergeant Morley Junior Brewer, RCAF, *27.2.45 (age 19)* [HARROGATE]

FROM THE EVIL TO COME HE IS TAKEN AWAY AND HIS MEMORY SHALL BE IN PEACE.
Sergeant Edward Max Bowman, RCAF, *28.1.45 (age 27)* [HARROGATE]

DEATH'S PAINS ARE PAST AND SORROWS CEASE, LIFE'S WARFARE CLOSED, HIS SOUL IN PEACE.
Private Roy Williams Collins, NNSH, *23.3.45 (age 19)* [GROESBEEK]

HE WILL NOT AGE. HIS SONG IS SUNG AND HE REMAINS FOREVER YOUNG.
Private John Herbert Bohan, SHC, *20.9.44 (age 27)* [CORIANO RIDGE]

SHORT LIFE, SHORT PAIN, DEAR BOY, WAS THINE; NOW JOYS ETERNAL AND DIVINE.
Corporal Isaac Stewart Eckford, HPER, *13.12.43 (age 24)* [MORO RIVER]

HE IS SUPREMELY BLEST, HAS DONE WITH SIN AND CARE AND WOE,
AND WITH HIS SAVIOUR RESTS.
Corporal Thomas John Cochrane, ESR, *21.11.44 (age 25)* [BRUSSELS TOWN]

POURQUOI PLEURER MON DÉPART PUISQUE LA MORT EST LA FIN DE MES SOUFFRANCES.
(Why weep at my departure since death is the end of my suffering.)
Captain Gérard Joseph Louis Perron, FMR, *17.10.44 (age 26)* [SCHOONSELHOF]

From the idea that death relieved the living of life's burdens it was a short step to the view, most memorably expressed by the poet Menander and widely repeated in literature ever since, that "those whom the gods love die young." Behind this lies the reasoning that to be taken in the bloom of youth, before the vicissitudes of life have sapped one's vitality and tarnished a worthy reputation, was a sign of divine favour confirming the excellence of the deceased. It also speaks for a time when people feared the decrepitude of old age more than the finality of death. Binyon's much quoted line "Age shall not weary them nor the years condemn" recycles an old theme that appears in many variations:

FOR EVER YOUNG.
Captain David Stephen Herbert Loughnan, RCIC, *19.2.45 (age 25)* [GROESBEEK]

A BELOVED SON AND BROTHER. "CROWNED WITH THE SUNSHINE OF IMMORTAL YOUTH."
Warrant Officer II George James Beresford, RCAF, 19.2.43 [KIEL]

FOR HIM NO SLOW DECLINING YEARS, NO LONG AND WEARY SPAN.
Pilot Officer Leonard Hunter Hogg, RCAF, 14.10.44 (age 21) [REICHSWALD FOREST]

STILL, MY DARLING, YOU WILL BE ALWAYS YOUNG AND DEAR TO ME.
Corporal Alexander Wallace Caldwell, 14th CH, 27.2.45 (age 30) [GROESBEEK]

YOUR DUTY DONE, FOR EVER YOUNG AND FREE, REST NOW, MY BELOVED SON, PEACEFULLY.
Flight Sergeant Edward Irvine Johnston, RCAF, 20.12.42 (age 21)
[AMSTERDAM NEW EASTERN]

'TIS SAD BUT TRUE, WE WONDER WHY THE BEST ARE ALWAYS FIRST TO DIE.
Corporal George Raymond Angove, 48th HC, 10.12.44 (age 21) [RAVENNA]

MANY WOULD ENVY HIS YOUTHFUL FAME, HIS CLEAN BRIEF LIFE, HIS HONOURED NAME.
Flight Lieutenant Alastair Clarence Watt, RCAF, 17.3.45 (age 21) [DURNBACH]

HE SHALL NOT GROW OLD. IN THE GLORY OF HIS YOUTH WE SHALL REMEMBER HIM.
Lance Corporal Chancey Alva Jones, RCCS, 16.12.44 (age 23) [BERGEN-OP-ZOOM]

THE LADS WHO WILL DIE IN THEIR GLORY AND NEVER BE OLD. (A.E. HOUSMAN)
Flying Officer William Stewart McLintock, RCAF, 21.9.44 (age 21) [BERGEN-OP-ZOOM]

Death and burial far from home exacerbated the pains of untimely death. The "terrible tyranny of distance" that prevented most families from visiting the grave, figures time and again in the epitaphs of both wars. The first example below expresses the only remedy for their predicament that most families had, an appeal to sympathetic passersby to do what those across the ocean could not, but the others show the mixture of resignation, longing, and pledges of spiritual union common to epitaphs mourning a loved one buried far from his kith and kin:

BREATHE A SILENT PRAYER FOR MY BELOVED SON WHO SLEEPS HERE SO FAR FROM HOME.
Private Ralph George Gremm, PR, 24.4.45 (age 26)

THOUGH THE SEAS OUR HEARTS DIVIDE, IN SPIRIT YOU ARE BY MY SIDE. WE'LL MEET AGAIN.
Lance Corporal Samuel Alexander Hazlett, RHLI, 13.4.45 (age 34)

WHERE LOVE ENDURES, THERE IS NO SEPARATION.
Sergeant William Oliver Douglas Baird, RCAF, 28.5.44 (age 33) [HARROGATE]

OUR ONLY BELOVED SON. MAY THE ANGELS FOR EVER GUARD FOR US THIS SACRED SPOT.
Private Ivan Renaud, ESR, 31.7.44 (age 21) [BRETTEVILLE-SUR-LAIZE]

THOUGH YOU LIE IN ENGLAND SO FAR AWAY, YOUR MEMORY IS IN OUR HEARTS FOR EVER.
MOTHER
Leading Aircraftman Edward Wahlers, RCAF, 21.12.44 (age 21) [BROOKWOOD]

THOUGH ALIEN EARTH YOUR HEART MAY PRESS, YOU LIVE AND SHALL NOT EVER LOVE ME LESS.
Corporal Harold Lavigne, LWR, 20.2.45 (age 28) [GROESBEEK]

PART OF US IS HERE WITH YOU. REST IN PEACE. YOUR WIFE EVA AND SON ALLAN.
Flight Sergeant Edward Vicary Davidson, RCAF, 3.10.43 (age 30) [HANOVER]

GOD BE WITH YOU, OUR BEST, BELOVED BY ALL, OUR OWN, BEYOND THE SALT-SEA WALL.
Private Walter Harold MacFadden, RCR, 17.5.44 (age 20) [CASSINO]
[CHRISTINA ROSSETTI, *BY THE SEA*]

To compensate for the soldier's absence from his native land, several families contributed epitaphs commending their loved ones to permanent rest alongside their comrades. The Imperial War Graves Commission had justified its decision not to repatriate the bodies of the dead for burial at home on the grounds that the soldiers themselves had stated their preference to be laid to rest among their friends and fellows. These families likewise thought it fitting that the servicemen who had fought and died together find honoured burial among their peers:

IT IS WELL WITH YOU AMONG THE CHOSEN FEW, AMONG THE VERY BRAVE, THE VERY TRUE.
Trooper Willard James Morris, 12th MD, 19.4.45 (age 23)

WE LEFT WITH A JEST OUR HOMES IN THE WEST, NOW HERE WITH THE BEST WE LIE AT REST.
Rifleman Gordon Branton, RRR, 6.6.44 (age 24) [BÉNY-SUR-MER]
Rifleman Ronald Branton, RRR, 8.7.44 (age 28) [BÉNY-SUR-MER]

WHEN DUTY CALLED WE DID OUR BEST AND HERE IS WHERE WE WISH TO REST.
Flying Officer Norman Roger Vatne, RCAF, 15.1.45 (age 21) [RHEINBERG]

THOUGH FAR AWAY FROM HOME MY BELOVED SON RESTS IN PEACE WITH HIS BUDDIES.
Private Leslie Cecil Wray, CSR, 7.10.44 (age 24) [ADEGEM]

AWAY IN THIS LAND A DEAR SON AND BROTHER LIES. HE DIED WITH HIS PALS THAT WE MAY LIVE.
Lance Corporal Orval Earl Brock, 48th HC, 23.5.44 (age 24) [CASSINO]

HERE IN ITALY IN A SOLDIER'S GRAVE LIES OUR DEAR SON AMONG THE BRAVE.
Private Forest Roy Himmelman, WNSR, 24.1.44 (age 25) [MORO RIVER]

GLORY GUARDS WITH SOLEMN ROUND THIS BIVOUAC OF THE DEAD.
Private Murdock Ross, RCAMC, 25.7.44 (age 24) [BÉNY-SUR-MER]

A LOVING SON AND BROTHER WITH GALLANT MEN AT REST WHO SERVED THEIR COUNTRY, GAVE THEIR BEST.
Flying Officer John Archibald Wilding DFC, RCAF, 9.9.44 (age 23) [BROOKWOOD]

IN HONOUR'S NAME I LIE IN KINDRED DUST.
Private Frederick Parkinson, BWC, 5.4.45 (age 36) [GROESBEEK]

Other families fell back on Rupert Brooke's averment that the soldier's grave made some corner of a foreign field forever England (or Canada, an emendation many felt free to make). Epitaphs crafted from his poem *The Soldier* have been noted in the previous chapter; given here is another example saying the same thing in slightly different words. In contrast, however, a Latin aphorism from the Roman poet Ovid (who in irrevocable exile bemoaned his fate to be buried among strangers far from home) is quoted on several headstones, offering the consoling thought that "to a brave man the whole earth is native land." The final quotation argues that distance helps to

A 17-year old Canadian soldier, killed four days before the end of the war.

An inscription in Dutch and English at Holten.

A photo left by the family at the grave of Private Emile Joseph Soens.

A private memorial left by the grave of Private Kenneth James Coughlan at Coriano Ridge War Cemetery, Italy.

Interesting details on the headstone of Private Harvey Edward Cullimore: "Archaeologist, authority on arts, crafts, symbols and life of North American Indians".

sustain happy memories of the deceased, but not many found it convincing. It occurs only once:

THIS HALLOWED GROUND WHEREIN HE LIES WILL BE FOREVER HIS BELOVED CANADA.
Flying Officer James Boustead Dallyn, RCAF, 23.5.44 (age 22) [REICHSWALD FOREST]

BELOVED SON OF PERCY & EDITH LUDLOW, BRANTFORD, ONTARIO.
OMNE SOLUM FORTI PATRIA.
Flying Officer Michael Thomas Robert Ludlow, RCAF, 10.8.43 (age 21) [DURNBACH]

"MEMORY, NO LESS THAN HOPE, OWES ITS CHARM TO THE FAR AWAY." BULWER-LYTTON
Flight Lieutenant Robert Joseph O' Sullivan, RCAF, 10.3.45 (age 25) [HANOVER]

A few families went to the trouble of supplying bilingual inscriptions, presumably on the assumption that the majority of people seeing the grave would be inhabitants of the country where the soldier was buried and hence unable to read the valedictions. This was a consideration in epitaphs entreating prayers or remembrance from passersby. A few words in the language of the country of burial, connecting the land where the soldier had died with the land of his birth, may also have been a symbolic way of closing the circle of his life. An epitaph in English echoed in Dutch at Holten has been cited above, and similar diptychs combining English inscriptions with French, Italian, Dutch, and German translations appear in the list below. In one noteworthy instance a French Canadian family had an inscription entirely in Dutch engraved on their son's headstone at Bergen-op-Zoom:

"I SAID, THOU ART MY GOD: MY TIMES ARE IN THY HAND." "J'AI DIT, TU ES MON DIEU:
MES TEMPS SONT EN TA MAIN."
Lieutenant James Rogerson McNeily, QORC, 18.7.44 (age 26) [BÉNY-SUR-MER]
[PSALM 31: 14–15]

LEST YE FORGET. PERCHE NON SI DIMENTICHI.
Captain Roger Llewellyn Stephens, LER, 6.8.44 [FLORENCE]

FOR ME TO LIVE IS CHRIST AND TO DIE IS GAIN. PHIL. I. 21. GESU E' INFALLIBILE.
(Jesus is infallible.)
Private Donald Maurice Foster, LRSR, 15.12.44 (age 21) [VILLANOVA]

ONVERGETELIJKE ZOON EN BROEDER VAN DEN HEER AND MEVROUW OVILA GOULET
EN DE FAMILIE.
(Unforgettable son and brother of M. and Mme Ovila Goulet and family.)
Private Joseph Emile Eugène Goulet, BWC, 13.10.44 (age 25) [BERGEN-OP-ZOOM]

ETERNAL REST GRANT UNTO HIM, O LORD. SCHENK HEM, O HEER, EEUWIGE RUST.
Private William Joseph Moore, CH, 8.2.45 (age 20) [GROESBEEK]

GOD LOVED HIM TOO AND TOOK HIM HOME WITH HIM TO REST. AUF WIEDERSEHEN, LIEBLING.
Sergeant Raymond John Baroni, RCAF, 16.12.43 [BERLIN]

PRAY FOR ME. BETEN FÜR MICH.
Pilot Officer Louis Curatolo, RCAF, 14.1.44 (age 20) [HANOVER]

A palliative to the sorrow of so many graves beyond the sea was the assurance that a loved one had received a decent burial or, if one of the missing, proper commemoration on a monument. The first visitors to the war cemeteries in the 1920s came away deeply impressed and inspired by the achievements not only of the architects but of the landscapers and horticulturalists who had transformed the burial grounds into veritable gardens of remembrance. The beauty of the cemeteries did much to reconcile the public to the policy of burying the dead where they had fallen; and for families unlikely to see the graves the image of a rustic, tranquil setting akin to the roadside tombs of the ancient world or the country churchyards cherished by the Romantics provided a measure of appeasement. The picture drawn by the first example below may be coincidental, but the reference to an olive tree is perfectly apposite on a headstone at the Moro River Canadian War Cemetery, where a pair of gnarled olive trees that survived the shelling were enclosed within the precinct, and where the architect laid out trellised walkways to integrate the burial ground into its setting among the olive groves and vineyards covering the headland opposite Ortona:

AS WE NOW OUR VIGIL KEEP 'NEATH YOUR OLIVE GENTLY SLEEP. "TILL WE MEET AGAIN."
Private Americo Quattrin, LER, 27.12.43 (age 21) [MORO RIVER]

WAY IN YONDER GRAVEYARD WHERE BIRDS SING OVERHEAD. GONE BUT NOT FORGOTTEN.
Private Gordon Gerald Kingshott, 48th HC, 16.9.44 (age 20) [CORIANO RIDGE]

The gentle scenes imagined in some epitaphs include appeals to the elements of nature to shelter the distant grave; one of the most tender of all conveys the family's love in these words:

MY DARLING SON. BLOW SOFTLY, WIND, OVER HIS DEAR YOUNG HEAD, WHISPER—OUR LOVE.
Private Edward Ramsay, CMSC, 10.11.44 (age 21) [ADEGEM]

In the end, however, the constant allusions in the epitaphs to the distance separating the mourners and the mourned expose the inadequacy of any words or images to satisfy one of the deepest needs of human beings. *"Multas per gentes et multa per aequora. . . "* opens one of the best known poems of the ancient world in which the poet Catullus describes his journey "through the lands of many peoples and over many seas" to "give the very last gift the dead receive" at the grave of his brother. The determination to come to the grave of a lost husband or kinsman, to satisfy a sense of duty, to express love and gratitude one last time, and above all, to say farewell directly, is poignantly attested in the war cemeteries. In 1994, seventy-seven years after Sergeant Tom Holmshaw of the Royal Engineers died of wounds, his daughter came to Lapugnoy War Cemetery to insert a plaque at the grave of a father she could barely recall, inscribed with these words: *"You left me, dear father, when I was three . . . now aged 81 I have travelled and seen your resting place since 1917."* Fifty-six years after Flight Sergeant John Victor Potter of the RCAF was killed on operations in July 1942, his brother travelled to the Kiel War Cemetery to place a token of remembrance at the grave: *Brother Jack, thank you. Bob. 1998.* That the passage of time did nothing to extinguish the desire to see a loved one's grave is plain from two Canadian inscriptions, both remarkable testaments to the family's fidelity to the memory of the deceased:

MISSING IN ACTION SINCE 13TH MAY 1943 BUT NEVER FORGOTTEN.
FEBRUARY 1973
Flight Sergeant Wesley Morey, RCAF, 13.5.43 [JONKERBOS]

IT TOOK 43 YEARS, DAD, BUT WE MADE IT. GOD REST YOUR SOUL.
KEITH, LARRY AND MOM, JULY 30 1987.
Private Elgin Ray Wilson, CHO, 6.9.44 [CALAIS]

The necessity, and the effect, of such a visit are most movingly recounted by Gregory Clark (1892–1977), a veteran of the First World War (who won the Military Cross at Vimy Ridge) and afterwards a popular columnist with the *Toronto Star* and other publications. His eldest son, Lieutenant John Murray Clark of the Regina Rifles, was killed outside Boulogne in September 1944. Nearly seven years to the day since his son's death in action, Clark made the journey to the Calais Canadian War Cemetery to see the grave. In a letter to his wife describing his visit he emphasizes from the beginning the calming aspect of the site:

> He sleeps in a garden.
> There can be no other name for it. On a high remote and rolling hilltop . . .
> amid roses, hydrangea, golden mimosa, dahlias of every colour on earth,
> so buried and embowered with flowers they can hardly be seen from one
> another, he sleeps in a scene of such utter peace and serenity that I wonder
> if I can ever tell you how different it is from anything we have ever seen.

The cemetery was in the final stages of completion when Clark arrived. The headstones had been stacked in a corner for insertion the following spring, and small metal crosses stood over each grave. Once the gardener had led him to the gravesite, the sight of his son's resting place, awash in flowers, triggered an outpouring of emotion that opened the way to the consolation he sought:

> I fell down to my knees and simply let go. I don't know how long it lasted.
> It was pretty terrible, this little metal cross, these roses, the dahlias yellow,
> red, white, mimosa, a tangle of the loveliest flowers you ever saw. I kept
> looking up and around, trying to get some sort of answer from the sky, the
> great garden, the little crosses of his young comrades, all of them, each one
> of them as dear to somebody as he was to us.
> I looked back over my shoulder at the cliffs of England so near. Then I
> looked at the ground and said: "Give me an answer!" And I found myself
> saying: "Thank you, God, for letting us have him for the years we did. He
> might never have been born. He might have been taken from us in childhood.
> Thank God for the years we were blessed by having him . . . "

Clark returned to the cemetery the following day to bring flowers and to leave money for the gardener to put flowers on the grave each September 1st, his son's birthday. As with so many other bereaved next of kin who made their own pilgrimages, it was the beauty and tranquility, enhanced by the isolation of the place, that steadied the turbulence of his emotions and enabled him to find and to extend comfort:

> Now, darling, there it is. Maybe I shall never see it again. But I feel in
> my heart it is so different from anything we could imagine, so untouchable,
> so remote and kindly, I would not hesitate some day to bring you . . . to see
> it as I have seen it. For you would get the same answer I got from it. Thank
> God for the years we did have him, for, as I knelt there, remembering for
> his birthday all the scenes of his life I could (starting first of all with that

*morning Sept. 1 either 29 or 30 years ago, when you, all dressed, came to
the door of the sunroom at the back of 147 Indian Rd., wakened me, smiled
down at me, and said: "Well, here we go!") and so on through his boyhood
and manhood, I could not help but realize that we were blessed indeed to
have had him and known him and shared him with nobody but God.*

*I hope with all my heart this letter does not distress you, but that you
may get the same answer I got, and some measure of the peace that fills me
now that the journey and this letter are done.*

In his letter Clark mentions the epitaph that he had selected from a poem written
by his son, but it is not the one that appears on the headstone. It would seem that
the experience of visiting the grave led Clark to choose another line of his son's
composition, one that kept a cherished link intact:

**AH, GENTLE SKY, IN THY BLUE BEND I SEE THEE STOOP TO KISS THAT SPOT
THAT'S DEAR TO ME. J.M.C.**
Lieutenant John Murray Clark, RRR, 17.9.44 (age 23) [CALAIS]

To return to Holten. As in any large war cemetery, the valedictions are numerous and
varied enough to illustrate the general trends within the epitaphs as a whole. Where
the previous chapter dealt with the profound influence of Great War commemoration
on the personal epitaphs of the Second, this chapter has attempted to place the
epitaphs in the broader context of sepulchral inscriptions and to show where they
express themes of consolation long embedded in the epitaphic tradition. The personal
inscriptions are affecting and memorable principally because they are where they are;
but they also point to the sources of consolation hallowed by time and custom which
preceding generations have turned to, and which those to come will no doubt continue
to draw from.

It has also been a purpose of this chapter to acknowledge the recurrence of formulae
or commonplaces in the epitaphs. These tend to become monotonous through
repetition, but we should remember that the families who contributed them were
not striving for originality or succinct character sketches—they wished to have some
appropriate words engraved on the headstone to honour the memory of someone they
loved, and their choice of valediction should not be discounted simply because it lacks
particularity. They felt obliged to say certain things, and if they borrowed such phrases
they could still be sincere and heartfelt in their grief. In his *Essays Upon Epitaphs*
William Wordsworth emphasized the paramount role of the reader's sympathy in
perceiving the significance of inscriptions which at first sight appear unexceptional. In
his view, such epitaphs were addressed to all, reminding all of our common nature and
upholding the values passed down the generations; if read with the requisite insight,
they also prompted the reader to pause over the larger story implicit in meagre or
commonplace details, whether the fate of the deceased or the effect on those who
loved them. In applying these considerations to the epitaphs at Holten and other war
cemeteries, we should note that they compel us to take due notice of the debt of
remembrance, seldom recognised, owed to the bereaved who chose to leave a dignified
record, not just of their loss, but of the principles and values for which their sons,
husbands, and fathers had died, and of the sort of men they were at their best. If some
of their tributes seem idealised or commonplace, let us not forget that it would be idle
to speak of ideals or a common humanity had these and other young men not defeated

the aims of Nazi Germany, as the Dutch who lived through the occupation can attest. The epitaphs, rarely giving way to bitterness and never cynical, say as much about the fortitude of the bereaved as about the sacrifice of the fallen when we remember the ones at home who bore the cost of victory:

YOU'VE BEEN AWAY A LONG, LONG TIME. MAY WE ALL MEET WHEN WE CROSS THE LINE.
Private Gordon Hume Hand, BWC, 5.4.45 (age 19)

YOUR PRESENCE IS EVER NEAR US, TED. YOUR LOVED ONES WILL NEVER FORGET.
Private Theodore Stafford Dunn, AR, 11.4.45 (age 30)

TO A LOVING SON. REST IN PEACE, DEAR SOLDIER BOY. YOU WILL NEVER BE FORGOTTEN.
Private Robert Jamieson, 48th HC, 16.4.45 (age 21)

OF YOUR CHARITY, PRAY FOR THE REPOSE OF HIS SOUL. GRANDPARENTS AND PARENTS
Private Lionel Valley, NS(NB)R, 7.4.45 (age 19)

YOU'RE LIKE A HAUNTING ECHO OF SWEET MUSIC, MY DEAR, FAR AWAY BUT EVER NEAR.
Rifleman Allan Robert Lawson Mylles, QORC, 11.4.45 (age 20)

LOVING YOU, MISSING YOU, SO PROUD OF YOU. GOD BLESS AND KEEP YOU.
MUM, DAD AND JACK
Captain Bruce Edward Ashton Caw MC & BAR, 1st Hussars, 13.4.45 (age 25)

IN THE MORNING AND THE EVENING WE WILL REMEMBER HIM IN OUR PRAYERS.
Private James Iverson Creelman, NNSH, 18.4.45 (age 19)

YOU, MY SON, I WILL NEVER FORGET AND ALL YOU HAVE DONE FOR ME.
Corporal Hugh Edgar, LSR, 22.4.45 (age 38)

NO MATTER WHAT I DO I'LL ALWAYS LONG FOR YOU. ALL MY LOVE,
MARION AND BABY GERALD
Private Gerald Walter Barnaby, CHO, 27.4.45 (age 26)

THERE IS A MOTHER WHO MISSES YOU SADLY AND FINDS THE TIME LONG SINCE YOU WENT.
Sapper Murray Albert Hodder, CRCE, 6.5.45 (age 30)

NO ONE KNOWS THE HEARTACHE OR THE GRIEF SILENTLY BORNE FOR THE ONE I LOVE SO
WELL. REMEMBERED BY HIS WIFE.
Sapper Frederick Charles Cheverie, CRCE, 19.5.45 (age 40)

LONELY IS OUR HOME WITHOUT YOU. HELP US, LORD, BEAR OUR CROSS. MOM AND DAD
Private Stanley Phillip Petersen, RCASC, 4.11.45

FURTHER READING:

The Book of War Letters. 100 Years of Private Canadian Correspondence. Compiled and edited by Audrey and Paul Grescoe. Toronto: McClelland & Stewart, 2005.

Copp, Terry. *Cinderella Army. The Canadians in Northwest Europe 1944–1945*. Toronto-Buffalo-London: University of Toronto Press, 2006.

Greene, Janet. *Epitaphs to Remember: Remarkable Inscriptions from New England Gravestones*. Chambersburg, Pennsylvania: Alan C. Hood & Company Inc., 1962.

Lattimore, Richmond. *Themes in Greek and Latin Epitaphs*. Urbana: University of Illinois Press, 1962.

Scodel, Joshua. *The English Poetic Epitaph. Commemoration and Conflict from Jonson to Wordsworth*. Ithaca-London: Cornell University Press, 1991.

Wordsworth, William. *Essays Upon Epitaphs* in: *The Prose Works of William Wordsworth*, ed. W.J.B. Owen and J.W. Smyser. Oxford: Clarendon Press, 1974. Volume II, pp. 45–119.

CHAPTER FIVE

"His spirit sought the stars"
Hanover War Cemetery, Germany

THY PEACE, O GOD, BE HIS TO SHARE WHOSE FIGHT HAS ENDED IN THE AIR.
Pilot Officer Arthur Harrison DFM, RCAF, *27.9.43 (age 19)*

Though the U-boat and the airplane added new dimensions to warfare during the First World War, the abiding image of the conflict remains the struggle in the trenches. The memoirs and poetry that have come to define the experience of the Great War, and the commemoration of the fallen, were focussed almost exclusively on the soldier rather than the sailor or the airman, since the burden of the fighting lay most heavily upon the armies. For Canadians, names like Bishop, Barker, Collishaw, MacLaren, Carter, McKeever, and Quigley garnished the country's war record, but the gallantry of Canada's aces savoured of a knightly tournament staged far above the mass, anonymous slaughter on the ground. Canadian pilots had given the Royal Flying Corps (reborn as the Royal Air Force in 1918) a vital boost in manpower and fighting prowess analogous to that given by the Canadian Corps to the British Army, at a much lower cost in lives. Of the 66,000 Canadian dead of the Great War, 1,500—less than three per cent—died on service with the air forces. A generation later, however, once the experiments in close ground support and strategic bombing during 1917–1918 had shown the way out of the impasse of trench warfare, the proportion of casualties marks the biggest single difference between the Great War and its sequel. Close to 45% of Canada's Second World War dead lost their lives on service with the Royal Canadian Air Force or its British parent. Six out of every ten belonged to Bomber Command.

Graves inscribed with the RCAF badge, new to the Second World War, mark the Canadian presence in every theatre of the war. They stand side by side with graves identifying the Australian, New Zealand, and other Commonwealth airmen who likewise served and died far from their native lands. Warrant Officer Lawrence Edgar Mathews (Trail, B.C., Canada) is one of three Canadian airmen buried at Suda Bay in Crete; "Native of Shelburne, Ontario, Canada" introduces the inscription on the grave of Flight Sergeant Ernest Caldwell McLean in the Esbjerg General Cemetery in Denmark. These are just two of many such unlikely convergences of Canadian hometowns with final resting places all over the world. Although they call attention to the often overlooked contribution of Canadian airmen to campaigns waged by British and fellow Commonwealth forces, notably North Africa and Burma, the efforts and sacrifice of the RCAF are most clearly registered in the archipelago of air force plots stretching across northwest Europe from the bases in the British Isles to the target areas in Germany:

OF 106 SQDN. BORN BERTHIER-EN-BAS, QUEBEC. SHOT DOWN OVER HAMBURG. R.I.P.
Flight Sergeant Joseph Rosario Arthur Coulombe, RCAF, 3.2.43 (age 23)

IN MEMORY OF A GALLANT BOMBARDIER. MAY HE REST IN PEACE.
Flying Officer Glenn Crawford Bellamy, RCAF, 14.10.44 (age 26) [REICHSWALD FOREST]

A NAVIGATOR SO YOUNG AND JUST. HE DIED TO PROVE HIS LOVE FOR US.
Flight Sergeant Ivor Derrick Jennings, RCAF, 4.9.43 (age 20) [BERLIN]

FIFTY THREE BOMBING MISSIONS. SOME DAY BEYOND THE STARS WE WILL MEET AGAIN. DAD
Flying Officer Raymond Alfred French, RCAF, 14.2.45 (age 25) [DURNBACH]

IN LOVING MEMORY OF OUR ONLY SON JACK, KILLED ON HIS 33RD TRIP.
Flight Lieutenant John Gifford Laurence Laffoley, RCAF, 4.3.45 (age 22) [HARROGATE]

HE GAVE HIS LIFE. HE BELIEVED IN THE CAUSE HE WAS FIGHTING FOR.
Flying Officer Edward Thomas Coles, RCAF, 16.11.44 (age 21) [RHEINBERG]

"A PILOT'S LIFE IS ALL I HAD TO GIVE, THAT BRITISH FREEDOM, JUSTICE, PEACE MIGHT LIVE."
Flying Officer Stanley William Smith, RCAF, 29.5.44 (age 27) [BROOKWOOD]

WILLINGLY, COURAGEOUSLY, HE FOUGHT AND FELL, A HERO IN THE BATTLE OF THE SKIES.
Sergeant William Henry McGuigan, RCAF, 29.5.44 (age 19) [BROOKWOOD]

HIS BROTHER GORDON, R.C.A.F., IS BURIED IN HARROGATE, ENGLAND.
"GOD WIPES AWAY ALL TEARS."
Flying Officer Richard Hartley Long, RCAF, 16.3.45 (age 22) [ADEGEM]

AT THE GOING DOWN OF THE SUN AND IN THE MORNING WE WILL REMEMBER HIM.
Sergeant Gordon Long, RCAF, 27.5.44 (age 20) [HARROGATE]

GREATER LOVE HATH NO MAN THAN THIS, HE GAVE HIS LIFE THAT WE MIGHT LIVE.
Flying Officer Lloyd Albert Hannah, RCAF, 14.10.44 (age 26) [HARROGATE]
Flying Officer Harold Allan Hannah, RCAF, 27.1.45 (age 24) [HARROGATE]

BORN IN HALIFAX, NOVA SCOTIA. OUR DEAR SONS ARE REUNITED. IAN, R.C.A.F., KILLED
JANUARY 1943 AND BURIED IN HIS HOME TOWN.
Warrant Officer II Donald Blair Machum, RCAF, 29.5.44 (age 20) [BROOKWOOD]

The memory of the bombing campaign sits uneasily in the minds of many today. Its conduct, purpose, and results have been heavily taxed by historians in the countries whose air forces reduced German cities to rubble and killed some 400,000 civilians, over half of them women and children. The head of Bomber Command, Sir Arthur Harris, has become the Douglas Haig of the Second World War, a commander vilified for his singleminded, inflexible aim to grind down the enemy with seemingly little concern for the losses sustained by his own forces. The firestorms that consumed Hamburg and Dresden, and the debates over the effects of area bombing on the German war effort, have in some quarters erased the moral distinction between the Allies and Nazi Germany and cast the bomber crews as unwitting agents of a cruel and immoral policy. For all the criticism of the bombing campaign, however, a number of hard questions may be asked in rejoinder. Should the Germans have been permitted to develop their weapons programs, including their quest for an atomic bomb, without hindrance, and should the Allies have thereby made the task of defeating Nazi Germany lengthier and more costly to themselves, if not impossible? Should the German people, in whose name Warsaw, Rotterdam, and Coventry had been mercilessly bombed to break the will of the Poles, Dutch, and English to resist, have been allowed to trust their leaders' cynical assurances that the war would not touch them? And would a present generation truly find it more morally acceptable to know that between 1940 and 1944 the Allies, though possessed of the means to strike at Germany, did not use every last weapon at their disposal to fight against a noxious regime that felt itself bound by no moral constraints whatsoever, meanwhile leaving the lion's share of the struggle to the Russians (with all the political consequences that would have entailed)?

HE ENJOYED THE LIFE HE GAVE FOR CANADA, HIS HOME WHICH HE LOVED DEARLY.
Flying Officer James Frank Gilbey, RCAF, 14.1.44 (age 22)

THROUGH LABOUR TO REST. THROUGH COMBAT TO VICTORY. "UNTIL THE DAY BREAK."
Flight Sergeant Arthur Cephas Worden, RCAF, 26.5.43 (age 32) [UDEN]

**IT IS OUR HOPE THAT IT WAS NOT IN VAIN WHEN INTO THE NIGHT YOU SOARED AWAY.
R.I.P.**
Pilot Officer Douglass-Smith Kirkwood, RCAF, 22.5.44 (age 22) [REICHSWALD FOREST]

Recent evaluations of the bombing campaign, by historians in the former Allied countries and Germany, have made a strong case for the crippling effect on German armaments, industry, and morale caused by the bombing campaign, as well as for its overall contribution to an Allied victory that came in 1945, not in 1947, 1948, or not at all, possibilities by no means out of the question during the war itself. It is important to take these considerations into account before proceeding to the epitaphs of Canadian airmen, for the controversy surrounding the bombing campaign has tended to obscure the courage and sense of duty among the RCAF crews who for much of the war were the only Canadians carrying the fight to the enemy. They did so at odds of survival far less hopeful than those faced by their comrades on land and at sea. *"He hath delivered my soul in peace from the battle that was against me"* states the epitaph on the grave of Pilot Officer Kenneth Watson MacDonald, one of 706 Canadians at rest in the Reichswald Forest War Cemetery, citing a verse from Psalm 55 that continues, *"for there were many with me."* True enough, for 13,000 Canadian airmen died on active service, another 4,000 in training or accidents. Of the 40,000 who served in Bomber Command, 10,000 did not return, a third of them listed for official purposes as "missing—presumed dead."

**HIS BROTHER WILLIAM, PILOT OFFICER, R.A.F., WAS LOST ON OPERATIONS 4.9.1942.
AGE 27.**
Sergeant Edward Wilson Foxlee, RCAF, 29.8.41 (age 20) [VLISSINGEN NORTHERN]

HIS BROTHER ALLAN P/O R.C.A.F. FAILED TO RETURN 29.7.44.
Pilot Officer Arthur Kenneth Clarke, RCAF, 12.4.44 (age 22) [HARROGATE]

AND IN MEMORY OF HIS BROTHER DAVID P. ROBERTS, FLIGHT SERGEANT, PILOT, R.C.A.F.
MISSING 22 JULY 1942, AGE 21.
Lieutenant Edward Lear Roberts, AR, 14.9.44 (age 25) [ADEGEM]

THREE WINGED, PROUD SONS SAILED ACROSS THE SEAS. ONE RETURNED. GOD REWARD.
Flying Officer John Joseph Pearson, RCAF, 13.8.44 (age 30) [DURNBACH]

It seems appropriate to base a chapter devoted to the epitaphs of Canadian airmen in one of the war cemeteries in Germany, where the wider implications of the strategic bombing campaign are never far from mind. Although, for reasons noted in the previous chapter, all but a few Canadian soldiers killed in Germany were reburied in the Netherlands, the Commission's policy of interring the dead where they had fallen held firm in the case of air crews. Over three thousand Canadian airmen, gathered from hundreds of crash sites and temporary graves, remain in the Commonwealth War Cemeteries built in Germany. One of them, Reichswald Forest, is the largest British cemetery of the Second World War. Two war cemeteries, at Kiel and Hamburg, are secluded within larger civil cemeteries; four mass graves in Hamburg's Ohlsdorf cemetery contain the thousands of civilians killed when the port city—like Kiel, a legitimate military target—was gutted by the Allied air forces in July 1943. The spacious Berlin war cemetery, not far from the site of the Nazi showpiece 1936 Olympics, was laid out in the sector allotted to the British when the flattened city was partitioned among the eastern and western Allies after the war. The short distance between Becklingen War Cemetery, where some of the first and last Canadian fatalities of the air war lie buried, and the Bergen-Belsen concentration camp, where the horrific scenes that greeted the British liberators defied description, magnifies the sacrifice of the fallen and issues a categorical reminder of the need to defeat Nazi Germany as utterly and as quickly as possible. The rest of the war cemeteries lie between the towns and industrial centres bombed repeatedly during the war, a story summarized on the headstones of the fallen:

"THE READINESS IS ALL."
Warrant Officer II Douglas McKay Wylie, RCAF, 2.9.43 (age 23)

GOD LET YOU LEAVE A NAME. . . AMONG THE VERY BRAVE, THE VERY TRUE.
Warrant Officer I Allan Heaney, RCAF, 22.9.43 (age 21)

HE HAD NOT LOVED US HALF SO MUCH LOVED HE NOT HONOUR MORE.
Warrant Officer II Kenneth Alexander Bernard McArthur, RCAF, 4.10.43

FOR YOU, DEAR SON, PEACE. FOR US, LOVING MEMORIES.
Warrant Officer II Jack Dunbar Newcombe, RCAF, 16.12.43

OUR DEAR BOY. A SWEETER BOY NEVER LIVED. HE GAVE HIS LIFE
THAT OTHERS MIGHT LIVE.
Flying Officer Gordon Robert Drimmie, RCAF, 14.1.44 (age 21)

HE DIED THAT LIFE, AS HE KNEW AND LOVED IT, MIGHT ENDURE UPON THE EARTH.
R.I.P.
Pilot Officer William John Douglas, RCAF, 21.1.44 (age 22)

I SOUGHT THE LORD AND HE HEARD ME, AND HE DELIVERED ME FROM ALL MY TROUBLES.
Warrant Officer II Roy Edwards Mogalki, RCAF, 31.3.44 (age 23) [PSALM 34: 4]

LORD OF LIFE, BE HIS THE CROWN, LIFE FOR EVER MORE.
Flight Lieutenant Roger Harrop Galbraith, RCAF, 16.1.45 (age 25)

The architects who designed the war cemeteries in northwest Europe and Italy were remarkably deft in harmonising architectural features of the host country with the fixed commemorative traditions of the War Graves Commission. At the Hanover War Cemetery, however, the clash between the white Stone of Remembrance and the dark granite shelters, rendered in Gothic style, that flank the entranceway heightens awareness that the fallen lie at rest in the land of the enemy. The rows of white headstones that rise with the slope include 333 RCAF crew members among the 2,400 British and Commonwealth burials. Several carry two or three names and as many air force badges showing the mix of nationalities typical in bomber crews. The loyalty between crew members and the shared risk that each crew faced stand out in the many collective burials, and in the valedictions from families aware of their son's close ties to his comrades. The first epitaph below, from Hanover, bids farewell to a young flight engineer buried alongside six of his crew and countrymen. Examples of the bond between aircrews include a pair of epitaphs commemorating twin brothers who served and died together. The last is inscribed on the graves of two friends buried side by side:

IN LOVING REMEMBRANCE OF OUR SON, WHO DIED WITH HIS COMRADES.
Sergeant Elwood Campbell Houlding, RCAF, 14.1.44 (age 22)

**GOD BE MERCIFUL TO MY SON. REUNITE HIS SOUL WITH THOSE OF HIS DAD & HIS PALS.
MOTHER**
Sergeant Jesse Clemence Brakeman, RCAF, 3.9.41 (age 21) [DUNKIRK]

"TO SAVE MANKIND YOURSELF YOU SCORNED TO SAVE."
Warrant Officer II Robert Ernest Tod DFM, RCAF, 23.6.43 (age 23) [MEDEMBLIK]

"YOUR MEMORY HALLOWED IN THE LAND YOU LOVED."
Warrant Officer II Richard Douglas Tod, RCAF, 23.6.43 (age 23) [MEDEMBLIK]

MAY HIS SOUL AND THE SOULS OF THE MEMBERS OF HIS CREW REST IN PEACE.
Flight Lieutenant James Anthony Sherry, RCAF, 31.12.44 (age 22) [NEDERWEERT]

IN LOVING MEMORY OF A GALLANT SON. GOD BLESS HIM AND HIS CREW.
Flying Officer Ross Orval Ellsmere, RCAF, 4.5.44 (age 22) [ST. DÉSIR]

REST IN PEACE WITH YOUR BRAVE COMRADES.
Sergeant Percy John Ireland, RCAF, 8.4.43 (age 30) [REICHSWALD FOREST]

HE HAPPILY GAVE HIS LIFE WITH HIS FRIENDS THAT WE MIGHT LIVE. GOD BLESS HIM.
Sergeant Douglas Layne Pocock, RCAF, 22.1.44 (age 19) [BERLIN]

WE WERE ENRICHED BY HIS LIFE AS WE WERE BEREFT BY HIS DEATH.
Flying Officer Donald Cameron Walker, RCAF, 2.12.43 (age 27) [HARROGATE]
Flying Officer William John Taylor, RCAF, 2.12.43 (age 25) [HARROGATE]

The bonds between air crews transcended nationalities. Most crews were a miscellany of British and Empire men serving in their various capacities as pilots, flight engineers, navigators, air gunners, and bomb aimers. Often a headstone bearing the air force insignia of a particular country notes the home country of the deceased. *Of Canada,*

Of South Africa, Of Jamaica, Of Rhodesia, Of Bermuda, Of Newfoundland appear in brackets below the names of airmen who came from all over the Empire to serve in the multinational Commonwealth air forces. At Hanover, as in every gathering of RCAF burials, a handful of headstones following this practice distinguish the nationality of men who crossed the border to join the armed forces of Canada in the years before their own country entered the conflict:

OF HIS OWN VOLITION HE FOUGHT FOR FREEDOM AGAINST TYRANNY AND OPPRESSION.
Flight Sergeant Francis Weatherford Peterkin (of USA*),* RCAF*, 22.10.43 (age 22)*

THAT ALL MEN MIGHT BE FREE.
Warrant Officer II Hugh MacLennan (of USA*),* RCAF*, 14.1.44 (age 24)*

Just over 6,000 Americans signed up with the RCAF in the twenty-seven months between the German invasion of Poland and the Japanese attack on Pearl Harbor. Of the roughly 9,000 Americans who enrolled in the RCAF during the war, well over half preferred to remain in Canadian service rather than transfer to the American air forces once Uncle Sam crooked his finger in their direction. The inscriptions on the headstones of Americans who died in Canadian uniform merit attention for the idealism they espouse. The sincerity of these declarations cannot be doubted, for the servicemen they commemorate headed north out of conviction and principle at a time when their own country showed no inclination to get involved. They were following a precedent set in the First World War when many Americans headed "over there" by way of Canada long before April 1917. *One of American Harvard vanguard, entering Canadian service in 1916* suggests that student idealism set Lieutenant Phillip Comfort Starr on his path to the Royal Engineers via the Canadian Expeditionary Force; Private Roy Emerson Marshall, A *citizen of the United States who fought and died for France,* seems to have taken Benjamin Franklin's dictum about a man having two countries, his own and France, very much to heart; but the most remarkable instance of an American taking matters into his own hands is Driver Leland Wingate Fernald, A *volunteer from the U.S.A. to avenge the Lusitania murder,* who served with the Canadian Field Artillery in Flanders until his death in May 1916. Although isolationism ran strong in the United States during the 1930s, there were Americans who were appalled by what Nazi Germany represented and felt themselves obliged to fight for their political and religious beliefs once the war in Europe began. The first pair of inscriptions below honour two of "Canada's Yanks" who did not live to see their country enter the fray in December 1941. All pay tribute to men of true moral courage:

VOLUNTEER U.S.A. DOING WHAT HE BELIEVED RIGHT IN THE EYES OF GOD AND FREE MEN.
Sergeant William Risdon Malkemus, RCAF*, 7.9.41 (age 20)* [REICHSWALD FOREST]

MAY THE FREE PEOPLES OF THE WORLD ALWAYS UNITE TO FIGHT TYRANNY.
Pilot Officer Robert Melville Burlinson (of USA*),* RCAF*, 18.9.41 (age 23)*
[AMSTERDAM NEW EASTERN]

HOME, SULPHUR SPRINGS, TEXAS, U.S.A. UNKNOWN BY HIS COUNTRY
BUT WHO GAVE MORE?
Pilot Officer William Stone Tyler, RCAF*, 15.4.42 (age 21)* [RHEINBERG]

IF WE DO NOT RETURN, WE WILL HAVE NO REGRETS.
Flight Sergeant Thomas Austin Withers (of USA*),* RCAF*, 27.7.42 (age 27)* [KIEL]

A SOLDIER TO THE END. HE GAVE ALL TO HELP SAVE THE WORLD FOR CHRISTIANITY.
Pilot Officer Howard Houston Burton (of USA*),* RCAF*, 20.9.42 (age 32)* [DURNBACH]

MAY THIS AMERICAN, SERVING IN THE CANADIAN AIR FORCE,
REST IN PEACE IN HOLLAND.
Warrant Officer I Edward Warren Murphy, RCAF*, 2.10.42* [NOORDWIJK]

BORN 23.11.1916, THOMASVILLE, GEORGIA, U.S.A.
KILLED IN ACTION NEAR BIERFELD, GERMANY.
Flight Sergeant Albert Andrew Tschantre (of USA*),* RCAF*, 17.4.43 (age 26)* [RHEINBERG]

"THE NOBLE DIE, LIKE CHRIST ON THE HILL. THEY DIE—THAT WE MAY LIVE."
Pilot Officer James Louis Rossignol (of USA*),* RCAF*, 21.4.43 (age 21)* [BERLIN]

FOR FREEDOM AND CHRISTIANITY. OUR HERO!
ONLY SON OF CAPT. D.H. VANCE, M.C., U.S. NAVY.
Warrant Officer I Fred Renshaw Vance (of USA*),* RCAF*, 13.7.43 (age 25)* [CATANIA]

ONE OF THE FIRST AMERICANS TO SERVE WITH THE CANADIANS.
MAY HE REST IN PEACE.
Flying Officer Harry Allen Danniger, RCAF*, 6.9.43 (age 26)* [DURNBACH]

CLAUDE WEAVER III. HIS BROTHER DAVID WAS KILLED IWO JIMA 5.3.45,
AGE 20 YEARS.
Pilot Officer Claude Weaver DFC, DFM & BAR *(of* USA*),* RCAF*, 28.1.44 (age 19)*
[MEHARICOURT]

"THE LISTENING SKY REMEMBERS HIM AND COMRADES TOO WHEN LIGHTS ARE DIM."
Flying Officer William Warfield (of USA*),* RCAF*, 3.12.44 (age 21)* [BRUSSELS TOWN]

AN AMERICAN HERO FAR FROM HOME.
JACKSON HEIGHTS AND BABYLON, NEW YORK, U.S.A.
Flight Sergeant Andrew Anthony Swihura, RCAF*, 21.2.45 (age 22)*
[REICHSWALD FOREST]

Studies of the bombing campaign are awash in numbers, ratios, tables, and statistics charting the sorties flown, tonnage of bombs dropped, percentage of attacking force lost, extent of area damaged, and so on. The details on the graves of the bomber crews, most in their late teens or early twenties, who night after night steered their heavy laden aircraft through the flak and nightfighters until the odds caught up with them, add a humanising coda to these quantifications. The ages at which they died explain why the overwhelming majority of inscriptions come from parents, not from the wives or children whom young men diverted by training and service in distant places had no chance to have. Their epitaphs echo the lamentations and consoling themes common among the farewells to their comrades in the other services, and tributes to their character and courage sound forth among the final professions of love and remembrance, gratitude and comforting thoughts, that put each loss in isolation. Yet many air force epitaphs stand apart as expressions of the pride that RCAF personnel took in their service, a pride as deep as any soldier felt towards his regiment. Valedictions incorporating the air force motto, *Per ardua ad astra,* or a variation of it, appear on many RCAF graves, as do epitaphs extolling the airman's devotion to a service with an aura of adventure and bravado uniquely its own:

"THRO' THE STARS TO GLORY." EVER REMEMBERED. MUM, DAD AND FAMILY.
TILL WE MEET AGAIN.
Sergeant Denis Everest, RCAF, 22.9.43 (age 21)

THROUGH DIFFICULTY TO THE STARS.
Flying Officer George Stapleford Palin, RCAF, 3.1.44 (age 21) [BERLIN]

HE FLEW HIS LAST KITE.
Flying Officer William George Hoar, RCAF, 29.3.43 (age 26) [SAGE]

HE RODE THE SKIES CLOSE TO GOD IN THE SERVICE HE LOVED.
Sergeant Walter Alexander Hill, RCAF, 10.8.42 (age 21) [EINDHOVEN (WOENSEL)]
Flying Officer Raymond Norman McCleery, RCAF, 17.12.42 (age 28) [DEN BURG]

HE GAVE HIS ALL TO HIS COUNTRY IN THE SERVICE HE LOVED.
Flying Officer George Stoudt Ragan, RCAF, 21.3.45 (age 21) [REICHSWALD FOREST]

HE HAS EARNED HIS WINGS.
Flying Officer William Kerluk, RCAF, 16.1.45 (age 21) [REICHSWALD FOREST]

"THE ENEMY AND THE SKIES LURED HIM, VENTURE HERSELF ENSNARED HIM!"
Flight Lieutenant Nelson Alexander Cobb DFC, RCAF, 29.6.43 (age 21) [RHEINBERG]

A GLORIOUS BAND, THEY CLIMBED THE STEEP ASCENT OF HEAVEN.
Flight Sergeant Harold Geoffrey Round, RCAF, 11.8.44 [BROOKWOOD]

"PROUD, THEN, CLEAR-EYED AND LAUGHING, GO TO GREET DEATH AS A FRIEND."
Flight Lieutenant Hugh Stinson Glassco, RCAF, 5.1.45 (age 25) [RHEINBERG]

YOUNG, FULL OF LAUGHTER AND GENTLENESS, FEARLESSLY THEY FLEW GUARDING US.
Warrant Officer II George Norman Matthews, RCAF, 30.1.44 (age 21) [BROOKWOOD]

"LET NOT THE THOUGHT OF ME BE SAD, REMEMBER THAT I DID NOT FEAR."
Flying Officer Charles Davis Brown, RCAF, 23.5.44 (age 25) [REICHSWALD FOREST]

Teeming with allusions to the euphoria of flight, and with citations from Scripture or poetry portraying the airman's experience metaphorically as the ascent of the soul or its search for safe haven, the RCAF epitaphs preserve the distinct spirit and character of the war waged by the fighter pilots and bomber crews. The first four examples from Hanover introduce a series of inscriptions repeating assurances of divine guidance that movingly evoke the image of air crews plotting their course through the night skies:

THE LORD SHALL GUIDE THEE: HIS WAY IS PERFECT.
Pilot Officer Orville Francis Compton, RCAF, 13.8.44 (age 22)
[ISAIAH 58: 11; PSALM 18: 30]

"THE LORD SHALL PRESERVE THY GOING OUT AND THY COMING IN. . . FOR EVER MORE."
Flight Sergeant John Anthony Leach, RCAF, 27.9.43 (age 22) [PSALM 121: 8]

THE LORD IS OUR LIGHT. IN HIM MUST WE TRUST.
Sergeant John Murray Morrison, RCAF, 27.9.43 (age 21) [PSALM 27: 1]

"I ONLY KNOW I CANNOT DRIFT BEYOND HIS LOVE AND CARE." JOHN GREENLEAF WHITTIER
Flight Sergeant Ronald William Miller, RCAF, 22.10.43 (age 19)

GOD WHO RULES THE AIR IS JUST AND I HAVE FOUND HIM BY MY SIDE.
Pilot Officer John Frederick Myrick, RCAF, 11.8.42 (age 21) [ESBJERG]

THE LORD, HE IT IS THAT DOTH GO BEFORE THEE; HE WILL BE WITH THEE. DEUT. XXXI.8
Pilot Officer William George Mann, RCAF, 15.10.44 (age 19) [KIEL]

I WILL BE WITH THEE: I WILL NOT FAIL THEE, NOR FORSAKE THEE. JOSHUA I. 5
Warrant Officer II Percy Gordon Williams, RCAF, 25.2.43 (age 20) [DURNBACH]
Flying Officer Lorne Franklin Curry, RCAF, 15.6.44 (age 27) [BRETTEVILLE-SUR-LAIZE]

"SO HE BRINGETH THEM UNTO THEIR DESIRED HAVEN."
Flight Sergeant Robert Gray MacDonald, RCAF, 12.3.43 (age 26)
[LONDON EXTENSION] [PSALM 107: 30]

"HE HAS NOT MISSED THE WAY. HE COULD BUT STEER THE COURSE OUR PILOT SET."
Pilot Officer Archibald MacArthur Barrowman DFC, RCAF, 15.3.44 [DURNBACH]

I'LL MEET THE WORLD'S BEST PILOT AT THE DAWN.
Warrant Officer I Glen Allen McMillan, RCAF, 13.5.43 (age 22) [RHEINBERG]

THE WORLD WAS ALL BEFORE HIM AND PROVIDENCE HIS GUIDE.
Sergeant Harry William Ingleson, RCAF, 16.5.44 (age 19) [CHESTER (BLACON)]

I AM NOT AFRAID. GOD IS MY GUIDE.
Flight Sergeant Stuart Walker Little DFC, RCAF, 25.5.44 (age 30) [RHEINBERG]

O SEND OUT THY LIGHT AND THY TRUTH: LET THEM LEAD ME. PSA. 43: 3
Pilot Officer Richard Alan Biggerstaff, RCAF, 5.3.45 (age 19) [HARROGATE]

For most of the war, the RAF and RCAF flew at night to avoid the higher loss rates suffered in daylight raids. To increase the accuracy and effectiveness of night bombing, new technology and tactics were developed and specialised squadrons, known as Pathfinders, were trained to go ahead of the main force to mark out the target areas. The first epitaph below refers to this role, cast now in spiritual terms, while the rest speak for the bomber crews who followed the pathfinder groups through the darkness onto the objectives:

TRULY A PATHFINDER.
Flight Lieutenant Orville Ray Waterbury DFC, RCAF, 12.3.43 (age 22)
[REICHSWALD FOREST]

HE FLEW INTO THE NIGHT AND TOUCHED THE HAND OF GOD.
Flight Sergeant Lionel Harry Williams, RCAF, 2.10.42 (age 24) [NOORDWIJK]

AS THEY FLEW THROUGH THE NIGHT THEY WERE NOT AFRAID FOR GOD WAS WITH THEM.
Flight Sergeant Russell Edward Adam, RCAF, 1.9.43 (age 27) [BERLIN]

HE LEAVES A WHITE UNBROKEN GLORY, A WIDTH, A SHINING PEACE UNDER THE NIGHT.
Flying Officer Kenneth Wallace Bolstad, RCAF, 24.11.43 (age 21) [PERSHORE]

HE PASSED FROM THE DARKNESS OF THE NIGHT INTO THE AWAITING ARMS OF GOD.
Warrant Officer II Leonard Thomas Kennedy, RCAF, 27.4.44 (age 25) [DURNBACH]

HE DIED AT NIGHT, THAT YOU MIGHT LIVE AT DAWN. REMEMBER HIM.
Pilot Officer Pierre Joseph Benoit Morel Madore, RCAF, 27.4.44 (age 22) [DURNBACH]

BEYOND THE DARKNESS LIES THE PERFECT DAY.
Flying Officer William John Boyce, RCAF, 12.6.43 (age 26) [RHEINBERG]

The spiritual overtones of flight and the gallantry associated with aerial combat that distinguish the epitaphs of airmen from those of soldiers and sailors carry on a tradition of personal commemoration that began in the Great War. Families whose first instinct was to turn to Scripture could find many richly allusive passages, especially in the Psalms, whereas others eulogised pilots in terms more suited to the Hundred Years War than to a modern conflict between industrialised nations. Although much of Great War flying involved routine work in mapping and artillery observation, and most aces went about their work as clinically as any sniper in the trenches, the chivalric image of aerial warfare that prevailed in public imagination is evident in the epitaphs of both wars:

WHO WILL GIVE ME WINGS LIKE A DOVE AND I WILL FLY AND BE AT REST.
Lieutenant Matthew Halligan, RFC, 18.11.17 (age 36) [DOULLENS] [PSALM 55: 8]

HE SHALL DEFEND THEE UNDER HIS WINGS.
Major George Bernard Ward MC, RFC, 21.9.17 (AGE 26) [CHOCQUES] [PSALM 91: 4]

EVER REMEMBERED. THE LAST FLIGHT OF A "LAD WITH WINGS."
Lieutenant Thomas Seaman Green, RFC, 13.2.17 (age 22) [HEILLY STATION]

WHERE DUTY BADE HE CONFIDENTLY STEERED.
Lieutenant William Anderson MC, RGA/RAF, 21.9.18 (age 21) [MENDINGHEM]

KILLED IN ACTION SINGLE HANDED AGAINST FIVE ENEMY PLANES ABOVE THIS SPOT.
2nd Lieutenant Iorwerth Roland Owen, RFC, 7.5.17 (age 20) [STE CATHERINE]

A LITTLE WHITE KNIGHT OF MERRIE ENGLAND.
2nd Lieutenant Frederick John Ewart Stafford, RFC, 22.4.17 (age 19) [ABBEVILLE]

HE WAS AN ENGLISHMAN, A KNIGHT OF WAR, WITHOUT FEAR, WITHOUT REPROACH.
Lieutenant Walter Anderson Porkess, RFC, 10.2.17 (age 29) [CHOCQUES]

"HE HAS OUTSOARED THE SHADOW OF OUR NIGHT." SANS PEUR ET SANS REPROCHE.
Squadron Leader Ronald Stanley Weir, RCAF, 6.8.44 (age 43) [BÉNY-SUR-MER]

The knights of the air of the First World War were succeeded by the fighter pilots who, in the words on the headstone of a British flyer, "*raised aloft the lamp of hope in freedom's darkest hour*" during the Battle of Britain. The heroic spirit of 1940, given voice in the speeches of Winston Churchill, sounds forth in the epitaphs of these British and Canadian airmen:

WITH THE FEW WHO SAVED THE MANY. MORE VICTORIOUS THAN THEY KNEW.
Pilot Officer Harold Leslie Atkin-Berry, RAF, 10.7.40 (age 20) [TERLINCTHUN]

IN LOVING MEMORY OF "ONE OF THE FEW."
Wing Commander Hugh William Eliot DSO, DFC, RAF, 11.3.45 (age 23) [ARGENTA GAP]

"HIS FINEST HOUR."
Flying Officer Maurice Gordon Moor, RCAF, 6.12.42 (age 23) [EINDHOVEN (WOENSEL)]

NEVER IN THE FIELD OF HUMAN CONFLICT WAS SO MUCH OWED BY SO MANY TO SO FEW.
Warrant Officer I Charles John Wyllie, RCAF, 8.5.42 (age 20) [BERGEN-OP-ZOOM]

NEVER HAVE SO FEW GIVEN SO MUCH FOR SO MANY, TO THE UTMOST, TO THE END.
Pilot Officer Arthur Cameron Thompson, RCAF, 29.1.44 (age 22) [BERLIN]

**YOU GAVE YOUR ALL, MY SON, THOUGH YOUNG IN YEARS, THE BLOOD AND SWEAT;
THE TEARS, MY SHARE.**
Pilot Officer Robert Kane Gillis, RCAF, 25.10.44 (age 22) [BROOKWOOD]

The use of Churchill's own words in the epitaphs point to an important difference between the commemoration of Great War airmen and that bestowed on their successors. Where the army had won the Great War, after tremendous exertions and losses, the pilots of Fighter Command had saved Britain in 1940 while the crews of Bomber Command had to all intents and purposes manned the Western Front in the air until the assault on Hitler's Fortress Europe could begin. The pilots of the Great War, for all their gallantry and distinction, had not tipped the balance of the conflict to anywhere near the extent that the air forces of the Second World War did in staving off defeat and conducting the only offensive campaign the western Allies could mount for much of the war. Recognition of the decisive part played by the RAF and its Commonwealth contingents is apparent in the epitaphs of these Canadian airmen which express their families' gratitude for the collective as well as the individual contribution they made to the war effort:

YOUR GALLANT SOUL PATROLS THE FREEDOM OF THE SKY.
Flight Sergeant George Allen Morley, RCAF, 24.6.42 (age 26) [BROOKWOOD]

HE DIED THE HELPLESS TO DEFEND, A FAITHFUL AIRMAN'S NOBLE END.
Pilot Officer Joseph Harvey Milton Lacelle, RCAF, 28.6.42 (age 20) [BERGEN-OP-ZOOM]

**THEIR SHOULDERS HELD THE SKY SUSPENDED; THEY STOOD,
AND EARTH'S FOUNDATIONS STAY.**
Flight Sergeant Lawrence Dennis Ryan, RCAF, 5.4.43 (age 26) [SAGE]

LET US PRAY TO BE WORTHY OF THEM WHO MET DEATH IN THE BURNING SKY.
Sergeant John Gillespie, RCAF, 27.4.43 (age 24) [SCHOONSELHOF]

LOYAL À MORT.
Flight Sergeant William Albert Sparrow, RCAF, 25.6.43 (age 27) [BERGEN-OP-ZOOM]

MAY HE FIND PEACE IN THE ETHEREAL HOME OF FREEDOM'S HEROES.
Flying Officer Francis Dalton Dwyer, RCAF, 29.9.43 (age 23) [BROOKWOOD]

HERO OF THE AIR SACRIFICED ALL FOR HIS COUNTRY'S FREEDOM.
Pilot Officer Joseph Léon Gibault, RCAF, 24.11.43 (age 38) [PERSHORE]

**THEIR GOLDEN YOUTH BLOTS OUT THE SKY AS EACH FLIES TO LIVE OR DIE
FOR COUNTRY AND FOR GOD.**
Pilot Officer James Duncan Fairbairn, RCAF, 7.12.43 (age 20) [BROOKWOOD]

**GOD BLESS THESE CAPTAINS OF THE TRACKLESS AIR WHO ON THEIR WINGS
THE FATE OF MANKIND BEAR.**
Pilot Officer Gordon Templeton Grieg, RCAF, 28.4.44 (age 21) [SCHOONSELHOF]

HIS BRAVE YOUNG LIFE ON EARTH FOR EVER ENDED. STILL WRAPT AROUND HIS HEART
THE FLAG HE DEFENDED.
Sergeant Albert Ormond Wedin, RCAF, 8.5.44 (age 21) [CHESTER (BLACON)]

WHO DIED VALIANTLY IN DEFENCE OF HIS COUNTRY AND LOVED ONES. REQUIESCAT IN PACE
Pilot Officer Charles Vernon Dymond, RCAF, 13.6.44 (age 20) [DUNKIRK]

TO THE GLORIOUS MEMORY OF A SON WHO FOUGHT AND DIED—A MAN.
Pilot Officer Clifford Eugene Leroy Cook, RCAF, 1.11.44 (age 19) [BERGEN-OP-ZOOM]

HE FOUGHT FOR HIS BELIEFS AND WON. HIS FLIGHT IS NOW COMPLETE. PSALM 23
Flying Officer George Jeffrey Symes, RCAF, 1.11.44 (age 27) [BERGEN-OP-ZOOM]

UNDAUNTED BY DEATH AS THOSE WITH WHOM HE DIED. TO HIM WE LOOK WITH PRIDE.
HIS LIFE YET SO YOUNG SHALL NEVER GO UNSUNG.
Flight Sergeant James Harold Preece, RCAF, 12.12.44 (age 20) [CHESTER (BLACON)]

NOBLY HE SERVED AND MET HIS FATE SO BRAVELY IN THE FEVERED SKY.
Flying Officer James Arthur Bleich, RCAF, 21.2.45 (age 23) [DURNBACH]

YOUR MISSION COMPLETED, O VALIANT SPIRIT. R.I.P.
Squadron Leader Eric Thomas Garrett, RCAF, 5.3.45 (age 24) [HARROGATE]

A HEROIC SKYPILOT WHO WILL ALWAYS BE LOVINGLY REMEMBERED.
Flight Lieutenant William George Davis, RCAF, 30.3.45 (age 21) [HOLTEN]

The literary heritage of the Great War lay heavily upon aspiring poets and writers in the Second World War who could add but little to the literature of modern war. Only aerial combat, a realm of experience outside the purview of most Great War participants or contemporaries (although Cecil Lewis's *Sagittarius Rising* and William Butler Yeats's *An Irish Airman Foresees his Death* rank high in Great War prose and poetry), offered relatively uncharted territory. Once again, the dichotomy between the works attempting to depict the reality of the war and those exalting the spirit of adventure and sacrifice separates the best known poems of the Second World War. Randall Jarrell's *Death of the Ball-Turret Gunner* transforms the anonymous air gunner suspended in the bomber's womb into the expendable progeny of the state—"when I died they washed me out of the turret with a hose." His lesser known but equally terse elegy to the bomber crews, *Losses*, reduces their war to its withering essentials: "in bombers named for girls, we burned the cities we had learned about in school—till our lives wore out." But just as the bereaved of the Great War turned not to Sassoon, Graves, or Owen, but to Kipling, Binyon, and McCrae for personal inscriptions, the families of fallen airmen found inspiration and solace in perhaps the most famous poem of the Second World War, John Gillespie Magee's *High Flight* (1941). One of the Americans who came north in 1940 to serve in the RCAF, Magee wrote the sonnet three months before he was killed in a mid-air collision over England. The first and last lines form the epitaph on his grave in Scopwick Churchyard; rare are the air force burial grounds without at least one headstone citing verses from what became the official poem of the RAF and RCAF:

OH, I HAVE SLIPPED THE SURLY BONDS OF EARTH . . . PUT OUT MY HAND
AND TOUCHED THE FACE OF GOD.
Pilot Officer John Gillespie Magee, RCAF, 11.12.41 (age 19) [SCOPWICK CHURCHYARD]

"OH, I HAVE SLIPPED THE SURLY BONDS OF EARTH, SUNWARDS I'VE CLIMBED."
Flying Officer John William Wallace, RCAF, 27.9.43 (age 28) [HARROGATE]

**"I'VE TROD THE SANCTITY OF SPACE, PUT OUT MY HAND
AND TOUCHED THE FACE OF GOD."**
Flying Officer Peter Harold Burne, RCAF, 22.2.45 (age 21) [BECKLINGEN]

HIGH IN THE SUNSET SILENCE . . . FLEW . . . PUT OUT MY HAND AND TOUCHED THE FACE OF GOD.
Flight Lieutenant Andrew Boyd Ketterson, RCAF, 4.3.44 (age 22) [WEVELGEM]

"SUNWARD I'VE CLIMBED . . . PUT OUT MY HAND AND TOUCHED THE FACE OF GOD."
Flying Officer Coran Cyman McPherson, RCAF, 6.9.43 (age 28) [RHEINBERG]

Other epitaphs drawn from literary sources touch on the ecstasy of flight and the intimations of immortality expressed so vividly in Magee's poem. Shelley's words in praise of his friend Keats, "He has outsoared the shadow of our night" provided an appropriate epitaph for airmen; the line "On joyful wings upwards I fly," from the hymn *Nearer my God to Thee*, also appears on many headstones. The spiritual connotations of flight were so engrained in poetry and hymns that the same motifs—the soul rising heavenwards in full flight into eternity, the vision of a celestial world beyond this one—are conveyed in many different ways:

THE HIGH SOUL CLIMBS THE HIGH WAY.
Flying Officer Richard Winter Taylor DFC & BAR, RCAF, 14.3.43 (age 22) [DURNBACH]

THEIR WINGS HAVE TOUCHED THE HEAVENS.
Sergeant Vincent James Dunnigan, RCAF, 14.10.43 (age 23) [CHESTER (BLACON)]

MY GRAVE IS IN THE ASHEN PLAIN, MY SPIRIT IN THE AIR.
Flying Officer Wallace Allan Smart, RCAF, 3.7.44 (age 26) [BROOKWOOD]

HE HAS CONQUERED EARTH'S CONFINING SOD AND GONE FORTH TO BE WITH GOD.
Pilot Officer Richard Hugh Chittim, RCAF, 2.1.45 (age 21) [DURNBACH]

THE ONE WHOSE GOING LEFT US LONELY IS SCALING THE HEIGHTS UNDREAMED OF YORE.
Flying Officer Raymond Alexander Rember, RCAF, 24.7.44 (age 24) [KIEL]

**FATHER IN HEAVEN, HAVE MERCY ON HIS SOUL AND KEEP HIS SPIRIT FREE,
FREE AS THE AIR ON HIGH. BR., THIS IS OUR PRAYER.**
Flight Sergeant William Henry Terwilliger, RCAF, 31.8.42 (age 25) [EVESHAM]

**HE RODE UPON THE CHERUBINS AND DID FLY. HE CAME FLYING UPON
THE WINGS OF THE WIND.**
Flying Officer Benjamin Charles Hunt, RCAF, 13.5.45 (age 31) [CHESTER (BLACON)]

IN THE SOLITUDE OF FLIGHT, THY BEAUTY AND GREATNESS WERE REVEALED.
Flight Sergeant Henry Edward Went, RCAF, 9.5.42 (age 24) [BERLIN]

"INTO THE INFINITE PASS FOR EVER KNOWING THE LIGHT OF LIGHTS FAILETH NEVER."
Flight Sergeant Gerald John Patrick Kearns, RCAF, 20.5.42 (age 23) [HEVERLEE]

**DEAR ARTHUR, DEAR SON AND BROTHER WHO DIPPED HIS WINGS AND FLEW
BEYOND THE HORIZON OF OUR SIGHT.**
Flying Officer Arthur Jeffrey Corriveau, RCAF, 13.5.44 (age 21) [BROOKWOOD]

AS ON YOUR LAST FLIGHT, YOU SOARED INTO ETERNITY. MOM, DAD AND DOROTHY.
Flying Officer Richard Herbert Fisher, RCAF, 31.3.45 (age 22) [BECKLINGEN]

Families listening to news of the war were accustomed to hearing that "x of our planes failed to return" from a bombing raid. In response the bereaved alleviated the pain of "failed to return" by speaking of their loved one's safe arrival in a heavenly home:

"O THOU, WHO DID CREATE THIS LAD, RECEIVE HIM NOW THAT HE TURNS HOME."
Flying Officer Murray Norman Firth, RCAF, 21.2.45 [RHEINBERG]

ONE OF OUR PILOTS IS SAFE. REST IN PEACE.
Flying Officer Charles Edward Tindall, RCAF, 22.3.44 [COLOGNE SOUTHERN]

GOD OPENED THE GATES AND AN AIRMAN SOARED INTO HEAVEN. HE WAS LOVED BY ALL.
Pilot Officer Robert Clarke Buckberrough, RCAF, 11.7.44 (age 22) [BROOKWOOD]

GONE ON A HIGHER FLIGHT WITH JESUS AS HIS PILOT.
Sergeant Calvin George Whittingstall, RCAF, 22.10.44 (age 20) [CHESTER (BLACON)]

HE WHO DARED THE TRACKLESS SKY HAS FOUND A FAITH MORE STRONG AND SURE.
Pilot Officer Maxwell Warren Coones, RCAF, 5.3.45 (age 20) [HARROGATE]

I HAVE FINISHED MY COURSE. MY SOUL SHALL WING ITS FLIGHT ON HIGH.
Flying Officer Norman Alexander Watt, RCAF, 1.7.43 (age 21) [SCOPWICK CHURCHYARD]

GONE BUT NOT FORGOTTEN. REJOICE IN THIS, THAT YOUR NAME IS WRITTEN IN HEAVEN.
Warrant Officer II Chester Charles Trudell, RCAF, 17.12.44 (age 21)
[AMERSFOORT (OUD LEUSDEN)] [LUKE 10: 20]

HE HAS HIGHER FLIGHT TO REACH, A FULLER LIFE TO HAVE WITH GOD.
Flying Officer Stewart Millen Bonter, RCAF, 15.3.45 (age 26) [REICHSWALD FOREST]

GOD LIFTED HIM UP.
Flying Officer Roy Gibson Madge, RCAF, 26.5.43 (age 23) [HEVERLEE]

FOR "BRIGHT EYES" BRIGHTER SKIES.
Flying Officer William Ransom Breithaupt DFC, RCAF, 13.9.44 (age 24) [RHEINBERG]

TO CHARLIE WHO PASSED THE PRAISING STARS TO MEET HIS GOD.
Flying Officer Charles Henry Love, RCAF, 21.11.44 (age 32) [REICHSWALD FOREST]

HE LOVED YOUR STARS. HE LEARNED THEM ALL BY NAME FOR USE IN ONE LAST JOURNEY.
Flight Sergeant John Hunter Carter, RCAF, 28.1.45 (age 22) [HARROGATE]

OUR ONLY SON. HE LEARNED THE STARS ALL BY NAME FOR HIS ONE LAST JOURNEY.
Flying Officer Bruce Alexander Parker, RCAF, 12.12.44 (age 20) [REICHSWALD FOREST]

"HE HAS FLOWN AS ONLY THE YOUNG CAN FLY, WHO HAVE HOMECOMING IN THEIR EYES."
Flying Officer Edward Granville Bayer, RCAF, 7.3.44 [HARROGATE]

HE MADE THE SACRIFICE SUBLIME. HIS SOUL SOARS ON ITS WAY, A TRYST TO KEEP.
Flying Officer George Gordon McGolrick, RCAF, 5.1.45 (age 23) [HARROGATE]

The religious comfort that families sought emerges from the prayers and Scriptural passages to which the airmen themselves often turned in times of need. Psalm 91 in

Kiel War Cemetery.

Allied plot in Hamburg's Ohlsdorf Cemetery.

RCAF graves at Berlin War Cemetery (Eric Reid).

British and Canadian crew members buried together on the Danish coast.

The heroic spirit of the air war on an RAF headstone.

The grave of Squadron Leader Ian George Armour McNaughton at Sage War Cemetery, Germany.

RCAF graves at Kirkeby Churchyard, Denmark.

particular was known as "the soldier's Psalm" for its promise of God's protection of His own and His triumph over the wicked. Recommended for all servicemen, Psalm 91 (and the hymn adapted from it) spoke in terms relevant to bomber crews—"surely He shall deliver you from the snare of the fowler . . . thou shalt not be afraid for the terror by night . . . nor for the pestilence that walketh in darkness . . . a thousand shall fall at thy side . . . but it shall not come nigh thee. . . for He shall give His angels charge over thee." It was one of several Scriptural texts invoking divine aid and protection that families used to commend their loved ones to the care of God:

HEAR THOU, O LORD, A NATION'S PRAYER FOR THESE THY CHILDREN OF THE AIR.
Pilot Officer John Walter Hawkey, RCAF, 24.1.44 (age 23) [CHESTER (BLACON)]

"THE LORD LOOKETH FROM HEAVEN; HE BEHOLDETH ALL THE SONS OF MEN."
Flying Officer Douglas Hitchcock, RCAF, 18.12.44 (age 27) [DIEPPE] [PSALM 33: 13]

"THE CHILDREN OF MEN PUT THEIR TRUST UNDER THE SHADOWS OF THY WINGS."
Pilot Officer Hedley de la Broquerie Young, RCAF, 29.8.44 (age 22) [PADUA] [PSALM 36: 7]

IN THE SHADOW OF THY WINGS WILL I MAKE MY REFUGE."
Flying Officer James Commodore Campbell, RCAF, 15.10.44 (age 28)
[REICHSWALD FOREST]
Flying Officer William James Windeler, RCAF, 15.6.44 (age 25) [BROOKWOOD]
[PSALM 57: 1]

HE THAT DWELLETH IN THE SECRET PLACE OF THE MOST HIGH. PSALM XCI. 1
Flight Sergeant George Weston Laut, RCAF, 7.3.45 (age 25) [RHEINBERG]

"HE SHALL COVER THEE WITH HIS FEATHERS AND UNDER HIS WINGS SHALT THOU TRUST."
Flying Officer George Frederick Radcliffe Jackson, RCAF, 19.4.43 (age 21) [BROOKWOOD]

"UNDER HIS WINGS SHALT THOU TRUST."
Pilot Officer Lloyd Wilson Kerr, RCAF, 31.8.43 [HEVERLEE] [PSALM 91: 4]

"UNDER HIS WINGS MY SOUL SHALL ABIDE."
Flying Officer William Herkis Jessiman, RCAF, 3.1.44 (age 28) [BRETTEVILLE-SUR-LAIZE]

UNDER HIS WINGS MY SOUL SHALL ABIDE, SWEETLY ABIDE FOR EVER."
Sergeant George Herkis Jessiman, RCAF, 20.12.43 (age 22) [RHEINBERG]
[HYMN, *UNDER HIS WINGS*, BY WILLIAM CUSHING]

"THE LORD UPHOLDETH ALL THAT FALL AND RAISETH UP ALL THOSE THAT BE BOWED DOWN."
Flight Sergeant Carl Heinrich Weicker, RCAF, 16.3.45 (age 21) [DURNBACH] [PSALM 145: 14]

"I BARE YOU ON EAGLES' WINGS, AND BROUGHT YOU UNTO MYSELF."
Warrant Officer I Philip Sibbald Ogilvie Brichta DFM, 16.9.42 (age 31)
[REICHSWALD FOREST] [EXODUS 19: 4]

"THEY SHALL MOUNT UP WITH WINGS AS EAGLES; THEY SHALL RUN AND NOT BE WEARY."
Flying Officer Geoffrey Winslow Hess, RCAF, 14.3.45 (age 29) [VENRAY] [ISAIAH 40: 11]

THE ETERNAL GOD IS THY REFUGE AND UNDERNEATH ARE THE EVERLASTING ARMS.
Warrant Officer I William Robert Tait, RCAF, 20.9.44 (age 23) [ARNHEM OOSTERBEEK]
[DEUTERONOMY 33: 27]

UNDERNEATH ARE THE EVERLASTING ARMS.
Squadron Leader Burton Norris Jost DFC, RCAF, 25.6.43 (age 31) [JONKERBOS]

"AND ONE OF THEM SHALL NOT FALL ON THE GROUND WITHOUT YOUR FATHER."
ST. MATT. X. 29
Flying Officer Ernest Borden McCutcheon, RCAF, 22.7.43 (age 25) [CASSINO]

I SHALL RISE AGAIN.
Flying Officer Leonard Douglas Proctor, RCAF, 22.3.44 (age 22) [DURNBACH]

HE BRAVED THE DANGERS OF THE AIR; GOD KEEP HIM SAFE. "UNTIL WE MEET AGAIN"
Flying Officer Earl Douglas Tait, RCAF, 10.2.45 (age 20) [BROOKWOOD]

"Born in the sun, for a brief moment they walked towards the sun," the epitaph on the grave of Flying Officer Otto Hjalmar Antoft, buried at Arnhem Oosterbeek, paraphrases a line from Stephen Spender's poem *I Think Continually of Those*, and invites the reader to take note of its continuation, *"and left the vivid air signed with their honour."* These words remind us of the esteem in which the families and the citizens of the Allied coalition held the airmen who waged the longest and most perilous offensive campaign of the war. Nor should we forget that the fleets of bombers flying overhead were also proof to the citizens of occupied Europe that liberation would come one day. The epitaphs extolling the spirit and conviction of the airmen restore the perspectives of the time when the urgency of the military and political situation, and the limited options for hitting back at the enemy, demanded the highest standards of fortitude and dedication from the personnel of Fighter Command and Bomber Command. It is no exaggeration to say that the Allies lost the first half of the war, and among the few fillips to morale were the valiant defence of Britain in 1940 and the blows struck at Germany by the bombers of the British and Commonwealth air forces.

WITH HEAVENLY WEAPONS I HAVE FOUGHT THE BATTLES OF THE LORD.
Flying Officer Norman Alexander Macaulay, RCAF, 31.3.44 (age 26) [DURNBACH]

"NOR WERE THEY BLIND TO THE DANGER, JUST AND NOBLE WAS THEIR RESOLVE."
Flying Officer Andrew MacFarlane Harrison Gain, RCAF, 15.1.43 (age 19) [PERSHORE]

Public support for the bombing campaign was strong throughout the war, but there were protests from clergymen and public figures (such as Vera Brittain and C.S. Lewis) against the use of air power against civilians. Controversies over the ethics and legality of area bombing arose intermittently, with matters reaching a head in 1943 when the Archbishop of York, Dr. Cyril Garbett, argued that "often in life there is no clear choice between absolute right and wrong; frequently, the choice has to be made of the lesser of two evils . . . and it is a lesser evil to bomb a war-loving Germany than to sacrifice the lives of thousands of our own countrymen . . . and to delay delivering millions now held in slavery." While the issue of area bombing continued to provoke intense debate in Britain, with opponents at full liberty to express their views, even as the lesser of two evils it paled before the greater. In October 1943 Heinrich Himmler gave his infamous speech at Poznan reassuring the SS officers involved in exterminating the Jewish race that "to have seen this, and . . . to have remained decent, has made us hard and is a page of glory never mentioned and never to be mentioned." In debates over the conduct of the bombing campaign and the role of the Canadian aircrews who supplied

20% of Bomber Command's manpower, the basic distinction between one side and the other should be borne in mind. Like the other secular ideologies of the twentieth century, Nazism had exiled conscience from its moral realm, and the Nazi leadership had from the war's outset made brazenly clear the means by which it intended to achieve its ends. To defeat this conscienceless enemy, thousands of young Canadians who had no wish to do what they were doing gave their lives in the belief that their efforts were necessary and justified when measured against the alternative. The duties they were called upon to perform in the face of evil evince the bitter realities of the human condition, but they were also means to a larger and more hopeful end. Two last epitaphs, one from Hanover, the other from a churchyard in England, express a wish and a prayer meaningful only in the event of the victory which the airmen sacrificed so much to achieve:

HE GAVE HIS LIFE THAT WE MIGHT LIVE, AND WHERE HE FELL MAY FREEDOM STAND.
Flying Officer Fred Moncrieff Carter, RCAF, 1.9.43 (age 26)

FATHER, MAKE US CLEARLY SEE THE PART WE HAD IN THIS. IN THY MERCY HEAL US ALL.
Flying Officer Ernest Stollery, RCAF, 20.12.42 (age 21) [ST. JOHN CHURCHYARD]

FURTHER READING:

Bashow, David. *No Prouder Place: Canadians and the Bomber Command Experience 1939–1945*. St. Catharines: Vanwell Publishing Limited, 2005.

_____ . "The Balance Sheet: The costs and the gains of the Bombing Campaign," *Canadian Military History* 15/3 & 4 (2006), 42–70.

Hall, David Ian. "'Black, White and Grey': Wartime arguments for and against the Strategic Bomber Offensive," *Canadian Military History* 7/1 (1998), 7–19.

Milberry, Larry. *Canada's Air Force at War and Peace* (3 volumes). Toronto: CANAV Books, 2000.

Robertson, Scot. "In the shadow of Death by Moonlight," in: *The Valour and the Horror Revisited*, ed. David J. Bercuson and S.F. Wise. Montreal-Kingston: McGill-Queen's University Press, 1994, pp. 153–179.

Eric Reid

CHAPTER SIX

Just another good soldier. . .
Adegem Canadian War Cemetery, Belgium

SHOULD TIME'S FINGERS BRUSH THE FOLDS OF DUST APART, YOU'LL FIND A
MAPLE LEAF ENGRAVED UPON HIS HEART.
Private Thomas Joseph Abdulla, QOCHC, 13.9.44 (age 21)

Bard Cottage, Bus House, Caesar's Nose, Cement House, Cheddar Villa, China Wall, Gunners Farm, Hop Store, Lancashire Cottage, Lone Tree, Motor Car Corner, Mud Corner, No Man's Cot, Packhorse Farm, Ration Farm, Rifle House, Sanctuary Wood, Suffolk, Talana Farm, The Huts, Tyne Cot, and the immortal trio of casualty clearing stations playing on the –ghem suffix of Flemish placenames, Dozinghem, Bandaghem, and Mendinghem (i.e. "dosing 'em," "bandage 'em," "mending 'em")— the distinctive, ironic, often homesick, toponymy of the Tommies lives on in the war cemeteries dotting the Ypres Salient where the armies of the British Empire held the line for forty-nine of the fifty-two months of the Great War. The names imprinted on the Flemish landscape attest the stoic jocularity of the Tommies that endears them to posterity while symbolising their resolve to see the war through to the end. "These men stood by their country the way that you stood by a pal whose luck was out," was the historian Denis Winter's colloquial but succinct explanation of the remarkable stamina shown by the British army, the only army of the Great War never to teeter on the brink of moral collapse despite the costly task of driving the Germans out of Flanders and Picardy. In Winter's view, the question "would you let Germany win?" kept the British soldier at his post even at the worst of times. In recognition of their steadfast defence of the Ypres Salient the architects of the Imperial War Graves Commission kept the names echoing the plucky, irreverent spirit of the Tommies that made the corners of a foreign field forever England.

PAST THE MILITARY AGE, HE RESPONDED TO THE MOTHER COUNTRY'S CALL.
Regimental Sergeant Major Stewart Godfrey, PPCLI, 18.4.16 (age 47)
[MENIN ROAD SOUTH]

MORTUUS EST PRO SCOTIA.
(He died for Scotland.)
Lance Corporal Harry Walker, 29th BCI, 20.10.15 (age 24)   [WULVERGHEM-LINDENHOEK]

OUR BOY, ENGLAND'S MAN.
Private Henry Griffin, 16th BCI, 28.4.17 (age 21)   [ORCHARD DUMP]

ONE OF CANADA'S GIFTS TO THE EMPIRE, A LIFE.
Private William Smith, 49th BCI, 29.9.18 (age 24)   [RAILLENCOURT]

WE MISS OUR BOY BUT IT HELPS TO KNOW THAT HE FELL FACING BRITAIN'S FOE.
Private Walter Newman, 43rd BCI, 28.10.18   [ABBEVILLE]

LOST LIFE, NOT HONOUR, AND DIED IN THE BRITISH WAY.
Private Hugh Gordon Ross, CE, 5.2.19 (age 22)   [TERLINCTHUN]

Corners of foreign fields are also forever Australia, India, New Zealand, South Africa, and Canada. Maple Copse, Maple Leaf, Toronto Avenue, and Canada Farm in Flanders join with the other outposts along the old Western Front—Adanac ("Canada" spelled backwards), Canada Cemetery, Canadian Cemetery No. 2, Dominion Cemetery, Manitoba Cemetery, Niagara Cemetery, Ontario Cemetery, Regina Trench Cemetery, Toronto Cemetery—to pay tribute to the role of the Empire's senior Dominion whose loyalty to Britain's cause was as reflexive and unwavering as that shown by her fellow Dominions. Not surprisingly, the professions of allegiance to the Mother Country in the epitaphs of Canadian soldiers abound, given that half the men of the Canadian Expeditionary Force had been born in the British Isles, but a number of epitaphs express the feeling throughout the Dominion that the British Empire and the ideals it represented summoned the loyalty of all its members, above and beyond the loyalty they felt to their own country or kind. Just three years before the Great War drew Britain into its first European conflict in a century, Canada's commitment to the British Empire had been tested in the election of 1911, when Canadians had reaffirmed their status as denizens of British North America by rejecting the reciprocity treaty with the United States. England, Britain, Empire, King and Country, all were synonymous with the interests of Canada when Canadians belonged to a legally united empire, and considered themselves first and foremost British subjects:

HE DIED FOR CANADA AND THE EMPIRE.
Private Robert Blake Allan, 16th BCI, 31.5.15 (age 20)   [CHOCQUES]

A CANADIAN BOY WHO GAVE HIS LIFE FOR THE EMPIRE AND FREEDOM.
Private Thomas Mills, 4th BCI, 12.4.16 (age 28)   [CHESTER FARM]

HE WAS DUTIFUL AND GAVE HIS LIFE FOR LIBERTY OF THE EMPIRE.
Private Joseph Craig, 2nd BCI, 26.4.16 (age 24)   [WOODS]

DIED FOR KING AND CONSTITUTION WITH WORLD WIDE LIBERTY. GOD IS LOVE.
Lieutenant William Joseph Sanderson Connor, CFA, 5.7.16 (age 31)   [VLAMERTINGHE]

HE GAVE HIS LIFE FOR LIBERTY AND THE BRITISH EMPIRE.
Private Ernest Fridlington, 5th BCI, 10.5.16 (age 36)   [WOODS]

ENGLAND CALLED, WHO IS FOR LIBERTY? WHO FOR RIGHT? I STOOD FORTH.
Private Sydney Howard Burgess, 10th BCI, 9.4.17 (age 26)   [NINE ELMS]

FOR ENGLAND, HOME AND DUTY, AND THE HONOUR OF HIS RACE.
Lance Corporal Arthur Walter Lake, 54th BCI, 10.4.17 (age 30)
[CANADIAN CEMETERY NO. 2]

SACRIFICED HIS LIFE TO UPHOLD THE HONOUR OF ENGLAND.
Private Robert James Connor, 78th BCI, 28.7.17 (age 18) [LA CHAUDIÈRE]

FOR ENGLAND, TRUTH AND BEAUTY.
Private William Kidd, 31st BCI, 9.8.18 (age 26) [CAIX]

INDIAN—TRIBE 6 NATIONS. DIED FOR HONOUR OF EMPIRE.
EVER REMEMBERED BY WIFE AND CHILDREN.
Sapper Lewis Wilson, CE, 31.8.18 (age 38) [AUBIGNY]

Loyal she began, loyal she remained to the common cause of the Empire, yet as the war went on and the reputation of the Canadian Expeditionary Force grew with each victory, Canada began to emerge from under the wing of the Mother Country. Side by side with the valedictions hailing the fallen for their sacrifice for the Empire are others displaying a newfound pride in Canada. It may be a commonplace that the First World War galvanised Canadian nationalism, but it is a commonplace amply supported by the epitaphs. Families made a point of noting the soldier's birthplace or enlistment in Canada, his service for Canada, and the country's contribution to the Allied cause. Examples of epitaphs recording the soldier's death in action on the Somme, at Vimy Ridge, Passchendaele and Cambrai were cited in Chapter Two; the final epitaph in the sample below refers to the Canadian breakthrough near Amiens on August 8 1918, the prelude to the Hundred Days which saw the Canadian (and Australian) Corps spearhead the Allied advance to victory:

FIRST CANADIAN CONTINGENT. R.I.P. WE WILL NEVER FORGET.
Private Austin Keens, 15th BCI, 28.4.16 (age 24) [WOODS]

ENLISTED AUG. 12, 1914, MOOSIMIN, SASK., CANADA.
Lance Corporal Henry Chilton, 5th BCI, 3.6.16 (age 34) [LARCH WOOD]

ONE OF CANADA'S BRAVE AND NOBLE SONS.
Private Joseph Gonzague Chalue, 60th BCI, 10.7.16 (age 18) [LIJSSENTHOEK]

BORN AT HUMBER BAY, CANADA, NOV. 25 1884. OF 74TH BN. FROM TORONTO,
SPRING 1916.
Private Septimus Herbert Hicks, 42nd BCI, 6.8.16 (age 32) [BOULOGNE EASTERN]

BELOVED SON, PROUD CANADIAN.
Private James Hayes, 24th BCI, 17.9.16 (age 18) [ADANAC]

VIVE LE CANADA. L.L. BELL, GRAND SAULT, N.B. EST MORT POUR L'EUROPE.
(Long live Canada. L.L. Bell, Grand Sault, N.B. died for Europe.)
Corporal Louis Leo Bell, 26th BCI, 4.10.16 (age 28) [CONTAY]

A CANADIAN HERO.
Private Joseph Aitchison, 38th BCI, 11.4.17 (age 18) [BRUAY]

A TORONTO BOY. OUR ONLY SON. HE LOVED PEACE. FOR CANADA HE SERVED.
Sergeant George Frederick Stone Hayden, CFA, 17.7.17 (age 26) [BOULOGNE EASTERN]

HE FOUGHT THE FOES OF CANADA AND DIED ON A BATTLE-FIELD.
Private William Henry Hill, 8th BCI, 15.8.17 (age 27) [RUE-PETILLON]

ONE OF THOSE WHO DIED FOR CANADA.
Private Lionel Arthur McIntosh, 19th BCI, 25.4.18 (age 19) [DOULLENS]

TOMORROW WILL BE CANADA'S DAY.
Lieutenant Colonel Elmer Watson Jones DSO & BAR, 21st BCI, 8.8.18 (age 44)
[LONGUEAU]

The first Canadians killed in action in the Great War died in the Ypres Salient near Ploegsteert Wood in January 1915, the last outside Mons minutes before the Armistice took effect. While the passage of time has lent perspective to the war, it has also distorted the significance and purpose of the conflict as contemporaries understood it. The Great War is not remembered today as a war of liberation or national survival, nor the triumphant Allied soldiers as liberators, in the way that the Second World War is remembered as a struggle to rescue the populations of occupied Europe; but for the people of Belgium and northeastern France, subjected to four years of occupation and exploitation unrelenting to the very end, the Allied victory of 1918 secured their release from the grip of a foreign invader. In the case of Belgium, not only had the Germans violated its neutrality and taken ninety per cent of its territory, they had also in their outrage at the Belgians' temerity to resist their advance in 1914 planned to annex the country and turn it into a Germanised province—a very real possibility well into 1918. The Canadians who entered Mons on the last day of the war were greeted as liberators by a populace whose enthusiastic reception prefigured the reactions of the French and Belgians to a second liberation in 1944.

**ALSO 2/LT. K.D. MURRAY 9/EAST SURREYS. THEY DIED FIGHTING
FOR GOD & RIGHT & LIBERTY.**
Sergeant Christopher Desmond Murray, 49th BCI, 30.10.17 (age 28)
[PASSCHENDAELE NEW BRITISH]

**IN FLANDERS NOBLY HE DIED BY THE PATH OF DUTY
THAT WE MIGHT ALL LIVE IN FREEDOM.**
Private Adelburt Samuel Green, 75th BCI, 23.1.18 (age 18) [VILLERS STATION]

GREATER LOVE HATH NO MAN THAN THIS, HE DIED FOR PEACE AND LIBERTY.
Corporal Frederick Ward, AR, 14.9.44 (age 37)

**BLESS, O LORD, OUR DEAR SON. "MAY BELGIAN SOIL BE UNTO THEE
AS THAT OF THY NATIVE LAND."**
Private John Richinski, HLIC, 9.10.44 (age 22)

HERE LIES A GOOD SON AND A GOOD CANADIAN.
Signalman George Seery, RCCS, 2.2.45 (age 23) [SCHOONSELHOF]

The war cemeteries bearing the dates 1939–1945 depart from their 1914–1918 models in tell-tale ways. None retains the colourful toponymy of the Great War burial grounds. The armies were not in one place long enough to bestow lasting nicknames on this or that feature, and for easy access the cemeteries of the second war were laid out along good roads and named after the closest settlement. For Canadians, and no doubt for the peoples of the other dominions, the cemeteries mark a further stage in their evolution as fully fledged countries. While the inscriptions on Canadian headstones still show Canada's attachment to Great Britain, very few note birthplaces in the British Isles. Though professions of loyalty to England or the Empire still occur, they run a poor second to those proclaiming allegiance to Canada. Ancestral ties are mentioned, but affection towards the Mother Country now seems more acquired than innate. Many epitaphs allude to the wives and children left behind in Britain when Canadian servicemen went into action after years of training and waiting. The long Canadian sojourn in Britain also bred warm feelings towards England and her people:

OUT OF THE STRESS OF THE DOING INTO THE PEACE OF THE DONE. HE DIED FOR ENGLAND.
Lieutenant John William Mallison, RCA, *21.12.43 (age 34)* [MORO RIVER]

HE RESTS IN A CORNER OF A FOREIGN FIELD THAT IS FOREVER ENGLAND.
Lance Corporal Leonard James Higgins, CPC, *5.12.43 (age 35)* [MORO RIVER]

HE LAID DOWN HIS LIFE FOR CANADA AND THE EMPIRE.
Trooper Douglas Milton Rexford, 14th CH, 15.12.41 (age 20) [BROOKWOOD]

MY DARLING SON WHO THOUGHT IT THE HIGHEST HONOR AND GLORY TO DIE FOR HIS GOD, KING AND COUNTRY.
Corporal Robert Clive Daly, RCR, *7.10.43 (age 21)* [BARI]

BORN AT ST. JOHN, NEW BRUNSWICK, CANADA. "BREATHE GENTLY ON HIM, ENGLAND. IT WAS FOR YOU HE STAYED."
Sergeant Richard Woffendale Lawton, RCAF, *17.12.42 (age 24)* [SILLOTH (CAUSEWAY)]

BREATHE GENTLY ON HIM, ENGLAND, IT WAS FOR YOU HE DIED.
Craftsman Robert McKenzie Gray, CRCEME, *21.7.44 (age 21)* [BROOKWOOD]

BURIED IN THE SOIL OF HIS ANCESTORS.
Private Sinclair Shalto Shatford, RCASC, *15.2.43* [BROOKWOOD]

OUR DEARLY BELOVED SON LIES FAR FROM HOME IN THE LAND HE LEARNED TO LOVE.
Pilot Officer Donald Kenneth Irvine MacNicol, RCAF, *10.10.44 (age 20)* [BROOKWOOD]

MAY HE REST IN PEACE IN THE LAND HE LOVED AND GAVE HIS LIFE FOR.
Gunner Harold Smith, RCA, *12.1.45 (age 40)* [BROOKWOOD]

Among the Canadians buried at Brookwood are two aboriginal soldiers whose epitaphs movingly record their fidelity to a distant sovereign:

DIED IN THE SERVICE OF "THE GREAT WHITE FATHER."
Private Teddy Manywounds, RCASC, *19.2.42* [BROOKWOOD]

BORN AT SIX NATION, INDIAN RESERVE, OHSWEKEN, ONT. CANADA. DIED ON HIS MAJESTY'S SERVICE.
Private David Elliot John, RCOC, *1.10.44 (age 31)* [BROOKWOOD]

The Canadians who assisted in the second liberation of Belgium during the autumn of 1944 did not have to fight the static, attritional battles that had consumed so many of their countrymen in Flanders a generation earlier. Nevertheless, the fighting along the Leopold Canal, followed by the battles in the Breskens Pocket and the clearing of the Scheldt estuary, involved the Canadian army in some of the hardest struggles of the victory campaign. Some of the Canadians who died freeing the port of Antwerp for Allied supply ships lie at rest beside their predecessors of the Great War in Brussels Town Cemetery and in Antwerp's Schoonselhof Cemetery, but the majority are buried in the Canadian war cemetery near Adegem. If their efforts and sacrifice often go unrecognised in accounts of the Allied campaign, the compensating gratitude of the inhabitants of west Flanders to the soldiers of First Canadian Army is recorded in the monuments put up by the locals in the surrounding towns and villages. The most impressive tribute is in Maldegem where at his own expense a private citizen established a museum dedicated to the Canadians whose arrival saved his father from arrest and certain death at the hands of the Gestapo.

DULCE ET DECORUM EST PRO PATRIA MORI.
Lance Corporal Omer Dubois, 22nd (FC)B, *20.2.16 (age 22)* [LA LAITERIE]

A GLORIOUS DEATH IS HIS WHO FOR HIS COUNTRY FALLS.
Private William Leonard Cousineau, ESR, *16.10.44 (age 23)* [BRUSSELS TOWN]

DULCE ET DECORUM EST PRO PATRIA MORI.
Gunner Roy William Leighton, RCA, *11.10.44 (age 28)*

HE GAVE HIS LIFE THAT OTHERS MIGHT LIVE IN PEACE. WHAT MORE HAS MAN TO GIVE?
Sergeant Alexander Clark, CSR, *27.10.44 (age 28)*

A BELOVED HUSBAND WHO WAS KILLED IN ACTION. SADLY MISSED BY WIFE AND DAUGHTER.
Rifleman James Hector Munn, RRR, *30.10.44 (age 28)*

IN FONDEST MEMORY OF MY HUSBAND WHO DIED IN BATTLE SO WE MAY LIVE IN PEACE.
Private Herman Henry Bendig, LWR, *16.9.44 (age 26)*

TO OUR SLEEPING SON. AS A HUSBAND, FATHER, SOLDIER, YOUR DUTY YOU FULFILLED.
Private Leonard Harold Saville, LWR, *4.10.44 (age 36)*

YOU CHOSE THE BEST. YOU SPRANG TO DUTY'S CALL, YOU BRAVELY STOOD THE TEST.
Private Gerald Leroy Nowe, NS(NB)R, *13.10.44 (age 23)*

IN LOVING MEMORY OF A PRECIOUS ONLY SON AND DEAR BROTHER. A LOYAL CANADIAN.
Lieutenant Charles Alfred Channell, RRC, *13.9.44 (age 29)*

TO SEE YOUR FACE, HOLD YOUR HANDS AND WHISPER, WE LOVE YOU.
WIFE, DAUGHTER AND SON
Trooper Francis Ross McKee, SAR, *19.9.44 (age 27)*

SACRED TO THE MEMORY OF CAMERON. FOR GOD, LOVED ONES AND COUNTRY HE GAVE ALL.
Lieutenant Cameron Collin Williams, RRR, *2.11.44 (age 24)*

A GOOD CATHOLIC, A BRAVE SOLDIER, AN HONOURABLE DEATH.
Lieutenant Kenneth George Muller, RRC, *3.10.44 (age 24)* [SCHOONSELHOF]

I GLADLY GAVE MY SON BECAUSE MY COUNTRY I LOVED.
Corporal George John Fletcher, BWC, *21.8.44 (age 28)* [BRETTEVILLE-SUR-LAIZE]

BELOVED SON OF LEO AND EMMA BOPPRE, WATERLOO, ONTARIO, CANADA.
"TO DIE WAS AN HONOR."
Sergeant Gerald Martin Boppre, AR, *21.11.44 (age 24)* [GROESBEEK]

Canadian toponyms on Great War cemeteries.

Quiet but firm patriotic sentiments on a British grave at the Sangro River War Cemetery, Italy.

(top) *South African patriotism on the grave of a young soldier buried at Castiglione War Cemetery, Italy.*

(bottom) *"He took his tank forward to help his comrades in trouble." Devotion to comrades on a British grave at Gradara.*

HE EVADED NOT CANADA'S CALL. HE FOUGHT AND DIED, GAVE HIS ALL FOR CANADA.
Trooper Frederick Ware, NBR, *10.12.43 (age 23)* [MORO RIVER]

THEIR HOPES AND DREAMS OF THE FUTURE WAS THE PRICE THEY PAID AS CANADIANS.
Corporal Douglas Walker Vollett, ASHC, *23.10.44 (age 21)* [BERGEN-OP-ZOOM]
Private Frederick Leslie Vollett, ASHC, *11.3.45 (age 21)* [GROESBEEK]

O CANADA, WE STAND ON GUARD FOR THEE.
Private William Arthur Boate, SDGH, *29.12.44 (age 25)* [GROESBEEK]

The soldiers who fought for Canada in the Second World War were the products of a society that deplored war—and knew its cost—as much as our own. Yet they also came from a society that believed that certain things were worth defending. The notion that it is sweet and proper to die for one's country, the quotation drawn from the Roman poet Horace that most today read through the lens of Wilfred Owen's indictment of "the old lie," *Dulce et decorum est,* is yet another of the Great War testaments to the fallen that seemed equally appropriate to the generation that went through the Second World War. It captures the ideals of duty and service to one's country that subjects of the British Empire were once taught to admire as the mainstay of the Roman Empire and an ideal to which they should aspire when their country called. As an epitaph Horace's maxim will in most cases say more about the values and ideals of his society than it does about the soldier's own outlook. On the headstones of Canadian soldiers and airmen who volunteered for overseas service when they were free to remain in home defence the commendation of their sacrifice should not be dismissed too quickly by a later generation wary of patriotic appeals and military involvements. Even if the risk of death in battle was intermittent, the men and women who went overseas were prepared to accept long, indefinite absences from their homes and families, and to interrupt the course of their own lives for a cause which they, in differing degrees and for varying reasons, saw as right. One of the myths about the Second World War holds that most Canadians enlisted to escape unemployment, when in fact eight out of ten who enlisted in the first three years of the war left jobs or occupations to sign up. Nor were the remainder all men in search of steady wages, since this group includes students who enlisted upon leaving school or those not yet ready to seek full employment. This is not to say that their motives were entirely idealistic, but neither were they unconsidered or desperate. There were men for whom the dictates of conscience, or the fundamental belief that Nazi Germany and its allies threatened their world or way of life, played a part in their decision to take up arms. Simple but firm statements on the headstones show the depth of these convictions:

A DUTY BRAVELY DONE AND APPRECIATED BY ALL LOVERS OF CHRISTIAN LIBERTY.
Sapper Robert Fisher, CRCE, *6.10.44 (age 23)*

"MAY MY LOVED ONES NOT PERISH."
Flight Lieutenant Vanegmond Robert Bell, RCAF, *6.3.45 (age 26)*

I THOUGHT IT WAS THE RIGHT THING TO DO.
Private Edward Andrew French, WR, *24.9.44 (age 25)* [CESENA]

"THERE IS A WAY WHICH SEEMETH RIGHT UNTO A MAN."
Sapper Harry Frederick Kean, CRCE, *24.4.45 (age 39)* [GROESBEEK] [PROVERBS 14: 2]

FOR I WAS BORN IN CANADA.
Flight Sergeant Frederick John Simpson, RCAF, 28.4.45 (age 21) [BROOKWOOD]

HE LOVED HIS COUNTRY.
Major Eric Albert Willis, RCAMC, 3.3.45 (age 28) [GROESBEEK]

A CANADIAN BORN AND BRED WHO DIED IN THE CAUSE OF FREEDOM.
WIFE, PARENTS & FAMILY.
Flying Officer Sydney Emmington Fern Higgs Smith, RCAF, 21.7.44 (age 31)
[WEVELGEM]

LIBERTY. I HAVE FOUGHT FOR IT. MAY GOD BLESS MY BELOVED CANADA.
Trooper Frank MacIlwraith, 4th PLDG, 20.9.43 (age 22) [BARI]

MORE THAN SELF HIS COUNTRY LOVED, MERCY MORE THAN LIFE. "OUR BEST PAL."
Sergeant Gordon Basil Heathfield, RCA, 24.9.44 (age 27) [CESENA]

Patriotic sentiments or assertions of loyalty to one's country are to be expected in war cemeteries. What sets many of them apart are the ingredients of patriotism and loyalty which they display. In some cases the epitaphs assert the ideals or values which the country represented, or state the principles which the soldier's family felt had factored in his choice to enlist; in others, the closer allegiances, to family and church, regiment and comrades, that impelled men to do their duty despite inclinations to the contrary, appear singly or collectively:

FOR GOD AND CANADA AND THE FREEDOM OF CANADIAN LIBERTY.
Private Alban Joseph Babineau, CSR, 7.10.44 (age 22)

"TOUT POUR LA GLOIRE DE DIEU, LE TRIOMPHE DE L'EGLISE, L'HONNEUR DE MA FAMILLE."
(All for the glory of God, the triumph of the Church, the honour of my family.)
Lance Sergeant Rosaire Lapointe, FMR, 9.9.44 (age 23)

"GREATER LOVE THAN THIS NO MAN HATH." CARITAS CHRISTI URGET NOS. R.I.P.
(The love of Christ constraineth us.)
The Reverend Thomas Edmund Mooney, CCS, 14.9.44 (age 38)
[JOHN 15: 13; II CORINTHIANS 5: 14]

RAYMOND WAS A ROMAN CATHOLIC.
Private Raymond Francis Benere, AR, 10.10.44

LATE OF THE LOYAL EDMONTON REGIMENT. "REST IN PEACE."
Corporal Robert Wilson Ellenwood MM, AR, 14.9.44 (age 42)

The elements of loyalty that the epitaphs combine to lay out resemble the threefold quality of *pietas* prized by the Romans. Devotion to the gods, to family, and to country gave one a moral anchor in a troubled world, keeping emotions and reactions in check, and undergirding the sense of duty when confronted by hard choices. The epitaphs at Adegem introduce similar declarations found in other war cemeteries that emphasize the soldier's service to one or all of these objects of loyalty. God, family, and native land figure in English Canadian epitaphs but are more often the core loyalties among staunchly Catholic French Canadians:

HIS ALL FOR GOD, HIS HOME AND CANADA.
Flight Sergeant James Allan Pirie, RCAF, 30.5.43 (age 22) [REICHSWALD FOREST]

I HAVE FOUGHT FOR GOD, FOR CANADA, AND FOR YOU, DEAR PARENTS. PRAY FOR ME.
Private Jean Paul Doiron, FMR, 23.8.44 (age 23) [BRETTEVILLE-SUR-LAIZE]
Private Romeo Hébert, CYR, 25.11.43 (age 23) [MORO RIVER]

THAT MAN IS GREAT WHO TRULY SERVES HIS GOD, HIS HOME, HIS NATION.
Lance Corporal Joseph Irwin Murray, CRCE, 24.10.43 [BARI]

I GAVE MY LIFE FOR MY GOD AND FOR MY COUNTRY.
Rifleman Samuel Joseph Gagné, QORC, 7.12.44 (age 25) [GROESBEEK]

HIS GOD, KING AND COUNTRY, HIS FAMILY AND NEIGHBOURS. HE LOVED THEM ALL AND DIED FOR THEM ALL.
Private Neil La Franier, HPER, 13.12.43 [MORO RIVER]

A SOLDIER WHO BRAVELY DIED FOR HIS LOVING WIFE ANNE AND SON HAROLD. BYNG INLET, ONTARIO, CANADA.
Private Leo Durocher, IRC, 29.9.44 (age 36) [CESENA]

A CEUX QUE JE NE DOIS PLUS REVOIR DITES BIEN QUE J'AI FAIT MON DEVOIR. ADIEU
(To those I am to see no more, be sure to say that I did my duty. Farewell.)
Private Roland Lavallée, RM, 13.8.44 (age 24) [BRETTEVILLE-SUR-LAIZE]

HE GAVE HIS LIFE FOR MAPLE CREEK, CANADA. GOD GIVE HIM REST.
Trooper Howard Kenneth White, CR, 10.12.43 [MORO RIVER]

FOUGHT AND DIED FOR JUDIQUE, THE LAND OF MY BIRTH.
Private Alexander Donald MacIsaac, ASHC, 19.8.44 (age 33) [BÉNY-SUR-MER]

Added to the mix was the pride in regiment that runs as a leitmotiv through the memoirs of Canadian soldiers. Many of the epitaphs noting the soldier's home town point to the close regional connections of the Permanent Force and militia units that made up Canada's army overseas. The deep loyalty that soldiers felt towards their regiment and its traditions is evident in the inscriptions consisting solely of the regimental motto—a practice much in evidence on the gravestones of Toronto's 48th Highlanders, particularly in the Canadian plot at Cesena. To be noted in all but one of the epitaphs below is the family's insistence on recording the soldier's "true" regiment:

FORMERLY OF THE ROYAL REGIMENT OF CANADA. SON OF JOHN AND ANNIE CHASE, PETERBOROUGH, ONTARIO, CANADA.
Lieutenant John Earle Chase, 48th HC, 1.8.43 (age 29) [AGIRA]

COMMISSIONED IN THE R.C.R. 24TH JULY 1940. TO P.P.C.L.I. 12TH DECEMBER 1943, TWO DAYS BEFORE HIS DEATH.
Captain John Blair Hunt, RCIC, 14.12.43 [MORO RIVER]

ORIGINALLY WITH HIGHLAND LIGHT INFANTRY. OF GALT, CANADA.
Captain Alexander Stewart, SDGH, 8.6.44 (age 35) [BAYEUX]

ROYAL MILITARY COLLEGE. ROYAL CANADIAN DRAGOONS. TRUTH, DUTY, VALOR.
Lieutenant Edward Samuel Stokes, RCD, 3.9.44 (age 23) [GRADARA]

"JAKEY" SERVED FOR THIRTEEN YEARS IN THE WESTMINSTER REGT.
Major John West Hughes, LRSR, 3.9.44 (age 28) [GRADARA]

FORMERLY SEAFORTH HIGHLANDERS OF CANADA. "TO US, HE IS LIVING YET."
Private Robert Butler, ESR, 26.5.45 (age 20) [HOLTEN]

Pride in regiment was matched by the pride of the various corps working alongside the infantry. The headstones of tank crewmen often cite the motto of the Royal Canadian Armoured Corps, those of gunners the motto of the Royal Canadian Artillery:

THROUGH MUD AND BLOOD TO GREEN FIELDS BEYOND.
Trooper Cameron Raymond Taite, TRR, 6.10.43 (age 18) [MORO RIVER]

BELOVED SON OF JOHN AND EDITH G. FIRTH. "TO GREEN FIELDS BEYOND." AMEN
Guardsman Richard Stanley Firth, CGG, 21.8.44 (age 22) [BRETTEVILLE-SUR-LAIZE]

UBIQUE QUO FAS ET GLORIA DUCUNT.
Lieutenant Reginald Donald Barker, RCA, 8.6.44 (age 36) [BÉNY-SUR-MER]

EVERYWHERE WHERE FAITH AND GLORY LEAD.
Lieutenant Alvin John Greenly, RCA, 14.10.44 (age 29) [GROESBEEK]

WHITHER RIGHT AND GLORY LEAD.
Captain Frederick William Drewry MC, RCA, 7.12.44 (age 23) [CORIANO RIDGE]

The inscription most often found on the graves of Canadian soldiers of either war comes from John 15: 13, "Greater love hath no man. . .," the words spoken by Jesus to the disciples as he bade farewell to them in contemplation of his impending death. The epitaphs usually follow through to the Scriptural conclusion "that a man lay down his life for his friends," but families often substituted other beneficiaries of the soldier's sacrifice, "for his country," "for his own," "for the cause," "for his friends and homeland," "for peace and liberty," "for his King and country," or even "for all of us." The widespread use of this citation is in keeping with the consoling image of the fallen soldier as the true follower of Christ—no greater proof of love and loyalty could there be than the willing offering of one's life for others, to die a death which, like Christ's, was painful and lonely, as much on behalf of a tormented, heedless world as it was for the soldier's friends and kin. The words could be applied broadly to all soldiers who fell for their country, and their recurrence gives them a generic character which can sometimes blind us to the fact that in some cases they were quite literally true. The Reverend Kenelm Edwin Eaton, buried on the threshold of the Gothic Line at Montecchio, stepped on a mine as he went to the aid of a wounded soldier; the Reverend Walter Leslie Brown, buried at Bény-sur-Mer, was out searching for the wounded when he was captured and subsequently murdered by troops of the 12th SS Panzer Division. A grave in Heverlee war cemetery bearing the Victoria Cross belongs to a British pilot who steadied his damaged plane so that his crew could bail out; and the Canadian plot in Brookwood contains the grave of Sergeant John Rennie who won a posthumous George Cross for attempting to fling a hand grenade, dropped during a training exercise, out of harm's way. All their headstones carry the citation from John, but a number of inscriptions refer directly to the act of self-sacrifice that cost the soldier his life. The first commemorates a British officer, the rest Canadian servicemen who gave their lives for others. Their epitaphs serve as a reminder that five of Canada's Victoria Cross winners received the Empire's highest decoration for service to their comrades—Topham for tending the wounded under fire, Foote for going into captivity with the men in his care, Osborne for falling on a grenade, Hornell for ceding his place in a lifeboat, and Mynarski for trying to rescue a trapped air gunner as their plane fell from the sky:

KILLED IN ACTION RESCUING HIS MEN FROM A BURNING TRUCK.
"GREATER LOVE HATH NO MAN."
Major Charles Vere Broke, RA, 6.8.44 (age 32) [BROUAY]

HE STAYED WITH HIS SHIP, SAVED HIS CREW, AND A VILLAGE.
WE ARE JUSTLY PROUD.
Flying Officer Martin Stewart Little, RCAF, 25.3.44 (age 23) [BROOKWOOD]

HE FELL IN ATTEMPTING TO RESCUE HIS COMRADE. FAITHFUL WARRIOR, WELL DONE.
Lance Corporal Wesley Arthur Roger Traill, SSR, 25.9.44 (age 20) [SCHOONSELHOF]

YOU SAVED A BUDDY BY GOING UNDER FIRE AND NO OTHER FAME COULD A HERO DESIRE.
Private Donald John MacKinnon, NNSH, 25.3.45 [GROESBEEK]

OUR DARLING SON AND BROTHER WHO LOST HIS LIFE TRYING TO SAVE HIS COMRADE.
Sergeant John Charles Forward, RRR, 30.3.45 (age 23) [GROESBEEK]

The epitaphs commemorating the serviceman's fidelity to his country, principles, family, and comrades are inscribed on the headstones of soldiers who were not just faceless pawns on a tactical chessboard, but ordinary young men wrenched from their lives at home and inserted into the alien, lethal world of war. The beliefs and values they had acquired at home, in church, in their communities had to be adapted to the cruel realities of war. While patriotism or abstract loyalties may have played a part in their decision to enlist, battle called upon the deepest reserves of moral strength. This entry in the North Shore Regiment's war diary, written by one of the company commanders who took part in the gruelling assault on the town of Carpiquet in July 1944, identifies the sources of courage that kept soldiers going in the worst moments:

> *I am sure that at some time during the attack every man felt he could not go on. Men were being killed or wounded on all sides and the advance seemed pointless as well as hopeless. I never realised until the attack on Carpiquet how far discipline, pride of unit, and above all, pride in oneself and family, can carry a man even when each step forward meant possible death.*

The epitaphs dwelling on the themes of loyalty and devotion to duty touch on the question of the soldier's motivation in battle. Ever since John Keegan's *The Face of Battle* put the study of military history on a new footing, historians have paid greater attention to the conduct and morale of soldiers on the battlefield, and the reasons why they confront the perils of combat. Keegan himself has noted that many soldiers, especially those conscripted into military service and subject to harsh disciplinary measures, have had little choice in the matter, or have been allowed to suppress their fears with alcohol or drugs; but more positively (and with greater relevance to a volunteer army filled by the country's citizens), soldiers wished to maintain their reputation among their comrades, friends, and family, even if it involved masking their fears. Conscience, the awareness that others were depending on them, also stood between a soldier's performance or dereliction of his duty. *He loved honour more than he feared death* is a common refrain in the epitaphs, as is *He had not loved us half as much had he not loved honour more*—their repetition should not obscure the important truth they contain. The first inscription below offers the highest praise soldiers could bestow; the second speaks for the dedication and courage shown by the officers who directed the fighting at close quarters. The third will be familiar to readers of Farley Mowat's *And No Birds Sang*. Alex Campbell strides through Mowat's narrative like "the big man" described by Keegan, a soldier whose lust for battle and force of personality exerted a powerful influence over the men around him. Yet the strain of combat told on him as well, so much so that during the fighting at Ortona he composed a poem in the form of a prayer asking God to help him conceal his fear as he led his men into battle:

RED WAS AN OUTSTANDING SOLDIER, RESPECTED, ADMIRED AND LIKED BY ALL.
MAY HIS REST BE PEACEFUL.
Sergeant Wallace Patrick Ducharme, HPER, 13.10.44 (age 22) [CESENA]

TO SAVE HIS MEN HE FACED DEATH UNAFRAID. MAY WE SO FACE THE EMPTY DAYS AHEAD.
Lieutenant Frederick Ernest Mullins, BWC, 29.9.44 (age 22) [BERGEN-OP-ZOOM]

HELP ME TO LEAD THEM IN THE FIGHT SO THEY WILL SAY HE WAS A MAN.
"PRAYER BEFORE BATTLE." A.R.C.
Major Alexander Railton Campbell, HPER, 25.12.43 (age 33) [MORO RIVER]

If the epitaphs are taken as a cross-section of the values and ideals esteemed by Canadians over sixty years ago, loyalty would rank close to the top. Loyalty to Britain guided Canada's decision to go to war; loyalty to Canada and what it stood for led Canadians to make a contribution to the Allied war effort out of all proportion to the country's population and place alongside the major powers. On the most fundamental level, loyalty to friends and comrades braced the morale and endurance of soldiers in battle, occasionally manifesting itself in exceptional acts of self-sacrifice or feats of arms, but for the most part enabling men to do their duty. Where some epitaphs speak of the heroism of a few, these last examples from Adegem speak for the unrecognised but necessary toil of the many:

JUST ANOTHER GOOD SOLDIER AND SON. MOM AND DAD
Corporal Joseph Pallister, CSR, 6.10.44 (age 21)

A FALLEN BUT NOT FORGOTTEN SOLDIER WHO HAS DONE HIS DUTY TO HIS COUNTRY.
Private James Alexander Armitage, LWR, 23.9.44 (age 20)

FURTHER READING:

Copp, Terry. *Fields of Fire: The Canadians in Normandy*. Toronto: University of Toronto Press, 2003.

Copp, Terry, and McAndrew, William. *Battle Exhaustion: Soldiers and Psychiatrists in the Canadian Army, 1939–1945*. Montreal: McGill-Queen's University Press, 1990.

Keegan, John. *The Face of Battle*. Harmondsworth: Penguin Books, 1978.

Winter, Denis. *Death's Men. Soldiers of the Great War*. Harmondsworth: Penguin Books, 1978.

Steve Douglas

CHAPTER SEVEN

"Into the mosaic of victory. . ."

The foregoing chapters have considered the sources of inspiration and principal themes in the epitaphs. It is time now to let them speak for themselves. This chapter consists simply of a list of inscriptions, given in chronological order, that might best be said to replicate a visit to any given war cemetery. Just as visitors meander through the rows of headstones, noting details in passing and occasionally pausing before those of particular interest, so here may readers browse through the valedictions at their leisure. Some will speak more affectingly to parents, others to wives, and even children, who will be attuned to the sorrow of their counterparts two generations ago. All will speak to Canadians, no matter their knowledge of the war, for the expressions of loss and consolation are universal; moreover, even if few today can put a face to the name of a fallen soldier, these men were ours, and their service to Canada is no less deserving of our gratitude and respect today than it was to the generation they served in its time of need.

IN LOVING MEMORY. LOST HIS LIFE IN THE VOLUNTARY DEFENCE OF HIS COUNTRY.
Lieutenant Leslie Ambrose Wheeler, CYR, 16.8.40 *(age 23)* [BROOKWOOD]

THE SOULS OF THE RIGHTEOUS ARE IN THE HANDS OF GOD,
AND NO TORMENT SHALL TOUCH THEM.
Pilot Officer Donald Eglinton Stewart (of Canada), RAF, 11.9.40 *(age 27)* [BECKLINGEN]

I AM GLAD IT IS MORNING, I AM COMING HOME TODAY.
Private John Henry, RCOC, 20.9.40 [BROOKWOOD]

GOD'S STRONG ARMS ARE ALL AROUND YOU. IN THE DARK HE SOUGHT AND FOUND YOU.
Signalman James Downs Doherty, RCCS, 28.9.40 *(age 28)* [BROOKWOOD]

"TIS BUT THE CASKET THAT LIES HERE, THE GEM THAT FILLED IT SPARKLES YET."
Lance Corporal John Ralph Murphy, CPC, 12.10.40 *(age 26)* [BROOKWOOD]

MOTHER DIED 1941. DAD DIED 1923.
Private John Melnyk, 48th HC, 16.2.41 *(age 26)* [BROOKWOOD]

IN LOVING MEMORY OF IAN. "WE WERE YOUNG, WE HAVE DIED: REMEMBER US."
Signalman Ian Hamilton Ferguson, RCCS, 21.2.41 (age 17) [BROOKWOOD]

"FAME IS THE SPUR."
Pilot Officer Huntley Donald Brander, RCAF, 30.6.41 (age 25) [BECKLINGEN]

WE THANK THEE, O LORD, FOR THE HONOR OF BEING MOTHER AND FATHER OF LORNE.
Pilot Officer Lorne Smith Christman, RCAF, 5.7.41 (age 24) [REICHSWALD FOREST]

"THE FRONTIERS OF THE DAWNING ARE YOURS TO GLIMPSE, FULFILMENT YOURS TO KNOW."
Major Sunley Gordon Hayward Steele MC, 9.7.41 (age 46) [BROOKWOOD]

DEAR GOD, THROUGH BOYHOOD TO MANHOOD WE BLESS THE YEARS WE CALLED HIM OURS.
Sergeant Harvey Lewis Crich, RCAF, 19.8.41 (age 22) [HEVERLEE]

"AS IN ADAM ALL DIE, EVEN SO IN CHRIST SHALL ALL BE MADE ALIVE."
I CORINTHIANS XV. 22
Flight Sergeant Jack Marshall Boyd, RCAF, 31.10.41 (age 25) [KIEL]

WAIT FOR ME, SAITH JEHOVAH, UNTIL THE DAY THAT I RISE UP TO THE PREY. ZEP. III. 8
Rifleman Leslie Revelle Hopgood, RRfC, 19.12.41 (age 19) [SAI WAN]

BROTHER OF LIEUTENANT L.W. MITCHELL, KILLED IN SAME ACTION. IN THEIR DEATH,
THEY WERE NOT DIVIDED.
Lieutenant Eric Lawson Mitchell, WG, 20.12.41 (age 23) [SAI WAN]

HE DIED THE NOBLEST DEATH A MAN COULD DIE, FIGHTING FOR GOD, RIGHTS, AND LIBERTY.
Sergeant Edward Herbert Rodgers, WG, 21.12.41 (age 30) [SAI WAN]

"I PRAY THEE, THEN, WRITE ME AS ONE THAT LOVES HIS FELLOW MEN." LEIGH HUNT
Captain Morgan Charles Hawkins, CADC, 8.2.42 (age 27) [BROOKWOOD]

"AND I GIVE UNTO THEM ETERNAL LIFE: AND THEY SHALL NEVER PERISH."
Pilot Officer William Forsythe Munn, RCAF, 25.4.42 (age 27) [ABBEVILLE]

SUCH A HAPPY, GOOD BOY, MISSED BY ALL WHO KNEW HIM. WAS HIS LIFE GIVEN IN VAIN?
Flight Sergeant Alfred Ernest McCoy, RCAF, 9.5.42 (age 21) [BERLIN]

"FOR THE SPLENDOUR OF A SINGLE THOUGHT."
Pilot Officer Samuel Richard Balden, RCAF, 15.5.42 (age 30) [SAGE]

"I WILL LIFT UP MY EYES UNTO THE HILLS FROM WHENCE COMETH MY HELP."
PSALM CXXI. 1
Pilot Officer Ralph Connors O'Brien, RCAF, 31.5.42 (age 24) [REICHSWALD FOREST]

GOD BLESS THOSE WHO HAVE DIED FOR US.
Flight Sergeant Allan Dease Robert, RCAF, 5.6.42 (age 23) [AMERSFOORT (OUD LEUSDEN)]
Corporal Warren Arless Robert, RCAF, 14.1.43 (age 22) [MONTREAL (MOUNT ROYAL)]

"O LOVE THAT WILT NOT LET ME GO, I REST MY WEARY SOUL IN THEE."
Flight Sergeant Milton Argue Fawcett, RCAF, 8.6.42 (age 23)
[AMERSFOORT (OUD LEUSDEN)]

A PAGE IN MY BOOK OF MEMORIES IS GENTLY TURNED TODAY. NORMAN JR.
Flight Sergeant Ernest Norman Jefferies, RCAF, 9.6.42 (age 28) [RHEINBERG]

GLORY DWELLETH IN EMMANUEL'S LAND.
Flying Officer William Donald McCulloch, RCAF, 23.6.42 (age 22) [SAGE]

GO WITH GOD.
Flight Sergeant Frederick Francis Duff, RCAF, 26.6.42 (age 20) [BECKLINGEN]

PSALM 23. HIS FAITH AND COURAGE NEVER FAILED.
Pilot Officer William James Ruddy, RCAF, 28.6.42 (age 25) [BECKLINGEN]

YOUR MEMORY HALLOWED IN THE LAND YOU LOVED, "CANADA."
Pilot Officer Robert Lorne Storey, RCAF, 4.7.42 (age 24) [ESBJERG]

"MASTER, THE TASK IS FINISHED; PAY WHAT WAGES THOU WILL."
Flight Sergeant George William Roney, RCAF, 22.7.42 (age 26) [EINDHOVEN (WOENSEL)]

A SON OF BRACEBRIDGE, ONTARIO. A COURAGEOUS ATHLETE WHO DIED FOR FREEDOM.
Pilot Officer Haddo Eric Von Bruce, RCAF, 26.7.42 (age 31) [UDEN]

"NIGHT SHALL FOLD HIM IN SOFT WINGS."
Pilot Officer Swante Oliver Hill, RCAF, 29.7.42 (age 21) [SAGE]

DO UNTO OTHERS AS YOU WOULD HAVE THEM DO UNTO YOU.
Flight Sergeant Rodney David Gibson, RCAF, 1.8.42 (AGE 23) [HEVERLEE]

"WHAT I DO THOU KNOWEST NOT NOW; BUT THOU SHALT KNOW HEREAFTER."
ST. JOHN XIII. 7
Private Albert George McKinley, RRC, 19.8.42 (age 29) [DUNKIRK]

MY SON! MY SON!
Warrant Officer II William Everett Lunan, RCAF, 12.8.42 (32) [SCHOONSELHOF]

HOW LOVED, HOW HONOURED ONCE AVAILS THEE NOT, TO WHOM RELATED,
OR BY WHOM BEGOT.
Warrant Officer Bernard Anthony Brophy, RCAF, 13.8.42 (age 32) [DURNBACH]

"THEY SHALL NEVER PERISH, NEITHER SHALL ANY MAN PLUCK THEM OUT OF MY HAND."
Sub Lieutenant Clifford Davidson Wallace, RCNVR, 18.8.42 (age 22) [DUNKIRK]

MENTIONED IN DESPATCHES, PUT TO DEATH BY THE ENEMY.
"HIS SPIRIT MUST BE OUR BANNER."
Sergeant John Oliver Payne, WG, 26.8.42 (age 23) [SAI WAN]
Lance Corporal George Berzenski, WG, 26.8.42 (age 26) [SAI WAN]
Private Percy John Ellis, WG, 26.8.42 (age 25) [SAI WAN]
Private John Henry Adams, WG, 26.8.42 (age 27) [SAI WAN]

ONE OF THOUSANDS WHO DID THEIR BEST FOR ALL THE PEOPLE IS NOW AT REST.
Sergeant Walter Alfred Hayes, RCAF, 29.8.42 (age 20) [BROOKWOOD]

"HE THAT OVERCOMETH SHALL INHERIT ALL THINGS; I WILL BE HIS GOD,
HE SHALL BE MY SON."
Warrant Officer II Rhys Hallam Morgan, RCAF, 2.9.42 (age 20) [ESBJERG]

THEY ARE NOT DEAD——THEIR HANDS CLASP YOURS AND MINE.
Pilot Officer Albert John Fawcett, RCAF, 16.9.42 (age 22) [EVESHAM]

"GIVE PEACE IN OUR TIME, O LORD."
Pilot Officer William Harry Donovan, RCAF, *20.9.42 (age 22)* [RHEINBERG]

WEEP NOT, MOTHER; HIS COUNTRY AT STRIFE, A SOLDIER WILLINGLY GIVES HIS LIFE.
Lance Sergeant Wesley James White, RCCS, *25.9.42* (AGE 22) [SAI WAN]

NOW THE LABOURER'S TASK IS OVER, THE BATTLE DAY IS PAST.
Rifleman William John Barclay, RRfC, *7.10.42 (age 20)* [SAI WAN]

**IT'S IN MY HEART TO SPUR ME ON, MY FAITH AND COURAGE TO RENEW
THE THOUGHT OF YOU.**
Corporal James McHaffie-Gow, CSR, *14.10.42 (age 28)* [BROOKWOOD]

HE RIDES ABOVE THE MOUNTAIN CREST WHERE SHADOWS FOLLOW TO THE WEST.
Flight Sergeant Arthur Geoffrey Lee, RCAF, *15.10.42 (age 28)* [BRUSSELS TOWN]

YOU'RE ONLY ONE OF MILLIONS. FOR MY GRIEF IS THIS RELIEF, I BORE A GALLANT SON.
Flying Officer Clifford Leonard Horncastle, RCAF, *3.11.42 (age 24)* [BROOKWOOD]

THEY NEVER DIE WHO, LIVING, GIVE UP LIFE THAT OTHERS MAY LIVE IN PEACE.
Flying Officer Harry Brooks, RCAF, *31.12.42* [SCOPWICK CHURCHYARD]

THE SHORT TIME SPENT WITH YOU, DARLING, WAS WONDERFUL. I WILL LOVE YOU ALWAYS.
Pilot Officer William Basil Cheale Thompson, RCAF, *1.1.43 (age 21)*
[SILLOTH (CAUSEWAYHEAD)]

O CANADA, WILT THOU DENY THE PRAYER OF THESE WHO DARED TO DIE?
Pilot Officer Gilbert Frederick Brown, RCAF, *28.1.43 (age 23)* [SCOPWICK CHURCHYARD]

**PEACE BE WITH THEE, SON OF MINE, AND IN HOURS OF SADNESS GREET US
AS A SPIRIT MAY.**
Private Ralph Townsend Smith, CFC, *8.2.43 (age 27)* [BROOKWOOD]

THEY HAVE WON TO LIFE UNDYING SINCE THEY DIED TO MAKE MEN FREE.
Flight Sergeant Ross Maddaugh Agnew, RCAF, *11.2.43 (age 34)* [SAGE]

"I WILL BE WITH THEE: I WILL NOT FAIL THEE, NOR FORSAKE THEE." JOSHUA I: 5
Warrant Officer II Percy Gordon Williams, RCAF, *25.2.43 (age 20)* [DURNBACH]

ONLY WHAT WAS OF EARTH RESTS HERE. HIS SPIRIT IS WITH GOD, FREE AND KINDLY.
Flight Sergeant Harold Roy Millson, RCAF, *3.3.43* [BECKLINGEN]

IN THAT GREAT CLOISTER'S STILLNESS, HE LIVES WHOM WE CALL DEAD.
Warrant Officer II Donald Cameron Plaunt, RCAF, *12.3.43 (age 20)*
[REICHSWALD FOREST]

**IN DREAMS WE SHALL ALWAYS SEE YOU, JIM, TRUE, KIND AND YOUNG.
MUM, DAD AND SISTERS**
Gunner James Alexander Webster, RCA, *28.3.43 (age 20)* [BROOKWOOD]

HE WAS THINE, NOT MINE. I THANK THEE FOR THY PRECIOUS LOAN.
Flying Officer George Floyd Mabee, RCAF, *30.3.43 (age 26)* [HANOVER]

BELOVED, IF GOD SO LOVED US, WE OUGHT ALSO TO LOVE ONE ANOTHER. I JOHN IV. 11
Flight Sergeant Allen Roderick Ross, RCAF, *17.4.43 (age 20)* [RHEINBERG]

"LO, I AM WITH YOU ALWAYS, EVEN UNTO THE END OF THE WORLD." ST. MATT. XXVIII. 20
Warrant Officer II Frederick Grant McCardle, RCAF, 17.4.43 (age 21) [DURNBACH]

"WHO ARE THESE LIKE STARS APPEARING, THESE BEFORE GOD'S THRONE WHO STAND?"
Flight Sergeant Ralph Edwin Powis, RCAF, 27.4.43 (age 20) [BARI]

IN MEMORY OF NORMAN FRANCIS, 18TH CANADIAN FORESTRY COY.
Private Norman Francis Meers, CFC, 29.4.43 (age 25) [BROOKWOOD]

TILL MORN AWAKES, YOUTH LONGS AND MANHOOD STRIVES, BUT AGE REMEMBERS.
Gunner James Henry Kinsella, RCA, 17.5.43 (age 21) [BROOKWOOD]

"NOT DISSATISFIED IF IT MADE THE WORLD A BETTER PLACE TO LIVE IN."
Warrant Officer II Charles Thomas Smith, RCAF, 26.5.43 (age 22) [RHEINBERG]

UNTIL THE DAY BREAK AND THE SHADOWS FLEE AWAY. SOLOMON II. 17
Flying Officer Henry Neville Petts, RCAF, 26.5.43 (age 25) [JONKERBOS]

OUR HEARTS, OUR HOPES, OUR PRAYERS, OUR TEARS, OUR FAITH TRIUMPHANT
O'ER ALL OUR FEARS, ARE ALL WITH THEE.
Flying Officer Graham Stanley Hynam, RCAF, 29.5.43 (age 22) [PERSHORE]

"BETTER IN DARKNESS JUST TO FEEL THY HAND, AND FOLLOW THEE."
Pilot Officer George Robert Densmore, RCAF, 12.6.43 (age 23) [EINDHOVEN (WOENSEL)]

THAT UNSELFISH LIFE, IT HAS NOT ENDED.
Pilot Officer Bernard Laird Tedford, RCAF, 13.6.43 (age 23) [TEXEL (DEN BURG)]

"HE HATH PREPARED FOR THEM A CITY." HEB. XI. 16
Flying Officer Douglas Stewart Milne, RCAF, 22.6.43 (age 28) [EINDHOVEN (WOENSEL)]

SOLA VIRTUS VERA NOBILITAS.
(Virtue is the only true nobility.)
Warrant Officer II Aymeric Essex Vidal, RCAF, 29.6.43 (age 33) [SCHOONSELHOF]

PRO ARIS ET FOCIS. "COME UNTO ME."
(For our altars and our hearths.)
Flying Officer Richard Michael Hastings Purdon, RCAF, 30.6.43 (age 21) [DUNKIRK]

"HE SHALL RISE UP AT THE VOICE OF THE BIRD AND ALL THE DAUGHTERS OF MUSIC
SHALL BE BROUGHT LOW."
Sapper Donald Lloyd McRae, CRCE, 18.7.43 (age 33) [BROOKWOOD]

HAPPILY I MET EACH DAY AND FEARED NOT DEATH, SO GRIEVE ME NOT,
FOR NOW I REST IN PEACE.
Flight Sergeant Dwain Nowell Hunter, RCAF, 30.7.43 [HAMBURG]

A TRUER FRIEND NO MAN EVER HAD. HE KEPT HIS FAITH AND NOW HE UNDERSTANDS.
Flight Sergeant Robert Alexander Leslie Scott, RCAF, 16.8.43 (age 34) [ST. DÉSIR]

O GIVE THANKS UNTO THE LORD, FOR HE IS GOOD; FOR HIS MERCY ENDURETH FOR EVER.
Flight Sergeant Raymond Arthur Kirk, RCAF, 24.8.43 (age 22) [SAGE]

WAITING ON JEHOVAH'S UNDESERVED KINDNESS FOR A HOPEFUL RESURRECTION.
Flight Sergeant Frederick George Painter, RCAF, 24.8.43 [BERLIN]

INTO THINE HAND I COMMIT MY SPIRIT, O LORD GOD. PSALM XXXI. 5
Pilot Officer Ernest Dean Cornelius, RCAF, 24.8.43 (age 25) [RHEINBERG]

BLOW, GOLDEN TRUMPETS, MOURNFULLY, FOR ALL THE GOLDEN YOUTH THAT'S FLED.
Flight Sergeant Martin Bailey, RCAF, 28.8.43 (age 27) [DURNBACH]

IN LOVING MEMORY OF ROBERT, KILLED ON ACTIVE SERVICE. GOD KEEPS FOREVER
THOSE WHO SERVE HIM.
Pilot Officer Robert Lloyd Henry, RCAF, 29.8.43 (age 23) [HARROGATE]

"O LORD OF HOSTS, BLESSED IS THE MAN THAT TRUSTETH IN THEE."
Flying Officer Iven Andrew Isfeld, RCAF, 31.8.43 (age 22) [REICHSWALD FOREST]

I WILL BE AS THE DEW UNTO ISRAEL: HE SHALL GROW AS THE LILY. HOSEA XIV. 5
Major Hugh Allen MacLean, CRCE, 1.9.43 (age 42) [BROOKWOOD]

SAY, WHY SHOULD FRIENDSHIP GRIEVE FOR THOSE WHO SAFE ARRIVE ON CANAAN'S SHORE?
Private George William Jacques, WNSR, 20.9.43 (age 19) [BARI]

SO THAT HE SEEMED NOT TO PASS OUT OF LIFE BUT OUT OF ONE HOME INTO ANOTHER.
Flying Officer William Norman Hamilton, RCAF, 27.9.43 (age 22) [HANOVER]

SICUT PATRIBUS SIT DEUS VOBIS. REQUIESCAT IN PACE.
MY HEART LIES HERE WITH YOU, SON. MOTHER
(God be with you as He was with your fathers. May he rest in peace.)
Private Frederick Douglas Goodchild, WNSR, 11.10.43 (age 23) [MORO RIVER]

"LORD, REMEMBER ME WHEN THOU COMEST INTO THY KINGDOM."
Private Ariel Booth, HPER, 17.10.43 (age 23) [MORO RIVER]

STEADFAST IN HIS DUTY——HE WAS A PERFECT PATRIOT AND A NOBLE FRIEND.
Flight Lieutenant Herbert John Southwood, RCAF, 24.10.43 (age 25) [ABBEVILLE]

IN MEMORY OF OUR DEAR SON WHO LAID THE WORLD AWAY AND GAVE UP THE YEARS TO BE.
Sergeant William John Moore, 48th HC, 31.10.43 (age 21) [MORO RIVER]

WE WILL DRAIN OUR DEAREST VEINS BUT THEY SHALL BE FREE. ROBERT BURNS
Bombardier James Davidson, RCA, 8.11.43 [MORO RIVER]

"TO BEAR ALL NAKED TRUTHS AND TO ENVISAGE CIRCUMSTANCE ALL CALM."
Flight Sergeant Ivan Steen Sollows, RCAF, 15.11.43 (age 20) [CHESTER (BLACON)]

"THE LORD IS THY KEEPER: THE LORD IS THY SHADE UPON THY RIGHT HAND."
PSALM 121. 5
Private Joseph William Colp, WNSR, 18.11.43 (age 24) [MORO RIVER]

HE FIRST GAVE HIMSELF TO THE LORD AND THEN TO HIS COUNTRY.
Flying Officer Rob Roy MacGregor, RCAF, 22.11.43 (age 26) [SAGE]

NO NIGHT CAN DARKEN THE SUNLIGHT OF THEIR MEMORY.
Pilot Officer Lorne Franklin Cook, RCAF, 24.11.43 (age 22) [PERSHORE]

"HE WILL BE OUR GUIDE EVEN UNTO DEATH."
Flight Lieutenant Victor Yelverton Haines, RCAF, 26.11.43 (age 25) [RHEINBERG]

BEING MADE PERFECT IN A SHORT SPACE, HE FULFILLED A LONG TIME. BOOK OF WISDOM.
Pilot Officer George Henry Rich, RCAF, 26.11.43 (age 24) [DURNBACH]

TO THE HONOUR OF MY DEAR AND ONLY SON WHO DIED FOR HIS PATRIE. LOVE, MOTHER
Trooper Maurice Chastenais, SFR, 29.11.43 (age 19) [BROOKWOOD]

ROCK OF AGES CLEFT FOR ME, LET ME HIDE MYSELF IN THEE.
Gunner Ronald Edward John White, 166th (Nfld.) FA/RA, 29.11.43 (age 24)
[SANGRO RIVER]

I SHALL REMEMBER WHILE LIGHT LIVES YET AND IN DARKNESS I SHALL NOT FORGET.
Flying Officer Gordon Harry Kay, RCAF, 2.12.43 (age 30) [BERLIN]

"THEY SHALL SEE HIS FACE, AND HIS NAME SHALL BE ENGRAVED ON THEIR FOREHEAD."
Squadron Leader Robert Geoffrey Cook DFC, RCAF, 4.12.43 (age 22) [BERLIN]

SOLDIER, SLEEP WELL. YOU'RE FOR THE KING'S GUARD IN THE MORNING.
Pilot Officer Fayette Williams Brown George Hingston, RCAF, 4.12.43 (age 25)
[BROOKWOOD]

FONDLY LOVED AND DEEPLY MOURNED. HEART OF MY HEART, I MISS YOU SO. WIFE RITA
Private Joseph Kendall, 48th HC, 8.12.43 (age 28) [MORO RIVER]

TREAD SOFTLY, MY DARLING SLEEPS HERE.
Corporal Gordon Cunueaude Parker, SLI, 11.12.43 (age 25) [MORO RIVER]

"MAN THAT IS BORN OF A WOMAN IS OF FEW DAYS AND FULL OF TROUBLE." JOB XIV. 1
Corporal William Chester Oaks, CR, 9.12.43 (age 24) [MORO RIVER]

IN LOVING MEMORY OF OUR DARLING SON. YOU GAVE YOUR LIFE, NEED MORE BE SAID.
Private Norville Carl Nowell, SHC, 11.12.43 (age 24) [MORO RIVER]

THE LAST ENEMY THAT SHALL BE DESTROYED IS DEATH. I CORINTHIANS XV. 26
Sergeant Richard Piercy, LER, 11.12.43 (age 38) [MORO RIVER]

MY SINCERE WISH IS THAT GOD'S RICH BLESSING MAY BE WITH MY SON AND HIS LOVED ONES.
Lance Corporal Gordon Rice, WNSR, 12.12.43 (age 24) [MORO RIVER]

THE SOUL, IMMORTAL AS ITS SIRE, SHALL NEVER DIE. MONTGOMERY
Trooper Morris Krasutsky, OR, 12.12.43 (age 22) [MORO RIVER]

IN THOUGHT, FAITH. IN WORD, WISDOM. IN DEED, COURAGE. IN LIFE, SERVICE.
Signalman John Douglas Pattison, RCCS, 15.12.43 (age 25) [MORO RIVER]
BRUCE HAS GONE TO HIS HEAVENLY HOME TO JOIN HIS BROTHER JOHN,
KILLED IN ITALY 15.12.1943.
Pilot Officer Allen Bruce Pattison, RCAF, 31.3.44 (age 23) [BROOKWOOD]

SO YOUNG, SO SIMPLE WAS HE YET, HE SCARCE COULD CHILDHOOD'S JOYS FORGET.
Private George Irvine McLean, SLI, 16.12.43 (age 23) [MORO RIVER]

YOUR SMILE WE SEE AND VOICE WE HEAR "HOME ON THE RANGE." YOUR LOVED ONES
Private Edgar Joe Ross, SHC, 17.12.43 (age 26) [MORO RIVER]

JESUS PERMITS US TO LOVE EVEN OUR OWN WHO ARE DEPARTED FROM THIS WORLD.
Private Wilfred Boudreau, HPER, 18.12.43 (age 27) [MORO RIVER]

"MINE EYES ARE EVER TOWARD THE LORD, FOR HE SHALL PLUCK MY FEET OUT OF THE NET."
Sergeant Leonard David Griese, RCAF, 19.12.43 (age 20) [HARROGATE]

A MOTHER'S HOPE, "THERE SHALL BE A RESURRECTION OF THE DEAD, BOTH OF THE JUST AND THE UNJUST."
Private Lawrence Bye, RCR, 19.12.43 (age 27) [MORO RIVER]

OUR OWN "PETE" GAVE ALL FOR FREEDOM. EVER WE HOLD IT SACRED. DAD AND FAMILY
Flight Sergeant Peter Robert Humphrys, RCAF, 19.12.43 (age 22) [HARROGATE]

MY DEAREST SON, LOVED AND CHERISHED BY ALL. EVERY 23RD DAY OF DECEMBER A MEMORABLE DAY.
Private Solomon Koloyian, HPER, 23.12.43 (age 20) [MORO RIVER]

IN MEMORY OF A DEAR SON. TIME SO FAR HAS ONLY PROVED HOW MUCH WE MISS YOU.
Private Donald Roderick McDonald, LER, 23.12.43 (age 22) [MORO RIVER]

"THE DEAD SHALL HEAR THE VOICE OF THE SON OF GOD, AND THEY THAT HEAR SHALL LIVE."
ST. JOHN V. 25
Private George Baluck, RCR, 24.12.43 (age 20) [MORO RIVER]

"LIGHTEN OUR DARKNESS, WE BESEECH THEE, O LORD."
Major Thomas Cullen Brown Vance, SHC, 24.12.43 (age 30) [MORO RIVER]

DEEP IN OUR HEARTS FOR EVER LIES TRIBUTE TO HIS SACRIFICE.
Corporal Murray Alexander Brown, 48th HC, 25.12.43 (age 34) [MORO RIVER]

DAY BY DAY WE SADLY MISS HIM. WORD WOULD FAIL OUR LOSS TO TELL. REST IN PEACE.
Sergeant John William Chapman, TRR, 28.12.43 (age 29) [MORO RIVER]

I WISH I COULD SEE YOU AGAIN BEFORE IT COMES TRUE. SWEET MEMORIES OF YOU.
Private Nick Witoshynski, SLI, 28.12.43 (age 41) [MORO RIVER]

IN ALL THE OLD FAMILIAR PLACES, LIGHT AND GAY, ALL DAY THRU' WE'LL BE SEEING YOU.
Sergeant Terence Graham Newcomen Watts, CPC, 28.12.43 (age 26) [MORO RIVER]

SOMEWHERE THE SUN IS SHINING, HUSH THY SAD REPINING. GOD LIVES, ALL IS WELL.
Private Harry Blake Stephenson, 48th HC, 29.12.43 (age 21) [MORO RIVER]

FOR LOVE'S SAKE HE GAVE ALL; VICTOR OVER FEAR HE STILL SERVES.
Major Winston Case Johnson, CYR, 29.12.43 (age 31) [MORO RIVER]

IN DISTANT LANDS ACROSS THE SEA MY LOVE, MY LIFE, I GAVE FOR THEE.
Private John Gilbert Morrison, 48th HC, 31.12.43 (age 23) [MORO RIVER]

HE DIED IN FAITH. NO MORE CAN WORDS EXPRESS TO SOOTHE OUR GRIEF, MAKE OUR SORROW LESS.
Flying Officer Wilfred Glen Cockwill, RCAF, 3.1.44 (age 23) [BERLIN]

TRIUMPHO MORTE TAM VITA.
(I triumph in death as in life.)
Flight Lieutenant John Allardyce Allen, RCAF, 3.1.44 (age 23) [BERLIN]

IT MATTERS NOT HOW LONG WE LIVE BUT HOW.
Flying Officer James George MacLeod, RCAF, 4.1.44 (age 24) [CHESTER (BLACON)]

MY LOVE GOES WITH YOU, MY DARLING.
Squadron Leader Edward Sudbury Alexander DFC, DSM, RCAF, 14.1.44 (age 24)
[BERGEN-OP-ZOOM]

HE GAVE HIS LIFE THAT HIS WIFE AND SON MAY BE FREE AND HAPPY: MAY GOD KEEP IT SO.
Private Norman Lloyd Douglas Hurrell, PR, 17.1.44 (age 25) [MORO RIVER]

MAY LIGHT ETERNAL SHINE UPON YOUR SOUL AND GOD BEFRIEND AND BLESS YOU, DARLING.
Private Ross Albert Chaisson, CBH, 17.1.44 (age 21) [MORO RIVER]

OUR DARLING DADDY IS JUST AWAY. FOR ME TO LIVE IS CHRIST AND TO DIE IS GAIN.
Flight Sergeant Leslie Lee Petry, RCAF, 19.1.44 (age 23) [HARROGATE]

TO THEE THE LORD HATH GIVEN GOODNESS AND STRENGTH. LOVE, DAD AND MOTHER.
Sergeant Robert William Edwards, RCAF, 21.1.44 (age 21) [BERLIN]

NON ILLE PRO CARIS AMICIS AUT PATRIA TIMIDUS PERIRE. HORACE, ODES IV-IX
(He was not one to fear dying for his dear friends or for his native land.)
Warrant Officer II William Penri Morris, RCAF, 21.1.44 (age 21) [VENRAY]

HERE RESTS IN HONOURED GLORY MY SOLDIER HUSBAND, A LOVING FATHER,
KNOWN BUT TO GOD.
Private Wilfred Joseph Rivait, RCR, 21.1.44 [MORO RIVER]

YOU SHALL HEAR HIS VOICE AND COME FORTH IN THE NEW WORLD. JOHN V. 28-29
Pilot Officer Lloyd William Wesley Jones, RCAF, 22.1.44 (age 22) [BERLIN]

OMNIA RELIQUIT UT PATRIAM SERVARET.
(He gave up everything to save his native land.)
Squadron Leader Lloyd Martin Linnell, RCAF, 29.1.44 (age 26) [BERLIN]

OUR DARLING. "O DANNY BOY, WE LOVED YOU SO."
Flight Lieutenant Warren Ainslie Roberts, RCAF, 30.1.44 (age 23) [BERLIN]

THE LORD STOOD WITH ME AND STRENGTHENED ME. 2 TIMOTHY 4. 17
Private Alexander Devitt, HPER, 30.1.44 (age 26) [MORO RIVER]

"OUR SOLDIER SLEEPS, HIS GOOD SWORD RUSTS; HIS SOUL IS WITH THE SAINTS,
WE TRUST." DAD
Private Gordon Stephens, HPER, 30.1.44 (age 21) [MORO RIVER]

ALL HE HAD HE GAVE. ONWARD, CHRISTIAN SOLDIER, ON TO VICTORY AND PEACE.
Private James Edward Albert Hurlock, PR, 5.2.44 (age 24) [MORO RIVER]

THIS IS OUR SHRINE IN THE TEMPLE OF TIME WHEREIN A LOVED ONE REPOSES.
Private John Revill, PR, 5.2.44 (age 20) [MORO RIVER]

HAD HE ASKED US, WITH TEARFUL EYES WE'D SAY, LORD, WE LOVE HIM, LET HIM STAY.
Private Ralph Chambers, RCR, 9.2.44 (age 24) [MORO RIVER]

BILLY. WITH A SMILE FOR EVERYONE. "STILL SMILING THROUGH." FRANCES AND DAD
Lieutenant William Waddell Morrow, CR, 17.2.44 (age 29) [MORO RIVER]

REST IN PEACE, DARLING. ALL OUR LOVE FOREVER.
Corporal Newton William Hanlan, LER, 20.2.44 (age 26) [BARI]

JESUS' HEART MOURNS FOR HIM.
Sergeant John Dixon, RCAF, 20.2.44 [HANOVER]

I AM THINKING TONIGHT OF THE PAST, DEAR SON. I PICTURE YOU IN MY MEMORY AS I SAW YOU LAST.
Pilot Officer William Forrest, RCAF, 21.2.44 (age 29) [DURNBACH]

SLEEP ON, SON. YOUR SONG IS ENDED. STILL THE ECHO LINGERS IN OUR HEARTS.
Lieutenant Robert Dalton Heard, IRC, 22.2.44 (age 26) [MORO RIVER]

AMONG HONORED COMRADES. OUR SON. "REST ON, THY DUTY DONE." FROM HIS HOME IN CANADA.
Sergeant Francis Elvin Wilt, RCAF, 29.2.44 (age 22) [HARROGATE]

DARLING DENNY. ALWAYS IN MY THOUGHTS. BROKEN-HEARTED OLIVE AND BABY.
Private Dennis Edgar Hayes, RCR, 3.3.44 (age 25) [BROOKWOOD]

"LORD, WHITHER SHALL WE GO BUT TO THEE? THOU HAST THE WORDS OF ETERNAL LIFE."
Warrant Officer I John Haig Broad, RCAF, 20.3.44 (age 21) [CHESTER (BLACON)]

"AND THE SPIRIT SHALL RETURN UNTO GOD WHO GAVE IT."
Pilot Officer Billie Herman Murdock, RCAF, 22.3.44 (age 18) [RHEINBERG]

BE STILL, MY SOUL.
Private Lewis Neil McQuitty, PPCLI, 22.3.44 (age 25) [MORO RIVER]

THERE IS A DIVINITY THAT SHARES OUR ENDS.
Warrant Officer II Raymond Hathaway Wilson, RCAF, 31.3.44 (age 22) [HANOVER]

TO BE REMEMBERED THUS IS NOT TO DIE.
Pilot Officer Gordon Lewis Preece, RCAF, 31.3.44 (age 19) [RHEINBERG]

HERE ALSO LIES HIS SON GEOFFREY EDMUND WHO DIED 28TH JAN. 1945, AGE 8 MONTHS.
Private Edmund Philip Baines, RCIC, 9.4.44 (age 32) [BROOKWOOD]

"SEIGNEUR, COMME UNE TERRE ALTÉRÉE, MON ÂME A SOIF DE TOI." PS. 143. 6
("Lord, my soul thirsteth after Thee, as a thirsty land.")
Trooper Roméo Napoleon Vézina, 4th PLDG, 9.4.44 [MORO RIVER]

DARLING, WE WILL LOVE YOU TILL THE END OF TIME. YOUR FAMILY BACK HOME IN CANADA
Private James Samuel Hall, IRC, 16.4.44 (age 18) [MORO RIVER]

DARLING TOMMY, WE DO NOT NEED A SPECIAL DAY TO BRING YOU TO OUR MIND. MOTHER, SISTERS AND BROTHERS
Trooper Thomas William James, LSH(RC), 18.4.44 (age 22) [BARI]

FOR THOU "WITH THE WIND ON THE HEATH" ART STILL.
Flying Officer Harold Keith Langrish, RCAF, 23.4.44 (age 25) [REICHSWALD FOREST]

DAVID WILL NEVER BE FORGOTTEN BY HIS FRIENDS AT NORTH KLESKUN, ALBERTA, CANADA.
Pilot Officer David Pickering, RCAF, 24.4.44 (age 22) [HARROGATE]

WE HOPE TO MEET AGAIN WHERE WARS AND HEARTACHES ARE NO MORE. MOTHER AND DAD
Pilot Officer Richmond Wesley Smith, RCAF, 24.4.44 (age 22) [HARROGATE]

SOFTLY YE WINDS, OVER HIS DEAR HEAD WHISPER A BENEDICTION FOR THE DEAD. R.I.P.
Lieutenant George Paul Damer, RCR, 27.4.44 (age 33) [NAPLES]

A FRIEND TO ALL WHO PASSED HIS WAY, GLAD WERE THEY SUCH A MAN TO KNOW. MOTHER
Flying Officer William Alexander Pope, RCAF, 2.5.44 (age 32) [HARROGATE]

I SEE YOU EVERY DAY, KEN, JUST AS YOU LEFT HOME. YOU DID YOUR BEST: NOW REST. DAD
Pilot Officer Kenneth Leverne Cannings, RCAF, 9.5.44 (age 20) [WEVELGEM]

HE LEAVES TO US THE RISING LIGHT AND GLORY OF HIS PAST. HIS DEVOTED FAMILY
Lance Corporal Douglas Desrochers, R22R, 19.5.44 [CASSINO]

QUE SON ÂME REPOSE EN PAIX. "IL ÉTAIT UN PATRIOTE EXEMPLAIRE."
(May his soul rest in peace. "He was an exemplary patriot.")
Pilot Officer Charles Marie Beauregard, RCAF, 23.5.44 [REICHSWALD FOREST]

OUR COMRADE DIED WITH THE GIFT OF COURAGE.
Corporal Anthony Adolph Brandel, WNSR, 25.5.44 (age 33) [CASSINO]

HIS LIFE WORK IS ENDED. HE HAS CROSSED THE SWELLING TIDE.
Sergeant Joseph Raymond Pollon, RCAF, 28.5.44 (age 17) [HARROGATE]

DEAR SON, YOU DIED FOR YOUR COUNTRY. MAY IT NEVER FORGET YOUR COURAGE. AMEN.
Lance Corporal Louis Philippe Martel, RCIC, 5.6.44 (age 20) [BROOKWOOD]

WHO HAS NOT DARED, LIVES NOT.
Lieutenant Hugh MacMillan Walker, 1st CPB, 6.6.44 (age 21) [RANVILLE]

"I KNOW THY WORKS: BEHOLD, I HAVE SET BEFORE THEE AN OPEN DOOR."
Flying Officer James Harrison Clark, RCAF, 7.6.44 (age 24) [HERMANVILLE]

HE LIVES AND SMILES BEYOND THE WALL. OUR BELOVED SON AND BROTHER LORNE.
Flying Officer Lorne Cheatham Flather, RCAF, 7.6.44 (age 26) [HERMANVILLE]

YOU WENT, IT SEEMS BUT YESTERDAY. YOU LINGER THERE—NOT DEAD, BUT JUST AWAY.
Rifleman George Thomas White, RWR, 8.6.44 (age 27) [BÉNY-SUR-MER]
Rifleman Robert Edward White, RWR, 8.6.44 (age 24) [BÉNY-SUR-MER]

FOR NOW WE SEE THROUGH A GLASS DARKLY, BUT THEN FACE TO FACE.
I COR. 13: 12
Rifleman Robert Munro Findlay, RWR, 8.6.44 (age 20) [BÉNY-SUR-MER]

MY DARLING HUSBAND, YOUR MEMORY TO ME IS A TREASURE. LOVING WIFE AUDREY
Rifleman Gordon Leroy Kimmel, RWR, 8.6.44 (age 28) [BRETTEVILLE-SUR-LAIZE]
GOD BE WITH YOU UNTIL WE MEET AGAIN.
Corporal Richard Kenneth Kimmel, RRR, 18.6.44 (age 28) [BÉNY-SUR-MER]
HE WAS A GOOD SON AND A GOOD SOLDIER.
Corporal Clifford Howard Kimmel, HPER, 5.12.44 (age 26) [RAVENNA]

"COMMIT THY WAY TO THE LORD; PUT THY TRUST IN HIM; AND HE SHALL BRING IT TO PASS."
Rifleman James Joseph Witt, RRR, 9.6.44 (age 19) [BÉNY-SUR-MER]

"NEVER BLOWS SO RED THE ROSE AS WHERE SOME BURIED CAESAR BLED." OMAR KHAYYAM
Captain Percy Royston Gilman, RCASC, 10.6.44 (age 33) [BÉNY-SUR-MER]

"HE SHALL NOT BE MOVED FOREVER; THE RIGHTEOUS SHALL BE IN EVERLASTING REMEMBRANCE."

Sapper George Alonzo Benner, CRCE, *11.6.44 (age 26)* [BRETTEVILLE-SUR-LAIZE]

HE CARED MORE FOR THE LONG AGE HE WILL NOT SEE THAN FOR THE LITTLE THAT HE HELD OF TIME.

Major Kenneth Siddons Osler, RCA, *12.6.44)* [BÉNY-SUR-MER]

I SOUGHT THE LORD AND HE HEARD ME, AND DELIVERED ME FROM ALL MY FEARS. PSALM XXXIV. 4

Warrant Officer II Ronald George Lemky, *13.6.44 (age 23)* [JONKERBOS]

"YEA, AND ALTHOUGH DEEP IN OUR HIDDEN SOULS WE KNOW THAT WITH HIM ALL IS WELL. . ."

Lance Corporal George Russell Boyd, 1st CPB, *16.6.44 (age 21)* [RANVILLE]

NOT FORGOTTEN, NOT ALONE.

Flying Officer Harold Beverly Brett, RCAF, *17.6.44 (age 27)* [AMERSFOORT (OUD LEUSDEN)]

THE STRIFE IS OVER, THE BATTLE WON.

Flying Officer Leonard George Hill, RCAF, *17.6.44 (age 30)* [AMSTERDAM NEW EASTERN]

THOU WILT KEEP HIM IN PERFECT PEACE WHOSE MIND IS STAYED ON THEE. ISAIAH XXXVI. 3

Pilot Officer Martin Morrison, RCAF, *22.6.44 (age 23)* [REICHSWALD FOREST]

THERE IS NO WEALTH BUT LIFE; HE GAVE HIS ALL. GREATLY LOVED AND MISSED. MOTHER

Trooper Tom.Huntington Widlake, OR, *24.6.44 (age 26)* [ASSISI]

IN LOVING MEMORY OF A DEAR BROTHER. IN THIS GREAT WAR HE GAVE HIS BEST.

Lieutenant George Alfred McDermott, RCIC, *26.6.44 (age 29)* [HOTTOT-LES-BAGUES]

HE VOLUNTEERED FOR OVERSEAS. "AT THE GOING DOWN OF THE SUN AND IN THE MORNING WE WILL REMEMBER HIM."

Signalman William Tadgell, RCCS, *29.6.44 (age 24)* [BÉNY-SUR-MER]

FOREVER HONOURED AND FOREVER MOURNED.

Private Owen Tadgell, NNSH, *8.7.44 (age 29)* [BÉNY-SUR-MER]

BELOVED SON OF HARRY AND CLARA YOUNG. "IN GLORY WILL THEY SLEEP."

Lieutenant Richard Oliver Young, RCIC, *29.6.44 (age 25)* [BÉNY-SUR-MER]
Lieutenant Peter Byrne Young, RCIC, *16.7.44 (age 19)* [BANNEVILLE]

THEY ARE NOT DEAD, OUR MEN WHO FOUGHT. THEY LIVE AGAIN IN THE HEARTS OF MEN.

Flying Officer John Raymond Daly, RCAF, *4.7.44 (age 23)* [RAVENNA]

IN LIFE LOVED AND HONORED. "FOR ALL THE BOUNDLESS UNIVERSE IS LIFE—THERE ARE NO DEAD."

Company Sergeant Major Joseph Henry O'Leary Louis Murray, NS(NB)R, *4.7.44 (age 32)* [BÉNY-SUR-MER]

GOD REMEMBERS WHEN THE WORLD FORGETS.

Lance Corporal Robert Harmon Halliday, RWR, *4.7.44 (age 20)* [BÉNY-SUR-MER]

TO MEMORY EVER DEAR. IF LOVE COULD SAVE THOU HADST NOT DIED.

Corporal William James Halliday, RWR, *25.10.44 (age 24)* [ADEGEM]

"GREATER LOVE HATH NO MAN THAN THIS." BY HIS BRAVERY HE CAN MAKE US BRAVE.
Sergeant Neil Scott Hurder, RCAF, 5.7.44 (age 20) [BROOKWOOD]

WHEN THE ROLL IS CALLED UP YONDER, I'LL BE THERE.
Private Francis Woodman, NS(NB)R, 5.7.44 (age 23) [BAYEUX]

"OUR SOUL WAITETH FOR THE LORD: HE IS OUR HELP AND OUR SHIELD." PSALM 33: 20
Sergeant Malcolm Sutherland Leeco, 1st CPB, 7.7.44 (age 26) [RANVILLE]

"I CRIED UNTO HIM WITH MY MOUTH AND HE WAS EXTOLLED WITH MY TONGUE."
Private Kenneth Joseph Branscombe, CSR, 8.7.44 (age 26) [BÉNY-SUR-MER]

"FOR THE END OF THAT MAN IS PEACE." PSALM XXXVII. 37
Lieutenant Nairn Stewart Boyd, SFR, 8.7.44 (age 26) [BÉNY-SUR-MER]
GREATER LOVE HATH NO MAN THAN THIS; HE LAID DOWN HIS LIFE FOR HIS FRIENDS.
Lieutenant Kenneth Archibald Boyd, 17th DY, 9.7.44 (age 21) [BÉNY-SUR-MER]

HIS GRAVE WE CANNOT SEE. SLEEP ON, DEAR. IN SILENCE I WILL ALWAYS THINK OF THEE.
Private Antoine Anthony Casey, NNSH, 8.7.44 (age 32) [BÉNY-SUR-MER]
Private Joseph Felix Casey, PR, 1.9.44 (age 26) [MONTECCHIO]

THIS WAS HIS GREATEST HOUR. LET IT NOT HAVE BEEN IN VAIN.
Lieutenant Hubert Murray Jones MBE, RCIC, 8.7.44 (age 22) [RYES]

"THE LORD IS MY STRENGTH AND MY SHIELD; MY HEART TRUSTETH IN HIM." PSALM XXVIII. 7
Private Foster Irvin Rogers, NNSH, 8.7.44 (age 20) [BÉNY-SUR-MER]

THE ALTAR OF OUR LOVE. A PARENT'S TRIBUTE TO A BRAVE YOUNG SON OF CANADA.
Lieutenant Brian Freeman Lynn, RCIC, 8.7.44 (age 21) [DOUVRES LA DÉLIVRANDE]

GOD GRANT THIS SUMMERSIDE BOY REST AND PEACE. GONE BUT NOT FORGOTTEN.
Private Charles James MacDonald, NNSH, 8.7.44 (age 28) [BÉNY-SUR-MER]
MAY THE SOUL OF THIS SUMMERSIDE SOLDIER REST IN PEACE.
Private Joseph Frederick MacDonald, WNSR, 15.9.44 (age 23) [CORIANO RIDGE]

LOVE'S AN ESSENCE OF THE SOUL WHICH SINKS NOT WITH THIS CHAIN OF CLAY.
Private Orville Edison Babcock, CSR, 8.7.44 (age 27) [BÉNY-SUR-MER]

"IS IT NOTHING TO YOU ALL YE THAT PASS BY?" R.I.P.
Corporal Francis Paul Fitzgerald Cope, SSTCA, 10.7.44 (age 26) [HOLTEN]

MY SON. "LET ALL THE PEOPLE PRAISE THEE, O GOD, LET ALL THE PEOPLE PRAISE THEE."
Private Ivan Samuel Wagner, RRC, 18.7.44 (age 27) [BRETTEVILLE-SUR-LAIZE]
Private Harry Everett Wagner, RRC, 12.8.44 (age 30) [BÉNY-SUR-MER]
Private Bruce Howard Wagner, ASHC, 31.1.45 (age 20) [GROESBEEK]

"WE ARE IN VERY TRUTH THAT WHICH WE LOVE, AND LOVE, LIKE NOBLE DEEDS, IS BORN OF FAITH."
Private Marshall Watts, CH, 18.7.44 (age 21) [BÉNY-SUR-MER]

NOT IN VAIN YOUR SACRIFICE AND WORK. THE WORLD'S HEARTS BEAT HIGH BECAUSE OF YOU.
Private Murray Robinson, NS(NB)R, 19.7.44 (age 20) [RANVILLE]

FORGIVE US OUR TRESPASSES, AS WE FORGIVE THEM THAT TRESPASS AGAINST US.
Pilot Officer Ingval Millar Hanon, RCAF, *21.7.44 (age 22)* [GROESBEEK]

WHO DIED IN VIOLENCE, REST IN PEACE.
Pilot Officer Walter Dennis Robertson, RCAF, *29.7.44 (age 19)* [BECKLINGEN]

HE STOOD FOR EVERYTHING THAT IS FINE IN LIFE.
Pilot Officer Robert William Robinson, RCAF, *29.7.44 (age 33)* [KIEL]

HINDER ME NOT. SEEING THE LORD HATH PROSPERED MY WAY . . .
THAT I MAY TO MY MASTER.
Pilot Officer John Unger, RCAF, *29.7.44 (age 23)* [BECKLINGEN]

"A CHEQUER-BOARD OF NIGHTS AND DAYS WHERE DESTINY WITH MEN FOR PIECES PLAYS."
Sergeant Charles Aldwin Benner, PR, *2.8.44 (age 31)* [NAPLES]

WE WILL NOT FORGET YOU; WE LOVE YOU TOO DEARLY FOR YOUR MEMORY
TO FADE FROM OUR LIVES LIKE A DREAM.
Sapper Joseph Thomas Walsh, CRCE, *7.8.44 (age 24)* [FLORENCE]

"IN QUIETNESS AND IN CONFIDENCE SHALL BE YOUR STRENGTH." ISAIAH XXX. 15
Lieutenant Andrew Fraser Bushell, RCIC, *8.8.44 (age 20)* [BAYEUX]

GOD'S WORK AND GLORY IS TO BRING IMMORTALITY AND ETERNAL LIFE TO MAN.
L.D.S. CHURCH
Gunner Lee Leishman, RCA, *8.8.44 (age 23)* [BÉNY-SUR-MER]

THE GLORY OF GOD IS INTELLIGENCE. DOC. AND COV. 93. 36
Signalman Phillip James Mount, RCCS, *9.8.44* [BÉNY-SUR-MER]

'TIS A LOVING FATHER CALLS THE WANDERER HOME. "WHOSOEVER WILL MAY COME."
Private Robert Leonard Lawrence NS(NB)R, *13.8.44 (age 20)* [BAYEUX]

HER LIFE WAS A WORDLESS SERMON IN COURAGE AND UNDERSTANDING.
Radio Officer Maud E. Steane, MN *(Canada), 14.8.44 (age 28)* [FLORENCE]

PLACEBO DOMINO IN REGIONE VIVORUM. PSALM 116 VERSE 9
(I shall please the Lord in the land of the living.)
Trooper George Smith-Loggie, 1st Hussars, 14.8.44 (age 22) [BÉNY-SUR-MER]

REMEMBRANCE, THE ONLY IMMORTALITY WE KNOW.
Warrant Officer II Dennis Budd Herman Lorenz, RCAF, *17.8.44 (age 26)* [KIEL]

WEEPING MAY ENDURE FOR A NIGHT BUT JOY COMETH IN THE MORNING. PS. XXX. 5
Corporal Lynn Sutton, SSR, *17.8.44 (age 24)* [BAYEUX}

WE'RE PROUD OF YOU, DADDY. WE LOVE YOU AND NEED YOU.
YOUR TWO LITTLE BOYS AND MUM.
Private Harold James Cosgrove, LER, *17.8.44 (age 29)* [FLORENCE]

TRUE LOVE'S A GIFT WHICH GOD HAS GIVEN TO MAN ALONE BENEATH THE HEAVEN.
Flying Officer George Scott, RCAF, *17.8.44 (age 32* [AABENRAA]

I LOVE YOU TRULY.
Sapper Peter Donald Clements, CRCE, *23.8.44* [ANCONA]

STAT MAGNI NOMINIS UMBRA.
(There stands the shadow of a great name.)
Private Walter Warner, CH, *23.8.44 (age 31)* [BRETTEVILLE-SUR-LAIZE]

AND IF IT PLEASE MINE HOST THAT I REPAIR ELSEWHERE AWHILE, THEN BE IT SO.
Lieutenant Robert Charles Foster, CRCE, *24.8.44 (age 29)* [ANCONA]

BRIEF IS LIFE, BUT LOVE IS LONG.
Sergeant Clyde Roswell Osborne, RCAF, *24.8.44 (age 24)* [HARROGATE]

HOW MANY NIGHTS AND DAYS HAVE GONE YET THE NIGHT OF OUR SORROW HAS NO DAWN.
Private Sam Edward Oakley, 48th HC, *26.8.44 (age 22)* [MONTECCHIO]

THOU WAST NOT BORN FOR DEATH. KEATS
Sergeant Irl William Shannon, CRCE, *26.8.44 (age 23)* [BRETTEVILLE-SUR-LAIZE]

BORN MONTREAL 20-10-15. "THEY ARE NEVER ALONE WHO ARE
ACCOMPANIED BY NOBLE THOUGHTS."
Lieutenant Ian MacMillan Crawford, 17th DY, *27.8.44 (age 28)* [BAYEUX]

BUAIDH LE BÀS, DUAIS A´ GHAIDHEIL.
(Victory with death is the Gael's reward.)
Private William Joseph Jamieson, HPER, *27.8.44 (age 19)* [MONTECCHIO]

COME, AND HE COMETH.
Private Bernard Barkase, SHC, *27.8.44 (age 26)* [ANCONA]

ONLY SON. BORN IN ENGLAND. EDUCATED STONEYHURST. CANADIAN CITIZEN. R.I.P.
Corporal Frederick Peliti, HPER, *28.8.44 (age 34)* [MONTECCHIO]

NO GREATER LOVE HATH ANY MAN THAN THIS. HE GAVE HIS LIFE FOR HIS COUNTRY.
Lance Corporal Robert Short, ASHC, *29.8.44 (age 19)* [BRETTEVILLE-SUR-LAIZE]
Corporal William Short, HLIC, *20.10.44 (age 25)* [ADEGEM]

WHAT IS LOVELY, NEVER DIES.
Sergeant Robert Austin Dutton, RCAF, *30.8.44 (age 21)* [HARROGATE]

GREATLY LOVING, GREATLY LOVED, SON OF MY SOUL, DEAR JEWEL OF MY LIFE.
Trooper Henry Foster Lockwood, BCD, *31.8.44 (age 25)* [MONTECCHIO]

"INASMUCH AS YE HAVE DONE IT UNTO THE LEAST . . . YE HAVE DONE IT UNTO ME."
ST. MATTHEW XXV. 40
Lieutenant Hugh James Russell, BCD, *31.8.44 (age 24)* [MONTECCHIO]

WHAT GIFT MORE WONDERFUL THAN TO HAVE KNOWN AND LOVED YOU. REST WITH JESUS.
Trooper James Allan Tucker, BCD, *31.8.44 (age 25)* [MONTECCHIO]

THE UNFORGOTTEN ARE NOT DEAD.
Flight Lieutenant Michael Kidston McGuire, RCAF, *31.8.44 (age 23)* [CHESTER (BLACON)]

HE GAVE HIS LIFE THAT WE MIGHT LIVE. WHERE GOD IS KNOWN THERE IS PEACE.
Lieutenant James Robert Henderson, PR, *31.8.44 (age 22)* [MONTECCHIO]

THE WILL OF GOD, NOTHING MORE, NOTHING LESS, NOTHING ELSE.
Lieutenant Irwin James Reed, SAR, *1.9.44 (age 22)* [RYES]

MY LOVE, THE JOB WAS GREAT. WARD DEAREST, YOUR MEMORIES WILL LIVE IN MY HEART.
Trooper Ward Wayne Kison, BCD, 1.9.44 (age 22) [GRADARA]

"THOU HAST BEEN MY HELP, THEREFORE IN THE SHADOW OF THY WINGS WILL I REJOICE."
Private Eric Alexander Johnston, CBH, 1.9.44 (age 27) [MONTECCHIO]

I AM PROUD THAT I CAN SAY HE WAS MY HUSBAND AND MY FRIEND.
Lieutenant Earle James Pritchard, LRSR, 2.9.44 (age 27) [GRADARA]

MAY HIS REWARD BE AS GREAT AS HIS SACRIFICE.
Private Arthur Heath, WR, 2.9.44 (age 26) [GRADARA]

SLEEP, SOLDIER, STILL IN HONOURED REST, YOUR TRUTH AND VALOUR WEARING.
Private Clayton Snyder, RCR, 4.9.44 (age 25) [ANCONA]

I WILL CLING TO OLD RUGGED CROSS AND EXCHANGE IT ONE DAY FOR A CROWN.
Private Bertram John Doggrell, RCR, 4.9.44 (age 23) [ANCONA]

HE GAVE HIS LIFE FOR HIS PAL AND THAT OTHERS MIGHT LIVE.
Private Roy Patrick Greenough, RCR, 4.9.44 (age 26) [ANCONA]

"I WILL LEAD THEM IN PATHS THAT THEY HAVE NOT KNOWN." ISA. XLII. 16
Sapper Douglas Cribb Lewis, CRCE, 4.9.44 (age 26) [GRADARA]

". . . HE FOUGHT FOR LOVE AND NOT FOR GAIN. MAY HIS SACRIFICE NOT BE IN VAIN." J.M. STAATS
Private James Montague Staats, HPER, 4.9.44 (age 19) [GRADARA]

"IN FAMINE HE SHALL REDEEM THEM FROM DEATH AND IN WAR FROM THE POWER OF THE SWORD."
Private Charles Robert Gray, PLDG, 6.9.44 (age 27) [MONTECCHIO]

HE WILL TEACH US OF HIS WAYS AND WE WILL WALK IN HIS PATHS. ISAIAH II. 3
Private Harvey Charles Parsons, RCR, 6.9.44 (age 20) [CORIANO RIDGE]

FOR THINE IS THE KINGDOM, THE POWER AND THE GLORY, FOR EVER AND EVER.
Corporal Arthur Lionel Benson, RCASC, 7.9.44 (age 22) [ANCONA]

HIS WAS A NOBLE LIFE FILLED WITH LOVING UNSELFISHNESS. A.L.S.
Lieutenant George Ewing Starke, CBH, 8.9.44 (age 32) [CORIANO RIDGE]

"THAT IN BLESSING I WILL BLESS THEE AND IN MULTIPLYING I WILL MULTIPLY THY SEED."
Private John Sawyer, ASHC, 8.9.44 (age 20) [ADEGEM]

"THE WAYS OF A MAN ARE CLEAN IN HIS OWN EYES: BUT THE LORD WEIGHETH THE SPIRITS."
Private Joseph Proctor, LWR, 9.9.44 (age 21) [ADEGEM]

THEY THAT SOW IN TEARS SHALL REAP IN JOY. PSALM CXXVI. 5
Private Gordon Hillier Sherman, LWR, 9.9.44 (age 22) [ADEGEM]

BY THEIR DEEDS YE SHALL KNOW THEM. THEY LIVE FOREVER IN GOD'S KINGDOM.
Private Alan Bruce Jarvis, ASHC, 9.9.44 (age 20) [ADEGEM]

"LIFE TRULY IS NOT MEASURED BY THE FIGURES ON THE DIAL."
MOTHER, FATHER AND SISTERS
Lieutenant William John Kotchapaw, RCIC, 10.9.44 *(age 20)* [GROESBEEK]

MAKE ME A CAPTIVE, LORD, FORCE ME TO RENDER UP MY SWORD
AND I SHALL CONQUEROR BE.
Private Avard Isaac Northrup, NS(NB)R, 11.9.44 *(age 19)* [ADEGEM]

I WAS A SON UNTO MY FATHER, TENDER AND ONLY BELOVED IN THE SIGHT OF MY MOTHER.
PROVERBS IV. 3
Major Ronald Rainey Counsell MC, QOCHC, 11.9.44 *(age 29)* [ADEGEM]

"DESIGNER INFINITE!—AH! MUST THOU CHAR THE WOOD ERE THOU CANST
LIMN WITH IT?" F.T.
Corporal Joseph Jerome McGarrity, QOCHC, 12.9.44 *(age 20)* [ADEGEM]

LOVE SHALL CLASP HIM WITH STRONG HANDS, PEACE SHALL FOLD HIM IN SOFT WINGS.
Lieutenant John Milne Roberts, SAR, 12.9.44 [ADEGEM]

"HIS LOVE, NOT MINE, THE RESTING PLACE; HIS TRUTH, NOT MINE, THE TIE."
Sergeant Roy Long, RCA, 12.9.44 *(age 28)* [GRADARA]

WHATSOEVER IS COMMANDED BY THE GOD OF HEAVEN LET IT BE DILIGENTLY DONE.
EZRA VII. 23
Private James Albert Kemp, BWC, 13.9.44 *(age 20)* [ADEGEM]

"HEAVEN AND EARTH SHALL PASS AWAY: BUT MY WORDS SHALL NOT PASS AWAY."
LUKE XXI. 33
Private Clifford Weirmeir, IRC, 14.9.44 *(age 19)* [GRADARA]

WE SHALL MEET AGAIN AROUND ONE COMMON MERCY SEAT.
Lance Corporal Grant Peck, CYR, 15.9.44 *(age 24)* [GRADARA]

FATHER, FORGIVE THEM.
Gunner Bruce Johnson, RCA, 15.9.44 *(age 23)* [CORIANO RIDGE]

MY DARLING DADDY. LOVINGLY REMEMBERED BY HIS SON EDWIN JOHN SULLIVAN,
AGE FIVE YEARS.
Lance Sergeant Edwin Sullivan, RCR, 16.9.44 [CORIANO RIDGE]

THE LAST GREAT CONFLICT ENDED, THEY GREET THE MORNINGTIDE.
Private Reginald Ernest Bent, 48th HC, 16.9.44 *(age 22)* [GRADARA]

BEAUTIFUL WORDS OF JESUS: COME UNTO ME ALL YE THAT LABOUR. . .
AND I WILL GIVE YOU REST.
Private Wilfred Joseph Harford, PPCLI, 17.9.44 *(age 23)* [CORIANO RIDGE]

HE THAT ENDURETH TO THE END, THE SAME SHALL BE SAVED. ST. MATTHEW X. 22
Private Charles Townsley, SHC, 17.9.44 *(age 38)* [CORIANO RIDGE]

IN DUTY, VALOROUS, IN ALL THINGS NOBLE, TO THE HEART'S CORE CLEAN. CANON SCOTT
Lieutenant Francis Joseph Bore, SSR, 17.9.44 *(age 31)* [ADEGEM]

MAY HIS NAME BE BRIGHTLY GILDED IN THE AUTOGRAPH OF GOD.
Private Stanley Kenneth Currie, SHC, 18.9.44 *(age 17)* [CORIANO RIDGE]

WE'LL CATCH THE BROKEN THREADS AGAIN.
Private David Wallace Stickley, SHC, 18.9.44 (age 19) [CORIANO RIDGE]

SLEEP ON, DEAR SON. IT IS TRUE YOU SUFFERED MUCH AND TOLD BUT FEW. MOM AND DAD
Lance Corporal William Wall, HPER, 20.9.44 (age 21) [CORIANO RIDGE]

ALL LOVELY THINGS BY THEE BELOVED SHALL WHISPER TO OUR HEARTS OF THEE.
Lieutenant Harold Cameron Phillips, LWR, 21.9.44 (age 23) [ADEGEM]

BELOVED HUSBAND OF AILEEN. FATHER OF GEORGINA ANNE, BORN IN ENGLAND 1944.
Captain George Richard Corkett, PPCLI, 22.9.44 (age 28) [CORIANO RIDGE]

THE LORD IS MY HELPER AND I SHALL NOT FEAR WHAT MAN SHALL DO UNTO ME. HEB. XIII. 6
Trooper Lawrence Stonefish, LSH (RC), 23.9.44 (age 37) [CESENA]

"HE ASKED LIFE OF THEE AND THOU GAVEST IT HIM." PS. XXI. 4
Private David Brian Hacking, RHLI, 23.9.44 (age 18) [SCHOONSELHOF]

"TO HONOR THE DEAD CHERISH THE LIVING." II SAMUEL IX. 1
Squadron Leader Henry Wallace McLeod DSO, DFC & Bar, RCAF, 27.9.44 (age 28)
[RHEINBERG]

LEAVING HIS WIFE AND TWO CHILDREN, LORRAINE AGE 3, DENIS AGE 2.
Trooper Antoine Gosselin, RCD, 27.9.44 (age 23) [GRADARA]

THE WAR IS OVER, FONSE, AND ITALY IS FREE. THESE THINGS IN HEAVEN SHOW
YOU NEED NO EARTHLY HERALDRY.
Private Alphonsus Francis Noah, CBH, 29.9.44 (age 27) [CESENA]

HE IS NOT DEAD, THE CHILD OF OUR AFFECTION.
Private Henry William Lester, RHLI, 30.9.44 (age 19) [BAYEUX]

IN ALL YOUR DEAR FAMILIAR HAUNTS, BILLIE, WE SHALL FIND YOU.
Private William Albert Oxley, RHLI, 3.10.44 (age 21) [SCHOONSELHOF]

THE ROSES DIE, THE MUSIC FADES, BUT STILL MY HEART REMEMBERS.
Sergeant William Lloyd Dudgeon, RHLI, 3.10.44 (age 25)) [SCHOONSELHOF]

GOD ONLY LOANED YOU TO US. THEN GOD CALLED YOU HOME, SON, BUT OH,
HOW WE LOVED YOU. MUM AND DAD
Gunner Frederick Albert Gordon Green, RCA, 4.10.44 (age 21) [CESENA]

CLIFF AND I LIVED A GLORIOUS LIFETIME TOGETHER IN FIVE SHORT MONTHS. VERA
Sergeant Clifford Vernon Hebner MM, CRCE, 5.10.44 (age 32) [SCHOONSELHOF]

THE ONLY LIFE THAT IS WORTH ANYTHING IS THE LIFE OF SERVICE TO HUMANITY.
Private Wallace Clifford Cosby, RHLI, 6.10.44 (age 29) [BERGEN-OP-ZOOM]

IN MEMORY OF OUR BELOVED AND ONLY SON HARRY WHO LOVED LIVING.
Private Harry Laughington, CH, 9.10.44 (age 19) [HOLTEN]

"THE LORD WILL NOT CAST OFF HIS PEOPLE, NEITHER WILL HE FORSAKE HIS INHERITANCE."
Rifleman Fred William McRitchie, RWR, 9.10.44 (age 19) [ADEGEM]

DEAR FATHER, SAFE FROM GRIEF AND PAIN. I WILL MEET YOU AGAIN. SON GRANT
Corporal Sydney Smead, ESR, 14.10.44 (age 39) [BERGEN-OP-ZOOM]

IN LOVING MEMORY OF A DEAR SON. "DEATH BEFORE DISHONOUR."
Private Earl Springett, HPER, 15.10.44 (age 23) [CORIANO RIDGE]

PLEASE GOD, LET HIM KNOW THAT WE DO NOT FORGET. WE LOVE AND MISS HIM SO.
MOTHER AND BROTHERS
Private Henry Howell, ESR, 16.10.44 (age 22) [BERGEN-OP-ZOOM]

THIS EARTH HAS NEVER BORNE A NOBLER MAN.
Private Frank Agnew, NS(NB)R, 16.10.44 (age 26) [ADEGEM]

"WHEN THOU LIEST DOWN THOU SHALT NOT BE AFRAID . . . AND THY SLEEP SHALL BE SWEET."
Corporal Einar Godtfred Pettersen, CHO, 18.10.44 (age 39) [ADEGEM]

THEY ARE NOT DEAD IN THE HEARTS OF THOSE WHOM THEY HAVE BLESSED. THEY LIVE AGAIN.
Private William Charles Alexander, CH, 18.10.44 (age 37) [BERGEN-OP-ZOOM]

YOU HAVE LEFT A LONELINESS THE WORLD CAN NEVER FILL. OUR LOVE WAS NOT FOR A
LIFETIME BUT FOR AN ETERNITY.
Private Allan Homer Trelford, CSR, 18.10.44 (age 23) [ADEGEM]

WE LOVED HIS COMFORTING PRESENCE. MAY HIS UNSELFISH SOUL BE NOW COMFORTED.
Private John Dougald MacDougall, SDGH, 18.10.44 (age 20) [ADEGEM]

A BOY'S YOUNG GALLANT GRAVE. HIS SPIRIT IS IN CANADA, HIS SOUL WITH GOD TO-DAY.
Lieutenant James Owrey William Weldon, TRR, 20.10.44 (age 31) [SANTERNO VALLEY]

GLORY TO GOD IN THE HIGHEST: AND ON EARTH PEACE TO MEN OF GOOD WILL. LUKE II. 14
Sergeant Robert Edward McWhirter, AR, 20.10.44 (age 25) [BERGEN-OP-ZOOM]

EVEN THOUGH WE MISS YOU SO, GOD ONLY TAKES THE BEST. THE WAR IS OVER NOW, MY SON.
Gunner Mathew Walter William McCarthy, RCA, 22.10.44 (age 21) [CORIANO RIDGE]

'TISN'T LIFE THAT MATTERS, 'TIS THE COURAGE YOU BRING TO IT.
Guardsman Robert Parent, LWR, 23.10.44 (age 32) [BERGEN-OP-ZOOM]

HIS BROTHER CEDRIC, ROYAL CANADIAN NAVY, WAS LOST IN THE ATLANTIC,
22ND OCTOBER 1940, AGE 27.
Sergeant Desmond Smith, RCAF, 23.10.44 (age 20) [HARROGATE]

WHILE VICTORY SHINES ON LIFE'S EBBING SANDS WHO WOULD NOT DIE WITH THE BRAVE.
Private James Nevin Bonar, QOCHC, 23.10.44 (age 29) [BERGEN-OP-ZOOM]

"AND JESUS CAME AND TOUCHED THEM, AND SAID, 'ARISE, AND BE NOT AFRAID.'"
Lance Corporal John Wilkinson, QOCHC, 23.10.44 (age 34) [BERGEN-OP-ZOOM]

GARTH DIED AS HE LIVED, HELPING OTHERS. HIS LIGHT STILL SHINES BEFORE MEN.
Private Garth Alford Witty, LWR, 25.10.44 (age 22) [BERGEN-OP-ZOOM]

SINCE YOU WERE CALLED TO REST HOW I REMEMBER THAT SAD DAY.
'TWAS I THAT LOVED YOU BEST.
Private William John Cosens, AR, 27.10.44 (age 22) [ADEGEM]

A BELOVED HUSBAND AND SON. DEATH HAS MOULDED INTO A CALM COMPLETENESS
THE STATUE OF HIS LIFE. R.I.P.
Private William Gill, CSR, 27.10.44 (age 32) [ADEGEM]

"SEEKING NOTHING, GIVING ALL, ANSWERING TO HONOUR'S CALL." LORD GORELL
Major Frederick Keith Amy, RCA, 29.10.44 (age 32) [BERGEN-OP-ZOOM]

"COME IN, COME IN: ETERNAL GLORY THOU SHALT WIN." PILGRIM'S PROGRESS
Lieutenant John Trelawney Scudamore, BCR, 29.10.44 (age 21) [BERGEN-OP-ZOOM]

GOD REST THEE, MY BELOVED, MY HEART IS THERE WITH YOU. YOUR LONELY WIFE WANDA
Private Harold Hussey, HLIC, 31.10.44 (age 36) [ADEGEM]

MY BILLY BOY. A GOOD BABY, A GOOD BOY, DIED A BRAVE SOLDIER.
Trooper William Walter Quinn, RCD, 31.10.44 (age 22) [GRADARA]

"THERE WAS A MAN SENT FROM GOD WHOSE NAME WAS JOHN." ST. JOHN I. 6
Private John Clarence Esselment, HLIC, 31.10.44 (age 28) [ADEGEM]

THE LORD IS MY PILOT, I SHALL NOT DRIFT. HE LIGHTETH ME ACROSS THE DARK WATERS.
Corporal Ernest Alexander Dixon, SDGH, 1.11.44) [ADEGEM]

"IF I CAN STOP ONE HEART FROM BREAKING I SHALL NOT LIVE IN VAIN."
Flying Officer William St. Clair Huskilson, RCAF, 2.11.44 (age 21) [RHEINBERG]

NOT THE ONLY ONE, 'TIS TRUE. OTHERS MADE THAT JOURNEY, TOO, NOT RETURNING WITH THE REST. DARLING SON, ONE OF THE BEST.
Rifleman Jarvis Alloun McRae, RRR, 2.11.44 (age 19) [ADEGEM]

LOVE ENDURETH AFTER DEATH.
Lance Bombardier Donald Laverne Minion, RCA, 2.11.44 (age 20) [BERGEN-OP-ZOOM]

"AND HE SAID UNTO HIM, ARISE, GO THY WAY, THY FAITH HATH MADE THEE WHOLE."
Lance Corporal John Allan Weatherson, GGFG, 3.11.44 (age 23) [SCHOONSELHOOF]

"BUT THESE WERE MERCIFUL MEN WHOSE RIGHTEOUSNESS HATH NOT BEEN FORGOTTEN."
Flying Officer Walter Franklin Moran, RCAF, 4.11.44 (age 29) [RHEINBERG]

"TO THIS END WAS I BORN . . . THAT I SHOULD BEAR WITNESS UNTO THE TRUTH." ST. JOHN XVIII. 37
Flying Officer Edwin Albert Love, RCAF, 4.11.44 (age 21) [VENRAY]

HIS INFLUENCE SHALL LIVE ON FOR GOOD.
Gunner Thomas Stanley Rowan, RCA, 4.11.44 [ANCONA]

DREAM ON; ONLY DREAMS ENDURE: LOVE, PEACE AND TRUTH— HEAVEN CAN HOLD NO MORE.
Flying Officer Harold Davison Durrant, RCAF, 7.11.44 (age 28) [ADEGEM]

HIS WAYS WERE WAYS OF GENTLENESS, HIS PATHS WERE PATHS OF PEACE.
Private Murdoch Ian Leslie Morrison, SSR, 15.11.44 (age 23) [GROESBEEK]

BELOVED ONE, THE WORLD BOWS ITS HEAD IN REVERENCE AT YOUR SACRIFICE.
Pilot Officer Charles Hamel, RCAF, 20.11.44 (age 21) [CHESTER (BLACON)]

DIED IN ACTION DOING HIS DUTY WHICH IS ONE OF THE GREAT ANCHORS OF THE SOUL.
Flying Officer Jack Harvey Johnston, RCAF, 21.11.44 (age 29) [REICHSWALD FOREST]

NEITHER COUNT I MY LIFE DEAR UNTO MYSELF. ACTS XX. 24
Pilot Officer Hartley Ernest Reynolds, RCAF, 21.11.44 (age 27) [HARROGATE]

IN THE REALM OF TIME, HOW BRIEF HIS EARTHLY LIFE, YET SO MOMENTOUS IN ITS ISSUE.
Flight Sergeant Owen Earle Venning, RCAF, 27.11.44 (age 20) [HARROGATE]

SADLY MISSED BY HIS LOVING WIFE CATHERINE, LEFT ALONE.
Private Sam Flundra, CSR, 28.11.44 (age 22) [GROESBEEK]

"THE LORD GAVE, AND THE LORD HATH TAKEN AWAY." OURS IT SEEMED, LORD, FOR JUST A DAY.
Pilot Officer Melvin Osborne Orr, RCAF, 29.11.44 (age 19) [RHEINBERG]

HE KNEW DEATH IS BUT A DOOR, KNEW HE WAS FIGHTING FOR A KINDER WORLD, A CLEANER BREED.
Corporal Alexander McNabb, WNSR, 2.12.44 (age 35) [RAVENNA]

SON OF IMMORTAL SEED, HIGH DESTINED MEN ARE WE.
Captain Samuel Ray Patte, RCA, 3.12.44 (age 26) [CORIANO RIDGE]

"FOR THOU, LORD, ART GOOD . . . AND PLENTEOUS IN MERCY UNTO ALL THEM THAT CALL UPON THEE."
Flight Lieutenant William Lee Saunders, RCAF, 3.12.44 (age 22) [REICHSWALD FOREST]

OUR BELOVED SON. BEHOLD, GOD IS MY SALVATION: I WILL TRUST AND NOT BE AFRAID.
Corporal William Keith Barlow, RCR, 5.12.44 (age 21) [RAVENNA]

HE WAS STRONG AND OF GOOD COURAGE. HE WAS NOT AFRAID, NEITHER WAS HE DISMAYED.
Captain Peder Harbo Anderdon Hertzberg, RCR, 5.12.44 (age 24) [RAVENNA]

BURIED IN FOREIGN SOIL BUT STILL AT HOME.
Private Henry Hohenleitner, WR, 5.12.44 [RAVENNA]

IF HONOR CALLS WHERE SHE POINTS THE WAY THE SONS OF HONOR FOLLOW AND OBEY. CHURCHILL
Flying Officer Jack Douglas Baird, RCAF, 6.12.44 (age 20) [CHESTER (BLACON)]

THY DEAD MEN SHALL LIVE, TOGETHER WITH MY DEAD BODY SHALL THEY ARISE. ISAIAH XXVI. 19
Trooper Basil Stillman, 12th MD, 6.12.44 (age 20) [BERGEN-OP-ZOOM]

NO PEN CAN WRITE, NO TONGUE CAN TELL MY SAD AND BITTER LOSS. MOTHER
Private Alexander Richard Roe, IRC, 8.12.44 (age 21) [ARGENTA GAP]

"HE LIVES! HE WAKES! 'TIS DEATH IS DEAD, NOT HE." LOVE NEVER FAILETH.
Private John David Mitchell, PR, 8.12.44 (age 18) [RAVENNA]

YOUR MEMORY AND LOVE WILL EVER LAST. EACH DAY IN OUR SON I FIND COMFORT.
Private Kenneth Eugene Conner, HPER, 8.12.44 (age 23) [RAVENNA]

EGO SUM RESURRECTIO ET VITA: QUI CREDIT IN ME, ETIAM SI MORTUUS FUERIT, VIVET.
(I am the resurrection and the life: he that believeth in Me, though he were dead, yet shall he live.)
Private John Caspar Gebert, CBH, 10.12.44 (age 22) [RAVENNA]

IN MEMORY OF A DEAR SON WHO GAVE HIS LIFE ON THE BATTLEFIELD IN HOLLAND.
Private Eugene Joseph Schnob, CH, 12.12.44 (age 20) [BROOKWOOD]

BORN NOT FOR OURSELVES ALONE BUT FOR THE WHOLE WORLD.
Corporal William Alfred van Koughnet, LSR, *12.12.44 (age 26)* [BERGEN-OP-ZOOM]

SEEK FIRST THE KINGDOM OF GOD.
Private Alexander John McLean, CBH, *13.12.44 (age 35)* [VILLANOVA]
Sapper Keith Mabin McLean, CRCE, *12.1.45 (age 24)* [VILLANOVA]

A MAN AMONG BRAVE MEN VINDICATING HONOUR, TRUTH AND RIGHT.
Private Edwin Russell Campbell, LRSR, *13.12.44 (age 25)* [VILLANOVA]

SI DIEU PERMET À LA MORT DE DÉTRUIRE, C'EST POUR RELEVER LUI-MÊME CE QUI TOMBE.
(If God allows death to destroy, it is to raise up Himself the one who falls.)
Private Philippe Chartier, LRSR, *14.12.44 (age 30)* [VILLANOVA]

DEAR DADDY, IN GOD'S KEEPING TILL JESUS COMES. WIFE AND SON.
SEE ST. JOHN III. 16.
Private William Ivan Duke, SHC, *14.12.44 (age 35)* [RAVENNA]

HE LOVED HIS COUNTRY MORE THAN HE FEARED DEATH.
Lance Corporal Lorne Smythe, CPC, *17.12.44 (age 19)* [CORIANO RIDGE]

MAY WE, REMEMBERING HIS EXAMPLE, FOLLOW THAT BRIGHT STAR INTO THE SUNRISE.
Major Eric Holland Thorne, RCR, *18.12.44 (age 38)* [ARGENTA GAP]

UNTOLD WANT, BY LIFE AND LAND NE'ER GRANTED, NOW VOYAGER, SAIL THOU FORTH
TO SEEK AND FIND.
Private John Bradley, WNSR, *18.12.44 (age 25)* [RAVENNA]

HOW SLEEP THE BRAVE WHO SINK TO REST BY ALL THEIR COUNTRY'S WISHES BLEST.
Lance Corporal James Wilfred Fountain, IRC, *20.12.44 (age 22)* [VILLANOVA]

A BRAVE CANADIAN SOLDIER. A LOYAL CITIZEN OF U.S.A. REST IN PEACE.
Private Robert Cameron, QOCHC, *20.12.44 (age 34)* [GROESBEEK]

"HE WHO WOULD VALIANT BE 'GAINST ALL DISASTER, LET HIM IN CONSTANCY
FOLLOW THE MASTER."
Pilot Officer Norman Ivor Freakley (of Canada), RAF, *24.12.44 (age 22)*
[REICHSWALD FOREST]

"A PARTAKER OF THE GLORY THAT SHALL BE REVEALED."
MOURNED BY WIFE AND THREE SONS.
Private Wilbert Carl Hart, BWC, *24.12.44 (age 37)* [GROESBEEK]

FAR FROM HOME BUT NEAR TO GOD. "LET NOT YOUR HEART BE TROUBLED."
Sapper Angus Lorne MacDonald, CRCE, *25.12.44 (age 25)* [VILLANOVA]

OUR JERRY. OUR ONLY CHILD. SAFE IN THE ARMS OF JESUS. MUM AND DAD
Trooper Gerald Class, GGHG, *27.12.44 (age 24)* [ARGENTA GAP]

THOU WILT KEEP HIM IN PERFECT PEACE BECAUSE HE TRUSTETH IN THEE. ISAIAH XXVI. 3
Private George Reid, IRC, *31.12.44 (age 29)* [ANCONA]

OUR BELOVED SON, A CANADIAN LOYAL AND TRUE, AT REST UNDER ITALIAN SKIES. R.I.P.
Lieutenant Daniels William Burns, RCR, *1.1.45 (age 26)* [ARGENTA GAP]

GOD BECKONED YOU: HE NEEDED A NEW STAR IN HEAVEN: NONE BRIGHTER EVER SHONE.
MOTHER
Private Neale Warren Merritt, NBR, 1.1.45 (age 23) [GROESBEEK]

YOU HAVE DONE YOUR SHARE. GOD GAVE US STRENGTH TO BEAR.
DAD, MOM, SISTERS AND BROTHERS
Private John Oliver Thibeault, CBH, 3.1.45 (age 23) [RAVENNA]

HE GAVE HIS LAST FULL MEASURE OF DEVOTION.
Private John Irving Clifford, IRC, 4.1.45 (age 19) [VILLANOVA]

"WAIT ON THE LORD: BE OF GOOD COURAGE, AND HE SHALL STRENGTHEN THINE HEART."
Lieutenant Keith Wilmot Hare, IRC, 4.1.45 (age 30) [RAVENNA]

OUR ONLY CHILD, BELOVED BEYOND WORDS. MAY HIS SOUL REST IN PEACE.
MOTHER & DAD, QUEBEC.
Lieutenant Matthew Ralph Kane, RCASC, 6.1.45 (age 24) [BERGEN-OP-ZOOM]

HE EARNED MORE THAN MORTALS PAY.
Private Joseph Ovila Marceau Belisle, PR, 8.1.45 (age 22) [ARGENTA GAP]

THERE IS A JOB TO DO. HE WHO LAID ASIDE HIS FEARS THAT WE MIGHT LIVE IN PEACE.
Flying Officer Kenneth Albert Stroh, RCAF, 8.1.45 (age 28) [DURNBACH]

DEAR GOD, OUR LOVE RETURNS HIM TO YOU FOR HIS GLORY AND FOR OURS.
Warrant Officer II Jean Jacques Marcel Simard, RCAF, 14.1.45 [HARROGATE]

LOST HIS YOUNG, HAPPY LIFE OBLIGING OTHERS. A HERO NEVERTHELESS. DAD
Pilot Officer James Firth, RCAF, 15.1.45 (age 21) [CHESTER (BLACON)]

THE YEARS TOUCH NOT THE LOVE THAT NEVER DIES. MOTHER
Lance Corporal Daniel Merrill Peppard, LSR, 20.1.45 (age 22) [GROESBEEK]

STANDETH GOD WITHIN THE SHADOW KEEPING WATCH ABOVE HIS OWN.
Squadron Leader Ronald Henry Stringer DFC, RCAF, 21.1.45 (age 25) [ARGENTA GAP]

SOFTLY THE LEAVES OF MEMORY FALL, GATHER THEM GENTLY AND TREASURE THEM ALL.
Private Charles Joseph Beaudry, LWR, 26.1.45 (age 28) [BERGEN-OP-ZOOM]

THY WORD IS A LAMP UNTO MY FEET AND A LIGHT UNTO MY PATH. PSALMS CXIX. 105
Gunner Edwin Arthur Pratt, RCA, 27.1.45 (age 20) [BERGEN-OP-ZOOM]

"THEY ARE NOT OF THE WORLD, EVEN AS I AM NOT OF THE WORLD." ST. JOHN XVII. 16
Private Joseph Harry Slater, LWR, 28.1.45 (age 23) [GROESBEEK]

WITH THE MORN THOSE ANGEL FACES SMILE WHICH I HAVE LOVED AND LOST, AWHILE.
Captain Richard Fowlke Dickie, LWR, 29.1.45 (age 21) [GROESBEEK]

"AND ALL OUR CALM IS IN THAT BALM—NOT LOST BUT GONE BEFORE."
Pilot Officer Arthur Malcolm Jones, RCAF, 2.2.45 (age 31) [REICHSWALD FOREST]

GONE TO VALHALLA. MAY HIS SOUL REST IN PEACE.
Flight Sergeant Edward Charles Dufresne, RCAF, 3.2.45 (age 18) [DURNBACH]

BORN FOR THE FUTURE, TO THE FUTURE LOST.
Pilot Officer Alfred Hector Morrison, RCAF, 3.2.45 (age 32) [REICHSWALD FOREST]

HE IS PART OF EVERY GOLDEN DAWN AND EVERY STAR.
Flying Officer Alan Quilliam Downward, RCAF, *3.2.45 (age 20)* [REICHSWALD FOREST]

FAIL HIM NOT. HE DIED THAT OTHERS MIGHT LIVE. GREATER LOVE HATH NO MAN.
Corporal Arthur Sidney Low, CSR, *9.2.45 (age 23)* [GROESBEEK]

HE IS MARCHING WITH HIS COMRADES SOMEWHERE ON THE ROAD AHEAD.
Private Bernard Merlyn Krislock, CSR, *9.2.45 (age 21)* [GROESBEEK]

MY DARLING SON WILLIAM, BRAVEST BOY GOD EVER MADE.
LOVED AND NOT FORGOTTEN. MOTHER
Private William Edgar Dunn, AR, *11.2.45 (age 19)* [BERGEN-OP-ZOOM]

ALL MY TRUST IN THEE, O LORD, I SAID, THOU ART MY GOD; MY LOTS ARE
IN THY HANDS. R.I.P.
Able Seaman Joseph Andrew Richard Gauthier, RCNVR, *14.2.45 (age 20)* [ADEGEM]

THE COST OF A THING IS THE AMOUNT OF LIFE WHICH MUST BE EXCHANGED FOR IT.
Flying Officer James David Sharples DFC, RCAF, *16.2.45 (age 23)* [DURNBACH]

THANKS FOR EVERYTHING, BOBBY. REMEMBERED BY MOM, DAD,
SISTERS AND BROTHERS.
Private Robert Linden Jensen, RWR, *16.2.45 (age 21)* [GROESBEEK]

CALMLY HE SLEEPS AS SLEEP THE BRAVE WHERE LIE THE NATION'S DEAD.
Private Robert Rufus Shearing, CSR, *18.2.45 (age 32)* [GROESBEEK]

KEPT BY AN ALL SUSTAINING POWER, HE LOANED HIS LIFE TO GOD.
Lance Corporal Henry Guaid Elam, CSR, *19.2.45 (age 25)* [GROESBEEK]

HE WAS SO YOUNG AND FAIR, SO TRUE, BORN WITH THE WILL TO DARE, THE WISH TO DO.
Lance Corporal Hugh Maitland Millard, ESR, *19.2.45 (age 24)* [GROESBEEK]

AND IN OUR LIVES LET THY REMEMBRANCE LINGER AS LIGHTLY AS A SUNBEAM
ON THE WATER.
Lieutenant Gordon Roseburgh Holder, RHLI, *19.2.45 (age 24)* [GROESBEEK]

EARTH CANNOT HIDE THE GLORY OF A NOBLE SOUL. HE DIED THAT HIS SON MIGHT LIVE.
Corporal Alan Robinson, RHLI, *21.2.45 (age 29)* [GROESBEEK]

"YOUR DEEDS REMEMBERED, HOMAGE TO THEE TENDERED, DEPARTED BUT NOT APART,
OF US THOU ART STILL."
Trooper Robert James Elliott, SFR, *21.2.45 (age 24)* [GROESBEEK]

"HE DID GOD'S WILL; TO HIM, ALL ONE, IF ON EARTH OR IN THE SUN." BROWNING
Flying Officer Colin John Pope Ramsey, RCAF, *21.2.45 (age 20)* [REICHSWALD FOREST]

IN MEMORY OF A DEAR HUSBAND AND FATHER. YOU DIED, BELOVED, THAT WE MIGHT LIVE.
Private Elmer Roland Johnson, LER, *22.2.45 (age 27)* [CORIANO RIDGE]

YOU SACRIFICED WHAT MEN CANNOT GIVE, BREATH OF YOUR LIFE, THAT WE MIGHT LIVE.
Lieutenant Thomas Edison Campbell, ESR, *24.2.45 (age 28)* [GROESBEEK]

THE LORD LIFT UP HIS COUNTENANCE UPON THEE AND GIVE THEE PEACE FROM WARS.
Gunner John Bradley, RCA, *24.2.45* [GROESBEEK]

British and Canadian graves at Reydarfjordur Cemetery, Iceland (David Noakes).

Graves of the Palestine Regiment (Jewish Brigade) at Ravenna War Cemetery.

Graves of the Airborne Regiment predominate at Ranville War Cemetery, Normandy
(Matt Symes).

Perth Regiment graves at Villanova Canadian War Cemetery, Italy.

Gunners of the 166th Newfoundland Field Artillery lie at rest at the Sangro River War Cemetery.

Canadian members of the First Special Service Force buried at Beach Head War Cemetery, Anzio, Italy.

A quotation from Alexander Pope on the grave of Lieutenant Donald William Chute at Ancona War Cemetery, Italy.

The graves of two wars stand side by side at Terlincthun War Cemetery in the Pas-de-Calais, France (Steve Douglas).

HEAR MY UNWORTHY PRAYER, PRESERVE FROM ALL DANGER, GIVE MY IMMORTAL SOUL
A PLACE AMONG THY CHOSEN.
Private Joseph Leopold Aubin, LER, 24.2.45 (age 21) [RAVENNA]

"GLORY, HONOUR, AND PEACE, TO EVERY MAN THAT WORKETH GOOD."
Private Thomas McDiarmid Orr, RHLI, 26.2.45 (age 32) [GROESBEEK]

MY DEAR HUSBAND EARL. MY GREATEST POSSESSIONS, MEMORIES OF YOU. LOVING WIFE MARY
Rifleman Earl James Elliot Messing, QORC, 26.2.45 (age 22) [GROESBEEK]

UNTIL I COME AND TAKE YOU AWAY TO A LAND LIKE YOUR OWN LAND. II KINGS XVIII. 32
Guardsman George Macbeth Young, CGG, 26.2.45 (age 21) [GROESBEEK]

"I HAVE GLORIFIED THEE ON EARTH: I HAVE FINISHED THE WORK THOU GAVEST ME."
Trooper Donald Nelson Wiggins, 1st Hussars, 26.2.45 (age 20) [GROESBEEK]

"CLOTHED WITH WHITE ROBES AND PALMS IN THEIR HANDS." REV. VII. 9
Private Victor Stewart, ASHC, 27.2.45 (age 23) [GROESBEEK]

A GOOD BOY AND A TRUE SON. HIS FAITH IN GOD & DUTY WAS SUBLIME.
REMEMBERED BY MOM & DAD.
Rifleman Thomas Patrick D'Iasio, RRR, 27.2.45 (age 22) [GROESBEEK]

BLESSED ARE THE EARLY DEAD.
Private William Harry Thomas Rankel, QOCHC, 27.2.45 (age 22) [GROESBEEK]

IF ALL MEN HAD HEARTS LIKE HIS, THERE WOULD BE NO MORE WAR.
Private Gordon Stewart Brown, AR, 28.2.45 (age 20) [GROESBEEK]

WITH SO MUCH TO REMEMBER, HOW COULD WE FORGET.
Flight Lieutenant Geoffrey Fitton Coward, RCAF, 1.3.45 (age 24) [BECKLINGEN]

"AND WHITE ROBES WERE GIVEN TO EVERY ONE OF THEM." REVELATION VI.2
Private Boyce Morcambe Alexander, ESR, 1.3.45 [GROESBEEK]

TO LIVE IN HEARTS WE LEAVE BEHIND IS NOT TO DIE. CAMPBELL
Sergeant Alfred Cadman, ESR, 1.3.45 (age 29) [GROESBEEK]

MAY YOU REST IN PEACE—OUR PRAYER. TO BE UNITED AGAIN—OUR HOPE.
Private Wilfred Melanson, NS(NB)R, 2.3.45 [GROESBEEK]

YOU WERE YOUR MOTHER'S TREASURE AND YOUR FATHER'S PRIDE. "DEATH, BE NOT PROUD."
Private Donald Montgomery, RHLI, 2.3.45 (age 23) [GROESBEEK]

BLESSED ARE THOSE THAT MOURN, FOR THEY SHALL BE COMFORTED. ST. MATTHEW V. 4
Private William Howard White, RHLI, 2.3.45 (age 38) [GROESBEEK]

AT PEACE WITH GOD AND THE WORLD. WIFE AND DAUGHTER
Gunner Earl Richard Russett, RCA, 2.3.45 (age 25) [GROESBEEK]

IN MEMORY OF MY DARLING HUSBAND LLOYD, AND COLIN, OUR ONLY SON, ALSO AT REST.
Lance Corporal Lloyd Bulger, CRCEME, 3.3.45 (age 24) [GROESBEEK]

WELL DONE, OUR GOOD YOUNG SON AND BROTHER. "LOVE AND FREEDOM LIVE."
Lance Corporal Abraham Alexander Moyer, QOCHC, 3.3.45 (age 33) [GROESBEEK]

HE OVERCAME BY THE BLOOD OF THE LAMB AND BY THE WORD OF HIS TESTIMONY.
Private Franklin Crosby Norman, SSR, 3.3.45 (age 30) [GROESBEEK]

"THAT MAN SHALL NOT LIVE BY BREAD ALONE, BUT BY EVERY WORD OF GOD." ST. LUKE IV.4
Lance Corporal John Henry Watson, RRC, 3.3.45 (age 27) [GROESBEEK]

"REMEMBER ME, O MY GOD, FOR GOOD ACCORDING TO ALL THAT I HAVE DONE
FOR THIS PEOPLE."
Warrant Officer II Company Sergeant Major Anthony Petta, AR, 3.3.45 (age 29)
[GROESBEEK]

THE PEACE YOU GALLANTLY DIED FOR BE WITH YOU FOREVER. WE SHALL NOT FORGET.
Private John Frederick Roffey, SDGH, 3.3.45 (age 19) [GROESBEEK]

HIS MOTTO, NOT MINE, BUT THY WILL BE DONE IN ALL THINGS. SO SAITH THE LORD.
Private Thearon Brown, AR, 3.3.45 [GROESBEEK]

HE HAS COME INTO HIS HERITAGE.
Flying Officer Humphrey Stanley Watts, RCAF, 5.3.45 (age 28) [HARROGATE]

FOR THOU SHALT REST AND STAND IN THY LOT AT THE END OF THE DAYS. DANIEL XII. 13
Private Helmer Ordell Renman, HLIC, 5.3.45 (age 20) [GROESBEEK]

A TRUE CHRISTIAN GENTLEMAN. A DEVOTED SON LOVED AND HONORED BY EVERYONE.
Flying Officer Robert George Smith, RCAF, 5.3.45 (age 21) [HARROGATE]

THE GLORY OF YOUR DEATH STANDS OUT BEFORE US. MOTHER, DAD, JACK AND BILL
Gunner Winston Hart Morehouse, RCA, 6.3.45 (age 38) [GROESBEEK]

"HE LINGERS WITH A BACKWARD SMILE TILL WE CAN OVERTAKE."
Pilot Officer Finley Ralph Leet, RCAF, 6.3.45 (age 20) [BROOKWOOD]

ABOVE THE CLOUDS THE SUN IS ALWAYS SHINING. HIS WIFE PEGGY AND PARENTS.
Flight Lieutenant Glenn Royal Harris, RCAF, 6.3.45 (age 25) [BROOKWOOD]

BLESSED ARE THE PURE IN HEART: FOR THEY SHALL SEE GOD. MATT. V. 8
Private Lawrence Ole Velve, LWR, 8.3.45 (age 21) [GROESBEEK]

DESTINY FULFILLED.
Private Robert Stephens McMillan, RHLI, 8.3.45 (age 25)) [GROESBEEK]

I HAVE SUFFERED.
Private James Harold Madden, RHLI, 8.3.45 (age 21)) [GROESBEEK]

OUR ETERNAL LOVE TO THOSE WHO FINISHED THEIR COURSE AND KEPT THE FAITH.
Flying Officer Graeme Alistair Robinson, RCAF, 15.3.45 (age 20) [BERLIN]

DEAR OLD PAL, HOW WE MISS YOU. WE ARE LONELY TONIGHT. MOTHER AND DAD
Flying Officer Earle Robert Evans DFC, RCAF, 15.3.45 (age 20) [NEDERWEERT]

YOU WERE TIRED BUT NOW YOU ARE AT REST. I'LL LOVE YOU ALWAYS. LOVING WIFE JUDY
Lieutenant Bruce Frederick Zimmerman, HLIC, 26.3.45 (age 24) [GROESBEEK]

WHEN NIGHT FALLS AND I AM ALL ALONE, MY HEART WHISPERS,
IF ONLY HE COULD COME HOME.
Gunner Robert Morton Robinson, RCA, 26.3.45 (age 23) [GROESBEEK]

FROM ME YOU WERE TAKEN. MY HEART WILL ALWAYS MOURN FOR YOU. REST IN PEACE, DEAR SON.
Private Frederick Lissoway, QOCHC, 30.3.45 (age 37) [GROESBEEK]

"I STAND TO GOD AND MY COUNTRY." ASTON
Private Edward Oliver Oberg, QOCHC, 30.3.45 (AGE 19) [GROESBEEK]

"BEING JUSTIFIED BY FAITH, WE HAVE PEACE. . . THROUGH OUR LORD JESUS CHRIST." ROM. V.1
Pilot Officer Albert Dorey, RCAF, 31.3.45 (age 27) [BECKLINGEN]

YOURS HAS THE SUFFERING BEEN: THE MEMORY SHALL BE OURS.
Private Archibald William Thompson, CH, 1.4.45 (age 20) [GROESBEEK]

THE BLESSINGS OF HIS QUIET LIFE FELL AROUND US LIKE THE DEW.
Rifleman Delmar Marvin Dowling, QORC, 3.4.45 (age 20) [GROESBEEK]

IN ALL THY WAYS ACKNOWLEDGE HIM AND HE SHALL DIRECT THY PATHS. PROVERBS III. 6
Private Joseph Smith Stewart, RRC, 3.4.45 (age 19) [HOLTEN]

YET LOVE WILL DREAM AND FAITH WILL TRUST THAT SOMEHOW, SOMEWHERE, MEET WE MUST.
Sergeant David MacIntyre, RRC, 4.4.45 (age 26) [HOLTEN]

SADLY TODAY I CLOSE MY EYES AND DREAM, AND ONCE AGAIN, MY SON, I SEE YOU SMILE. MOTHER
Private Robert Edward Bailey, RRC, 4.4.45 (age 34) [HOLTEN]

KATHY MAE'S DADDY.
Corporal John James Currie, RRC, 5.4.45 (age 29) [GROESBEEK]

I THANK MY GOD AT EVERY REMEMBRANCE OF YOU. PHILIPPIANS I. 3
Flight Lieutenant Gareth Allen Barker, RCAF, 6.4.45 (age 22) [BECKLINGEN]

"HE WILL SWALLOW UP DEATH IN VICTORY." ISAIAH XXV. 8
Flying Officer Stanley Ernest Messum, RCAF, 6.4.45 (age 29) [REICHSWALD FOREST]

GOD HAS HIS MYSTERIES OF GRACE, WAYS WE CANNOT TELL. GOOD NIGHT, JACK
Private John Caullay, SHC, 8.4.45 (age 20) [GROESBEEK]

SON, GO WORK TO-DAY IN MY VINEYARD. MATT. XXI. 28
Warrant Officer II Thomas William Fry, RCAF, 9.4.45 (age 21) [HARROGATE]

TILL THE FIRST DAY.
Pilot Officer George Frederick Peterson, RCAF, 11.4.45 (age 22) [ARNHEM (OOSTERBEEK)]

FIND PEACE IN THE LAND BEYOND, O GALLANT WARRIOR OF CANADA. WE MISS YOU, SON.
Private Ronald Olivier, 48th HC, 12.4.45 (age 20) [HOLTEN]

LOVE'S STRENGTH STANDETH IN LOVE'S SACRIFICE AND WHO SO SUFFERS MOST HATH MOST TO GIVE.
Private Ivan Roy Pindar, HPER, 13.4.45 (age 22) [HOLTEN]

ALBERTA'S SOD, AND HERE HE PLOWED WITH FURROW STRAIGHT FOR YOU AND GOD.
Sergeant Glen Miller, LER, 13.4.45 (age 23) [HOLTEN]

HE WILL LIVE IN OUR HEARTS FOREVER AND BE GREAT AMONG YOU, HAVING SERVED.
Private Allan Robert McMillan, LSR, 14.4.45 (age 20) [HOLTEN]

LIFE AND ALL IT POSSESSES IS A TRUST FROM ALMIGHTY GOD.
Private Robert May, SHC, 14.4.45 (age 36) [HOLTEN]

"MY PRESENCE SHALL GO WITH THEE AND I WILL GIVE THEE REST."
Private Ronald Victor Hyson, 48th HC, 16.4.45 (age 24) [HOLTEN]

"LEAD KINDLY LIGHT . . . THE NIGHT IS DARK, AND I AM FAR FROM HOME.
LEAD THOU ME ON."
Gunner James Duncan Wilson, RCA, 17.4.45 [GROESBEEK]

OUR HEARTS EVER CHERISH HIM IN FOND REMEMBRANCE AND ARE HUMBLE WITHIN US.
Flying Officer Alexander Graham Scott, RCAF, 19.4.45 (age 19) [HAMBURG]

"HE MAKETH PEACE IN HIS HIGH PLACES." JOB XXV. 2
Private Leslie Alban Cross, RCASC, 19.4.45 (age 30) [GROESBEEK]

"FOR EVER TO HOLD YOU SO CLOSE TO OUR HEARTS."
Flight Sergeant Roger Thomas Bridger, RCAF, 20.4.45 (age 24) [HARROGATE]

"TO THEE ALL PRAISE AND GLORY BE. HOW SHALL WE SHOW OUR LOVE TO THEE WHO
GAVEST ALL?"
Corporal John Thomas Shedden, LWR, 22.4.45 [HOLTEN]

ALL THE WORLD—UNTIL TOMORROW.
Lieutenant Walter Allan Westwood, BWC, 28.4.45 (age 23) [HOLTEN]

MISSED BY ALL WHO KNEW HIM. ALSO FOND MEMORIES OF HIS BROTHER JACK,
LOST AT SEA.
Flight Sergeant Stuart Berryman, RCAF, 30.4.45 (age 23) [CHESTER (BLACON)]

WE STREW WITH LOVING MEMORIES THE PATHS HIS FEET HAVE TROD, BLESS THE YEARS
HE WAS OURS, AND LEAVE THE REST TO GOD.
Flying Officer Anthony Arthur Clifford, RCAF, 18.5.45 (age 21) [BROOKWOOD]

HER SUN WENT DOWN WHILE IT WAS YET DAY.
Wren Margaret Airlie McGill, WRCNS, 24.5.45 (age 33) [BROOKWOOD]

LORD, TEACH US TO COMMIT OURSELVES TO THY WILL EVEN IN DIFFICULT TIMES.
Gunner Esa Rinne, RCA, 28.5.45 (age 26) [BERGEN]

VALIANT SON OF PRINCE EDWARD ISLAND, CANADA.
Private Alfred Joseph Arsenault, LSR, 5.6.45 (age 28) [HOLTEN]

AND O'ER EACH SON A MOTHER'S TEARS WOULD SAY, O GOD! I GAVE MY BEST.
Captain Donald Norval Eddy, CRCEME, 16.7.45 (age 27) [GROESBEEK]

OUR SON. THE WAR WAS OVER, HIS WORK WELL DONE. GOD CALLED HIM TO
HIS HEAVENLY HOME.
Corporal George William Beattie, RCAF, 21.7.45 (age 23) [BROOKWOOD]

HIS LIFE WAS AN INSPIRATION, HIS END A BENEDICTION.
Lieutenant John Jones Etheridge, RCIC, 12.8.45 (age 21) [BROOKWOOD]

WHAT IS TO BE, IS TO BE; WHAT IS WRITTEN, IS WRITTEN. IN FOND MEMORY, PEGGY AND KIP
Captain Kelso James Johnston, RCAPC, 30.8.45 (age 35) [GROESBEEK]

"DID THE HAND THEN OF THE POTTER SHAKE?"
Squadron Leader Alfred Ernest Webster DFC, RCAF, 4.11.45 (age 36) [MUNSTER HEATH]

THEY SAY TIME HEALS. PERHAPS IT DOES, BUT MEMORIES LAST AND SO DOES LOVE.
Pilot Officer Walter Fred Conley, RCAF, 5.11.45 (age 25) [HARROGATE]

A CHEERFUL, GENEROUS FRIEND TO ALL WHO KNEW HIM AT ELGIN HOUSE, MUSKOKA, ONTARIO, CANADA.
Captain Howard Oliver Love, RCASC, 9.1.46 (age 32) [BROOKWOOD]

FOIS SHIORRUIDH DO T'ANAM.
(Eternal peace to thy soul.)
Private John Angus Beaton, RCASC, 27.1.46 (age 32) [HOLTEN]

THERE SHALL BE A REWARD, AND THY EXPECTATION SHALL NOT BE CUT OFF. PROV. XXIV.14
Trooper John Raymond Warren, RCAC, 19.4.46 (age 20) [BROOKWOOD]

Among the thousands of valedictions from the Second World War are some that are indescribably moving. Of all the ones that I have seen, however, this inscription on the headstone of a young British soldier buried at the Orvieto War Cemetery in Italy made the deepest impression. It speaks for the tragedy that descended on countless people, decent, principled human beings who suffered from the cruel ambitions of warlords impervious to mercy and intent on exacting revenge for the wrongs supposedly done to their countries. Like so many of the bereaved, these parents did not renounce their beliefs or the teachings of their faith when struck by the loss of a son, barely beyond his boyhood, that could just as easily have left them permanently embittered. We could do worse than take to heart the act, no less than the prayer, of forgiveness indelibly recorded in this epitaph:

FORGIVE US, AS WE FORGIVE THEM. WE HAVE FORGIVEN THEM; WE KNOW YOU DID, GEORGE.
Private George Sidney James Whife, The Buffs, 21.6.44 (age 20)

CHAPTER EIGHT

Je me souviens
Gradara War Cemetery, Italy

LE CANADA FRANÇAIS, FIERS DE TOI. DE LAC-AU-SAUMON.
TU FUS UN AUTRE DE NOS HÉROS.
(French Canada is proud of you. From Lac-au-Saumon.
You were another of our heroes.)
Private Ernest Loof, R22R, 15.9.44 (age 29)

The assault on the Gothic Line in September of 1944 was the fourth major operation the Canadians had undertaken in Italy since the invasion of Sicily fourteen months before. By this time the regiments that had fought at Ortona and in the Liri Valley had seen their companies shrivel to less than two thirds of their fighting strength. The D-Day landings and the campaign in northwest Europe brought the dispiriting realisation that the Canadians in Italy were second in line for replacements already shown to be insufficient for one theatre, let alone two. The last battles of the Canadian campaign in Italy were fought by exhausted, understrength units reinforced by rear echelon soldiers hastily converted into infantrymen or by men wounded in action and sent back to the front lines, sometimes before they had fully recovered.

In 1946 a soldier who had fought in Italy published an account of his company's actions in the Gothic Line battle. After describing the loss of a section in a brave but ill-starred attack on a German position, he paused to put their fate in a broader context:

> How many will remember these valiant boys who fell for liberty and
> humanity, who fell to keep far from Canada and their loved ones the danger
> and threat of a tyranny which had to be defeated beyond our borders. They
> and thousands of others gave their lives while a number of their countrymen
> refused to enter the frontline with them or to bolster their strength. Perhaps
> people will give them a fleeting thought on November 11, and no doubt
> wreaths will be laid at the tomb of the unknown soldier, but that will not
> bring them back. They can no longer inhale the fragrant scent of the roses
> which adorn their common grave where a volley is fired in salute.
>
> Perhaps if certain Canadians had been more generous, more conscious
> of their duty to their country and their fellow citizens in arms, we would

have had more reinforcements and more forces to attack and overcome the enemy. Instead of attacking fortified positions with ten or fifteen men to a platoon, we would have had platoons of thirty or thirty-five, the way we should have, which would have made our task easier. We would have had fewer wounded, fewer dead, and one man would not have had to do the fighting of two or even three. Unfortunately, here in this country, people debated conscription and compulsory service, and political parties engaged in bloody battles where nary a drop of blood spilled forth. Meanwhile, we were at the end of our tether, worn out, without reinforcements, and our blood was flowing.

These words convey the anger felt by many veterans at the unwillingness of the soldiers conscripted for home defence to volunteer for service overseas and the government's reluctance to send them overseas. The fear of dividing French and English Canada for the second time in a generation over the issue of compulsory service lay behind the government's hesitation; but the soldiers who had seen their comrades driven beyond the limits of endurance for lack of trained reinforcements felt betrayed by the politicians and opponents of conscription at home indifferent to the plight of the men in the front lines. The memoirs of the Italian campaign by Farley Mowat, Stan Scislowski, Syd Frost, and others record with no little bitterness the effects of a mishandled reinforcement policy on the morale and performance of men called upon to risk their lives time and again without hope of relief.

If the criticism is typical, however, the source is not. The passage cited comes from the pen of a French Canadian officer, Major Gaston Poulin, whose *696 Heures d'enfer avec le Royal 22e Régiment* is one of several eyewitness accounts describing the experiences of French Canada's soldiers in the Second World War. As a French Canadian proud of his lineage, Poulin might have been expected to share his compatriots' antipathy to conscription. As a frontline soldier and, more tellingly, an officer of the Van Doos ever mindful in battle to uphold his regiment's illustrious reputation, he spoke instead on behalf of his comrades who had deserved greater support from their government and fellow citizens. His reproach acts as a reminder that French Canadian attitudes towards military service, and to the war in general, were not as monolithic as is sometimes supposed. Poulin's memoirs combine with those of Jean-Victor Allard, Claude Châtillon, Gérard Marchand, Lucien Dumais, Charly Forbes, Leo Gariépy, among others, to present a side of French Canada's war largely, and unjustly, neglected in the country they served. Their writings, steeped in the sensibilities of a French Canada that no longer exists, complement the epitaphs chosen by the families of French Canadian soldiers whose sacrifice, like that of Poulin's comrades, has been overshadowed by the controversies and divisions within Canada.

The soldiers killed in the Gothic Line lie in the war cemeteries marking the stages of the Allied advance from the Metauro River to the Lombard plain. Two hundred and eighty-nine Canadians, whose lives were the first instalment in the most expensive Canadian operation in Italy, are buried in the small battlefield cemetery between Montecchio and Osteria Nuova, on the glacis of the Gothic Line. Another 427 were laid to rest in the spacious confines of the Coriano Ridge War Cemetery, where the stately, classicising entranceway gives onto a view over the burial ground and the two ridges beyond, San Martino and San Fortunato, where a good many of the soldiers in the Canadian sections died in battle. Headstones inscribed in French appear in the

Canadian sections in both cemeteries, but the memory of the Van Doos is carved into the saga of the Gothic Line most prominently at Gradara War Cemetery.

Italy is home to some of the most impressive war cemeteries designed by the War Graves Commission architects. The five stone-girded burial grounds built in the mountain pastures of the Asiago plateau by Sir Robert Lorimer were judged the most beautiful of the Great War cemeteries, and the achievements of his successor, Louis de Soissons, are no less noteworthy for their harmonisation of setting with aesthetic effects. At Gradara, temporary burials had been laid out on a hillside long terraced for agriculture; de Soissons improved on the site by sculpting the hillside into even tiers and arranging the headstones in curved rows undulating with the contours of the ground. At the foot of the hill, he constructed a grand threshold in the shape of a battlement, creating a visual echo with the Castle of Gradara which dominates the skyline opposite. The wall, with its three rounded bastions, is an apt feature historically as well as architecturally, for it draws the cemetery into the orbit of the castle famous as the scene of the doomed love of Paolo and Francesca, immortalised by Dante in Canto V of his *Inferno*.

Nearly one third of the 369 Canadians buried on the upper terraces at Gradara belonged to the Royal Canadian Artillery or to the Van Doos. A row of over fifty headstones occupies one level where soldiers from homes in Montreal, Bagotville, Ste Anne de Beaupré, St. Hilaire, Victoriaville, Acton Vale, Matane are commemorated in the language and traditions of the other Canada:

LE SOLDAT QUI MEURT POUR SAUVER SES FRÈRES ATTEINT AU PLUS HAUT
DEGRÉ DE LA CHARITÉ.
(The soldier who dies to save his brothers reaches the highest level of Christian love.)
Private Morris Brown Vuillermet, RCASC, 12.9.44 (age 30)

COMME UN LYS À PEINE ÉPANOUI SON ÂME A ÉTÉ CUEILLI POUR LES DÉMEURES
ÉTERNELLES.
(Like a lily scarcely bloomed, his soul was taken up to an eternal abode.)
Private Albert Emilien Roger Turcotte, R22R, 14.9.44 (age 19)
Private Joseph Rosaire Marcel Lebrun, R22R, 14.9.44

ORIGINAIRE DE VICTORIAVILLE, QUÉBEC, CANADA. REPOSE EN PAIX.
(Native of Victoriaville, Quebec, Canada. Rest in peace.)
Private René Langlois, R22R, 14.9.44 (age 20)

INTERCÈDE POUR NOUS AUPRÈS DE DIEU. AU REVOIR AU CIEL. RITA, JACQUES, CLAUDE.
(Intercede with God on our behalf. See you in heaven. Rita, Jacques, Claude.)
Private Roger Gaudet, R22R, 14.9.44 (age 24)

PARENTS AIMÉS, J'AI GARDÉ LA FOI ET COMBATTU LE BON COMBAT. AU REVOIR AU CIEL.
(Beloved parents, I kept the faith and fought the good fight. See you again in heaven.)
Private Louis Gérard Coutu, R22R, 14.9.44 (age 21)

REQUIESCAT IN PACE. DE PROFUNDIS, PATER AVE GLORIA.
Lance Corporal Narcisse Santerre, R22R, 14.9.44 (age 28)

LA BONTÉ DE SON CARACTÈRE LUI FIT DE NOMBREUX AMIS. QUE DIEU LE PROTÈGE.
(The goodness of his character won him many friends. May God protect him.)
Private Charles Ouimet, R22R, 14.9.44 (age 24)

PAR SON HÉROÏSME IL A SU SAUVER SA PATRIE, LE CANADA. DIEU SAUVE SON ÂME.
(By his heroism he was able to save his native land, Canada. God save his soul.)
Private Raoul Jacques, R22R, 14.9.44 (age 23)

ROGER, QUI N'AVAIT FOI QU'EN DIEU, PAYS ET LIBERTÉ, LES A DÉFENDUS HÉROÏQUEMENT.
(Roger, who had faith only in God, country, and freedom, defended them heroically.)
Private Roger Cousineau, R22R, 15.9.44 (age 18)

EN MÉMOIRE DE NOTRE DISPARU, TUÉ AU COMBAT À RIMINI. AU REVOIR AU CIEL.
(In memory of our departed one, killed in battle at Rimini. See you again in heaven.)
Private Marcel Lemieux, R22R, 15.9.44 (age 26)

VOUS QUI PASSEZ ICI PRIEZ POUR CE GLORIEUX HÉROS QUI REPOSE LOIN DES SIENS.
(You who pass by, pray for this glorious hero who lies at rest far from his loved ones.)
Private Léonard Langlois, R22R, 15.9.44 (age 21)

LE TEMPS FAIT SÉCHER LES PLEURS, MAIS NE PEUT ADOUCIR LA DOULEUR.
(Time makes dry the tears, but it cannot ease the pain.)
Private Joseph Lucien Hormisdas Faubert, R22R, 16.9.44 (age 20)

**SANS UN MOT D'ADIEU TU NOUS QUITTA. REÇOIS TA RÉCOMPENSE
BIEN MÉRITÉE—LE CIEL.**
(You left us without a word of farewell. Accept your well deserved reward—heaven.)
Private Lionel Pelletier, R22R, 17.9.44 (age 29)

IL A DONNÉ SA VIE POUR SON PAYS ET POUR LA PROTECTION DE CEUX QU'IL AIMAIT.
(He gave his life for his country and for the protection of those he loved.)
Private Joseph René Ouellet, R22R, 20.9.44 (age 26)

IL A PASSÉ SON ENFANCE ET FAIT SES ÉTUDES À MONTRÉAL, CANADA. UNE PRIÈRE, S.V.P.
(He spent his childhood and did his studies in Montreal, Canada. A prayer, please.)
Private Marcel Deschênes, R22R, 22.9.44 (age 21)

FAMILLE ÉPLORÉE DÉPOSENT ÉTERNEL HOMMAGE SUR LA TOMBE DE ROGER.
(A grief-stricken family lays everlasting tribute upon the grave of Roger.)
Lieutenant Roger Dussault, R22R, 24.9.44 (age 23)

The valedictions at Gradara encompass the traits and sentiments common in French Canadian epitaphs. Most are spiritual in form, composed as prayers, intercessions, or requests for prayers, in keeping with the uniformly Catholic faith of French Canadian servicemen. Where the absence of a religious symbol indicates the atheistic or ideological leanings among English Canadian soldiers, a French Canadian grave without a cross is a rare find. In other ways, though, English and French Canadian epitaphs echo one another. Proverbs and formulae are found in both languages, and there were French and English Canadians who commemorated the fallen in closely similar terms, seeking comfort in the thought that a loved one had died for the principles of democracy, for peace and liberty, or for some greater good:

LE PLAISIR DE MOURIR SANS PEINE VAUT BIEN LA PEINE DE VIVRE SANS PLAISIR.
(The pleasure of dying without pain is well worth the pain of living without pleasure.)
Private Alcide Godin, R22R, 2.1.44 (age 21) [MORO RIVER]

The memorial to New Brunswick's North Shore Regiment at Carpiquet, Normandy.

Rome War Cemetery, nestled against the Aurelian Wall.

Gradara Castle, seen from the upper terraces of the war cemetery.

A German bunker on the parapet of the Gothic Line, near Montecchio, Italy.

Ruins of a dwelling destroyed in the battle for the Hitler Line in May, 1944.

The entrance to Agira Canadian War Cemetery, Sicily.

The extended horizontal perspective at Villanova Canadian War Cemetery, Italy.

The Verrières ridge today, seen from the Canadian memorial on Point 67.

THE GREAT USE OF A LIFE IS TO SPEND IT FOR SOMETHING THAT OUTLASTS IT.
Flying Officer Kenneth White, RCAF, *30.6.42 (age 21)* [AMSTERDAM NEW EASTERN]

HE SERVED AND DIED THAT HIS COUNTRY CANADA MIGHT LIVE.
Private Patrick Thériault, RC, *9.2.45 (age 34)* [GROESBEEK]

TO THE MEMORY OF A BRAVE MAN WHO DIED THAT HIS COUNTRY MIGHT LIVE.
Private George Anies Sanderson, WNSR, *13.10.43 (age 25)* [BARI]

MON FILS A DONNÉ SA VIE POUR UN MEILLEUR MONDE.
(My son gave his life for a better world.)
Private Joseph Arthur Guy, IRC, *28.9.44 (age 19)* [CESENA]

FOR HUMILITY, WISDOM, COURAGE, FAITH, AND FOR VICTORY AND A BETTER WORLD.
Flying Officer Allison Stewart Woolaver, RCAF, *4.7.44 (age 23)* [BROOKWOOD]

POUR DIEU, POUR LE CANADA, POUR LA LIBERTÉ.
(For God, for Canada, for freedom.)
Lieutenant Albert Edmond Brosseau, RM, *28.7.44 (age 25)* [BRETTEVILLE-SUR-LAIZE]

HERE LIES A SON OF CANADA WHO GAVE HIS LIFE FOR FREEDOM.
Corporal Thomas Henry Corbett, HLIC, *24.3.45* [GROESBEEK]

PUISSE MON SACRIFICE ASSURER À MES FRÈRES, LES HUMBLES, UNE VIE PAISIBLE.
(May my sacrifice assure my brethren, the lowly, of a life of peace.)
Private Wilfrid Bourget, R22R, *18.12.43* [MORO RIVER]

**HE DIED FOR HIS BELIEF THAT WE, THE LITTLE PEOPLE OF THE WORLD,
MAY LIVE A FREE AND HAPPY LIFE.**
Corporal Dallas Alexandra Hill Carsell, SHC, *26.12.43 (age 24)* [MORO RIVER]

The epitaphs also bring out the differences between the two Canadas. French Canadian epitaphs present the image of a more compact society, united around its core elements of Church, people, and family. More significantly, in their assertion of ancestral pride and identity, and in their profound allegiance to the beliefs and traditions of their society, the epitaphs of French Canada's fallen display the elements of a distinctly French Canadian patriotism. Amidst the vicissitudes of popular and historical memory, these epitaphs combine with the memoirs of French Canadian soldiers to preserve an unchanging record of a lesser known side of French Canada's war. They enable the present generation of Canadians, French and English, to look back across the rift formed by the passage of time, or by linguistic and cultural differences, and to appreciate the ways in which French Canadians perceived the war, their stake in the conflict, and the meaning of their loss.

Perhaps no issue brings the two solitudes into sharper contrast than the memory of the World Wars. For a time after the Great War, in the flush of victory and international renown, there were Canadians of English and French descent who hoped that a shared legacy of valour would transcend the differences between the two founding peoples. Nor did the dream of a new national unity forged by the war lack common foundation. English and French Canadians had fought side by side on the Somme, at Vimy, and on to victory during the Hundred Days. Among the headstones of the nation's fallen were these testaments to French Canada's presence:

UNIS DANS LA MORT COMME ILS L'ÉTAIENT DANS LA VIE.
(United in death as they were in life.)
Lance Corporal Charles Guy Destrubé, Royal Fusiliers, 17.2.17 *(age 27)*
Private Paul Jean Destrubé, Royal Fusiliers, 17.2.17 *(age 26)* [SERRE ROAD NO. 1]

QUE TON SACRIFICE ET NOS PRIÈRES T'OUVRENT LES PORTES DU CIEL. LA FAMILLE
(May your sacrifice and our prayers open the gates of heaven to you. The family.)
Private Armand Crevier, RCR, 9.4.17 *(age 28)* [LA CHAUDIÈRE]

J'AI FAIT MON DEVOIR.
(I did my duty.)
Private Francis Laflamme, 4th CMR, 11.4.17 *(age 30)* [BARLIN]

DORS EN PAIX, BOBI, SOUS LE SOL DE TES PÈRES.
(Sleep in peace, Bobby, beneath the soil of your fathers.)
Private Robert Joseph Georges, 102nd BCI, 8.6.17 *(age 21)* [VILLERS STATION]

NÉ À AYLMER, CANADA. MORT POUR SON ROI. R.I.P.
(Born in Aylmer, Canada. Died for his King. R.I.P.)
Private Alfred Gibeault, 47th BCI, 18.2.18 *(age 27)* [SUCRERIE ABLAIN ST. NAZAIRE]

MÈRES DE LÀ-BAS, AYEZ PITIÉ DE MOI; EN PASSANT REGARDEZ ET PRIEZ.
(Mothers over yonder, take pity on me; as you go by, look on and pray.)
Private Wilfrid Picard, 42nd BCI, 14.4.18 *(age 27)* [SUCRERIE ABLAIN ST. NAZAIRE]

ICI REPOSE MON FILS UNIQUE MORT POUR SA PATRIE SUR LE CHAMP D'HONNEUR.
(Here rests my only son who died for his country on the field of honour)
Private Pascal Leo LeBlanc, 38th BCI, 2.9.18 *(age 33)* [DURY MILL]

IL A TOUT DONNÉ. MOURIR LOIN DE SON FOYER, C'EST DEUX FOIS MOURIR.
(He has given all. To die far from hearth and home is to die twice.)
Lieutenant Edouard Bouchette, 87th BCI, 30.9.18 *(age 26)* [CANTIMPRÉ]

A FRENCH CANADIAN'S LOVE OF MOTHER AND CANADA.
Gunner Alexander Wilfred Laurier Chenette, CFA, 5.12.18 *(age 23)* [VALENCIENNES]

About 35,000 French Canadians served in the Canadian Expeditionary Force. Although they made up just five per cent of the army's numbers, the gallantry of French Canada's soldiers stood out nonetheless. The reputation of the Royal 22nd Regiment was born at Courcelette in September 1916, and the courage subsequently displayed by the sole French-speaking battalion in the CEF stemmed from the conviction among its officers and men that the honour of their people rested on their shoulders. A generation later, in September 1944, Poulin and his fellow officers would invoke the legacy of the old 22nd Battalion to inspire their men and to commend their courage in the arduous passage through the Gothic Line: "*So ended the bloody episode at the Marano, an episode which coincided with the exploits of the first boys of the 22nd at Courcelette during the Great War. Our fathers had marked the way well for us, and we had followed and reddened it with our blood.*"

DÉCÉDÉ À LA BATAILLE DE COURCELETTE. A SA DOUCE MÉMOIRE.
(Died in the battle of Courcelette. To his gentle memory.)
Private Emile Gascon, 22nd (FC)B, 17.9.16 *(age 19)* [COURCELETTE]

NOUS NOUS SOUVENONS.
(We remember.)
Private Charles Palma Charron, 22nd (FC)B, *2.10.16* [CONTAY]

Today in the fields near the village of Chérisy, southeast of Arras, two small burial grounds, Valley Cemetery and Quebec Cemetery, preserve the memory of the contribution made by French Canadian soldiers to the Allied victories on the road to Cambrai in 1918. Here, and on the other battlefields where its soldiers fought, the esprit de corps of the 22nd (French Canadian) Battalion resonates:

O DIEU, PRENEZ MA VIE POUR VOTRE GLOIRE ET CELLE
DU CANADA-FRANÇAIS.
(O God, take my life for Thy glory and the glory of French Canada.)
Lieutenant Joseph Oméril Hudon, 22nd (FC)B, *3.11.16 (age 28)* [TRANCHÉE DE MECKNES]

"MON ÂME À DIEU, MON CŒUR À MA MÈRE, À MA PATRIE MON SANG ET MA VIE"
("My soul to God, my heart to my mother, to my country my blood and my life.")
Private Omer Mallette, 22nd (FC)B, *17.6.1916 (age 23)* [LIJSSENTHOEK]

A LA FLEUR DE L'AGE IL SACRIFIA HÉROÏQUEMENT SA VIE POUR SON PAYS.
(In the bloom of youth he sacrificed his life heroically for his country.)
Captain Maurice Edouard Bauset, 22nd (FC)B, *16.9.16 (age 27)* [SUNKEN ROAD]

AU ROI ET À LA PATRIE UN FILS DU CANADA A NOBLEMENT TOUT DONNÉ.
(To King and country a son of Canada has nobly given all.)
Private Joseph Charland, 22nd (FC)B, *19.7.17 (age 22)* [LOOS]

ADIEU, PARENTS, JE MEURS POUR DIEU, LE ROI ET MA PATRIE.
(Farewell, parents, I die for God, the King and my country.)
Private Eugène Bariel, 22nd (FC)B, *15.8.17 (age 22)* [AIX-NOULETTE]

POUR SA PATRIE IL A DONNÉ SA JEUNESSE ET SA VIE.
(He gave his youth and his life for his country.)
Lance Sergeant Dalvaine Lamarche, 22nd (FC)B, *27.8.18 (age 20)* [WANCOURT]

DANS LES MOMENTS CRITIQUES JE DISAIS TROIS FOIS
"JE VOUS SALUE, MARIE."
(At critical moments I would say three times, "Hail, Mary.")
Lieutenant Pierre Eugène Guay MC, 22nd (FC)B, *1.5.18 (age 24)* [WAILLY ORCHARD]

FILS DE G.F.B. ET D'A. LAFRANÇOIS, VERCHÈRES, P.Q., CANADA.
LATE DEPUTY MINISTER OF CANADA.
Private Pierre Baillairge, 22nd (FC)B, *4.5.18 (age 20)* [WAILLY ORCHARD]

DITES LEUR QUE J'AI FAIT MON DEVOIR.
(Tell them that I did my duty.)
Lieutenant Louis Rodolphe Lemieux MM, 22nd (FC)B, *29.8.18 (age 20)* [LIGNY ST. FLOCHEL]

MORT GLORIEUSEMENT AU CHAMP D'HONNEUR À NEUVILLE-VITASSE, ARRAS.
(Died gloriously on the field of honour at Neuville-Vitasse, Arras.)
Corporal Joseph Kaeble VC, MM, 22nd (FC)B, *9.6.18 (age 25)* [WANQUETIN]

FILS DE JOSEPH BRILLANT. ENROLÉ VOLONTAIREMENT À RIMOUSKI, PROVINCE DE QUÉBEC.
TOMBÉ GLORIEUSEMENT SUR LE SOL DE SES AÏEUX. BON SANG NE PEUT MENTIR.
(Son of Joseph Brillant. Enlisted voluntarily at Rimouski,
Province of Quebec. Fell gloriously on the soil of his forefathers.
A worthy nature cannot conceal itself.)
Lieutenant Jean Brillant VC, MC, 22nd (FC)B, 10.8.18 *(age 28)* [VILLERS-BRETONNEUX]

"It will be to their eternal glory . . . to have awakened in us all the fighting virtues of our ancestors—bravery, endurance, tenacity, impulse, French exaltation—to have, in a word, given us a soul." The accolades that greeted the 22nd Battalion on its return home made manifest the pride that French Canadians took in their soldiers' achievements. But the battlefields of France and Flanders were far away, and distant military exploits soon receded in memory as French Canada dwelt instead on the more immediate domestic controversies the war had raised. Far from bringing French and English together in a shared national epic, the war left French Canada embittered and estranged, with a sense of injury that persists to this day. Already disaffected by the strident opposition to French-language education in Manitoba and Ontario, French Canadians saw the bigotry and intransigence of the English military establishment, capped by the introduction of conscription in 1917, as proof of English Canada's innate hostility to their language and faith. And so as the memory of the war took shape, one side chose to remember what the other preferred to forget. In cultivating the myth of the war as a heroic, nation-building rite of passage, English Canadians glossed over the conscription crisis and the recriminations hurled at French Canada's supposed lack of commitment to the war effort; but these were the episodes, not the gallant stand at Ypres or the breakthrough at Amiens, that defined the war for most French Canadians. Much as they admired their courage, their compatriots looked upon Brillant, Kaeble, and their comrades with some bewilderment. Why enlist voluntarily, as Brillant's epitaph makes a point of stating, why pour out your life's blood in an English war, for a country so inimical to your own people? Ironically, if the memory of the Great War galvanised English Canada's sense of nationhood, it also played a part in transforming French Canada into Quebec.

The resentment and aloofness engendered by the experience of the First World War lingered on in Quebec's guarded response to the Second World War. The approach of a second European conflict in which Canada was all but certain to be involved awakened the old ghost of conscription and the attendant fears that participation might accelerate the changes—industrialization, urbanisation, secularism—already seen to be eroding the foundations on which rural, clerical Quebec was built. The prospect of war raised troubling questions in the minds of French Canadian politicians and clerics. Might not a national war effort serve as a pretext for federal encroachment upon provincial autonomy, French Canada's bulwark against the English majority? Would not military life, with its propensity for alcohol, blasphemy, and licentiousness, corrode the morals of the young? Was not the English-speaking military the vanguard preparing the way for the eventual anglicisation and assimilation of the French Canadian minority?

Only twenty years removed from the upheavals of the First World War, wary of English Canada and her imperial ties to Great Britain, and believing that a war between European powers posed no direct threat to French Canada, most of the clerico-nationalist leaders advocated neutrality, or limited participation at most, when hostilities broke out in 1939. Even appeals on behalf of France seemed forced, for Quebec had been the colony of royalist France and had little in common with *la patrie* transformed by the Enlightenment and the Revolution, least of all with the ill-begotten socialist, anti-clerical Third Republic. As for loyalty to a mother country, what claim did France have after leaving *les canadiens* to fend for themselves under an unloved British step-parent for the better part of two centuries?

In this climate there was much to deter enlistment among French Canadians. In statistical terms, the rate of enrolment in Quebec (about 26%) was just over half that recorded for the English-speaking provinces. In human terms, this calculation translates into roughly 90,000 French-speaking Quebecers who came from all corners of the province, some never to return to their homes and families:

FILS DE FRANÇOIS TREMBLAY ET DE FEU MATHILDA GIRARD DE JONQUIÈRES, QUÉBEC.
MORT POUR LA CIVILISATION.
(Son of François Tremblay and the late Mathilda Girard of Jonquières, Québec. He died for civilisation.)
Sapper Adélard Tremblay, CRCE, 17.8.41 *(age 31)* [BROOKWOOD]

MON CHER FILS JOSEPH MAURICE. NÉ LE 5 OCTOBRE 1915, LAC AU SAUMON,
PROV. QUÉBEC. ENROLÉ LE 7 SEPTEMBRE 1940.
(My dear son Joseph Maurice. Born October 5 1915, Lac-au-Saumon, Prov. of Quebec. Enlisted September 7 1940.)
Flight Sergeant Joseph Maurice Paradis, RCAF, 18.12.44 *(age 29)* [HARROGATE]

FILS DE JOSEPH ET DE MARIA SARRAZIN. ST. FRANÇOIS DU LAC, COMTÉ D'YAMASKA, QUÉBEC.
Private Paul Emile Sarrazin, RC, 5.3.45 *(age 21)* [GROESBEEK]

PAROISSE DE NOTRE-DAME DE L'ISLE VERTE, QUÉBEC, CANADA. "QU'IL REPOSE EN PAIX."
Corporal Joseph Edgar Adéodat Guichard, R22R, 14.12.43 [MORO RIVER]

SON OF CAPTAIN LEO A. TOUGAS, QUEBEC FIRE BRIGADE, AND AMANDA ANGERS.
Lance Sergeant Jean Paul Tougas, R22R, 27.7.43 *(age 26)* [AGIRA]

PRIEZ POUR LE REPOS DE L'ÂME DE WILFRID, DE ST. EUSÈBE,
CO. TÉMISCOUATHA, P.Q., CANADA.
Private Wilfrid Lemieux, R22R, 2.12.44 *(age 32)* [FAENZA]

NÉ À CAUSAPSCAL, P. QUÉ., CANADA. MORT AU CHAMP D'HONNEUR. R.I.P.
Private Maurice Boucher, RC, 26.2.45 *(age 29)* [GROESBEEK]

NÉ À NEUVILLE, QUÉBEC, CANADA LE 27 NOVEMBRE 1920. BLESSÉ À CAEN LE 9 AOÛT 1944.
(Born in Neuville, Quebec, Canada, November 27, 1920. Wounded at Caen, August 9, 1944)
Private Armand Leveille, RM, 10.8.44 *(age 23)* [BAYEUX]

BORN AT ST. EUGENE, QUEBEC, CANADA. A SOLDIER. A RELIGIOUS BOY.
Private Bruno Henry Bernique, RM, 3.3.45 *(age 29)* [GROESBEEK]

ICI REPOSE LE CORPS D'ARMAND, FILS D'HUBERT HUET, CAP AUX MEULES,
ILES DE LA MADELEINE.
Gunner Armand Huet, RCA, 8.8.44 *(age 24)* [BRETTEVILLE-SUR-LAIZE]

Sayabec, St. Romuald, Trois Rivières, Lac St. Jean, Saguenay, Beaudry, Pont de Québec, Coaticook, St. Henri, Squateck, St. Jean de Cherbourg, Joliette, Bienville de Lévis, La Salle, St. Narcisse, Rimouski . . . towns, villages, counties, parishes synonymous with the heartland of French Quebec, where the influence of the outside world rarely intruded. But the response to the war in Quebec and the recruitment of French-speaking soldiers from that province do not tell the whole story of French Canada's role in World War II. There were soldiers from other regions of Canada where the descendants of French explorers and settlers had preserved their language and identity in communities dispersed throughout the Maritimes, Ontario, and the Prairies:

A LA MÉMOIRE DE ANTOINE, DE MONT CARMEL, I.P.E., CANADA.
(To the memory of Antoine, of Mont Carmel, P.E.I., Canada.)
Private Antoine Hermas Gallant, WNSR, 31.8.44 *(age 22)* [MONTECCHIO]

TOMBÉ AU CHAMP D'HONNEUR. CHER LIONEL, TON SOUVENIR RESTE DANS LE CŒUR DES TIENS Á CARAQUET, N.B., CANADA.
(Fallen on the field of honour. Dear Lionel, your memory remains in the hearts of your loved ones in Caraquet, N.B., Canada.)
Private Lionel Parisé, CYR, 4.12.44 *(age 28)* [BOLOGNA]

DAVID, FILS DE LUC ET DE MARIE ROBICHAUD À ROGERSVILLE, N.B.
MORT AU SERVICE DE SON PAYS.
*(David, son of Luc and Marie Robichaud of Rogersville, N.B.
Died in the service of his country.)*
Private David Robichaud, FMR, 10.8.44 *(age 28)* [BRETTEVILLE-SUR-LAIZE]

SON OF DESITHE AND MONIQUE MAZEROLLE OF PORTAGO RIVER, N.B., CANADA.
PAX VOBISCUM.
Private Achille Mazerolle, CYR, 13.12.43 *(age 20)* [MORO RIVER]

FILS BIEN AIMÉ DE M. ET MME JOSEPH ANDRÉ, SMITH'S FALLS, ONTARIO, CANADA.
Corporal Alabert André, GGFG, 2.3.45 *(age 22)* [GROESBEEK]

NÉ À RAITH, ONTARIO. FILS DE LÉON LALIBERTÉ ET EVELINA GODBOUT. R.I.P.
Private Clement Joseph Laliberté, RCAMC, 29.7.45 *(age 21)* [HOLTEN]

RENÉ LAISSE POUR LE PLEURER SON PÈRE, SA MÈRE, CINQ FRÈRES, UNE SOEUR, TOUS À TORONTO, ONTARIO.
(To mourn him René leaves his father, mother, five brothers, one sister, all in Toronto, Ontario.)
Private René Chateauvert, RCAMC, 13.6.44 *(age 21)* [CASSINO]

BELOVED SON OF HENRI & EUGENIE MASSON, CALLANDER, ONTARIO. MAY HE REST IN PEACE.
Lance Corporal Lucien Masson, FMR, 3.3.45 *(age 25)* [GROESBEEK]

FILS D'AURÈLE BEAULIEU ET MALVINA LANDREVILLE. NÉ À ST. LÉON, MANITOBA. R.I.P.
Private Laurent Thomas Joseph Beaulieu, QOCHC, 23.11.44 *(age 22)* [GROESBEEK]

NÉ À STE GENEVIÈVE, MANITOBA. FOI SINCÈRE, DÉVOUEMENT SANS BORNES.
(Born in Ste Genevieve, Manitoba. Faith sincere, devotion beyond measure.)
Private Henri Jean Richard, QOCHC, 28.8.44 *(age 23)* [BRETTEVILLE-SUR-LAIZE]

SON OF ULRIC AND YVONNE COULOMBE, PINE FALLS, MANITOBA, CANADA. R.I.P.
Private Edmond Coulombe, FMR, 30.3.45 *(age 22)* [GROESBEEK]

HERE LIES LOUIS, BELOVED SON OF CYPRIEN AND VERONIQUE CHARTRAND, CAMPERVILLE, MANITOBA, CANADA.
Rifleman Louis Chartrand, RWR, 8.6.44 (age 26) [BÉNY-SUR-MER]

DE WILLOW BUNCH, SASKATCHEWAN. BLESSÉ À DIEPPE EN 1942. TUÉ ACCIDENTELLEMENT. PATER AVE GLORIA.
(From Willow Bunch, Saskatchewan. Wounded at Dieppe in 1942. Killed in an accident. Pater ave Gloria.)
Lance Sergeant Jules Rainville, SSR, 2.5.43 (age 37) [BROOKWOOD]

An estimated 70,000 French Canadian volunteers came forward from the English provinces. Calculations suggesting that these men enlisted at rates equal to or above those of their English Canadian neighbours unveil yet another side of French Canadian attitudes towards military service in provinces where support for the war was higher than it was in Quebec. French-speaking soldiers, with names like Cormier, Robichaud, Bouthillier or Chiasson proclaiming their Acadian origins, made up nearly half of the North Shores from New Brunswick, while one company of the Carleton and Yorks was almost entirely francophone. The Essex Scottish from Windsor counted a good many Franco-Ontarians among its ranks, and one Franco-Manitoban family put a record ten brothers in arms. Three did not return. Troop Sergeant Wilfrid Robert Cantin died on home service; Flying Officer Clement Francis Amedée Cantin is commemorated on the El Alamein memorial; and a third brother is one of 527 Canadian airmen buried in Berlin:

BELOVED ONE, MAY GOD GRANT THAT YOUR SACRIFICE HAS NOT BEEN IN VAIN.
Flight Lieutenant Maurice Raoul Cantin, RCAF, 26.11.43 (age 21)

Even descendants of the French Canadians who had emigrated to the United States returned to serve in both world wars:

BORN IN SPENCER, MASS., U.S.A. 1885. WOUNDED THREE TIMES, KILLED IN ACTION.
Private George Girouard, 22nd (FC)B, 18.6.18 (age 34) [WAILLY ORCHARD]

FILS DE CAROLINE BANVILLE ET DE MOISE PIGEON. NÉ À FALL-RIVER, MASS. LE 5 AVRIL 1897.
Private Arthur Pigeon, 22nd (FC)B, 28.8.18 (age 21) [QUEBEC]

NÉ À SANFORD, MAINE, U.S.A. LE 17 MARS 1924. FILS D'ALFRED ROUX ET ROSE EMMA COTÉ.
Private Maurice Roux, RM, 1.8.44 (age 20) [BRETTEVILLE-SUR-LAIZE]

MAY HE REST IN PEACE AND LET PERPETUAL LIGHT SHINE UPON HIM. AMEN
Flight Sergeant Robert Henry Galipeau (of USA), RCAF, 14.9.42 (age 22)
[KIRKEBY CHURCHYARD]

The epitaphs recording the origins of French Canadian servicemen lead to a broader selection casting light on the values or principles which they believed worth defending. Why did they go, or more pertinently, why would they have gone? Their language, their society, and their Catholicism made them strangers to English Canadians, many of whom harboured the old grudge that their French-speaking fellow citizens refused to give their full support to the war effort. English Canadians were too quick to equate opposition to conscription with opposition to the war; nor were they, in their ready loyalty to Great Britain, willing to concede that the question of going to war presented itself in different terms to some of the peoples within the Empire:

"O CANADA, MON PAYS, MES AMOURS, MÊME S'IL N'Y A PAS DE RETOUR."
(O Canada, my country, my love, even if there is no coming back.)
Private Reginald Paul Simard, PR, 31.8.44 (age 21) [MONTECCHIO]

GEANTWOORD OP JOU ROEPSTEM, GEOFFER WAT JY VRA, VIR JOU SUID AFRIKA.
(Responded to your call, offered what you ask, for you, South Africa.)
Corporal Dirk van der Berg, South African Engineer Corps, 5.6.44 (age 30) [CASSINO]

IL NOUS ÉTAIT PRÊTÉ MAIS DIEU L'A REPRIS.
(He was lent to us but God reclaimed him.)
Private Edgar Leclerc, FMR, 23.10.44 (age 30) [BERGEN-OP-ZOOM]

**RUS EN VREDE GELIEFDE SEUN. DAT GOD JOU AAN ONS TOEVERTROU
HET WAS 'N SEËN.**
(Rest in peace, beloved son. That God entrusted you to us was a blessing.)
Corporal M.C. Davids, Witwatersrand Rifles, 7.4.45 (age 26) [CASTIGLIONE]

IL DORT LOIN DES SIENS MAIS SA MÉMOIRE RESTERA VIVACE À SON PAYS LE CANADA.
(He sleeps far from his own, but his memory will remain alive in his country, Canada.)
Private Richard Daudelin, RC, 6.4.45 (age 20) [HOLTEN]

**ONS SAL DIE SOET ONTHOU DIE SWAAR VERDRA. OP VREEMDE GROND 'N
STUKKIE VAN SUID AFRIKA.**
*(We shall remember the sweetness to bear the burden. On foreign soil
a piece of South Africa.)*
Major E. Liebenberg, Special Services Battalion, 10.6.44 (age 28) [BOLSENA]

Like the Afrikaans-speaking, Calvinist Boers, French Canadians were reluctant members of the British Empire, descendants of a conquered people long cut off from their ancestral land who could hardly be expected to respond to the call of an imperial overlord from which they felt alienated by history, language, and faith. "I have sometimes felt to the point of suffocation the bitter loneliness of my people in the world," André Laurendeau once wrote, capturing the predicament of a cautious, instinctively self-protective minority haunted by the fear of its disappearance. They were more North American in outlook than English Canadians, more conscious of their separation from Europe, and deeply attached to their own corner of the world. If Canada were threatened directly, there was no doubt that French Canadians would rally en masse to her defence; but the issue was the relative proximity of the threat. In his *Carnets de guerre*, an elegantly written memoir weaving meditations and poems into a narrative of his experiences with the Van Doos in Italy, Claude Châtillon assessed the implications of the conflict, and the choice before him:

> As a Franco-Ontarian, I have felt the weight of provincial regulations
> oppressing my language. The marks of incomprehension and condescension
> from the English-speaking majority with regard to my ancestors all through
> the history of French Canada remain in me like deep scratches. Keep in
> mind that since September '39 the daily papers have been full of official
> propaganda and calls for sacrifice directed towards England's woes and the
> dangers she is going through. By contrast, English Canadians care nothing

> *at all about the survival of their French-speaking countrymen as a people. This language is ignored, often scorned, even within the departments of the federal government, and especially in the armed forces. The English Canadian feels the tug on his heartstrings when he hears the clocktowers of London, whereas I ask myself about the dreadful silence of France. . . . Tradition, patriotism, security, a future—everything induces me not to stir.*

The following day, however, he returned to the question:

> *There can be no denying that there are events going on over there that touch what is deepest inside me, my principles and my convictions. I cannot, and will not, avoid this reality any longer. A great killing match is taking place over there, but above all, so is a war of ideas, a tussle of beliefs, about liberty, of rights, without discrimination as to origins, age, or colour. The domination of the majority leads to eventual assimilation; what I fear here in my country, in my province, to be precise, is spreading, increasing by leaps and bounds, swiftly gaining ground in Europe, and with savage cruelty. In our democracy, we are still free to react and to resist to save our culture. On the other continent, the Nazis are crushing all resistance to their dominating ideology, primitive and inhumane, like a steamroller. They make a mockery of treaties and borders—where will they stop? Today Europe, tomorrow Canada. If we wish to preserve our language and culture, we must logically begin by defending our basic principles over there. To know but to do nothing is to glaze over in mind and to clog every impulse in your heart to act. From this point of view, a simple life here is no longer possible for me; it takes on a sickening banality. I will sign up.*

The decision to serve overseas was the most important one that thousands of young French Canadians ever made, and one that bore against the tide of opinion in French Canada's clerico-nationalist circles. Given that many felt themselves to be second-class citizens in the Canada of the time, it is all the more noteworthy that as many as 160,000 French Canadians did enrol in the armed forces. Their motives will have varied considerably, of course, some joining up in seach of adventure, advancement, steady pay, or escape, some eagerly, others reluctantly or by force of circumstance, all in the welter of ideals, calculation, and doubts rendered by Gabrielle Roy in the concluding scenes of *The Tin Flute*. But they were also members of a tenacious, proud society that predicated the overriding issue of *la survivance* on the alliance of Church, nation, and family. Like Châtillon, there were other young French Canadians devoted to their people and way of life, who went to war to protect them from the threat, however distant, posed by Nazi Germany. Among the epitaphs of French Canada's soldiers we find patrimonial sentiments rooted in the traditions and sensibilities of *l'Amérique française*, where the words *Canada* and *canadien* refer to a homeland and people defined by their French heritage and Catholic faith. Encased within the allegiance to Church and nationality was an intense loyalty to parish and kin:

IL A CRU SAUVER LA RELIGION CATHOLIQUE ET LA RACE CANADIENNE FRANÇAISE.
(He believed that he was saving the Catholic religion and the French Canadian race.)
Private Paul Emile Brisebois, RC, 22.10.44 (age 23) [ADEGEM]

CHER RENÉ, TOI SI BRAVE ET SI BON, TU AS DONNÉ TA VIE POUR PROTÉGER LES NÔTRES.
(Dear René, so brave and so good, you gave your life to protect our people.)
Private Joseph Philippe René Jarry, RC, 16.8.44 (age 22) [BAYEUX]

MORT EN CHRÉTIEN POUR LA LIBERTÉ DE SES PARENTS, SA PATRIE, SA RELIGION.
(Died as a Christian for the freedom of his parents, his country, his religion.)
Private Rosario Joseph Dumais, RC, 6.3.45 (age 18) [GROESBEEK]

BRAVE CANADIEN, SA DERNIÈRE PENSÉE FUT POUR SON DIEU, SA MÈRE ET SA PATRIE.
(A brave French Canadian, his last thought was for his God,
his mother, and his native land.)
Private Antonin Raoul Lussier, IRC, 5.3.44 (age 32) [MORO RIVER]

IL A DONNÉ SA JEUNE VIE POUR SAUVEGARDER LA CHRÉTIENTÉ ET SA PATRIE.
(He gave his young life to safeguard Christianity and his native land.)
Pilot Officer Joseph Paul Roger Boileau, RCAF, 30.1.44 (age 22) [BERLIN]

SES MOTS D'ADIEU, "JE MEURS EN CHRÉTIEN D'ABORD ET EN PATRIOTE ENSUITE."
(His parting words, "I die as a Christian first, and then as a patriot.")
Flight Sergeant Joseph Marcel Wenceslas Fortin, RCAF, 2.6.42 (age 23) [REICHSWALD]

POUR DIEU ET MON CANADA.
(For God and my country Canada.)
Private Charles Eugène Belzile, FMR, 23.10.44 (age 22) [BERGEN-OP-ZOOM]

POUR DIEU, LA PATRIE ET L'HUMANITÉ. UNE PRIÈRE, S.V.P.
(For God, native land, and humanity. A prayer, please.)
Lieutenant Romuald Lucien St. Onge, R22R, 19.5.44, (age 34) [CASSINO]

MON ÂME À DIEU, MA VIE À MA PATRIE, MON CŒUR À MES PARENTS. PRIEZ POUR MOI.
(My soul to God, my life to my country, my heart to my parents. Pray for me.)
Private George Emile Poissant, FMR, 21.11.44 (age 22) [GROESBEEK]

BRUNO EST MORT EN HÉROS POUR SON DIEU, SA PATRIE, SA FAMILLE.
QU'IL REPOSE EN PAIX.
(Bruno died a hero for his God, his country, his family. May he rest in peace.)
Pilot Officer Joseph Jacques Bruno Cardinal, RCAF, 28.5.44 (age 24) [HEVERLEE]

BON FILS, INTRÉPIDE SOLDAT FIDÈLE À SA RELIGION, À SA PATRIE, MÉRITE LE CIEL.
(A good son, a fearless soldier faithful to his religion and his native land,
deserves heaven.)
Lance Sergeant Charles Tourand, RWR, 4.7.44 (age 25) [BÉNY-SUR-MER]

A DIEU, SON ÂME DE CHRÉTIEN. A LA FRANCE, SES CENDRES. TON PÈRE ET MÈRE,
FRÈRE ET SOEUR.
(To God, his Christian soul. To France, his ashes. Your father and mother,
brother and sister)
Trooper Dénis Ouellette, SAR, 21.8.44 (age 23) [BRETTEVILLE-SUR-LAIZE]

JE MEURS AU SERVICE DE MON PAYS, DE MA PAROISSE, DE MA FAMILLE. ADIEU!
(I die in the service of my country, my parish, and my family. Farewell!)
Private Paul Parent, FMR, 26.2.45 (age 24) [GROESBEEK]

"J'AI COMBATTU LE BON COMBAT" ST. PAUL. JE MEURS POUR MA PATRIE.
("I have fought the good fight" St. Paul. I die for my country.)
Private Jean-Paul Dumoulin, RCAMC, *20.7.44 (age 22)* [BRETTEVILLE-SUR-LAIZE]

DIEU ET CANADA. TELLE ÉTAIT MA DEVISE. LOIN DES MIENS J'AI LAISSÉ MA VIE.
(God and Canada. That was my motto. Far from my loved ones
I have laid down my life.)
Lance Sergeant Zénon Massé, R22R, *30.1.44* [BARI]

MARTYR DU DEVOIR, HÉROS DE LA PATRIE, HONNEUR DE SA FAMILLE, REPOSE EN PAIX.
(Martyr in the performance of your duty, hero of your country, honour of your family,
rest in peace.)
Corporal Jean Joseph Albert Racicot, RCAMC, *19.8.42 (age 34)* [DIEPPE]

DANS TA JEUNESSE EN FLEUR TU SACRIFIAIS TA VIE POUR LE PAPE ET LA PATRIE.
(In the bloom of youth you were sacrificing your life for the Pope and your
native land.)
Private Gaston Larouche, R22R, *20.5.44 (age 20)* [CASSINO]

If Private Larouche's epitaph might have startled even Catholic English Canadians, less given to the ultramontane Catholicism of French Canada, it would also strike many Quebecers today as an echo of the all but vanished world inhabited by their grandparents. The Quiet Revolution of the 1960s saw the old French Canada give way to a modernising, secular Quebec which, in the way of societies reoriented by social and political change, cast off the traditions and ways of the past, chief among them the influence of the Catholic Church. The religiosity so pronounced in French Canadian epitaphs is the most obvious trait distancing *les canadiens* from their *québécois* descendants. This break with the past goes some way to explain the indifference towards French Canada's servicemen on the part of a later generation that discarded the religious identity and habits of their forebears:

CATHOLIQUE ROMAIN.
Private Marcel Leclaire, NS(NB)R, *11.7.44 (age 20)* [BÉNY-SUR-MER]

A BRAVE CATHOLIC. HIS MEMORY WILL BE FOR EVER ENGRAVED IN THE HEARTS OF HIS
MOTHER AND FATHER.
Lance Sergeant John Haché, R22R, *2.12.44 (age 25)* [RAVENNA]

SA VIE FUT CELLE D'UN CATHOLIQUE CONVAINCU, SA MORT CELLE D'UN HÉROS.
(His life was that of a devout Catholic, his death that of a hero.)
Lieutenant Joseph Raymond Yves Morrissette, FMR, *23.10.44 (age 29)*
[BERGEN-OP-ZOOM]

O DIEU, VOUS ÊTES DE VOS SOLDATS LA RÉCOMPENSE ET LA COURONNE. LITURGIE.
R.I.P.
(O God, You are Your soldiers' reward and their crown. Liturgy. R.I.P.)
Trooper Laval Turgeon, 4th PLDG, *22.5.44 (age 20)* [CASSINO]

QUE LE DIEU DES ARMÉES DAIGNE SE SOUVENIR DE CEUX QUE J'AI TANT AIMÉS.
(May the Lord of hosts be so kind as to remember those I have loved so greatly.)
Lieutenant Roland Falardeau, RCR, *16.10.44 (age 24)* [CESENA]

TOUJOURS PRÊT POUR DIEU, MES PARENTS, MA PATRIE. AVE MARIA.
(Always prepared for God, my parents, my country. Hail Mary.)
Sergeant Joseph Jules Jean Jacques Vennes, RCAF, 26.11.43 *(age 21)* [PERSHORE]

JÉSUS, MARIE, JOSEPH, JE VOUS DONNE MON CŒUR, MON ESPRIT ET MA VIE.
(Jesus, Mary, Joseph, I give you my heart, my spirit, and my life.)
Private Jacques Lucien Benoit, 1st CPB, 20.8.44 *(age 28)* [RANVILLE]

We are not inclined in our secular day and age to credit religious conviction as a motive for taking up arms, yet the record of the epitaphs leaves no doubt as to the central place of religion in the world view of French Canadian soldiers and their families. During the war, such prominent spokesmen as Cardinal Villeneuve and Georges Vanier had framed their arguments in favour of participation in strongly spiritual terms, countering the opponents of the "English war" by portraying the conflict as a just war waged against an evil, godless aggressor. French Canadians had a duty to go to the rescue of Catholic countries overrun by the Nazis and to defend the Church from her enemies. Christian civilisation, not the British Empire, hung in the balance. The reception to appeals transmitted along these frequencies is apparent in French Canadian epitaphs casting the soldier's death in battle as fulfilment of a religious duty:

MOURIR POUR SON PAYS EST LE PLUS GRAND ACTE DE CHARITÉ ET DE BRAVOURE.
(To die for one's country is the greatest act of Christian love and bravery.)
Private Gérard Gilbert, AR, 24.10.44 *(age 27)* [BROOKWOOD]

MOURIR POUR SA PATRIE EST MOURIR POUR SON DIEU. SEIGNEUR, AIDEZ SON ÂME.
(To die for his native land is to die for his God. Lord, tend to his soul.)
Private Maurice Jodoin, R22R, 19.12.44 *(age 19)* [RAVENNA]

O JÉSUS, QUE MON SACRIFICE SERVE AU SALUT DES MIENS ET DES CANADIENS.
(O Jesus, may my sacrifice assist in the salvation of my loved ones and Canadians.)
Corporal Roma Cardinal, FMR, 6.10.44 *(age 30)* [BERGEN-OP-ZOOM]

LE SACRIFICE EST MA RECOMPENSE. PRIEZ POUR MOI.
(The sacrifice is my reward. Pray for me.)
Major Robert Fernand Major, GGFG, 23.10.44 *(age 27)* [BERGEN-OP-ZOOM]

SEIGNEUR, AGRÉEZ LE SACRIFICE DE MA VIE POUR VOTRE GLOIRE.
(Lord, accept the sacrifice of my life for Your glory.)
Rifleman Antoine Saint-Jacques, RRR, 8.10.44 *(age 23)* [ADEGEM]

C'EST PAR LE CHEMIN ARIDE DE L'ÉPREUVE QU'ONT MARCHÉ TOUS LES SAINTS.
(It is by the barren path of trial that all the saints have walked.)
Rifleman Sylvio David, RWR, 9.10.44 *(age 29)* [ADEGEM]

EN PLEINE ACTION, FACE AU DEVOIR À SON DIEU, IL EST ALLÉ TÉMOIGNER DE SA FOI.
(In the midst of action, facing his duty to his God, he went to give proof of his faith.)
Lieutenant Joseph Damase Raymond Racine, RM, 24.7.44 *(age 24)*
[BRETTEVILLE-SUR-LAIZE]

L'AMOUR DE DIEU REGNANT DANS SON CŒUR ET AVEC LUI L'AMOUR DU DEVOIR.
(The love of God ruling in his heart, and with it the love of duty.)
Corporal Antoine Lorenzo Huard, R22R, 18.4.44 *(age 35)* [MORO RIVER]

J'AI DONNÉ MA VIE POUR UNE CAUSE SACRÉE. UNE PRIÈRE POUR MOI ET LES MIENS.
(I gave my life for a sacred cause. A prayer for me and for my loved ones.)
Private Conrad Dubé, R22R, 29.12.43 (age 26) [MORO RIVER]

AIMANT DIEU ET SA PATRIE IL A DONNÉ SA VIE POUR LA LIBERTÉ DES AUTRES.
(Loving God and country he gave his life for the liberty of others.)
Private Armand Marquis, LWR, 23.4.45 (age 20) [HOLTEN]

ICI REPOSE CELUI QUI POUR LA DÉLIVRANCE DE L'OPPRESSEUR SACRIFIA SA VIE.
(Here rests a man who for deliverance from the oppressor sacrificed his life.)
Lieutenant Albini Jacques Dalpe, ASH, 21.8.44 (age 24) [BRETTEVILLE-SUR-LAIZE]

POUR QUE L'AMOUR DE DIEU ET LA PAIX REGNE ENFIN SUR LA TERRE.
(So that the love of God and peace may finally reign on earth.)
Private Joseph Arcade Georges Deneault, RC, 4.7.44 (age 19) [BÉNY-SUR-MER]

QUE SON HÉROÏSME SOIT COMME UNE SEMENCE DE CHARITÉ ET DE JUSTICE. R.I.P.
(May his heroism be like a sowing of charity and justice. R.I.P.)
Private Walter Walsh, R22R, 14.12.43 (age 19) [MORO RIVER]

QUE PAR SON SUPRÊME SACRIFICE LA CONCORDE ET L'HARMONIE REGNE À JAMAIS. TES PARENTS, FRÈRE ET SŒURS.
(Through his supreme sacrifice let concord and harmony reign for ever. Your parents, brother and sisters.)
Private Jean Paul Salmon, IRC, 2.1.45 (age 26) [VILLANOVA]

PARENTS CANADIENS, CONSOLEZ-VOUS, CAR JE SUIS MORT EN HÉROS ET EN CHRÉTIEN.
(Parents in Canada, be consoled, for I have died as a hero and a Christian.)
Private Adélard Larocque, RC, 18.7.44 (age 26) [BRETTEVILLE-SUR-LAIZE]

The memoirs of Father Gérard Marchand, who accompanied the Régiment de Maisonneuve from Normandy to the Rhine, describe the role and duties of a French Canadian chaplain ministering to soldiers in the front lines. The modest, unembellished account of his experiences during the hard fighting of 1944–45 portrays the emotional duress of a padre in close attendance upon his "walking parish" while being fully exposed to the dangers of the forward areas. His initiation to the gruesome sights and sounds of the battle zone was as nerve-wracking as that of any novice in combat, but recourse to his faith and a high sense of dedication to his flock guided his passage through the trial. Even though subject to fits of trembling under shellfire, or to feelings of anger and vengefulness towards the Germans who were killing the men in his care, Marchand spared no effort to hear confession and to hold services no matter how close he found himself to the enemy. He gives this description of his first service before battle:

> Towards ten o'clock on the morning of Tuesday, July 19, I was instinctively drawn to D company under Major Leon Brosseau. He was very busy assembling his 120 soldiers. Since the order for the company's departure was set for 10:00 hours, I was afraid of getting in the way, but Major Brosseau told me to wait a moment. Soon the whole company was in front of me in flawless uniform, carrying their rifles, small spades, PIATs (anti-tank weapons.), with clean, shining earphones over their ears. In a loud

*voice the Major gave the command, "Attention!"; and then he added, "The
padre is here. He's going to give us general absolution—make sure you do it
as though it were the last time." Emotion took hold of me. All together we
recited the Act of Contrition preceded by the "I confess unto God." I recited
the words of Absolution in the plural form, "In the name of Our Lord Jesus
Christ, I absolve you of all your sins, in the name of the Father, the Son, and
the Holy Ghost." Major Brosseau responded "Amen" each time. I will never
forget this touching, meaningful ceremony. At 13:00 hours the same day, a
number of them were killed on the start line at Fleury.*

Major Brosseau was one of the Maisonneuves killed in action shortly after receiving
absolution, on the regiment's first day in battle. The epitaph on his headstone, in
the Bretteville-sur-Laize Canadian War Cemetery, incorporates the regimental motto.
Further testimony to the faith that sustained French Canadian soldiers in battle
appears in two inscriptions found in the Canadian war cemetery at Groesbeek:

FIDÈLE À SA DEVISE, "BON CŒUR ET BON BRAS," JUSQU'À L'APPEL SUPRÊME!
(Faithful to his motto, "Stout heart and strong arm," until the final roll call!)
Major Léon Joseph Brosseau, RM, 19.7.44 (age 33)

A LA LIGNE DE FEU LA PRIÈRE EST LA MEILLEURE ARME QU'UN SOLDAT PUISSE AVOIR.
(In the line of fire prayer is the best weapon that a soldier can have.)
Lieutenant Robert Talbot, FMR, 26.2.45 (age 25)

IL A VU VENIR LA MORT AVEC LE CALME ET LE COURAGE QUE DONNE LA FOI.
(He saw death come with the calm and the courage which faith gives.)
Lieutenant Paul Henri Boutin, FMR, 7.4.45 (age 24)

On the occasion of the Maisonneuve's demobilisation in Montreal, Marchand gave
a farewell address to the soldiers and families in which he assured the bereaved that
no man in his regiment had gone into battle spiritually unprepared, and that no
family need be troubled that a loved one's salvation had been imperilled for lack of
the requisite rites. This was an important message to pious Catholic families who
could take comfort in the assurance that a fallen son, husband, or brother was with
God, as many inscriptions venture to say. We should bear in mind, too, that the older
doctrines on Purgatory still applied at this time, two decades before the reforms of the
Second Vatican Council. The requests for prayers issued from the belief that the living
should assist in the work of salvation through intercessory prayers and the purchase
of masses for the dead, all the more so since the soldier had given his life on their
behalf. Entreaties to family, friends, and even to passing strangers to pray for the soul
of the deceased are frequently put in the mouths of the fallen, as are promises to
await their loved ones in heaven. True to the ways of an older Catholicism, a number
of families preferred to use Latin, still the liturgical language of the Church, in their
valedictions:

IL A COMBATTU POUR NOUS, NOUS PRIERONS POUR LUI. SA FAMILLE
(He fought for us, we shall pray for him. His family.)
Private Wilfred Roy, RCASC, 28.10.45 (age 38) [GROESBEEK]

MÈRE, NE PLEUREZ PAS. JE VAIS À DIEU ET JE VOUS ATTENDRAI AU CIEL.
(Mother, do not weep. I go to God and I will await you in heaven.)
Pilot Officer Joseph Louis Raymond Cartier, RCAF, 29.3.43 (age 21) [REICHSWALD]

LES AILES L'ONT PORTÉ DANS L'ÉTERNEL AZUR POUR L'ÉTERNEL REVOIR.
(His wings have carried him into the eternal blue to an eternal reunion.)
Flight Sergeant Joseph Paul Henri Dubé, RCAF, 17.11.43 (age 22) [RHEINBERG]

FRÈRE BIEN AIMÉ, MORT POUR DIEU ET PATRIA, REPOSE EN PAIX AU CIEL. UNE PRIÈRE.
(Beloved brother, who died for God and native land, rest in peace in heaven. A prayer.)
Private Jules Gagnon, R22R, 1.9.43 (age 33) [AGIRA]

FILS BIEN-AIMÉ DE M. ET MME. DAMAS DÉSORMEAUX. SON SERVICE A ÉTÉ CHANTÉ
EN PLUS AU SAULT-AU-RECOLLET.
*(Beloved son of Mr. and Mrs. Damas Désormeaux. A mass was also recited for him
in Sault-au-Recollet.)*
Private Paul Désormeaux, FMR, 8.4.42 (age 32) [BROOKWOOD]

DIEU L'A PERMIS. IL FAUT SE TAIRE. IL NE NOUS RESTE QU'À PRIER. DE SA FAMILLE,
EN MÉMOIRE.
*(God allowed it; we must keep silence. It remains to us only to pray.
From his family, in memory.)*
Major Armand Joseph Brochu, FMR, 1.3.45 (age 30) [GROESBEEK]

POUR MOI L'HEURE FATALE EST SONNÉE, MAIS NE PLEUREZ PAS, JE VAIS À DIEU.
MON JÉSUS MISÉRICORDE.
(For me the fatal hour has sounded, but do not weep, I go to God. Jesus, have mercy.)
Private Paul Emile Bernier, RC, 12.7.44 (age 25) [BÉNY-SUR-MER]

GARDEZ MON SOUVENIR ET LAISSEZ LA PRIÈRE EN DIEU NOUS RÉUNIR.
(Keep my memory and let prayer reunite us in God.)
Guardsman Jean Marie Simard, CGG, 26.4.45 (age 25) [HOLTEN]

NOUS PRIONS POUR TOI. ON NE T'OUBLIERA JAMAIS. FAIS DE MÊME LÀ-HAUT.
(We pray for you. We will never forget you. Do likewise above.)
Corporal Engelbert Arbour, RM, 6.8.44 (age 27) [BRETTEVILLE-SUR-LAIZE]

QUE SES SOUFFRANCES NE LUI SOIENT INUTILES, O MON DIEU!
(O God, may his suffering not be of no avail to him!)
Private Joseph Edmond Robicheau, R22R, 14.4.45 (age 21) [HOLTEN]

QUE TON SANG VERSÉ POUR LA PATRIE CONSOLE CEUX QUE TU AS LAISSÉS AU CANADA.
(May your blood shed for your native land console those you left behind in Canada.)
Sergeant Rosaire Chouinard, RWR, 25.9.44 (age 24) [CALAIS]

QUE SON SACRIFICE UNI À CELUI DE CHRIST NOUS SOIT UNE SOURCE DE BÉNÉDICTION.
(May his sacrifice, joined to that of Christ, be a source of blessing to us.)
Private Henry Cormier, FMR, 19.1.45 (age 27) [GROESBEEK]

TON SACRIFICE FUT SUBLIME, NOTRE RÉSIGNATION CONSOLANTE. ADIEU
(Your sacrifice was sublime, our acceptance consoling. Farewell.)
Captain Joseph Arthur Raymond Bourget, RCIC, 8.7.44 (age 21) [BÉNY-SUR-MER]

A TOUT AMI CATHOLIQUE, UNE PRIÈRE S'IL VOUS PLAIT.
(To every Catholic friend, a prayer please.)
Private Marcel Arsenault, R22R, 19.10.43 (age 23) [AGIRA]

QUAND VOUS VERREZ TOMBER LES FEUILLES, SI VOUS M'AVEZ AIMÉ, PRIEZ POUR MOI.
(When you see the leaves fall, if you loved me, pray for me.)
Major Joseph Guy Savoie, RC, 1.11.43 *(age 29)* [BROOKWOOD]

VOUS TOUS QUI ÊTES SES AMIS, PRIEZ POUR LUI ET POUR LE CANADA.
(All of you who are his friends, pray for him and for Canada.)
Private Alphonse Proulx, FMR, 29.11.44 *(age 24)* [GROESBEEK]

PRIEZ POUR LUI, QUI LOIN DE SA PATRIE EXPIRA SANS ENTENDRE UNE PAROLE AMIE.
(Pray for him, who far from his native land breathed his last without hearing a friendly word.)
Gunner Léopold Gauthier, RCA, 6.10.44 *(age 21)* [ADEGEM]

MOTHER MARIA, I NEVER FORGET MY BELOVED SON. I PRAY FOR HIM EVERY DAY.
MOTHER, SISTERS AND BROTHERS.
Private Joseph Firia Jean Paul Gauthier, RCASC, 12.3.45 *(age 28)* [ADEGEM]

NIL SINE NUMINE.
(Nothing without divine guidance.)
Private Joseph Pierre Rosaire Landry, RM, 8.10.44 *(age 38)* [BERGEN-OP-ZOOM]

"QUIA APUD DOMINUM MISERICORDIA: ET COPIOSA APUD EUM REDEMPTIO."
R.I.P. AMEN
("Because with the Lord there is mercy and with Him plentiful redemption.")
Private Gaston Simard, R22R, 19.5.44 *(age 20)* [CASSINO] [PSALM 129/130: 7]

DEUS NOBISCUM, QUIS CONTRA?
(If God is for us, who is against us?)
Lieutenant Joseph Henri Maxime Dupuis, CHO, 7.6.44 *(age 34)* [BÉNY-SUR-MER]
[ROMANS 8: 31]

FLORET IN DEO FILIUS NOSTER CANADIENSIS. UTINAM CUM ILLO FLOREAMUS ET NOS.
(Our Canadian son flourishes in God. Come the day that we too may flourish with him.)
Sergeant Raymond Edmond Petitpas, R22R, 30.7.43 *(age 20)* [AGIRA]

DOMINE, IN NOS HUMANUS FUIT; IN EUM MISERICORS ESTO.
(Lord, he was kind to us; be Thou merciful unto him.)
Lieutenant Emile Roger Pellerin, R22R, 24.11.43 *(age 25)* [MORO RIVER]

Canada came out of Second World War less divided than she had been after the Great War. The country had sidestepped a second conscription crisis, if clumsily, and the barbarity of the Nazi regime left little doubt as to the rightness of the decision to go to war. Yet even though Canada had once again played a role out of all proportion to her population in the rescue of Europe, the Second World War did not forge a common bond between French and English Canadians, any more than the First had. The two peoples continued to lead parallel lives and to cultivate different memories of the years between 1939 and 1945. It is sad to think that one of French Canada's most ardent advocates of national unity after the First World War, the parliamentarian and Quebec Supreme Court Justice Lucien Cannon, was to lose a son in the Second. Captain Lawrence Cannon of the Royal 22nd Regiment died on May 24, 1944, in the battle to break the Hitler Line. He lies buried at Cassino: *Beloved son of the Hon. Mr. Justice Cannon and Mrs. Lucien Cannon, Quebec. R.I.P.*

OF NINE BROTHERS WHO SERVED IN WORLD WAR II HERE RESTS
THE ONLY ABSENTEE.
Flight Sergeant Joseph Wilfrid Aldéric Senez, RCAF, 9.11.42 (age 22) [BECKLINGEN]

The contribution of French Canada's servicemen to the national war effort, underappreciated among English Canadians, has never fit comfortably in the memory of their compatriots. Despite the number and quality of the sources recounting their experiences, the men who went overseas found themselves exiled to the periphery of popular memory in Quebec. They came home to a society uneasy with the subject of the war, especially once the revelation of the death camps and the murderous policies of Nazi Germany confronted the opponents of the war with overwhelming evidence refuting their views of the conflict and its implications. With the Quiet Revolution came a generation which tended to interpret the past in the light of the new nationalism asserting Quebec's differences and alienation from English Canada. In postwar novels and films, the focus was not on the soldier who fought but on the little guy who refused to take part in a war waged in the interests of the high and mighty or *les Anglais*. The real heroes were the ones who did not fight, who championed Quebec's resistance to the domineering English majority by avoiding military service. Together with the anti-heroism exemplified in *La Guerre, Yes Sir!* went the preference of nationalist historians who insisted on Quebec's "non-participation" in the Second World War. Insofar as the war is treated in the standard histories of Quebec—and there are textbooks in both languages which do not mention the war at all—it has been to emphasize French Canada's opposition, the conscription crisis, the effects of the war effort on society and the economy, federal-provincial relations, the incarceration of Camillien Houde—in short, everything except the thousands of French Canadians who made the decision to fight for their country. Fifty years after the war, the historian Jean-Pierre Gagnon spoke for the forgotten: "They felt that they were serving in the Canadian army as French Canadians and representing their fellow French Canadians," he declared, "and it is time that we recognised that these men were Québécois, French Canadians, that they fought for liberty and justice, and that the ones who enlisted out of principle or conviction had more vision and broader perspectives than the nationalists who opposed taking part in the war." Canadians of either language would do well to remember that these men made up four infantry battalions, one tank regiment, one medium field artillery regiment, and supplied much needed manpower to the RCAF, the Royal Canadian Navy, and a range of other arms and services. They, too, fought and died at Hong Kong and Dieppe, in Italy and northwestern Europe, and in other lands where the memory of French Canada's sacrifice in World War II endures:

SES VINGT ANS SONT TOMBÉS SUR LE SOL IMMORTEL D'OU JAILLIRENT SES AÏEUX.
(His twenty years have fallen on the immortal soil from which his forefathers sprang.)
Lieutenant Joseph Philippe Rousseau, 1st CPB, 7.6.44 (age 23)
NÉ À MONTRÉAL, CANADA. EPOUX D'AGNES HORNBY. MORT À IGNEY, MEURTHE-EN-MOSELLE.
(Born in Montreal, Canada. Husband of Agnes Hornby. Died at Igney, Meurthe-en-Moselle.)
Lieutenant Joseph Maurice Rousseau, 1st CPB, 20.9.44 [RANVILLE]

J'AI COMBATTU COURAGEUSEMENT. BONHEUR, ESPOIRS, J'AI TOUT SACRIFIÉ POUR LA LIBERTÉ.
(I fought with courage. Happiness, hopes, I sacrificed everything for liberty.)
Private Lucien Caron, FMR, 9.10.44 *(age 21)* [BERGEN-OP-ZOOM]

BIEN QUE REMPLI DE NOBLES AMBITIONS IL EST MORT POUR DIEU ET LES SIENS.
(Although full of noble aspirations, he died for God and his loved ones.)
Private George Henri Dion, RCASC, 17.4.45 *(age 29)* [HOLTEN]

CE HÉROS A LAISSÉ SA VIE ET SON ÉPOUSE QU'IL AIME LE PLUS CHER POUR LA VICTOIRE.
(This hero gave up his life, and his wife whom he loved most dearly, for victory.)
Corporal Etienne Boisclair, RM, 30.7.44 *(age 33)* [BRETTEVILLE-SUR-LAIZE]

IL A BRAVÉ LES TOURMENTS DE LA GUERRE POUR NOUS DONNER LIBERTÉ ET BONHEUR.
(He braved the torments of war to give us liberty and happiness.)
Private Fernand Breton, RM, 6.4.45 [HOLTEN]

I LEFT MY WIFE AND CHILD, DEAREST ON EARTH TO ME, FOR PEACE. MAY THEY PRESERVE IT.
Private Joseph Arthur Aimé Lachapelle, RC, 4.7.44 *(age 21)* [BRETTEVILLE-SUR-LAIZE]

CALLED BY CANADA. DIED FOR PEACE AND COMFORT OF HER PEOPLE.
Gunner Charles Eugène Lévesque, RCA, 23.4.45 *(age 28)* [HOLTEN]

HE FREELY GAVE HIS ALL TO GUARD HIS COUNTRY'S BANNER IN ANSWER TO HER CALL.
Private René Joseph Légère, NS(NB)R, 8.1.45 *(age 19)* [GROESBEEK]

QUE LA LIBERTÉ DU CANADA RECOMPENSE LE SACRIFICE DE SA VIE.
(May the liberty of Canada be the reward for the sacrifice of his life.)
Sergeant Roland Philip Dehase, BWC, 28.8.44 *(age 22)* [BRETTEVILLE-SUR-LAIZE]

HÉROS DE TA PATRIE, FIDÈLE JUSQU'À LA MORT, À TOI LA GLOIRE DE LA VICTOIRE.
(Hero of your country, faithful unto death, to you the glory of victory.)
Lieutenant Daniel Paré, RC, 16.1.45 *(age 24)* [GROESBEEK]

TA MORT DONNA AU MONDE LA PAIX, À TON PAYS LA VICTOIRE, À TA FAMILLE, LA GLOIRE.
(Your death gave peace to the world, victory to your country, and glory to your family.)
Warrant Officer II Viateur Bruno Paré, RC, 6.4.45 *(age 27)* [HOLTEN]

TA FILLE—TA FEMME—TES PARENTS, LE CANADA HONORERONT TA GLORIEUSE MÉMOIRE.
(Your daughter, your wife, your parents, and Canada will honour your glorious memory.)
Pilot Officer Lucien Marcel Soublière, RCAF, 15.8.45 *(age 28)* [BRUSSELS]

In the last few years French Canada's soldiers have finally begun to emerge from the shadows. The past decade has witnessed a resurgence of interest in *les héros oubliés* among francophone historians and writers who have sought to restore these men to their rightful place in the annals of French Canada. The forgotten heroes include men of all ranks who distinguished themselves in battle—Dollard Ménard, René Tessier, Michel Gauvin, Jacques Ostiguy, Pierre Sévigny, Jacques Dextraze, Pierre Potvin—while countless others resolutely and anonymously did their duty:

EN HÉROS? ENSEVELI DANS UN PAYS ÉTRANGE, QUE MON SACRIFICE
NE SOIT PAS EN VAIN.
(Like a hero? Buried in a foreign land, may my sacrifice not be in vain.)
Private Georges Simpson, RC, 31.10.44 *(age 18)* [ADEGEM]

FROM THE LAND OF THE MAPLE LEAF HE CAME AND DIED THAT OTHERS MIGHT LIVE.
Lieutenant Joseph George Beaulieu, RCA, 11.4.45 (age 30) [GROESBEEK]

D'UNE FAMILLE TRÈS DISTINGUÉE. LE SOLDAT MAURICE PÉRUSSE DONNE SA VIE POUR LA PATRIE.
(From a very distinguised family. The soldier Maurice Perusse gave his life for his country.)
Private Maurice Perusse, R22R, 12.12.44 (age 22) [RAVENNA]

POSTHUMOUSLY AWARDED "OPERATIONAL WINGS" FOR GALLANT SERVICE IN ACTION AGAINST THE ENEMY.
Flight Sergeant Jules Joseph La Bossière, RCAF, 17.9.42 [GROESBEEK]

IL A RÉPONDU À L'APPEL. IL A FAIT SON DEVOIR. IL DORT ICI EN PAIX.
(He answered the call. He did his duty. He sleeps here in peace.)
Lieutenant Joseph Alfred Blanchard, WNSR, 23.11.43 (age 22) [MORO RIVER]

IL AIMAIT SA CARRIÈRE. RIEN NE L'A FAIT RECULER DEVANT SON DEVOIR.
(He loved his service career. Nothing made him shrink before his duty.)
Lieutenant Louis Maurice Malouin, CHO, 7.6.44 (age 24) [BÉNY-SUR-MER]

TOMBÉ APRÈS CINQ ANS DE SERVICE POUR LA DÉFENSE DE SON PAYS.
(Fallen after five years of service in the defence of his country.)
Private Paul Cormier, RC, 9.8.45 (age 25) [GROESBEEK]

IL VOULAIT SERVIR SON PAYS. CECI EST PREUVE QU'IL L'A FAIT.
(He wished to serve his country. This is proof that he did so.)
Pilot Officer Fernand Leo Jolicoeur, RCAF, 28.1.45 (age 20) [DURNBACH]

BELOVED HUSBAND OF AGNES BOULRICE AND FATHER OF PAUL WHO ALSO SERVED.
Warrant Officer I Joseph Alexandre Napoleon Raymond, RCASC, 25.7.44 (age 44) [BÉNY-SUR-MER]

A LA DOUCE MÉMOIRE DE ADRIEN, DÉCÉDÉ EN ALLEMAGNE.
(To the gentle memory of Adrien who died in Germany.)
Lance Corporal Adrien Lévesque, RC, 26.2.45 (age 26) [GROESBEEK]

BORN IN MONTREAL, CANADA. KILLED ON DUTY AT KEEVIL, WILTSHIRE.
Sergeant Joseph Jacques Louis Dion, RCAF, 15.11.44 (age 24) [BROOKWOOD]

ICI REPOSE LE CORPS DE ALPHONSE, TOMBÉ EN SERVICE ACTIF EN FRANCE.
(Here rests the body of Alphonse, who fell on active service in France.)
Private Alphonse Couillard, NS(NB)R, 8.8.44 [BRETTEVILLE-SUR-LAIZE]

HERE LIES RAYMOND WHO DIED GLORIOUSLY FOR HIS COUNTRY IN THE SECOND WORLD WAR.
Sapper Raymond Rousseau, CRCE, 3.11.44 (age 22) [GROESBEEK]

IL S'ÉTAIT NOMMÉ LE REPRÉSENTANT DE LA FAMILLE.
(He had appointed himself the representative of the family.)
Private Louis Valmont Roy, RC, 6.6.44 (age 21) [BÉNY-SUR-MER]

DIED ON THE BATTLEFIELD. SON OF CLAUDIA CARON AND THE LATE J.B. JUBINVILLE.
Private Irène Henry Claude Jubinville, RM, 23.8.44 (age 20) [BRETTEVILLE-SUR-LAIZE]

IL ÉTAIT UN DE CES BRAVES CŒURS, DÉVOUÉ ET TOUJOURS SOURIANT.
(He was one of those brave hearts, devoted and always smiling.)
Private Joseph François Marius Pelletier, FMR, 28.2.45 *(age 30)* [GROESBEEK]

A LA MÉMOIRE DE NOTRE FILS BIEN-AIMÉ, DÉCÉDÉ EN SERVICE ACTIF. PARENTS ET AMIS,
PRIEZ POUR LUI. R.I.P.
(To the memory of our beloved son who died on active service. Relatives and friends,
pray for him. R.I.P.)
Captain Jean Pierre Antoine Normandin, RC, 26.6.43 *(age 23)* [BROOKWOOD]

ADIEU MAMAN, FRÈRES, SŒURS, J'AI COMBATTU JUSQU'À LA MORT.
UNE PRIÈRE, S'IL VOUS PLAIT.
(Farewell, mother, brothers, sisters, I fought until death. A prayer, please.)
Private Roméo Gosselin, PPCLI, 12.4.45 *(age 24)* [HOLTEN]

SOYEZ BRAVES AU FOYER COMME NOUS L'AVONS ÉTÉ SUR LES CHAMPS DE BATAILLE.
(Be brave at home, as we were on the field of battle.)
Lieutenant Jean Robert Grégoire, RC, 5.7.44 *(age 22)* [BÉNY-SUR-MER]

The recognition of French Canada's effort and sacrifice in the war should also take into account the trying experience of the families who had to cope with the absence from their homes of a son, brother, father or husband, and to live with the apprehension, sadly borne out in many cases, that they might never see them again:

SEIGNEUR, NOUS VOUS AVIONS SUPPLIÉ DE NOUS LE RAMENER MAIS VOTRE
VOLONTÉ DEVAIT ÉTEINDRE NOTRE DÉSIR.
(Lord, we had entreated You to bring him back to us, but it was Your will
to extinguish our wish.)
Sergeant Raymond Francoeur, RC, 4.7.44 *(age 23)* [BÉNY-SUR-MER]

REPOSE EN PAIX, BRAVE CANADIEN. LA FAMILLE TE PLEURE ET PRIE POUR TOI.
(Rest in peace, brave French Canadian. The family weeps and prays for you.)
Private Roger Taillefer, FMR, 3.3.45 *(age 18)* [GROESBEEK]

ADIEU, CHER FILS, NOTRE PENSÉE TE SUIVRA TOUJOURS MAIS NAVRE DE DOULEUR.
(Farewell, dear son, our thoughts will go with you forever,
but they ache with sorrow.)
Trooper Roland Joseph George Isidore Dion, TRR, 18.12.43 *(age 25)* [MORO RIVER]

JE T'AI BEAUCOUP AIMÉ. TU ES PARTI. JE NE T'AI PAS OUBLIÉ.
(I loved you very much. You have gone. I have not forgotten you.)
Private Pierre Blais, R22R, 11.1.44 *(age 30)* [MORO RIVER]

TON COURAGE ET TA BRAVOURE SONT POUR NOUS UN EXEMPLE DE GÉNÉROSITÉ.
(Your courage and your bravery are to us an example of generosity.)
Flight Sergeant Joseph Fernand Rolland Hurteau, RCAF, 23.4.44 *(age 28)* [EINDHOVEN]

LES LARMES DE CEUX QUI L'ONT AIMÉ SONT ICI-BAS SA LOUANGE.
UNE PRIÈRE, S.V.P.
(The tears of those who loved him are his praise down here. A prayer, please.)
Private Cassien Desrochers, FMR, 24.9.44 [HEVERLEE]

CHER FILS, TON SOUVENIR EST GRAVÉ DANS MON CŒUR. TA MÈRE INCONSOLABLE.
(Dear son, your memory is engraved within my heart. Your inconsolable mother)
Private Phillipe Dussault, RM, 6.3.45 (age 25) [GROESBEEK]

MON CŒUR EST ICI, MON BEAU JEAN PAUL; PROTÈGE TA MAMAN COMME AUTREFOIS.
(My heart is here, my fair Jean Paul; keep watch over your mother as you did before.)
Private Jean Paul Bélanger, RM, 5.4.45 (age 19) [HOLTEN]

NÉ LE DERNIER, AU CIEL LE PREMIER.
(Born the last, to heaven the first.)
Flight Sergeant Joseph René Larivière, RCAF, 18.12.44 (age 24) [HARROGATE]

CHER ÉPOUX, CHER PAPA. NOUS NOUS SOUVIENDRONS TOUJOURS DE TOI,
SI BON, SI CHARITABLE.
(Dear husband, dear papa. We will always remember you, so good, so kindly.)
Trooper Aurèle Delisle, RCAC, 9.2.45 (age 23) [GROESBEEK]

IL RESTE ENFERMÉ DANS NOS CŒURS, CHÉRI ET INOUBLIÉ.
(He remains enclosed in our hearts, cherished and unforgotten.)
Gunner Livin Fred Hébert, RCA, 18.6.44 (age 26) [BÉNY-SUR-MER]

BIEN JEUNE ENCORE, SON PÉLERINAGE EST DÉJÀ FINI. NOUS NOUS RETROUVERONS AU CIEL.
(Still so young, his pilgrimage is already over. We will meet again in heaven.)
Private Hubert Bénard, RC, 13.1.45 (age 23) [GROESBEEK]

O MON DIEU, AYEZ PITIÉ DE CEUX QUI S'AIMAIENT ET QUI ONT ÉTÉ SÉPARÉS.
DONNEZ À TOUS L'ESPÉRANCE ET LA PAIX. AINSI SOIT-IL.
*(O God, have mercy on those who loved each other and were parted.
Give hope to all, and peace. So let it be.)*
Private Yvon Dufresne, R22R, 16.4.45 (age 20) [HOLTEN]

MICHELE ET MOI, TA FEMME, T'ADORERONT ET SERONT TOUJOURS AVEC TOI.
(Michele and I, your wife, will treasure you and always be with you.)
Pilot Officer Joseph Hervé Théodore Bertrand, RCAF, 2.3.44 (age 19) [HARROGATE]

SEIGNEUR, DONNEZ LUI EN FELICITÉ CE QU'IL NOUS A DONNÉ EN TENDRESSE.
(Lord, give him in bliss what he gave to us in tenderness.)
Corporal Jean Octave Guimond, FMR, 29.4.45 (age 31) [HOLTEN]

A LA MÉMOIRE DE MON CHER ÉPOUX. NOUS NE T'OUBLIERONS JAMAIS. CÉCILE, SUZANNE.
(To the memory of my dear husband. We will never forget you. Cecile, Suzanne.)
Private Roger Fernand Lalonde, FMR, 4.3.45 (age 26) [GROESBEEK]

CE SOLDAT EST LE FILS D'EDMOND ET HÉLÈNE POIRIER QUI PLEURENT SA MORT.
(This soldier is the son of Edmond and Helene Poirier who mourn his death.)
Company Quarter Master Sergeant Eugène Poirier, RM, 22.9.44 (age 32) [SCHOONSELHOF]

CHER FILS, TU ÉTAIS NOTRE ORGUEIL. LE DESTIN A VOULU QUE TU SOIS UN HÉROS.
(Dear son, you were our pride. Fate willed that you be a hero.)
Warrant Officer II Yvon Jean Baptiste Guépin, RCAF, 14.5.43 (age 21) [RHEINBERG]

LE TEMPS APAISE LA DOULEUR, MAIS JAMAIS IL N'EFFACERA TA MÉMOIRE. "LES TIENS"
(Time eases the pain, but it will never erase your memory. "Your loved ones")
Private Jean Paul Dubreuil, FMR, 2.3.45 (age 19) [GROESBEEK]

CHER ADRIEN, TON SOUVENIR RESTE GRAVÉ À VIE DANS NOTRE COEUR MEURTRI.
(Dear Adrien, your memory is engraved for life in our broken hearts.)
Private Joseph Arthur Adrien Tremblay, FMR, *17.12.44 (age 22)* [GROESBEEK]

BIEN AIMÉ RÉAL, TON SOUVENIR SERA TOUJOURS PRÉSENT DANS LE CŒUR DE TES PARENTS.
(Beloved Réal, your memory will be ever present in your parents' heart.)
Warrant Officer II Joseph Robert Réal Gingras, RCAF, *14.1.45 (age 21)*
[HARROGATE]

GOD LENT HIM TO ME, TOOK HIM FROM ME. MAY HIS NAME BE BLESSED! PEACE BE WITH HIM.
Major Joseph Charles Ovila Garceau, R22R, *24.5.44 (age 31)* [CASSINO]

LAISSE SA FEMME YVETTE FULLUM, SES ENFANTS RAYMOND, DENISE, GISELLE, MICHELINE.
(Leaves his wife Yvette Fullum and his children Raymond, Denise, Giselle, Micheline.)
Private Donat Ellenberg, R22R, *5.1.45 (age 31)* [FAENZA]

EPOUX BIEN AIMÉ D'YVETTE GRENIER, PÈRE DE JACQUES, MICHELINE ET CLAUDETTE.
(Beloved husband of Yvette Grenier, father of Jacques, Micheline and Claudette.)
Private Arthur Lavoie, SLI, *1.1.44 (age 35)* [MORO RIVER]

EPOUX DE FLEURETTE HOULE, NÉE COMTOIS, LAISSANT TROIS ENFANTS,
VICTOR, PIERRE, CLAUDE.
(Husband of Fleurette Houle, née Comtois, leaving three children, Victor, Pierre, Claude.)
Private Germain Houle, RM, *14.4.45 (age 30)* [HOLTEN]

GÉRARD, DIEU A MESURÉ TA VALEUR À LA GRANDEUR DE TON SUPRÊME SACRIFICE.
(Gérard, God has measured your worth by the greatness of your supreme sacrifice.)
Private Gérard Jourdain, RC, *6.4.45 (age 22)* [HOLTEN]

NOUS SOMMES FIERS DE TOI.
(We are proud of you)
Private Roger Legendre, RC, 11.6.44 (AGE 26) [BÉNY-SUR-MER]

"It was a real thrill to watch the battle-wise Van Doos march straight forward, spread out and half crouching—they never dug in," wrote one English Canadian soldier who witnessed his French-speaking countrymen advance through the Liri Valley. "A real fighting outfit" was another soldier's admiring verdict. The soldiers of the Royal 22nd Regiment upheld the reputation of the old French Canadian Battalion, adding to their record of courage at the Casa Berardi and the San Fortunato ridge. When the First Division was transferred to northwestern Europe, the Van Doos rejoined the other French-speaking battalions raised in Quebec, the Maisonneuves, the Chaudières, and the Fusiliers Mont-Royal, which have left proud testimony to their contribution to the victory campaign:

"FILS DE LA CHAUDIÈRE, LOIN DE TON CANADA, EN TERRE DE FRANCE, REPOSE EN PAIX"
*("Son of the Chaudière, far from your native Canada, rest in peace in
the earth of France")*
Private Léger Laplante, RC, *4.7.44 (age 28)* [BÉNY-SUR-MER]

REPOSE EN PAIX, O HÉROS DE MAISONNEUVE, NOUS NE T'OUBLIERONS JAMAIS.
(Rest in peace, hero of the Maisonneuve regiment, we will never forget you)
Lance Corporal Gilles Lanteigne, RM, *9.3.45 (age 21)* [GROESBEEK]

San Fortunato Ridge, the scene of the Royal 22nd Regiment's most famous exploit in the Gothic Line battle, looms behind the Coriano Ridge War Cemetery.

The Cross of Sacrifice standing before the battlements and terraces at Gradara War Cemetery.

Montecchio War Cemetery at the foot of the ridgeline marking the bastion of the Gothic Line.

The stone-girded Barenthal War Cemetery on the Asiago Plateau in northern Italy.

"He believed he was saving the Catholic religion and the French Canadian race..."

Valley Cemetery with the village of Chérisy in the background.

Graves of the 22nd (French Canadian) Battalion in Quebec Cemetery.

The fleur-de-lys monument beside the Casa Berardi where Captain Paul Triquet won the Victoria Cross during the battle of Ortona.

IL EST NÉ D'UNE RACE FIÈRE, BÉNI FUT SON BERCEAU. LE CIEL A MARQUÉ SA CARRIÈRE
DANS UN MONDE NOUVEAU OÙ SE REPOSE NOTRE HÉROS.
(He was born of a proud race, blessed was his birthplace. Heaven has charted
his course in a new world where our hero rests.)
Private Raymond Bouley, FMR, 29.4.45 (age 19) [HOLTEN]

The headstones tabulating French Canada's sacrifice in World War II have a poignancy of their own. They mark the places of young men who volunteered to fight in a war which their own people did not fully endorse. In the armed forces of their own country, they were virtually foreigners, compelled to adapt to the language and ways not only of English Canada's military establishment, but of the Allied coalition as a whole. To Claude Châtillon, memorials to French Canadian soldiers held a special significance when viewed against the factors that set their war experience apart:

> I cannot help but think that a French Canadian who received a military decoration or met his death in battle has the right to a particular respect, if one bears in mind that he did his military service while having to express himself and to fight for a cause in circumstances and surroundings dissociated from his language and way of life, and from his Canada. I have great admiration for all Canadians who took part in the war, each in his own way, but it should not be held against me if I feel especially moved before a cross for bravery or a cross in the cemetery of a French Canadian soldier. To react otherwise would be false to my sincerity and convictions, and a betrayal of my faith in my country.

His words carry greater force when followed by the epitaphs of servicemen whose families wished them to be commemorated as French Canadians, identified as such in simple statements or in words rich in associations with French Canada's heritage:

A FRENCH CANADIAN.
Trooper Lorenzo St. Louis, TRR, 24.6.44 (age 33) [ASSISI]

ICI REPOSE SIMÉON. CANADIEN. R.I.P.
(Here rests Siméon. French Canadian. R.I.P.)
Private Siméon Picard, FMR, 24.9.44 (age 32) [BERGEN-OP-ZOOM]

SOLDAT CANADIEN. NÉ À ST. DÉNIS, QUÉBEC. MORT AU CHAMP D'HONNEUR.
(A French Canadian soldier. Born in St. Denis, Quebec. Died on the field of honour)
Private Laurier Chapdelaine, R22R, 14.12.43 (age 30) [MORO RIVER]

FROM ALL THOSE WHO LOVED HIM. FATHER-MOTHER. FRENCH CANADIAN OF QUEBEC.
Captain Joseph Dosithée Lucien Rhéaume, RCA, 28.2.45 (age 25) [GROESBEEK]

ENFANT DE THÉODULE PERRIER. UN CANADIEN FRANÇAIS DE TIMMINS,
ONTARIO, CANADA.
(Son of Theodule Perrier. A French Canadian from Timmins, Ontario, Canada)
Private Maurice Perrier, R22R, 15.12.43 [MORO RIVER]

I REGRET THE LOSS OF MY SON AND MISS HIM VERY MUCH. FRENCH CANADIAN BORN.
MRS. EMMA FINN
Gunner Lionel Joseph Finn, RCA, 27.1.44 (age 22) [MORO RIVER]

SOUVENEZ-VOUS D'UN CANADIEN FRANÇAIS QUI A DONNÉ SA VIE POUR LA PAIX.
(Remember a French Canadian who gave his life for peace.)
Private Arthur Groulx, RHLI, 8.3.45 (age 23) [GROESBEEK]

FILS DE FRANÇAIS, DEUXIÈME TOMBÉ AU CHAMP D'HONNEUR. REQUIESCANT IN PACE.
FILS DE FRANCE, LE DEUXIÈME TOMBÉ AU CHAMP D'HONNEUR. "REQUIESCANT IN PACE."
(Son of France, the second to fall on the field of honour. May they rest in peace.)
Private Jean François Roger Pichard, RC, 11.6.44 (age 21) [BÉNY-SUR-MER]
Private Bernard Pichard, RM, 26.2.45 (age 20) [GROESBEEK]

PETIT-FILS DE FRANÇAIS, TU SERAS TOUJOURS EN LA MÉMOIRE DU CANADA FRANÇAIS.
(Grandson of France, you will always be in the memory of French Canada.)
Private Réal Jean Paul St. Laurent, FMR, 24.9.44 (age 19) [BERGEN-OP-ZOOM]

CANADIEN-FRANÇAIS. MON ÂME À DIEU POUR LE CANADA SUR LA TERRE DE FRANCE.
(French Canadian. My soul to God for Canada on the soil of France.)
Private Joseph Latour, RC, 8.7.44 (age 22) [BÉNY-SUR-MER]

TON FRONT EST CEINT DE FLEURONS GLORIEUX; TA VALEUR PROTÉGERA
NOS FOYERS ET NOS DROITS.
*(Thy brow is wreathed with garlands of glory; thy valour will protect our homes
and our rights.)*
Sapper Adélard Fournier, CRCE, 4.6.45 [GROESBEEK]

The words above, taken from the French version of the national anthem, lead to a
last epitaph citing the motto of the province of Quebec. The simple yet richly evocative
phrase, inscribed on the headstone of a Franco-Ontarian soldier buried in Hong Kong
and of an airman from Quebec buried on the other side of the world in Germany, lays
a debt of remembrance on all Canadians:

JE ME SOUVIENS.
(I remember.)
Rifleman Gérard Joseph Pelletier, RRfC, 23.10.42 (age 31) [SAI WAN]
Warrant Officer Class I Joseph Henri Roger Ledoux, RCAF, 31.3.45 (age 29) [BECKLINGEN]

FURTHER READING:

« Actes du colloque: La participation des canadiens français à la deuxième guerre
mondiale. » *Bulletin d'Histoire politique*, vol. 3, nos 3 et 4, 1995.

Auger, Geneviève, and Lamothe, Raymonde. *De la poêle à frire à la ligne de feu. La
vie quotidienne des québécoises pendant la guerre '39–'45.* Montreal: Boréal Express,
1981.

Cantin, Robert. *Le sacrifice du Royal 22e Régiment (de 1914 à 1999).* Sainte-Foy:
Société de Généalogie de Québec, 2004.

Castonguay, Jacques. *C'était la guerre à Québec, 1939–1945.* Montreal : Art Global,
2003.

Châtillon, Claude. *Carnets de guerre. Ottawa-Casa Berardi, 1941–1944*. Ottawa: Les Editions du Vermillon, 1987.

Copp, Terry, and Hamelin, Christine. "Le Régiment de Maisonneuve: A profile based on personnel records," *Canadian Military History* 8/4 (1999), 17–25.

Cormier, Ronald. *Les Acadiens et la second guerre mondiale*. Moncton : Editions d'Acadie, 1996.

Dutil, Patrice A. "Against isolationism: Napoléon Belcourt, French Canada, and 'La Grande Guerre'," in: *Canada and the First World War. Essays in Honour of Robert Craig Brown*. Ed. David MacKenzie. Toronto : University of Toronto Press, 2005, pp. 96–137.

Filteau, Gérard. *Le Québec, le Canada et la guerre 1914–1918*. Montreal : Editions de l'Aurore, 1977.

Gagnon, Jean-Pierre. "Les historiens canadiens-français et la participation canadienne-française à la Deuxième Guerre Mondiale," *Bulletin d'Histoire politique*, vol. 3, nos 3 et 4, (1995), 25–42.

———. *Le 22e bataillon (canadien français.) 1914–1919. Etude socio-militaire*. Ottawa-Quebec: Laval University Press, 1986.

Jones, Richard. "Politics and Culture: The French Canadians and the Second World War," in: *The Second World War as a National Experience*, ed. S. Aster. Ottawa: The Canadian Committee for the History of the Second World War, 1981, pp. 82–91.

Loyal Service. Perspectives on French-Canadian Military Leaders. Ed. Colonel Bernd Horn and Dr. Roch Legault. Canadian Defence Academy Press, Kingston. Toronto, The Dundurn Group, 2007.

Marchand, Gérard. *Le Régiment de Maisonneuve vers la victoire, 1944–1945*. Montreal: Les presses libres, 1980.

Pariseau, Jean. "La participation des canadiens français à l'effort des deux guerres mondiales," *Canadian Defence Quarterly*, Autumn 1983, 43–48.

Poulin, J.-G. *696 Heures d'enfer avec le Royal 22ᵉ Régiment. Récit vécu et inspiré d'un journal tenu tant bien que mal au front*. Quebec City: Editions A.–B., 1946.

Richard, Béatrice. "La participation des soldats canadiens-français à la Deuxième Guerre Mondiale : Une histoire de trous de mémoire," *Bulletin d'Histoire politique*, vol. 3, nos 3 et 4, spring/summer 1995, 383–392.

Vanier, Georges. *Paroles de guerre*. Montreal: Editions Beauchemin, 1944.

Vennat, Pierre. *Dieppe n'aurait pas dû avoir lieu*. Montreal: Editions de Meridien, 1991.

———. *Les héros oubliés. L'histoire inédite de Canadiens-français de la deuxième guerre mondiale. Tome I : De la mobilisation à Dieppe. Tome II : De Septembre 1942 à la veille du « Jour J ». Tome III : Du « Jour J » à la démobilisation*. Montreal: Editions du Méridien, 1997–1998.

Wade, Mason. *The French Canadians 1760–1945*. New York: The MacMillan Company, 1955.

CHAPTER NINE

"For our freedom and yours"
Cassino War Cemetery, Italy

LET ALL THE NATIONS SEE THAT MEN SHOULD BROTHERS BE
THE WIDE WORLD O'ER.
Sergeant Alan Hughes Ransom, RCA, 24.5.44 (age 27)

Rome was the first of the Axis capitals to fall to the Allies, nearly a year after the landings in Sicily opened what was to be the longest and least rewarding of the Allied campaigns in western Europe. Beside the Pyramid of Gaius Cestius four large plaques have been attached to a section of the Aurelian Wall. They were placed there in tribute to the Allied units and local resistance groups that paved the way for the liberation of Rome on the 4th–5th of June, 1944. Among the Allied soldiers welcomed by the populace were the Canadians of the First Special Service Force, an élite unit formed of American and Canadian volunteers. A plaque featuring the distinctive Canada-U.S. shoulder patch worn by men of either nationality records the part played by the Special Service Force in pushing rapidly into the city and securing the Tiber bridges. A list of placenames summarises the role of the SSF in the battles around Cassino and in the Anzio beachhead during the long struggle that preceded the Allied entry into the Eternal City.

The SSF won a fearsome reputation among the Germans who are said to have dubbed it "The Devil's Brigade." This moniker in turn served as the title of a 1968 film purportedly based on the unit's exploits in Italy. Despite the embellishment and distortion typical of Hollywood storytelling, the film holds a particular interest for Canadians as being one of very few American or British war movies to recognise the Canadian presence in the Allied coalition. Lasting evidence of the price paid by the Canadians of the SSF is on display in two of the seven Commonwealth war cemeteries keeping vigil over the Allied route from Naples to Rome. One is Beach Head War Cemetery, by the road which branches south from the Via Appia and leads to the seaside resort of Anzio. Here, in a burial ground criss-crossed with walkways and pergolas, lie the Canadians who died in the static fighting along the Mussolini

Canal between February and May 1944, when the undermanned SSF held a sector normally allotted to a division, and subsequently in the breakout from the beachhead and the advance on Rome. All soldiers are young, but the ages on the headstones of the Forcemen who fell in battle, especially the officers, underline the strength and vigour of youth required in such highly trained units:

GARNET. LOVED SON OF VIOLET AND THE LATE SGT. DANIEL RICHARDSON.
"HIS MEMORY WE ALWAYS KEEP."
Staff Sergeant Garnet Cecil Richardson, SSTCA, 9.2.44 (age 22)

TRUE TO DUTY, HIS GOD AND COUNTRY. HIS LIFE A SACRIFICE TO FAMILY AND OUR FUTURE.
Sergeant George Oliver Godin, SSTCA, 22.2.44 (age 25)

HIS EYES WERE TRUE, HIS LAUGH WAS CLEAR, HE HELD HIS TRUTH AND HONOUR DEAR.
Sergeant Keith Garfield Garratt, SSTCA, 16.4.44 (age 20)

OF THIS BAD WORLD THE LOVELIEST AND THE BEST HAS SMILED, SAID GOODNIGHT AND
GONE TO REST.
Captain Frederick Blake Atto, SSTCA, 22.5.44 (age 25)

SO WILL HE LONG BE HONORED BY HIS COUNTRY, A HERO IN THE CAUSE OF LIBERTY.
Private Donald MacDonald, SSTCA, 23.5.44 (age 23)

YOU WERE MINE AND I LOVED YOU. SADLY MISSED BY HIS MOTHER. "GOD'S WILL BE DONE"
Private Harry Oliver Molesworth, SSTCA, 24.5.44 (age 19)

"IF GOD CHOOSE, I SHALL BUT LOVE THEE BETTER AFTER DEATH."
Private Wallace Arthur Tourangeau, SSTCA, 28.5.44 (age 21)
[ELIZABETH BARRETT BROWNING, SONNETS FROM THE PORTUGUESE]

FOR NOWHERE IS FAR FROM GOD. PRAY FOR ME AT THE ALTARS OF GOD WHEREVER YOU GO.
Sergeant James Emmett Guerin, SSTCA, 28.5.44 (age 32)

The SSF was involved in the battle for Rome from the beginning. The headstones of the Forcemen buried at Cassino face back towards the Mignano Gap and the mountain fastnesses on either side where the American Fifth Army came up against the German outposts denying passage along the principal route from Naples to Rome. It was to evict the Germans from these strongholds that the SSF, rigorously trained in mountain warfare, was brought to Italy in November of 1943. In the six weeks from the beginning of December to the middle of January 1944, the SSF undertook three assaults to root out the enemy garrisons perched in the mountains. The epitaph of a Canadian soldier killed in the unit's first engagement, the assault on the Monte Camino massif, cites a line penned by a venerable Canadian figure of the First World War, Frederick George Canon Scott:

THE ANGUISH AND THE PAIN HAVE PASSED, AND PEACE HATH COME TO THEM AT LAST.
Sergeant William Kotenko, SSTCA, 3.12.43 (age 20)

Scott's poem *Requiescant* is the other *In Flanders Fields*. He wrote it in April 1915, "in a field near Ypres," after witnessing the first Canadian attack of the war at Kitchener's Wood. Not far away, and about the same time, his compatriot John McCrae was composing one of the most famous poems in the English language.

The popularity of McCrae's poem has relegated the works of his contemporaries to obscurity, among them Canon Scott's war poetry and memoir, *The Great War As I Saw It*, which during the interwar period did as much as any literary piece to sanctify the memory of Canada's war effort. Echoes of Flanders seem most appropriate at Cassino, where the long, wearying stalemate made the name to Allied soldiers in Italy what Ypres or Passchendaele had been to their forebears on the Western Front—shorthand for the misery and frustration of a campaign in which the results never seemed to justify the expenditure in lives.

Cassino War Cemetery is the largest and most symbolic of the Commonwealth war cemeteries in Italy. It is tapered to the slope overlooking the stretch of the Gari River where the Germans welded fast their chain of defences across the corridor to Rome. With the town of Cassino forming its strongest link, the Gustav Line held firm for six months as a succession of Allied forces—American, French, Polish, New Zealand, British, Indian—found themselves obliged to fight on the usurious terms imposed by the terrain and the defenders. The raised entrance to the cemetery faces east, back over the mountains and the scenes of a battle that would eventually exact one third of the 321,000 Allied casualties in Italy. Stretching away to the west, the mountain walls frame the straitened corridor of the Liri Valley. To the north, on a spur of the Monte Cairo massif, the rebuilt Abbey of Monte Cassino broods over the site where 4,266 British and Commonwealth servicemen lie at rest. Nearly three hundred are unidentified, plain testimony to the intensity of the fighting around Cassino. They count among the 4,044 soldiers of the Italian campaign "to whom the fortunes of war denied a known and honoured grave" and whose names are inscribed on the memorial forming the centrepiece of the cemetery.

The Cassino Memorial deserves a moment's pause. In scope and design it is a far cry from the grandiose memorials created in the wake of the Great War to give individual commemoration to the droves of war dead known simply as "the missing." The most famous of these monuments, the Menin Gate at Ypres (54,000 names) and the Thiepval Memorial on the Somme (73,000 names), are but two of seventeen catalogues in stone listing what Siegfried Sassoon decried as "the intolerably nameless names," the only vestiges of the multitudes obliterated along the Western Front. Monuments without precedent, they translate, into various architectural forms, the annihilating power of a war unprecedented in its mobilisation of destructive energies. The second conflict did not oblige the architect of the Cassino Memorial, Louis de Soissons, to work on the same colossal scale—the vast majority of "the missing" of the Second World War being the civilians immolated in the bombing campaigns or the peoples exterminated in the death camps—but he faced a challenge of a different order in creating a register of names appropriate to a country as rich in architectural traditions as Italy. He departed from the massive structures of his Great War predecessors, turning instead to the Roman past for inspiration. Twelve tall plaques of green marble, recording the names of the missing, stand on either side of a sunken garden centred on an ornamental pool. The plant beds and pathways flanking the pool, and the geometric mosaics decorating the patios, recreate the aspect of the courtyard gardens found in the villas at Pompeii, and lend to the memorial a similar aura of repose and serenity. The memorial is aligned on the strong central axis fixed by the Stone of Remembrance and the Cross of Sacrifice, giving the cemetery as a whole a unifying focal point while establishing the memorial as a separate space commemorating those present in spirit only.

Two modern buildings now stand opposite the southeastern corner of the cemetery.

They mark the return of normalcy and prosperity to a region which six months of fighting had bludgeoned into a desolate, shell-cratered moonscape. Beyond, the saddle-shaped ridge connecting Monte la Difensa and Monte la Remetanea can be seen from the graves of these soldiers who died in battle on those peaks in December of 1943:

I ALWAYS WILL ADORE THAT GUY WHO TAUGHT MY HAPPY HEART TO FLY.
Sergeant Austin Ole Gunderson, SSTCA, 3.12.43 (age 24)

OUR SON. GOD BLESS HIM. MOTHER AND DAD
Private Gordon Mitchell Brady, SSTCA, 5.12.43 (age 19)

PASSANT, UNE PRIÈRE POUR LE PLUS AIMANT DES FILS ET LE PLUS BRAVE DES SOLDATS.
(Passerby, a prayer for the most loving of sons and the bravest of soldiers)
Corporal Jean-Marc Violette, SSTCA, 12.12.43 (age 24)

On the other side of the Mignano Gap, behind the worn anvil of Monte Trocchio, rises Monte Sammucro where the SSF spent Christmas of 1943 sweeping the German defenders from the western slopes. Further to the north, on the far side of the Rapido River, a range of peaks clusters around Monte Maio and the scenes of the SSF's subsequent operations in the Cassino sector. These inscriptions commemorate the soldiers buried within sight of the places where they died in battle. Even the simplest farewells become more poignant at dawn or dusk, when the light softens the contours of the rugged landscape:

WITH COURAGE HIGH HE SERVED THE CAUSE AND DIED THERE WITH HIS COMPANY.
Warrant Officer II Daniel Green, SSTCA, 24.12.43 (age 24)

HE GAVE HIS ALL IN WAR THAT OTHERS MIGHT LIVE IN PEACE.
Sergeant Jack Frederick Glenn, SSTCA, 25.12.43 (age 21)

GREATER LOVE HATH NO MAN THAN THIS, THAT A MAN LAY DOWN HIS LIFE FOR HIS FRIENDS.
Private Victor Innanen, SSTCA, 11.1.44 (age 17)

HIS COURAGE AND DEVOTION HELD EVER IN FOND MEMORY BY SUZIE AND ROXIE ANNE.
Sergeant Clinton Fyfe Joy, SSTCA, 13.1.44 (age 31)

BORN IN OTTAWA, CANADA. MAY HIS SOUL REST IN PEACE.
Private Francis Bernard Wright, SSTCA, 15.1.44 (age 19)

Aside from the troops of the SSF, Canadians saw action only in the final phase of the campaign, when in May 1944 the newly constituted 1st Canadian Corps spearheaded the Eighth Army's drive through the Liri Valley. Three and a half weeks of fierce fighting cost the Canadian Corps over 3,700 casualties, including nearly a thousand dead. Little remains in tribute to the Canadians who died in the struggle to prise open the way to Rome, leaving the inscription on the graves of two brothers, one buried in the Rome War Cemetery, the other in Assisi, to speak for all their comrades who fell:

BY THE ROAD TO ROME HE'LL REST FOR ALL ETERNITY, A LONG, LONG WAY FROM HOME.
Trooper James Roy Hurst, OR, 13.6.44 (age 20)
Trooper Allister Richard Hurst, OR, 2.7.44 (age 21)

The Canadian road to Rome was the Via Casilina, known in antiquity as the Via Labicana and in 1944 as Highway 6. Under these names it had for centuries served as the main artery connecting Rome with Naples and southern Italy. Since the war this ancient road has been superseded by the modern A1 expressway, the Autostrada del Sol, which has reduced the drive from Rome to Naples to a couple of hours. The Canadian traveller heading to Cassino from Rome will pass over the SS6 several times as it entwines with the autostrada. Past the Alban Hill mass a series of exit signs announces the names of towns that chart the Canadian path in reverse order. The first few, Colleferro, Anagni, Ferentino, Frosinone, Ceccano, Arnara, Pofi, were the scenes of brief clashes as Canadian columns snapped at the heels of the Germans, methodical and unhurried as ever, as they withdrew towards Rome; but the placenames appearing along the autostrada from Ceprano to Cassino are associated with battles which some veterans deemed even worse than Ortona:

FELL AT THE MELFA RIVER CROSSING. LOVED AND REMEMBERED ALWAYS.
Private Walter McKenzie Drummond, WR, 24.5.44 (age 26)

GOD CALLED OUR LOVED ONE, BUT WE LOSE NOT WHOLLY WHAT HE HAS GIVEN.
Trooper Israel Alex Chaval, LSH (RC), 24.5.44

THERE ALWAYS COMES A LONGING, DEAR SON, IF ONLY YOU COULD COME HOME. MOTHER
Private John William Mullen, WR, 24.5.44 (age 23)

NOW THE BATTLE IS O'ER, SLEEP, WARRIOR, SLEEP.
Trooper Lloyd Wilfred Bigham, LSH (RC), 24.5.44 (age 26)

IN LIFE HE ALWAYS LIVED FOR OTHERS, AND GAVE HIS LIFE FOR OTHERS TOO.
Private Eric Herbert Moore, WR, 24.5.44 (age 37)

O MAY GOD KEEP YOU IN HIS DEAR CARE, O MY SOLDIER LADDIE WHO'S OVER THERE.
Trooper George Merton McComb, LSH (RC), 25.5.44 (age 33)

GLORY TO THEM THAT DIED IN THIS GREAT CAUSE. GOD GRANT HIM ETERNAL REST.
Trooper James Joseph Burns, LSH (RC), 25.5.44 (age 19)

IN LOVING MEMORY OF A BRAVE AND COURAGEOUS SON AND BROTHER.
MOTHER, SISTERS AND BROTHERS
Private Nickolo Fruno, WR, 25.5.44 (age 29)

Not many who speed over the long viaduct crossing the Melfa River know that they are passing directly over the place where Major John Mahony of the Westminster Regiment won the Victoria Cross for his actions in securing a bridgehead vital to the Eighth Army's breakout from the Liri Valley. Nor, further on, is there anything to indicate that the towns signposted on either side of the autostrada, Aquino and Pontecorvo, once anchored the Hitler Line, the second thicket of defensive emplacements stretched across the Liri Valley, which the Canadian Corps had no choice to attack but by direct frontal assault. The breaching of this line stands as one of the finest displays of courage and perseverance by Canadian soldiers in the war. The date of the Hitler Line attack, 23rd May, 1944—just two weeks before the Normandy landings eclipsed the war in Italy—preponderates in the Canadian sections at Cassino, particularly among the westerners of the 2nd Brigade whose losses were the highest suffered by a Canadian brigade on any single day of the Italian campaign. A hardbitten memoir of one soldier's experience in Italy, Charles Monroe Johnson's *Action with the Seaforths*, opens with a platoon of Seaforth Highlanders talking amongst themselves the night before the attack. In reply to a friend's question about his reasons for signing up, Johnson relates his story as an American who had come north out of principle to enlist in the Canadian army, and the train of events that brought him to the fringes of the Hitler Line. When the attack goes in, Johnson is badly wounded in the torrent of shells let loose upon the advancing infantrymen, and afterwards learns in hospital that nearly every member of his platoon has become a casualty.

The Hitler Line has dimmed in Canadian memory, and 23 May 1944 is one of many days submerged in the history of a campaign that after June 1944 was consigned to secondary importance in the Allied war effort. Traces of the fighting remain in the *membra disiecta* of abandoned houses and pockmarked buildings where the Hitler Line once stood. It is still possible to find concrete turrets and bunkers gazing forbiddingly over the approaches to Pontecorvo and Aquino. In the central squares, as in the other towns and hamlets in the Liri Valley where a swath of destruction preceded liberation, public monuments list the names of the inhabitants whose lives were claimed by a war they had wanted no part of, but there is nothing to acknowledge the Canadians who ran the gauntlet through the obstacles, minefields, and killing zones cunningly laid before them. The men who died their "lonely, jagged deaths" in the Hitler Line were buried in battalion groups at Cassino. The messages of farewell on their headstones swell into a litany for one of the country's hardest days of the war:

IN THE SERVICE OF HUMANITY.
Lieutenant John Kenneth Hentig, SHC, 23.5.44 *(age 30)*

UNDISHONOURED, CLEAR OF DANGER, CLEAN OF GUILT, PASS HENCE AND HOME.
Corporal Edward Sinclair Weston, SHC, 23.5.44 *(age 22)*
[A.E. HOUSMAN, *A SHROPSHIRE LAD*]

HERE LIES OUR SON. HIS WORK ON EARTH IS DONE, SO REST IN PEACE, VICTORY IS WON.
Lance Corporal Joseph Victor Warner, SHC, 23.5.44 *(age 26)*

YOU FOUGHT A GOOD FIGHT, SON. IN GOD WE TRUST YOU REST.
DAD, MOTHER AND BROTHERS
Private Edward Louis Girardin, SHC, 23.5.44 *(age 20)*

WE HAVE LOVED IN HIM IN LIFE, LET US CONDUCT WITH OUR PRAYERS INTO THE
HOUSE OF THE LORD.
Private Louis John Street, SHC, 23.5.44 *(age 27)*

HE DIED DOING HIS DUTY FOR HIS LOVED ONES.
Lance Corporal Clarence Francis Bangle, PPCLI, 23.5.44 *(age 21)*

WENT THE DAY WELL? HE DIED AND NEVER KNEW. WELL OR ILL, FREEDOM,
HE DIED FOR YOU.
Lance Corporal George Amos, PPCLI, 23.5.44 *(age 44)*

SLEEP AND REST, DEAR SON, IN A LAND YOU DIED TO SAVE. WE WHO LOVE YOU
SADLY MISS YOU.
Private Morton Slemmon, PPCLI, 23.5.44 *(age 25)*

MAY HIS SOUL AND THE SOULS OF ALL HIS COMRADES REST IN PEACE WITH THEE, O LORD.
Private Leonard Nelson, PPCLI, 23.5.44 (age 23)

FOREVER WE'LL CARRY SADNESS IN OUR HEARTS FOR THE ONE WE LOVED.
Private George Clifford Quartly, PPCLI, 23.5.44 (age 21)

LEONARD. YOU STILL LIVE WAY IN THE SKY. WHAT JOY ONE DAY TO MEET IN PARADISE.
Private Leonard Urquhart, PPCLI, 23.5.44 (age 23)

NOT LOST, BUT LIVING IN THE REALM OF PEACE.
Private George Ronald Watson, PPCLI, 23.5.44 (age 21)

OUR HAROLD. WE MISS THY PRESENCE. EVERYWHERE THE VOICE WE LOVED IS STILLED.
Private Harold Roscoe Monson, PPCLI, 23.5.44 (age 24)

I WILL ALWAYS REMEMBER YOUR LOVELY FACE, MY DARLING. YOUR LOVING WIFE
Private Ernest Victor Smallpiece, PPCLI, 23.5.44 (age 23)

SON OF MAX LANG AND THERESA HINGER, RAYMORE, SASKATCHEWAN, CANADA.
MAY HE REST IN PEACE.
Private Karl Lang, LER, 23.5.44 (age 33)

LOVINGLY REMEMBERED BY THE FAMILY, CAMROSE, ALBERTA. "HE LIVED TO SERVE"
Private John Bruce "Peter" Price, LER, 23.5.44 (age 29)

HE BORE HIS CROSS AND HE HAS WON HIS CROWN. HE IS SAFE IN THE ARMS OF JESUS.
Private William Charles Brown, LER, 23.5.44 (age 25)

SINCE HE WHO KNOWS OUR NEED IS PEACE, LET NOT OUR EFFORTS EVER CEASE.
Private Wilfred Nicholas Delorey, CYR, 23.5.44 (age 31)

"HE DIED THAT WE MIGHT LIVE." HIS FRESH YOUNG LIFE HE GAVE.
HE LIES IN A SOLDIER'S GRAVE.
Private Ian Alexander Horne, CYR, 23.5.44 (age 21)

REJOICING IN HOPE, PATIENT IN TRIBULATION, CONTINUING INSTANT IN PRAYER.
ROMANS XII. 12
Lance Corporal James Henry Walter Johnson, 48th HC, 23.5.44 (age 25)

WHEN WE ASUNDER PART, IT GIVES US INWARD PAIN, BUT STILL JOINED IN HEART,
WE HOPE TO MEET AGAIN.
Private Albert Lewers, 48th HC, 23.5.44 (age 23)
[JOHN FAWCETT, *BLEST BE THE TIE THAT BINDS*, HYMN]

HIS HEART BRAVE AND TRUE, HE DIED TO SAVE HIS COUNTRY, LIKE OTHERS DID, FOR YOU.
Private Reginald John Rees, 48th HC, 23.5.44 (age 20)

FOR FREEDOM'S CAUSE HE COULD NOT GIVE MORE. HE GAVE HIS LIFE.
Lance Corporal John James Gillan, HPER, 23.5.44 (age 23)

THANK YOU, SON, FOR WHAT YOU HAVE DONE. EVER REMEMBERED. DAD AND MUM
Private Frank Leonard Reed, RCR, 23.5.44 (age 23)

ONLY A BOY, BUT DIED MANFULLY. GAVE HIS LIFE TO SAVE OURS. BERTHA, VERA MCGINN.
Gunner Francis McGinn, RCA, 23.5.44 (age 30)

"WE ARE IN THE CALM AND PROUD POSSESSION OF ETERNAL THINGS."
Sergeant Gordon Wallace Doak, RCOC, 23.5.44 (age 31)
[GEORGE WILLIAM RUSSELL, 1867–1935, BABYLON]

WEEP NOT BECAUSE I HAVE GONE BEFORE; WEEP RATHER THAT YOU COME NOT WITH ME.
Sapper William Henry Francis Standish, CRCE, 23.5.44 (age 27)

Nearly every nation of the British Empire is represented at Cassino War Cemetery. The emblems on the headstones issue the last great roll call of Britain's imperial army, which only two generations ago could still summon a host of peoples from around the globe to fight within its ranks—Australians, New Zealanders and Maoris from the Antipodes, South Africans of English, Dutch, and native descent, Rhodesians, Cypriots Greek and Turkish, Maltese, the Sikhs, Hindus, Muslims, and Gurkhas of the Indian Army, a world unto itself, as well as Newfoundlanders, English and French Canadians from North America—an assembly of languages, sects, and races whose silent presence makes Cassino the reliquary of an empire now as seemingly remote as the *imperium romanum*:

HIS SILENCE SPEAKS FOR ENGLAND AND HIS CROSS TELLS THE STORY OF OUR NOBLE DEAD.
Sergeant John Thomas Lane, The Royal Fusiliers, 12.5.44 (age 28)

BELOVED SON OF DUDLEY AND MARGARET CLARKE OF BARBADOS, BRITISH WEST INDIES.
Captain George Lawrance Alleyne Clarke, LSH (RC), 25.5.44 (age 24)

DAAR WAS GEEN AFSKEIDWOORD, GEEN VAARWEL OF GROET. BEDROEFDE EGGENOTE EN DOGTERTJE.
(There was no parting word, no farewell or greeting. Bereaved wife and little daughter)
Warrant Officer II Willem C. Bouwer, South African Artillery, 9.5.44 (age 27)

CLASSICAL SCHOLAR, PERSE AND MAGDALENE, CAMBRIDGE. VIVIT VIDEBIMUS.
Lieutenant Kenneth Johnston, 6th Rajputana Rifles, 10.3.44 (age 22)

LA MORT L'A CUEILLI LOIN DE SA PATRIE, LOIN DE SES AMIS. PASSANT, PRIEZ POUR LUI.
(Death culled him far from his native land, far from his friends. Passerby, pray for him.)
Corporal Dieudonné Adrien Lauzon, CR, 15.5.44 (age 28)

By the end of the Italian campaign, no less than twenty-six nationalities had appeared in the Allied order of battle. The polyethnic Commonwealth cemeteries form one group within a constellation of national war cemeteries dedicated to the men who fell in the battles for Rome. A joint Christian and Muslim burial ground at Venafro honours the French and colonial troops who played a major role in driving the Germans from the Aurunci mountains, and a shrine at Monte Lungo pays homage to the Italians who died fighting on the Allied side. The unrepatriated American dead rest beneath a forest of crosses in the great collection cemetery at Nettuno, not far from the better known town of Anzio. More than 20,000 German soldiers were gathered into collective graves on a knoll north of Cassino. The most affecting monument, however, is the Polish cemetery sculpted into the hillside facing the Abbey of Monte Cassino. Crosses draped with rosaries stand over the graves of more than a thousand Polish soldiers, the tragedy of their sacrifice heightened by the bitter irony that they were fighting for a homeland which their gallantry could not rescue. Recognition that other, more fortunate lands benefited from the courage exhibited by the Poles in Italy and northwestern Europe lies behind the words engraved in all Polish war cemeteries: ZA NASZA I WASZA WOLNOŚĆ —"For our freedom and yours."

By fitting coincidence, at a place sacred to Poland, the same words are found on the headstone of a Polish Canadian soldier buried at Cassino:

ZA NASZA I WASZA WOLNOŚĆ. CZEŚĆ JEGO PAMIĘĆI.
(For our freedom and yours. Honour his memory)
Lance Sergeant Edward Julian Hauptman, LER, *25.5.44 (age 24)*

A Polish inscription on the grave of a Canadian soldier highlights the demographic mixture that set Canada apart from the other dominions. The 1941 census draws a profile of the country that would surprise many today accustomed to thinking of multicultural Canada as a postwar phenomenon. Long before the term was coined, Canada was home to thirty different national groups, spread among the 2,300,000 Canadians not of British or French lineage. The diversity of the Dominion's population is echoed in the polyphony of Canadian headstones. Besides the official English and French, over a dozen languages express the parting words offered by families who chose to bid farewell in the language which they had always spoken to their son, brother or father, and whose rhythms and cadences they felt most deeply. These inscriptions preserve a record of overlapping allegiances, of ancestral traditions and influences, that casts light on the ways in which Canadians of non-British backgrounds viewed the war and their stake in it. At Cassino, as in any collection of Canada's fallen, professions of imperial loyalty to the Mother Country are matched by other affirmations of dual loyalty:

IN LOVING MEMORY OF A DEVOTED HUSBAND AND DEFENDER OF THE BRITISH EMPIRE.
Private Frank David Cook, LER, *23.5.44 (age 36)*

THUS BRITAIN CRIES, NO BEATEN WHINE BUT PROUDLY, "FREEDOM SHALL BE MINE"
J.B.McB.
Lieutenant Joseph Bullman McBride, GGHG, *26.5.44 (age 22)*

GREATER LOVE HATH NO MAN THAN THIS, THAT A MAN LAY DOWN HIS LIFE FOR HIS
KING AND COUNTRY.
Private James Clowater, PR, *26.5.44 (age 20)*

YOUR NAME SHALL LIVE FOR EVER AS A BRAVE UKRAINIAN CANADIAN SOLDIER.
Sergeant John Dykun, SSTCA, *6.12.43 (age 23)*
Private Peter Husak, AR, *7.3.45 (age 25)* [GROESBEEK]

Eastern European names are the most numerous among the nationalities dispersed throughout the Canadian sections at Cassino. Ochrymowich, Koscielny, Azarkiewicz, Sochowski, Polinsky, Oshowy, Wocalewski, Sawatzky, Biech appear among a score or so of Polish names scattered among the 855 graves marked by a maple leaf. Other names—Fediuk, Sawchuk, Wityshyn, Drushkiw, Yavis, and Kolcun identify soldiers of Ukrainian ancestry, whereas Sundstrom, Forsberg, Oerlemans, Eisenman, Beitz, Zuber, Siebls, Suotaila, Janzen, de Vries, and de Baeremaeker originate from northern European homelands. A handful—Tessaro, Drillio, Gamba, Fidiadis—point to a rising tide of immigrants from southern Europe which would increase dramatically after the war. The Italian roots of this Canadian soldier are evident in the prayer of his mother:

O VERGINE SANTA, NELLE TUE MANI HO RIPOSTO MIO FIGLIO. FA CHE REPOSI IN PACE.
(O holy Virgin, in your hands I have laid my son. Grant that he rest in peace.)
Gunner Mario Zecca, RCA, 16.5.44 (age 27)

Several headstones in Cassino carry inscriptions offering the bare details of the soldier's hometown and parentage. One is of a Ukrainian Canadian soldier who, like so many of his fellows, hailed from the Prairies:

SON OF ANNIE KOLINIAK OF MAYFAIR, SASKATCHEWAN.
Gunner Nick Koliniak, RCA, 24.5.44 (age 20)

By themselves, these inscriptions are of passing interest, but when gathered into a compilation of names and homes they mirror the history of immigration to Canada before the Second World War. Occasional references to immigrant communities in the Maritimes or French Quebec contrasts with the ubiquity of ethnic minorities elsewhere in the country. Homes in the bigger towns and cities are sometimes mentioned, as in an epitaph below of a soldier of Lithuanian origin. The hometowns cited in the inscriptions of Italian and Jewish Canadian servicemen reflect the preference of these groups for urban destinations. Most of the inscriptions, of course, concentrate around the largest immigrant groups, the Slavs, Germans, Scandinavians, and Dutch who came as farmers, miners, and lumberjacks to Ontario or as homesteaders to the Prairies—the "stout backs and willing hands" drawn by Clifford Sifton's ambitious plan to fill Western Canada with imported settlers capable of bringing its vast expanses under cultivation:

BELOVED SON OF OLIUS AND STANISLAVA BALSIS, MONTREAL, CANADA.
Private Frank Balsis, BWC, 2.4.45 (age 22) [GROESBEEK]

BELOVED SON OF THE LATE D. DI PIETRO AND M. DI PIETRO, FORT ERIE, ONTARIO, CANADA.
Private Tanferio Thomas Di Pietro, 4th PLDG, 25.9.44 (age 27) [CESENA]

THIRD SON OF W. AND C. KOROPCHUK, MILLGROVE, ONTARIO, CANADA.
Private George Koropchuk, RCASC, 19.3.44 (age 29) [BROOKWOOD]

BORN HASKERHORNE, FRIESCHLAND, HOLLAND. JOB 19, 25, 26.
MILLGROVE, ONTARIO, CANADA.
Private Gaele Visser, AR, 23.4.45 (age 24) [HOLTEN]

OF TIMMINS, CANADA. HUSBAND OF JANICA MAVRETIC. NATIVE OF BREZJE, JUGO-SLAVIA.
Private Nickola Doljac, CFC, 10.7.42 (age 35) [BROOKWOOD]

BELOVED SON OF K. AND K.M. TRUSKOSKI, CREIGHTON MINES, ONTARIO, CANADA.
Private Ted Truskoski, RCR, 19.4.44 (age 17) [MORO RIVER]

OF POLISH DESCENT. BORN IN WINNIPEG, MANITOBA, CANADA, 24TH SEPTEMBER 1922.
Pilot Officer Ignatius Thomas Pelechaty, RCAF, 30.9.44 (age 22) [REICHSWALD FOREST]

BORN MARCH 17TH 1923, GARDENTON, MANITOBA, CANADA.
Private Metro Zytaruk, CBH, 29.9.44 (age 21) [CESENA]

BORN IN CALIENTO, MAN. SURVIVED BY MOTHER, TWO BROTHERS.
FATHER PASSED AWAY IN 1924.
Private Walter Koshelanyk, RRC, 24.10.44 (age 22) [BERGEN-OP-ZOOM]

"HE DIED THAT WE MAY LIVE." ELPHINSTONE, MANITOBA, CANADA
Flying Officer Arthur Paul Haacke, RCAF, 23.6.44 (age 24) [HARROGATE]

OF ITUNA, SASKATCHEWAN, CANADA.
Private Nick Smysniuk, QOCHC, 21.7.44 (age 26) [BRETTEVILLE-SUR-LAIZE]

SON OF MR. & MRS. JOHN SCHAFF, PRELATE, SASK. BORN 9TH JANUARY 1923 AT KRUPP, CANADA.
Flight Sergeant Leonard Schaff, RCAF, 14.10.44 (age 21) [REICHSWALD FOREST]

ROUMANIAN ORIGIN. ORTHODOX FAITH. FROM PIERCELAND, SASK., CANADA.
Private Steve William Toma, NNSH, 25.7.44 (age 31) [BÉNY-SUR-MER]

BORN IN YORKTON, SASKATCHEWAN, CANADA. REST IN PEACE.
Rifleman Emanual Bishoff, RWR, 8.6.44 (age 18) [BÉNY-SUR-MER]

IN LOVING MEMORY OF ANTHONY. BELOVED SON OF ROKO AND MARIA PAVELICK, KENASTON, SASKATCHEWAN, CANADA.
Private Anthony Pavelick, PPCLI, 3.2.45 (age 31) [RAVENNA]

ІВАН ГУЛЯК, РОДЖЕНИЙ ДНЯ 14 ЧЕРВНЯ РОКУ 1923, ДНЕІПЕР, САСК. КАНАДА
(Ivan Hulyak, born 14 June in the year 1923, Dnieper, Sask., Canada.)
Gunner John Elmer Gulak, RCA, 8.9.44 (age 21) [GRADARA]

BORN AT SHEPENGE, ALBERTA, CANADA.
Private George Kuchuiran, CH, 1.11.44 (age 22) [BERGEN-OP-ZOOM]

HERE RESTS IN PEACE WILLIAM THE LOVING SON OF JOHN DROZDIAK, EDSON, ALBERTA, CANADA.
Sergeant William John Drozdiak, RCAF, 8.11.44 (age 18) [CHESTER (BLACON)]

ONE OF THE BOYS FROM BARRHEAD, ALBERTA. "HE SHALL GIVE HIS ANGELS CHARGE OVER THEE."
Private Kost Suchow, CH, 12.7.44 (age 30) [BÉNY-SUR-MER]

The impact of the war on these small ethnic communities can be gauged from one example. The hamlet of Rama, in eastern Saskatchewan, was home to a mix of Polish and Ukrainian settlers. Even today Rama numbers less than a hundred souls, and yet three of its young men lie buried in three different countries:

SON OF MR. AND MRS. JACOB YAWORSKI OF RAMA, SASKATCHEWAN, CANADA.
Warrant Officer I Adolf Edward Yaworski, RCAF, 25.3.44 [REICHSWALD FOREST]

OF RAMA, SASKATCHEWAN. EVER REMEMBERED BY HIS SISTER ANTONIA OLLINIK.
Private Louis Swiderski, SSR, 20.7.44 (age 27) [BRETTEVILLE-SUR-LAIZE]

BORN AT RAMA, SASKATCHEWAN. SON OF DMETRO AND NETTIE KOWALCHUK, NOBLEVILLE, CANADA.
Rifleman Wasyl Kowalchuk, RRR, 18.2.45 (age 24) [GROESBEEK]

Studies devoted to the experience of ethnic communities in Canada during World War II have inclined to the view that the non-British peoples did not see Canada's war, in other words, Britain's war, as their concern. At first glance, there were good reasons why this would have been so. Although the 1941 census lists nearly half a million Germans and over 300,000 Ukrainians, most of the minorities were small in number, tightly knit, and isolated by language or customs from the majority. They resided on the margins of Canadian society, and as members of unfamiliar ethnic or religious groups were regarded as outsiders impervious to the ways of a still very British country. Amidst the political and economic upheavals of the interwar period, the red banners unfurled by factions within the ethnic populations heightened wariness of foreign elements within Canada. Once the war began, latent xenophobia could harden into hostility and mistrust, leading to police surveillance and temporary detention, as in the case of German and Italian immigrants, or the internment of citizens and the confiscation of their property, as in the case of the Japanese. The response of the ethnic communities in the conscription plebiscite in 1942 came as a displeasing revelation that opposition to compulsory overseas service was not restricted to French Canadians. Preoccupation with the two solitudes veiled the larger truth that Canada was in fact home to many solitudes, in a day and age before government policies had begun to bring these minorities into the national mainstream.

GEROEM ZAGINUV U BOYU ZA CANADU I ZA SIMEISTVU SVOYU. TSARSTVO YOMU NEBESNE.
(Like a hero he died in battle for Canada and for his family.
The Kingdom of Heaven be his.)
Pilot Officer Nicholas Novack, RCAF, 29.7.44 (age 19) [BECKLINGEN]

To emphasize the aloofness of the ethnic minorities in Canada, however, is to look at just one side of the ledger. By the 1930s most immigrant groups had been in Canada for thirty or forty years, or longer, enough time to develop an attachment to the country and for a second, Canadian-born, generation to narrow the gap between their parents' world and the society around them. Epitaphs at Cassino commemorating soldiers of various national backgrounds proclaim the same universal principles or patriotic sentiments found on many English Canadian headstones. The first two inscriptions honouring soldiers of German and Polish descent introduce a wider sample of epitaphs from other war cemeteries which leave no doubt as to the loyalty felt by immigrant groups to Canada, or to a common set of ideals:

LOVING MEMORY OF MY DEAR SON WHO FREELY GAVE HIS LIFE SERVING HIS COUNTRY.
MAY HIS SOUL REST IN PEACE.
Private Harry Andrew Dollmaier, CBH, 26.5.44 (age 18)

HE GAVE HIS LIFE FOR FREEDOM.
Trooper Joseph Jurykovsky, RCD, 25.5.44 (age 23)

HIS FOES WERE THINE. HE KEPT US FREE. MAY GOD MAKE HIM WELCOME: THIS IS HE.
Rifleman William Kachafanas, QORC, 26.2.45 (age 23) [GROESBEEK]
[TENNYSON, ODE ON THE DEATH OF THE DUKE OF WELLINGTON]

FOR LIBERTY OF THE PEOPLE YOU GAVE YOUR LIFE. REST IN PEACE, DEAR BROTHER.
Private Walter Szewczuk, HPER, 14.6.44 [MINTURNO]

"ONLY BY SACRIFICE CAN WE ACHIEVE."
Private John Henry Stiefelmeyer, HLIC, 27.2.45 (age 22) [GROESBEEK]

HE WAS TAKEN AWAY LEST DECEIT BEGUILE HIS SOUL.
Private Adolph Schiele, SSR, 5.8.44 (age 30) [BRETTEVILLE-SUR-LAIZE]

SON OF MR. AND MRS. LOUIS BORKOFSKY. HE DIED FOR THE LOVE OF HIS COUNTRY CANADA.
Flight Sergeant Edward Borkofsky, RCAF, *6.10.44 (age 22)* [REICHSWALD FOREST]

OUR DEAR SON MADE THE SUPREME SACRIFICE IN THE CAUSE OF LOYALTY, FREEDOM, JUSTICE.
Gunner Paul John Misiurka, RCA, *5.8.44 (age 22)* [ROME]

I FOUGHT AND DIED FOR VICTORY AND PEACE FOR CANADA AND THE WORLD.
Private Casmier Syntak, CRCEME, *11.2.45 (age 32)* [GROESBEEK]

HE GAVE HIS LIFE SO HE COULD KEEP US FREE. O GOD, KEEP HIM CLOSE AND
CLOSER TO THEE.
Private Walter Wojnowicz, WNSR, *13.12.44 (age 24)* [RAVENNA]

THERE WAS A JOB TO DO AND I DID MY BEST.
Gunner Ivan Rayburn Nilsson, RCA, *1.4.45 (age 21)* [GROESBEEK]

BORN IN HOLLAND 4TH NOVEMBER 1922. HIS LIFE WAS EARNEST, HIS ACTIONS KIND. R.I.P.
Private Petrus Jacobus van Poele, 48th HC, *16.9.44 (age 21)* [CORIANO RIDGE]

IN LOVING MEMORY OF OUR SON PETER, FALLEN IN THE STRUGGLE FOR ALL
DEMOCRATIC COUNTRIES.
Private Peter Sam Holukoff, LER, *18.10.44 (age 23)* [CESENA]

DEAR ONLY SON OF SAMUEL SEREDIAK. HE GAVE HIS YOUTHFUL LIFE FOR KING AND COUNTRY.
Private Alexander Serediak, CSR, *14.4.45* [HOLTEN]

REST IN PEACE FOR A CAUSE THAT WAS WORTHY.
Private Jack Sokoloski, RCASC, *14.9.44 (age 23)* [CORIANO RIDGE]

FALLEN FOR HIS GOD, HIS KING, AND THE FREEDOM OF HIS COUNTRY.
Trooper Nestor Probizanski, 12th MD, *11.4.45 (age 22)* [HOLTEN]

FOR CHRIST AND CANADA. EVER REMEMBERED BY FAMILY.
Corporal Stanley Tschirhart, RCR, *6.9.44 (age 24)* [CORIANO RIDGE]

HE GAVE HIS ALL THAT OTHERS MIGHT LIVE. WHAT MORE, WE ASK, COULD A LOYAL BOY GIVE.
Private Aldo John Campagnolo, CH, *26.7.44 (age 19)* [BRETTEVILLE-SUR-LAIZE]

"IT IS MORE BLESSED TO GIVE THAN TO RECEIVE." HE GAVE HIS LIFE TO SAVE OTHERS.
Lance Sergeant Rocco Andrew Speziali, QOCHC, *30.3.45 (age 26)* [GROESBEEK]

MYTODY DIED A HERO'S DEATH FOR CANADA, THE COUNTRY HE LOVED.
Corporal Mytody Litvinchuk, ESR, *16.10.44 (age 23)* [BERGEN-OP-ZOOM]

GOD IS ONE AND LOVE IS ONE. WAR IS WON! WE LOVE YOU, JOHN. THE KRUPSKI FAMILY.
Gunner John Michael Krupski, RCA, *4.2.45 (age 22)* [ANCONA]

LEST WE FORGET, GUIDING STAR, CONVICTIONS LIKE YOURS COMPLETED THE WORK.
Pilot Officer Peter Warywoda, RCAF, *23.4.44* [BRUSSELS]

"LET US THEREFORE FOLLOW AFTER THE THINGS WHICH MAKE FOR PEACE." ROMANS XIV. 19
Private Miroslaw Stawnychka, SSR, *20.12.44 (age 25)* [GROESBEEK]

If the ethnic minorities, understandably, did not feel the reflexive loyalty to Britain that English Canadians did, it does not necessarily follow that they saw no role for themselves in the conflict. The question of loyalty posed itself in different terms to different groups. Canadians of European stock could not look with indifference upon the course and consequences of a European war in which the very existence of their ancestral lands or peoples was threatened. One conviction that people of eastern and northern European descent shared with a good many English Canadians, and with those French Canadians stirred by the fall of France, was that by enlisting in Canada's forces they were rallying to the defence of their own mother countries—many of which, by the end of the first year of the war, were suffering under Nazi occupation:

IN LOVING MEMORY OF ONE WHO GAVE HIS LIFE TO SAVE HIS MOTHERLAND AND ADOPTED COUNTRY. GONE BUT NOT FORGOTTEN. HIS LOVING WIFE AND CHILDREN, MOTHER AND RELATIVES.
Private Albert Hughes, ESR, 13.4.45 (age 35) [HOLTEN]

MON FILS EST MORT EN BRAVE POUR SON PAYS, LE CANADA, ET POUR LA FRANCE.
(My son died as a brave man for his country, Canada, and for France.)
Corporal René Emond, RC, 2.3.45 (age 22) [GROESBEEK]

DIED FOR FREEDOM OF CANADA. UMARŁ ZA WOLNOŚĆ POLSKI.
(Died for the freedom of Poland.)
Rifleman John Klacza, QORC, 26.2.45 (age 20) [GROESBEEK]

Poles had been arrriving in Canada for decades before a new influx of immigrants arrived during the 1920s, bringing the number of Canadians of Polish origin to over 100,000 by the time of the 1941 census. The link to the land of their birth remained strong, and the German invasion of Poland in September 1939, followed by one of the most brutal occupations imposed on any conquered country, provided ample motivation for Polish Canadian recruits. Their sacrifice on behalf of their native and adoptive lands appears in the inscriptions which follow:

A POLISH CANADIAN.
Warrant Officer II Vincent Ronald Polowy, RCAF, 7.2.44 (age 23) [HARROGATE]

TU SPOCZYWA LUDWIK KLIMCZAK SYN JÓZEFA I ZOFII KLIMCZAKÓW. LAT 42. URODZONY W POLSKE, WIEŚ OBLIEKOŃ, POWIAT KIELCE.
(Here rests Ludwik Klimczak, son of Joseph and Zofia Klimczak. 42 years of age. Born in Poland, village of Obliekon, district of Kielce.)
Private Ludwik Klimczak, RCOC, 10.4.44 (age 42) [BROOKWOOD]

TU SPOCZYWA W BOGU, ZA KRAJ I NAROD POLSKI, NASZ KOCHANY I NIGDY NIEZAPOMNIANY SYN I BRAT.
(Here resting in God, for the land and people of Poland, lies our beloved and never forgotten son and brother.)
Flying Officer Zygmunt Jan Zabek, RCAF, 14.2.44 (age 21) [BROOKWOOD]

CZEŚĆ JEGO PAMIĘĆI. HE IS NOT DEAD TO US WHO LOVED HIM. HE IS WITH US IN MEMORY.
(Honour his memory.)
Private Joseph Czach, 48th HC, 16.4.44 (age 24) [MORO RIVER]

CAME TO CANADA FROM POLAND, IN 1929. DIED BRAVELY IN BATTLE BY CAEN.
Private Nick Kaminski, NNSH, 8.7.44 (age 22) [BÉNY-SUR-MER]

IN LOVING MEMORY OF WILLIAM. BORN 1903, IN POLAND. DIED 1945, FOR CANADA.
Private William Nahornyk, LWR, 26.1.45 (age 42) [GROESBEEK]

JEDNEGO MY MIELI, I TEGO STRACILI, UMARŁ BOHATERSKO, BY INNI ŻYLI.
RODZICE
(One we loved and lost died heroically so that others might live. Parents)
Private Walter Juszkiewicz, RRC, 10.3.45 (age 24) [GROESBEEK]

FELL FOR FREEDOM, DEMOCRACY, AND FATHERLAND POLAND.
Lance Corporal Stanley Joseph Kobylas, BWC, 2.4.45 (age 22) [GROESBEEK]

A last pair of epitaphs connects Cassino with another place where Canadians and Poles fought side by side. The first occcurs on the headstone of a Polish Canadian soldier buried in the large Canadian war cemetery beside the road to Falaise, only a couple of miles from the Polish war cemetery at Grainville-Langannerie. The second honours a Polish Canadian airman buried in England. The words speak for all the Poles who fought for the liberty of Italy, France, Belgium, and Holland, and who for decades after the war were denied recognition in their own country:

DIED FOR OUR FREEDOM AND YOURS.
Private Kizer Kubian, SSR, 20.7.44 [BRETTEVILLE-SUR-LAIZE]

JEDYNY NASZ SYN POLEGŁ W WALCE ZA WOLNOŚĆ NASZA I WASZA.
(Our only son fell in the struggle for our freedom and yours.)
Sergeant Albert Volny, RCAF, 6.12.44 (age 20) [CHESTER (BLACON)]

Of all the nationalities enumerated in Canada's armed forces, the Ukrainians formed the largest contingent, with estimates running as high as 35,000 enrolments. Even if this rough calculation exaggerates, it is nevertheless clear that Ukrainian Canadians volunteered in considerable numbers. Motivation varied. The Depression had hit the Prairies hard, nudging young men of all backgrounds in the direction of the recruiting stations when the war broke out. The German attack on the Soviet Union in June 1941 gave an added boost to recruiting drives calling upon Ukrainian Canadians to rally to the cause of their kinfolk and allies in the occupied Ukraine. The assertions of Ukrainian identity, whether by choice of language or content, in the epitaphs supplied by the soldiers of these families attest the loyalty to country and homeland of perhaps the most self-conscious of the ethnic groups in wartime Canada. It is worth remembering that the insistence on Ukrainian loyalty, and sacrifice, came from parents who belonged to a generation that had seen former subjects of the Austro-Hungarian empire, including as many as 5,000 Ukrainian immigrants, treated as enemy aliens and interned during the First World War:

ТУТ СПОЧИВАЕ РАБ БОЖИЙ ФЕДОР МАКОВІЙЧУК. ВЕЧНАЯ ЕМУ ПАМЯТЬ.
(Here rests the servant of God, Fedor Makowichuk. Eternal memory to him.)
Private Fred Makowichuk, CSR, 9.7.44 (age 26) [DOUVRES-LA-DÉLIVRANDE]

CANADIAN UKRAINIAN.
Private John Kendzierski, QOCHC, 18.1.45 (age 20) [HOLTEN]

UKRAINIAN NATIONAL. GOD REST HIS SOUL.
Private Michael Sherbanuik, CH, 22.9.44 (age 24) [BERGEN-OP-ZOOM]

UKRAINIAN NATIONAL. AS LONG AS MEMORY LASTS WE WILL REMEMBER THEE. MOM, DAD & FAMILY.
Private Mike Fedina, BWC, 31.10.44 (age 19) [BERGEN-OP-ZOOM]

SLEEP, DEAR SON, YOU GAVE YOUR YOUNG LIFE FOR FREEDOM OF WORLD AND UKRAINA.
Corporal Alexander Bondoluk, GLCA, 19.11.44 (age 29) [BERGEN-OP-ZOOM]

ХАЙ БОГ ПРИЙМЕ ЖЕРТВУ ТВОЮ ЗА НАРОД І ВІТЧИЗНУ. IN LOVING MEMORY OF OUR SOLDIER SON.
(May God accept your sacrifice for your people and fatherland.)
Private Stanley Werniuk, SHC, 12.4.45 (age 23) [HOLTEN]

The Ukrainian origins of this soldier are hidden by the anglicised name, but the commitment of the Strynadka family of Rossburn, Manitoba, to the war effort is plain from the inscription:

ONE OF EIGHT BROTHERS IN THE SERVICES. GEORGE, THE FIFTH, FELL AT THE POST OF DUTY.
Corporal George Strank, 14th CH, 27.2.45 (age 24) [GROESBEEK]

The religious distinctions evident in the epitaphs may seem moot to Canadians of national heritages whose identity or survival have never been at risk. Before the 1920s the Eastern European peoples listed in the 1941 census had come to Canada not as citizens of established countries but as subjects of the polyglot Austro-Hungarian and Russian empires. The definition "Ukrainian" covered Ruthenians, Bukovinians, or Galicians who would have identified themselves as much by faith as by nationality. Language was one badge of identity which these groups cherished, but religious affiliation had long been the mainstay of national and cultural survival for populations living under foreign domination. The allegiance to the Catholic Church that preserved the idea of Poland throughout that country's tormented history accounts for the prayers and supplications on the headstones of these Polish Canadian servicemen:

TU SPOCZYWA ZDISL RUDSKI. WIECZNY ODPOCZYNEK PROSZĘ ZMOWIĆ ZA JEGO DUSZĘ.
(Here rests Zdisl Rudski. Please say an 'eternal repose' for his soul.)
Private Zdisl Rudski, CSR, 28.3.45 (age 24) [GROESBEEK]

REQUIEM AETERNAM DONA EI, DOMINE; ET LUX PERPETUA LUCEAT EI. TWOJ BRAT
(Eternal rest grant unto him, o Lord; and let light perpetual shine upon him. Your brother)
Rifleman Mike Leonard Szumski, RWR, 29.3.45 (age 24) [GROESBEEK]

BEATI MORTUI QUI IN DOMINO MORIUNTUR. REQUIESCAT IN PACE.
(Blessed are those who die in the Lord. May he rest in peace.)
Pilot Officer Sigmund Bernard Bandur, RCAF, 22.5.44 (age 28) [BROOKWOOD]

The Ukrainians to the east lived along the dividing line between the rival Catholic and Orthodox jurisdictions. Orthodox in ritual and doctrine, they styled themselves Ukrainian Catholics since they recognised the supremacy of the Pope which the other Orthodox churches rejected. After settling in Canada, however, a number of Ukrainian groups, concerned at the shortage of Ukrainian priests and fearing absorption by the "Latins"—i.e. French or Polish Catholics—broke away to form a Ukrainian Orthodox

Church, initially known as Greek Catholic Orthodox. The two inscriptions below reveal the split between Ukrainian Canadians wrestling with the question of religious affiliation:

SON OF MIKE AND MARGARET. UKRAINIAN CATHOLIC. BORN 1920,
WHITESAND, SASK., CANADA.
Lance Corporal William Fedun, CH, 22.9.44 (age 23) [BERGEN-OP-ZOOM]

DIED FOR HIS COUNTRY, CANADA, AND FOR HIS CHURCH, GREEK CATHOLIC ORTHODOX.
Warrant Officer I Stanley Mydaski, RCAF, 15.3.44 (age 22) [DURNBACH]

It is difficult, sometimes impossible, for the bereaved to find words for their grief. The repetition of formulae, and the vacant spaces, on so many headstones display this symptom of loss. One's heart goes out to the parents who laboured to compose an epitaph in a language not their own, and to those who could find words only in their mother tongue. A grave in the war cemetery at Bayeux shows how one Ukrainian family sought to enshrine their son's memory while easing the task of the engravers in carving an inscription in an unfamiliar language and script. Private Peter Zigolyk of the Royal Canadian Army Medical Corps died of wounds on July 24, 1944, at age 24. His parents in Blaine Lake, Saskatchewan, requested that these five words be incised on his headstone:

NECHAI ZEMLIA
BUDE TOBI PEROM

Its simplicity makes this one of the most moving valedictions, not just for what it says but even more so for the scene it suggests. The words translate closely into English as *"This earth be thy record,"* or more grandly, *"Let this earth be thy memorial."* The lettering, however, is Roman, not the Cyrillic in which Ukrainian is normally written, as though the parents chose an epitaph which they could express most eloquently in their native tongue, and then carefully converted each word into the Roman alphabet as they filled in the form to be sent back to the War Graves Commission.

Faced with thousands of inscriptions, some rendered in foreign languages requiring the use of special scripts and accents, it was inevitable that the engravers would make mistakes. An inscription on the grave of a young soldier of Czech descent, seems to be missing a few words. His parents' despair is palpable nonetheless:

KDYŽ ODEJMUL NAM OSUD TEBE, JEJŽ MELI JCME VROUCNĘ. RADI TU NE NEZBYLO,
NAM NIC JINEHO.
(When fate took you from us … we loved him dearly. There is no joy left,
nothing remains to us now.)
Guardsman Ladislau William Ondracka, GGFG, 7.9.44 (age 21) [CALAIS]

Professions of loyalty to their ancestral lands appear less often in the epitaphs of soldiers of Scandinavian origin, perhaps because the Danes, Norwegians, Swedes, and Icelanders had found the adjustment to life in Canada less trying. Inscriptions in the Scandinavian languages, particularly Danish, outnumber all other foreign-language inscriptions from the First World War. The name of a *Dansk frivillig* (Danish volunteer) killed in 1916, Private Victor Hugo Sørensen, shows strongly francophile inclinations, but most of the men from neutral Denmark who enlisted in the CEF likely did so out of anti-German feelings dating from the annexation of Schleswig-Holstein by Bismarck's

Prussia in 1864. A random selection of Scandinavian epitaphs from the Second World War displays the traits typical of English Canadian inscriptions, although a residual loyalty to home countries occupied by the Nazis appears in the epitaphs of Danish and Norwegian servicemen:

IN LOVING MEMORY OF KNUTE. BORN IN SWEDEN. REST IN PEACE.

Private Knute Emanuel Ahlstrom, CSR, 9.6.44 (age 22) [BRETTEVILLE-SUR-LAIZE]

DU TAPPRE SON! SORJD, SAKNAD. MA MANNISKORS ORO VIKA OM FRID
SKALL VARA.

(You brave son! Mourned, missed. May the sorrows of humanity end so that there shall be peace.)

Sapper Ture Adolph Nilsson, CRCE, 10.8.44 (age 38) [BRETTEVILLE-SUR-LAIZE]

HIS ABSENCE: UNSPEAKABLE SORROW. LOVE AND REMEMBRANCE LAST FOREVER.

Private Thomas Ferdinand Aastrom, BWC, 27.2.45 [GROESBEEK]

FOR ME A BLOOD-BOUGHT FREE REWARD, A GOLDEN HARP FOR ME.

Private Olaf Edmund Nystrom, CSR, 25.8.44 (age 30) [BRETTEVILLE-SUR-LAIZE]
[HYMN, *THERE IS A FOUNTAIN FILLED WITH BLOOD*, BY WILLIAM COWPER, 1772]

FOR NORWAY AND CANADA AND THOSE HE LOVED.

Private Halvor Taralson, PPCLI, 15.3.44 (age 20)[Moro River]

DIED WITH HONOUR FOR HIS COUNTRY.

Sapper Karl Christensen, CRCE, 10.4.45 (age 43) [HOLTEN]

WE ARE PROUD OF YOU. LOVING WIFE JOSEPHINE, SASKATCHEWAN,
AND MOTHER IN DENMARK.

Gunner Vadn Ludwig Frederickson, RCA, 10.6.44 [BRETTEVILLE-SUR-LAIZE]

HERREN ÄR MIN HERDE.

(The Lord is my shepherd)

Lance Bombardier Alf Herbert Josephsson, RCA, 23.4.45 (age 34) [HOLTEN]

BEST WISHES. FATHER, MOTHER AND DENMARK.

Private Oluf Olsen, LER, 14.12.44 (age 36) [RAVENNA]

KÆMP FOR ALT HVAD DU HARKÆRT, DØ OM SAA DET GÆLDER.

(Fight for all you hold dear, even though it may mean death.)

Private Christian Christiansen, CH, 1.8.44 (age 39) [BRETTEVILLE-SUR-LAIZE]

The Icelanders were the smallest of the Scandinavian groups in Canada, numbering just over 21,000 in 1941, but their record of service in both world wars deserves notice. Nearly a thousand men of Icelandic origin went overseas between 1914 and 1918. Although no overall figure has been calculated for the Second World War, a bimonthly magazine, the *Icelandic Canadian*, began in 1942 to include a section on Icelandic families with more than one member in the armed forces, both Canadian and American. Two families contributed six members; four families reported five members in uniform; fifty-seven sent three; and no less than one hundred and five sent two. When it is noted that this tally of multiple enlistments was by no means exhaustive, and that the magazine kept only a partial register of single enlistments, the response of the Icelandic communities in North America becomes even more astonishing. Fifty-four Canadians of Icelandic origin died on active service during the war, including one young man whose parents bade farewell in their own language:

HVÍL Í FRIÐI, ÁSTKÆRI SONUR. ÁSTVINIR BLESSA MINNINGU ÞINA. MOÐIR OG FAÐIR
(Rest in peace, beloved son. Loved ones bless your memory. Mother and father)
Rifleman Eggert Stefansson, RWR, 8.6.44 (age 21) [Bény-sur-Mer]

THE LORD IS MY SHEPHERD, I SHALL NOT WANT. 23RD PSALM OF DAVID.
Private Harold Thorkelsson, RCASC, 3.10.44 (age 23) [Adegem]

GOD OF ALL NATIONS, LET NOT THIS SACRIFICE HAVE BEEN IN VAIN.
Private Joel Theodore Bjornson, PPCLI, 18.9.44 (age 25) [Coriano Ridge]

HE GAVE HIS LIFE TO HELP MAKE A BETTER WORLD. A BELOVED SON AND BROTHER.
Lance Corporal Rurick William Thorsteinson, FGH, 8.8.44 (age 22)
[Bretteville-sur-Laize]

WHEN THE MORNING DAWNS WE WILL MEET AGAIN, MY DARLING. SVAVA
Gunner Peter Hoffman Hallgrimson, RCA, 20.10.45 (age 25) [Holten]

The spiritual valedictions offered in memory of servicemen descended from northern European settlers reveal the changes to the old devotion wrought by the Protestant Reformation. The Lutherans in Scandinavia, along with the Calvinist and Reformed Churches in Holland, had discarded the rituals of the Roman Church and its prayers for the souls of the departed, reverting instead to the assurances of Scripture. The austere Lutheran insistence on justification by faith alone, and the comfort sought from Biblical passages, stand on the headstones of two brothers who died in Normandy. They came from a Norwegian community in North Star, Alberta:

AND GOD SHALL WIPE AWAY ALL TEARS FROM THEIR EYES. REV. XXI. 4
Private Bert Julian Braaten, RRR, 6.6.44 (age 27) [Bény-sur-Mer]
THE LORD GAVE AND THE LORD HATH TAKEN AWAY. BLESSED BE THE NAME OF THE LORD.
JOB I. 21
Private Lester Lorian Braaten, BWC, 8.8.44 (age 21) [Bretteville-sur-Laize]

Dutch Canadian epitaphs show the same recourse to the assurances of Scripture. The plain reference to a Biblical passage on the headstone of a soldier buried in Cassino is one of several such inscriptions assuming the reader's familiarity with the Word of God. Another condenses a central passage in the development of Protestant doctrine:

REVELATION XXI.4
Lance Corporal Tys Feenstra, SHC, 31.5.44 (age 24) [Cassino]

SAVED THROUGH FAITH. EPHESIANS II.8
Private Abe Bruinsma, LER, 5.12.43 (age 29) [Moro River]

Canadians of Eastern European backgrounds were aware that they could fight for their mother countries only indirectly, yet there were soldiers who did assist in the deliverance of their ancestral lands. The epitaphs of these Dutch Canadian soldiers, killed during the liberation of the Low Countries, become more moving in their setting. All three are buried in Holland:

HIER LIGT ONZE GELIEFDE ZOON EN BROEDER YNTE. RUST EN VREDE.
(Here lies our beloved son and brother Ynte. Rest in peace.)
Private Ynte Peter Obbema, QOCHC, 5.10.44 (age 34) [BERGEN-OP-ZOOM]

HIJ GAF ZIJN LEVEN OM ONS VRIJHEID TE GEVEN. MOGE ZIJNE ZIEL IN VREDE RUSTEN.
(He gave his life to give us freedom. May his soul rest in peace.)
Lance Corporal Fidelis van Acker, NS(NB)R, 27.12.44 [BERGEN-OP-ZOOM]

U VERGETEN ZULLEN WIJ NOOIT. MOEDER, BROEDERS, ZUSTERS
(We shall never forget you. Mother, brothers, sisters)
Private Cyril van der Vennet, ASHC, 26.2.45 (age 25) [GROESBEEK]

Similarly, a soldier born in Belgium lies in the earth of his native land. Two others, of French and Flemish stock respectively, are buried in Normandy:

FILS DE MATHIEU DICKENSCHEID, OUGRÉE, LIÈGE. REPOSE EN PAIX
Private Jean Paul Dickenscheid, RC, 19.10.44 (age 22) [ADEGEM]

DESCENDANT DE RACE BELGE.
(Descendant of the Belgian race.)
Private Albert Joseph Bonfond, RHLI, 27.8.44 (age 27) [BRETTEVILLE-SUR-LAIZE]

PETER. BORN IN BELGIUM 24-10-1919. BELOVED SON OF ARMAND AND CLEMANTINE VANDEVELDE.
Private Peter Vandevelde, HLIC, 12.8.44 (age 24) [BRETTEVILLE-SUR-LAIZE]

The war had contrary effects among the ethnic populations in Canada. It eased the way of the groups whose home countries were allied with Canada. Their support for the war effort, whether in the workplace or in the armed forces, received wide publicity, and in the eyes of most their loyalty to Canada dovetailed with their attachment to their ancestral lands. Even so, during the war and after, servicemen with "foreign-sounding" names suspected that promotion had come more slowly to men not of British ancestry. The prevalence of privates and corporals among the soldiers whose epitaphs have been cited does not contradict this impression. There were ethnic minorities who faced an even harder road.

Germans made up the largest immigrant group in Canada. As with other labels, "German" referred not to a single country of origin but to a broader linguistic and cultural identity. Only about twenty percent of German Canadians traced their lineage back to Germany itself. The majority came from the German-speaking regions of central and eastern Europe that had been absorbed into the countries created after the First World War, although such distinctions mattered little to the general populace. Nevertheless, in spite of the fears of fifth columnists and compromised allegiances, Hitler's regime was repudiated by German Canadians who remained overwhelmingly loyal to their new homeland. The willingness of German Canadians to serve Canada is evident in the survey of foreign languages spoken in the armed forces, which showed that German ran a close second to Ukrainian. Yet for reasons which hardly need elaboration, the search through the war cemeteries yields only one inscription in German. It is the simplest of farewells:

AUF WIEDERSEHN.
Private George Paul Ethofer, RCAMC, 6.6.44 (age 36) [BROOKWOOD]

Many German Canadians who found entry into the workplace or the services made more difficult by their association with the enemy opted to change or anglicise their names. A soldier belonging to another enemy nationality translated his family name into English:

WHO GAVE HIS LIFE TO HIS COUNTRY. MAY HIS SOUL REST IN PEACE.
Gunner James V. White, RCA, 12.9.44 (age 30)

In civilian life, Gunner James White was Nicolo Vincezzo Bianco, the son of Nicolo and Olimpia Bianco, from Peterborough, Ontario. He is buried in Italy, on the terraced hillside at Gradara. Two other Italian Canadian soldiers who died in northwestern Europe are commemorated in Italian:

TORINDO! QUANTI CI MANCHI. INCONSOLABILI PREGANO, MAMMA, PAPA E SORELLE.
(Torindo! How much we miss you. Inconsolable mamma, papa and sisters pray.)
Private Torindo Bisaro, BWC, 28.7.44 (age 21) [BRETTEVILLE-SUR-LAIZE]

MORTO PER LA PATRIA. DOLENTI MAMA, PAPA, SORELLA E FRATELLO.
RIPOSI IN PACE
(Died for his country. Sorrowing Mama, Papa, sister and brother. Rest in peace.)
Private Ernest Guiseppe Monaco, ASHC, 28.2.45 (age 19) [GROESBEEK]

German and Italian Canadians were not alone in finding their reputations as loyal citizens sullied by association with the enemy. By the end of 1941 Canada found herself at war against six countries and faced a more complicated situation at home with regard to the treatment of enemy aliens. Hours before the Japanese attack on Pearl Harbor, Canada declared war on three countries—Finland, Hungary, and Rumania—which had thrown their lot in with the Germans in the attack against the Soviet Union. Soviet pressure on Britain to declare war on Germany's allies of convenience induced Canada's reluctant decision to follow suit. The Finns had been lionised for their gallant fight against the Russian behemoth in 1940, and no one could seriously believe that distant Hungary and Rumania posed the slightest threat to Canada. Although members of these nationalities were required to register with the police, the hand of the authorities lay light upon them, in large measure because the government departments concerned had begun to adopt more informed and flexible policies towards the country's minorities. It will be noted, however, that the epitaphs of Finnish Canadian soldiers do not allude to patriotic loyalties, keeping instead to religious themes or expressions of personal loss:

IN SWEET MEMORY OF A BRAVE YOUNG SOLDIER WHO WILL NEVER BE FORGOTTEN.
Rifleman Eino Makela, RWR, 8.6.44 (age 19) [BRETTEVILLE-SUR-LAIZE]

"IN MY FATHER'S HOUSE ARE MANY MANSIONS: ... I GO TO PREPARE A PLACE FOR YOU."
Private William Pitkanen, RHLI, 8.3.45 (age 31) [GROESBEEK] [JOHN 14: 2]

HOWEVER LONG WE LIVE, WHATEVER JOYS OR GRIEFS BE OURS,
WE WILL REMEMBER YOU.
Rifleman William Wilfred Aalto, RWR, 16.2.45 (age 34) [GROESBEEK]

The three soldiers whose epitaphs are cited below came from a triangle of towns in northern Ontario, Foleyet, Sudbury, and South Porcupine, where Finnish immigrants had found work in the lumber camps and mines:

RAKASTETTU ELÄISSÄSI KAIVATTU KUOLTUASI.
(Loved in life, missed in death.)
Private Vilho Gabreal Laitila, LSR, 11.5.43 *(age 21)* [BROOKWOOD]

ELON KEVÄÄSÄ VARHAIN JATIT SOTAISEN MAAN NYT LUONA HERRAN ILOITA SAAT.
(Early in the spring of life, you left the war-torn earth; now you can rejoice with the Lord.)
Private Olavi Nenonen, RRC, 18.7.44 *(age 21)* [BÉNY-SUR-MER]

LEPÄÄ RAUHASSA VIERAAN MAAN MULLASSA ISÄMME ARMAS.
(Rest in peace in the soil of a foreign land, our dear father Armas.)
Sapper Armas Poikkimaki, CRCE, 14.6.45 *(age 36)* [HOLTEN]

The Hungarian epitaphs each touch on different themes. Private Kerek's inscription emphasizes the ideological, as opposed to the national, contest that the members of many ethnic communities believed to be the paramount issue of the war. It is also surprising that it was not the habit of staunchly Catholic Hungarians to commemorate their fallen with the prayers and intercessions so common on the graves of Polish and French Canadian Catholics:

ITT NYUGSZIK GÀBOR JÓZSEF AKI HÖSI HALÀLT HALT HAZÀJÀÉRT. BÉKE PORAIRA.
(Here rests Jozsef Gabor who died a hero's death for his country. Peace be on his ashes.)
Rifleman Joseph Mitchell Gabor, RRR, 18.6.44 *(age 20)* [BÉNY-SUR-MER]

HARCOLT A FASIZMUS ELLEN ÉS MEGHALT, HOGY MÁSOK ÉLHESSENEK SZABADON.
(Fought against fascism and died so that others will live in freedom.)
Private Albert Kerek, LER, 20.9.44 *(age 24)* [CORIANO RIDGE]

GYÀSZOLJAK BÀNATOS SZÜLEI SZARKA JÓZSEF ÉS NEJE PAPP MARIA ÉS TESTVÉREI.
(Sadly mourned by his parents Jozsef Szarka and his wife Maria Papp, and by his siblings.)
Private Alex Szarka, CBH, 1.5.45 *(age 24)* [HOLTEN]

The discretion and understanding increasingly shown towards Canada's ethnic communities during the war did not extend to the peoples of Asian descent. The forced relocation of the Japanese Canadians, and the long process of redress, present a troubling reminder that in times of crisis democratic countries can fail to uphold the working principles of democracy. One part of the story that stands in reproach to the country that treated its citizens so unjustly was the readiness of Japanese Canadians to volunteer for active service, even in face of the prejudice and discrimination barring their way. The few whose persistence won them admission into the armed forces found it nearly impossible to reach the front lines, despite their wish to emulate the proud record of service bequeathed by Japanese Canadian soldiers in World War I. His father's example may have inspired this young man's decision to enlist:

'TIS A TOKEN OF LOVE AND REMEMBRANCE OF A SON WHO WAS ONE OF THE BEST.
Trooper Minoru Tanaka, FGH, 20.2.45 *(age 25)*

Trooper Tanaka was the son of Taisuku and Toku Tanaka of Wymark, Saskatchewan.

A plaque honouring the American and Canadian members of the Special Service Force, placed on the Aurelian wall near the Porta San Paolo.

The Cassino Memorial, listing the names of the Commonwealth servicemen who died on active service in Italy and "to whom the fortunes of war denied a known and honoured grave."

Cypriot soldiers of Greek and Turkish ancestry side by side.

A remnant of the Hitler Line.

Cyrillic lettering on a Canadian grave in Normandy.

The grave of Flying Officer Joseph Hong in Bretteville-sur-Laize Canadian War Cemetery.

Taisuku Tanaka had gone overseas a generation earlier and had been wounded at Vimy Ridge. His son lies buried in Groesbeek Canadian War Cemetery, within sight of Germany and the final stages of the victory campaign. He was the only Japanese Canadian to die in battle in the Second World War.

UNION OF A CHINESE HEART WITH A CANADIAN SPIRIT.
Flying Officer Joseph Hong, RCAF, 23.5.44 (age 23)

Joseph Hong was one of the first Chinese Canadians to serve in the RCAF, which until 1942 had rejected men of non-European backgrounds. The army and navy had been similarly reluctant to take Chinese Canadian volunteers, on the grounds that they would not be accepted within the ranks, while some politicians opposed the enlistment of Chinese Canadians for fear that a record of military service would give added weight to the demands of these and other Asian Canadians for full citizenship, including the right to vote. Nevertheless, roughly four hundred men and women of Chinese ancestry served in the armed forces. Contrary to expectation, many found greater acceptance in the military than they had in civilian life. A photograph of Flying Officer Hong with his fellow crew members shows the bonds that developed between aircrew as they went through training and faced the same risks together. On the night of 22-23 May, 1944, the Whitley bomber carrying Flying Officer Hong and five other crewmen was shot down near Alençon. All were killed. After the war, their remains were transferred to a collective grave in the Bretteville-sur-Laize Canadian War Cemetery, where they were laid to rest among their countrymen.

IN MEMORY OF "BILL." RACE OR CREED MEANT NOTHING TO HIM.
HE WAS A FRIEND TO ALL.
Private William James Thomas Shepherd, RCIC, 25.8.44 (age 36)
[BRETTEVILLE-SUR-LAIZE]

The story of the ethnic groups in the national war effort must acknowledge episodes such as the treatment of the Japanese Canadians, or the indifference to the plight of Jewish refugees, that tarnish the country's record of conduct during the Second World War. These failings contradict, but they do not invalidate, the principles and ideals for which thousands of Canadians, of all origins, gave their lives. Then as now, ignorance and prejudice competed against the worthier elements of a common humanity and decency among the population. To take one group as a microcosm, Charles Johnson's aforementioned *Action With the Seaforths* sketches the range of characters in his battalion. The naïve and uneducated rubbed elbows with the worldly and broadminded; a few turned out to be malingerers and cowards, or simply incompetent, whereas most proved to be conscientious and battleworthy. In this assortment of citizen soldiers, the man Johnson held in highest regard was his platoon leader, Jimmy Needham, who emerges from the narrative as a thoughtful, courageous young man guided by a steady moral compass. Lance Sergeant James Gerard Needham died on 23 May, 1944, by the road between Pontecorvo and Aquino, choosing to fight on rather than surrender when his platoon's position was overrun by German armour and infantry. He lies buried with his fellow Seaforths at Cassino, beneath a headstone inscribed with his family's prayer for the repose of his soul. The principles for which he fought, however, stand as his epitaph, in words recalled by Johnson when he reflected that "the war was a means to the end of a peace wherein, as Jimmy Needham had so aptly said, there would be truth, justice and freedom for everybody and for all time." The same universal hope, transcending the differences of race or background, dignifies the memory of Flying Officer Joseph Hong's younger brother, a Canadian soldier at rest in Italy:

SO THAT ALL PEOPLES MAY LIVE IN PEACE AND FREEDOM. BORN WINDSOR, ONTARIO, CANADA
Private George Hong, WNSR, 8.9.44 (age 18) [ANCONA]

FURTHER READING:

Dreisziger, N.F. "Rallying Canada's immigrants behind the war effort, 1939–1945," in: *Forging A Nation: Perspectives on the Canadian Military Experience*. Ed. Bernd Horn. St. Catharines: Vanwell Publishing Limited, 2002, pp. 177–194.

————. "7 December 1941: A turning point in Canadian wartime policy toward ethnic groups?" *Journal of Canadian Studies* 32/1 (1997), 93–111.

Dreisziger, N. F. (with M.L. Kovacs, Paul Bödy, Bennett Kovrig). *Struggle and Hope. The Hungarian Canadian Experience*. Toronto: McClelland and Stewart, 1982.

Icelandic Canadian, Winnipeg, years 1942–1952.

Lindström, Varpu. *From Heroes to Enemies. The Finns in Canada, 1937–1947*. Beaverton: Aspasia Books, 2000.

On Guard for Thee: War, Ethnicity, and the Canadian State, 1939–1945, ed. Norman Hillmer, Bohdan Kordan, Lubomyr Luciuk. Ottawa: Canadian Committee for the History of the Second World War, 1988.

Palmer, Howard. "Ethnic relations in wartime: Nationalism and European minorities in Alberta during the Second World War," *A Nation of Immigrants: Women, Workers and Communities in Canadian History, 1840s-1960s*. Ed. F. Iacovetta, P. Draper, R. Ventresca. Toronto: University of Toronto Press, 1998, pp. 451–481.

Prymak, Thomas M. *Maple Leaf and Trident. The Ukrainian Canadians during the Second World War*. Toronto: Multicultural History of Ontario, 1988

Taylor, Mary. A *Black Mark. The Japanese-Canadians in World War II*. Ottawa: Oberon Press, 2004.

Wong, Marjorie. *The Dragon and the Maple Leaf. Chinese Canadians in World War II*. London, Ont.: Pirie Publishing, 1994.

CHAPTER TEN

"For Israel and Canada"
Agira Canadian War Cemetery, Sicily

O ISRAEL, HERE LIES YOUR SERVANT; DEFENDER OF TRUTH,
JUSTICE AND BROTHERHOOD.
Private Issie Bell, HPER, 25.7.43 (age 24)

Curiosity towards the place where their war began, and the reactions to their baptism of fire in an ancient land, animate the Canadian accounts of the Sicily campaign. The anticipation of battle and the eagerness of the young soldiers to prove themselves in action lend a dramatic intensity to the narratives left by the soldiers and regimental historians. So do the impressions of the strange world they had entered. Descriptions of the landscape and its inhabitants were vivid, if not always favourable. The Canadians found themselves on the move through a land whose severity and primordial habitation exceeded anything they had known before. Unremitting heat oppressed them, the dust enveloped them, and the hardship of the Sicilian peasants who coaxed an existence from the parched soil could surprise men who had grown up during the Depression. And yet, as every step forward took them a step back in time, some were able to discern behind the desolation and squalor "a Biblical beauty and setting" as the island's long history revealed itself in the traces left by a parade of invaders and overlords over three millennia. The historian of the 48th Highlanders spoke for the men's awareness of their fleeting passage across an old stage when he wrote that "the Highlanders could sense age. They dimly knew that Sicily's yesterdays were so full that what was happening today was only a scratch on Sicily's time; this war was only a passing disturbance which would soon be swallowed up, too, by time."

A HERO SLEEPS.
Private James Alexander Cameron, LER, 21.7.43 (age 33)

ASLEEP BENEATH SICILIAN SKIES IN AN HONOURED SOLDIER'S GRAVE IS THE SON WE LOVED
AND MISS. HE RESTS AMONG THE BRAVE.
Corporal James Michael Vincent Dilio, TRR, 5.8.43 (age 21)

The 38-day battle for Sicily forms a nigh imperceptible layer in the island's historical stratigraphy. It would hardly occur to anyone visiting Sicily today that the largest amphibious operation ever undertaken had brought over 160,000 Allied soldiers to the southeastern quarter of the island on the night of July 9-10, 1943, or that the plush orchards and olive groves blanketing the lower slopes of Mount Etna had seen some of the fiercest fighting of the war. Among the temples, castles, and palaces displaying Sicily's long history of foreign invasion and conquest, the contest waged by the Allied and Axis forces has left few traces. And yet, even if within the greater context of the Second World War the campaign may now seem peripheral, the invasion of Sicily was of more than transitory importance at the time. It was part of a train of events, set in motion by the Eighth Army's landmark victory at El Alamein in November 1942, that restored the reputation of British arms and marked the change of the war's tide in 1943. After four years of defeat and desperate defence, the western Allies were at long last carrying the land war to the Axis powers. The Sicily campaign coincided with other momentous turns in the Allies' favour—the shift in the battle of the Atlantic, the escalation of the bombing campaign, and the failure of the last great German offensive on the Eastern Front—to make final victory certain, if not yet imminent.

The announcement of the Allied landings in Sicily came as a welcome tonic to morale in Canada. Alongside the British and American forces were 25,000 soldiers of the First Canadian Division and First Army Tank Brigade who swarmed ashore along the concave rim of the Costa dell'Ambra, not far from the town of Pachino. No longer were the country's soldiers sitting idle in England, mired in the disappointments of Hong Kong and Dieppe. Now mustered into the ranks of the fabled Eighth Army they were finally taking the fight to the enemy. Sicily imposed a hard apprenticeship on a novice army, demanding exceptionally high standards of endurance simply to cope with the torrid climate and rumpled ground, and pitting the Canadians against tough German formations adept in the use of terrain for defensive warfare. The young volunteers, however, hailing from one end of the country to the other, rose to the challenge of their first campaign, advancing further than any other formation in the Eighth Army and performing some of the country's most stirring feats of arms in the hilltop towns west of Mount Etna.

SLEEP ON, BRAVE WARRIOR. THE YEARS CAN NEVER DIM YOUR MEMORY, VALOUR, SACRIFICE, AS NOW YOU REST IN HIM.
Corporal Harold Wilfred Lawson, HPER, 10.7.43 (age 21)

LIFE IS IMMORTAL, LOVE IS ETERNAL, DEATH IS ONLY AN HORIZON. MOM, KAY, AND TONY
Private Raymond Henry Hunter, SHC, 10.7.43 (age 23)

I KNOW THAT YOU ARE SLEEPING WITH THE NOBLE AND THE BRAVE.
Trooper Edward Myers, TRR, 17.7.43 (age 39)

FOR THEM THE FORMER THINGS HAVE PASSED AND NOW THEY SLEEP IN PEACE.
Sergeant Bernard Bates Thompson, HPER, 18.7.43 (age 21)
Corporal Harold Trueman Thompson, SDGH, 17.9.44 (age 25) [CALAIS]
[REVELATION 21: 4]

BELOVED, SLEEP AND TAKE THY REST. GOOD NIGHT, GOOD NIGHT.
MOTHER, WIFE, SON JOHN, FAMILY
Private Gordon Warnica, SHC, 21.7.43 (age 23)

IN LOVING MEMORY OF MY BOY WHO IS SADLY MISSED.
Gunner John Osborne, RCA, 21.7.43 (age 17)

SOME TIME, SOME DAY, OUR EYES SHALL SEE THE ONE WE KEEP IN MEMORY. GOOD NIGHT.
Private Richard William Strangeway, SHC, 21.7.43 (age 23)

O LORD, FROM THE SKIES, COMMAND US TO RISE SO WE CAN SEE THE LOVED ONES AGAIN.
Private Sergie Zilnic, LER, 22.7.43 (age 19)

JOE. ONE OF THE BEST. LOST FIGHTING FOR PEACE. GOD KNOWS HOW MOTHER MISSES YOU.
Private Patrick Joseph McKenna, HPER, 25.7.43

WE THOUGHT HIS LIFE TOO SOON DONE; ENDED, INDEED, WHEN SCARCELY YET BEGUN.
Private Daniel James Murray, 48th HC, 25.7.43 (age 20)

IN THE PRIME OF LIFE I LEFT THIS WORLD, MY BELOVED WIFE AND DEAR LITTLE GIRL.
Corporal Joseph Ernest Norton, RCR, 26.7.43 (age 23)

A MEMORY DEARER THAN GOLD OF A DADDY WE LOVED AND WILL NEVER FORGET.
PHYLLIS AND SYLVIA
Sapper Clement Irwin, CRCE, 31.7.43 (age 33)

DEAR KEN, REST IN PEACE FROM THE ROAR OF BATTLE. LOVE, AUNT MARY
Private Kenneth John Earnshaw, RCR, 1.8.43 (age 21)

OUR ONLY SON WHOM WE HAVE SORELY LOST. SADLY MISSED BY
HIS FATHER AND MOTHER.
Lance Corporal John Frolis, HPER, 3.8.43 (age 23)

WE ARE WAITING, FRANKIE LAD. MOTHER AND DAD
Sapper Oscar Frank Foster, CRCE, 4.8.43 (age 22)

THOUGHTS THAT DO OFTEN LIE TOO DEEP FOR TEARS.
Private Herbert Clayton Jones, LER, 5.8.43 (age 21)

I HAVE NOT KNOWN THEE FROM MYSELF, NEITHER OUR LOVE FROM GOD.
Private Arthur Parry, SHC, 5.8.43 (age 36)
[DANTE GABRIEL ROSSETTI, THE HOUSE OF LIFE V; HEART'S HOPE]

The Agira Canadian War Cemetery, set in the lonely, rugged terrain of eastern Sicily, pays tribute to Canada's first major campaign of the war. The burial ground was chosen by Canadian graves registration officers shortly after the campaign as the most appropriate place to concentrate 490 of the 562 men who fell in Sicily. Agira is the first of three war cemeteries in Italy designated as Canadian, but it holds the distinction of being the sole cemetery of the Second World War in which Canadians only are buried. Although the fallen lie in the most beautiful of the Canadian war cemeteries, their true monument resides not in the work of human hands but in the surrounding landscape. Long after the armies have passed into history, the cliff face at Assoro, the jagged ridgelines beyond Nissoria, and the hills enclosing the Salso river valley will remain indelible testaments to the achievements of the Canadians who fought in Sicily.

IF OUR TIME BE COME LET US DIE MANFULLY FOR OUR BRETHREN;
LET US NOT STAIN OUR HONOUR.
Major George Richard Smerger Drought, The Cameronians, 10.7.43 (age 32)
[SYRACUSE] [I MACCABEES 9: 10]

DIED IN THE CAUSE OF HUMANITY'S LIBERATION. UNFORGOTTEN BY HIS FAMILIES.
Fusilier Isaac Louis Goldstein, The Royal Scots Fusiliers, 10.7.43 (age 30) [SYRACUSE]

A HERO OF DUNKIRK, EL ALAMEIN, SICILY.
Private David Henry Hayes, East Yorkshire Regiment, 18.7.43 (age 23) [CATANIA]

50TH DIVISION, EIGHTH ARMY.
Lieutenant David Hemersham Cox, Chesire Regiment, 16.8.43 (age 23) [CATANIA]

Agira belongs to a triad of Commonwealth war cemeteries perpetuating the memory of the Sicily campaign. Over a thousand British graves in the Syracuse War Cemetery, and another two thousand in its counterpart at Catania, record the ferocity of the Eighth Army's struggle against the German defenders nestled into the southern slopes of Mount Etna. *He was proud to serve with the Eighth Army* proclaims an epitaph at Syracuse. *Killed on active service with the Eighth Army* reads another at Catania. These testimonials to the spirit of Britain's most famous formation, forever identified with its commander, General Bernard Montgomery, correspond with the esprit de corps sounding forth from the Canadian headstones. *"Dileas gu brath." Faithful forever* is a first example at Agira of many 48th Highlander graves in Italy bearing the regimental motto. *"A soldier at heart"* concludes the epitaph of Lance Corporal Harold Hill of the Princess Patricias, while *A soldier's glory lives beyond the grave* commemorates Private Stanley John Miller of the Seaforth Highlanders. Homes in New Brunswick noted on the headstones of Carleton and Yorks, or Quebec towns on the graves of French-speaking Van Doos, recall the close regional affiliations of the First Division's battalions and the comradeship forged among friends and familiars who came to look upon their regiment as a second family. Regimental pride also bred a high sense of duty among the commissioned officers. They stood apart from the rank and file as career soldiers, university graduates, or the scions of military families, who held themselves to exacting standards of courage and leadership. It was a symptom of conspicuous bravery not yet tempered by experience that many officers in Sicily took risks that more seasoned soldiers might have avoided. Bold leadership made the difference in a number of engagements, but excessive gallantry came at a price:

GLORY IS THE LEAST OF THINGS THAT FOLLOW THIS MAN HOME.
Lieutenant Edward Martin MacLachlan, 48th HC, 15.7.43 (age 31)
[RUDYARD KIPLING, LORD ROBERTS]

NON OMNIS MORIAR.
(Not all of me shall die.)
Lieutenant Joseph Beverley Starr, CYR, 18.7.43 (age 25) [HORACE, ODES III.30]

THE LORD IS MY SHEPHERD, THEREFORE CAN I LACK NOTHING.
Major John Henry William Pope, RCR, 18.7.43 (age 30)
[PSALM 23: 1, IN THE BOOK OF COMMON PRAYER]

HERE, MY BELOVED, ENGLAND LIVES; GO TELL THE ENGLISH WHY I DIED.
Captain Maurice Herbert Battle Cockin, HPER, 21.7.43

HE THAT DWELLETH IN THE SECRET PLACE OF THE MOST HIGH SHALL ABIDE UNDER THE SHADOW OF THE ALMIGHTY.
Lieutenant Colonel Ralph Marston Crowe, RCR, 24.7.43 (age 31) [PSALM 91: 1]

'FIDELIS'
Lieutenant Robert Free Osler, 48th HC, 26.7.43 (age 32)

HE DIED AS FEW MEN GET THE CHANCE TO DIE, FIGHTING FOR A WORLD'S MORALITY.
Captain George Turnbull Whitelaw, 48th HC, 1.8.43 (age 23)

IN MEMORY OF MY SON. HE FACED DESTINY AS HE DID LIFE, WITH COURAGE AND A SMILE.
Lieutenant Earl John Christie, LER, 5.8.43 (age 26)

Agira cemetery is small enough to create an air of intimacy. A walk along each row of headstones makes the visitor familiar with accounts of the campaign pause at certain graves. Company Sergeant Major Charles Nutley was the first Canadian to die in Sicily, killed by a stray round while wading ashore on the wrong beach. The shell that killed Lieutenant-Colonel Bruce Sutcliffe and Captain Herbert Battle Cockin as they explored the road winding up to Assoro led to the bold decision to scale the undefended heights on the town's eastern side. Major William Bury died while leading a company of Edmontons against an enemy outpost on the western fringe of Agira; and Private Sidney Cousins singlehandedly eliminated two machine gun posts on a knoll outside Leonforte, an action which might well have earned him a Victoria Cross had he not been killed by a shell shortly afterwards. Many names, of course, do not appear in the narratives. They belong to young men who died carrying out the orders given to them, and whose epitaphs are all that remain to give meaning to their brief lives:

MAN IS ONLY AS GREAT AS HE IS KIND.
Private James Nelson Rasmussen, LER, 15.7.43 (age 28)

"AND WE KNOW THAT ALL THINGS WORK TOGETHER FOR GOOD FOR THEM THAT LOVE GOD."
SOMETIME WE'LL UNDERSTAND.
Sapper Joseph Daigle, CRCE, 22.7.43 (age 28) [ROMANS 8: 28]

BLESSED ARE THE PEACEMAKERS: FOR THEY SHALL BE CALLED THE CHILDREN OF GOD.
Private Willard Snow, RCOC, 22.7.43 (age 30) [MATTHEW 5: 9]

IN HOC SIGNO VINCES.
(In this sign shalt thou conquer.)
Trooper William Charles Palmer, TRR, 24.7.43 (age 38)

HE MADE THE SUPREME SACRIFICE FOR THE LOVE OF GOD AND HUMANITY.
Private Arthur Morton, 48th HC, 25.7.43 (age 25)

THEY THAT WAIT UPON THE LORD SHALL RENEW THEIR STRENGTH. ISAIAH XL. 31
Private Byron Randolf Mailman, WNSR, 31.7.43 (age 22)

R.I.P. O VALIANT HEART, NO LAGGARD THOU. IN REMEMBRANCE YOUR LIFE SHINES ON.
Private Cyril George Peck, LER, 3.8.43 (age 22)

The wider implications of the Sicily campaign become apparent at Agira. The valedictions on the headstones grow in meaning in a land where the many markers and memorials do much to explain why these young men came to be buried so far from home. Street names common to every Sicilian and Italian town read like a primer of the nation's history since Reunification—Corso Garibaldi, Via Cavour, Via XX Settembre, Corso Vittorio Emmanuele, Viale Plebiscito, Via XXIV Maggio, Piazza IV Novembre—the last two commemorating Italy's entry into the First World War in

1915 and the day on which the conflict ended in victory in 1918. Every town square or public park contains a monument to the locals who did not return from the Italian version of the Western Front in the mountainous killing grounds along the Piave River. This inscription honours the sons of a small town on the western coast of Sicily:

> *Within her nurturing maternal embrace*
> *Erice receives*
> *The elect spirits of all her sons*
> *Who in falling not in vain*
> *For the sacred goals of Italy*
> *Have passed from life into history.*

The words "not in vain" took on bellicose overtones in Italy after 1922. Side by side with the memorials to Italy's 600,000 war dead are others displaying the malignant aftereffects of the First World War. The perceived humiliations of the Versailles treaty were grist to Hitler's mill, but the settlement also left two victorious countries, Italy and Japan, nursing grievances at having been denied their rightful rewards by their British and French allies. Resentment at the "mutilated victory" helped to fuel Mussolini's rise to power in the chaotic years after the war, and much of the monumental architecture of the Fascist era invoked the memory of the sons fallen for the sacred goals of Italy to justify Il Duce's claims to *"Italia irredenta"*—the lands across the Adriatic deemed to be Italian by historical right—as well as to a greater Mediterranean empire. Unlike Germany, where all insignia of the Nazi regime have been expunged, the Ozymandian remnants of Mussolini's Italy still abound today, bombastically promoting the aesthetic, social, and militaristic agendas of the Fascist movement. "Many enemies, much honour," "To you, Duce, we dedicate our youth," "Italy finally has her empire," bray the captions inlaid among the mosaics in the Foro Italico depicting Mussolini's invasion of Ethiopia in 1935, a wanton act of aggression that pointed the way ahead to his cynical decision in June of 1940 to throw his lot in with Nazi Germany. With Europe at Hitler's feet, and Britain isolated, Mussolini reckoned that "a few thousand corpses" would entitle Italy to a second helping of the spoils when his partner rewrote the ending to the First World War. He badly miscalculated, of course, overestimating Hitler's position, underestimating British resolve, and overrating the capacity of his armed forces to wage his parallel war of conquest. "Believe, obey, fight," was the motto of the Fascist movement, yet it was war that exposed the moral hollowness of Mussolini's regime which collapsed within two weeks of the Allied landings in Sicily.

HE LIVED AS HE DIED, TO KEEP PEACE IN THIS WORLD.
Private John Thomas Ferguson, SHC, 21.7.43 (age 24)

"BELOVED, NOW ARE WE THE SONS OF GOD: . . . WHEN HE SHALL APPEAR
WE SHALL BE LIKE HIM."
Lance Corporal Spencer Kay McElhoes, SHC, 21.7.43 (age 30) [I JOHN 3: 2]

"THE LORD REDEEMETH THE SOUL OF HIS SERVANTS: AND NONE OF THEM THAT
TRULY TRUST IN HIM SHALL BE DESOLATE."
Sergeant Arthur Wallace Eatman, CYR, 22.7.43 (age 23) [PSALMS 34: 22]

ALIKE IN PEACE AND WAR ONE PATH HE TROD. HIS LAW WAS DUTY AND HIS GUIDE WAS GOD.
Private Wilbert Roy Boulton, PPCLI, 23.7.43 (age 24)

V ČIZINE SE NARODIL, V ČIZINE MLADÝ SVŮJ ŽIVOT ZA DEMOKRACII POLOŽIL.
(He was born in a foreign land, and in a foreign land he lay down his
young life for democracy.)
Private Steve Slavik, RCR, 24.7.43 (age 30)

J'AI COMBATTU POUR L'HONNEUR, LA GLOIRE ET LA JUSTICE.
J'ATTENDS DE DIEU MA RECOMPENSE.
(I fought for honour, glory, and justice. I await my reward from God.)
Private Albert Perreault, RCOC, 25.7.43

THE FIGHT FOR RIGHT IS WON AND HE HAS PAID HIS DEBT. THE KING OF KINGS
HAS SPOKEN, THOU FAITHFUL ONE, WELL DONE.
Sergeant Peter Birnie, 48th HC, 25.7.43 (age 35) [CF. MATTHEW 25: 23]

HE DIED FOR DEMOCRACY, FREEDOM, LIBERTY AND JUSTICE.
Private Martin Alleman, LER, 3.8.43 (age 49)

The epitaphs in Agira make their own reply to the slogans and stated intentions of
Fascist Italy and Nazi Germany. The brutal friendship between the dictators united
two strains of a toxic ideology that in its arrogant militarism and crude worldview
repudiated the worth of the individual, religious faith, and peace among nations. It
does lasting credit to the common sense of the Canadians who volunteered for overseas
service that even after the dismal performance of the democracies during the political
and economic crises of the 1930s they nevertheless rallied in defence of democratic,
civilised principles. This is not to say that their motives were entirely idealistic. It is
to say that there were many volunteers for whom religious and moral convictions, or
the basic but firmly held belief that the Axis powers threatened their security and
values, guided their decision to take up arms. Sprinkled among them were men whose
epitaphs leave no doubt as to the sincerity of their political or religious motives:

IN LOVING MEMORY OF AN ANTI-FASCIST FIGHTER. HELEN AND MOTHER
Private Hugh Reid Anderson, RCR, 18.7.43 (age 28)

FOR ISRAEL AND CANADA. EVER REMEMBERED BY MOTHER, FATHER, SISTERS AND BROTHER.
Private Jack Besserman, 48th HC, 18.7.43 (age 29)

Private Anderson's epitaph recalls the ideological polarisation of the late 1930s when
the growing alliance between Italy and Germany mobilised opposition from the other
end of the political spectrum in the form of a popular front movement open to all anti-
fascist forces. It united die-hard Communists, socialists, and moderate sympathisers in
an international alliance, first congregated in the Spanish Civil War, whose members
saw the opportunity to take up the anti-fascist struggle in the service of their countries.
The absence of a cross on Private Anderson's grave confirms the commitment to the
cause of the proletariat, as does the first epitaph below, inscribed on the headstone of
a soldier who died in the battle to break the Hitler Line:

DIED THAT FASCISM BE DESTROYED AND THAT WORKERS MIGHT BUILD A NEW WORLD.
Private Arthur Edgar Harris, SHC, 23.5.44 (age 31) [CASSINO]

TILL JUSTICE RULES THERE IS NO LIBERTY. I DIED FOR IT.
Flight Lieutenant Arthur Grant Longwell, RCAF, 14.2.43 (age 29) [JONKERBOS]
[FROM "MEN OF THE SOIL," IN THE SOCIALIST SONGBOOK]

The Sicily campaign did more than confront Fascism in the country of its birth. Once the Germans took up the battle from their faltering Italian allies it brought Jewish Canadian soldiers face to face with the enemy whose aim to annihilate their people was by this time well known. Private Besserman's is one of seven Jewish graves at Agira, but the story of his death in action illustrates the added incentive that Jewish soldiers carried into battle. When the 48th Highlanders came up against a network of German outposts on a ridgeline south of Valguarnera, small groups of infantrymen worked their way forward to eliminate the enemy positions. The history of the 48th records that a six-man section rushed the main gunpit. One of the attackers was "Bessie" Besserman, "his Jewish hatred of the Nazis driving him into the position with a stabbing bayonet. He was killed in the hand-to-hand melee, but first paid off racial scores." Another Jewish soldier from Toronto, Private Max Lampert, also died in this brave action that forced the Germans to give up Valguarnera and allowed the Canadian advance to resume. The regimental chaplain who saw to the placement of a Star of David over the graves of the two Jewish soldiers sent a letter of condolence to Besserman's mother extolling him "as a true son of ancient Israel . . . to exterminate the evil that was Naziism was his single purpose."

The Star of David accompanying the maple leaf on Canadian headstones and the emblems of the other Allied nations displays the allegiance of Jewish servicemen to their co-religionists that complemented their loyalty to their native countries. In other cases it speaks for the awareness among European Jews that they no longer had a country, and that solidarity before the scourge of Nazism now superseded national loyalties. Their choice underlines a significant difference between the First and Second World Wars. In the First World War, the Jews had fought for their countries against their co-religionists fighting for theirs on the far side of no man's land. Small stone tablets among the crosses in the German cemeteries issue a reminder that twenty-two thousand German Jews died for their fatherland between 1914 and 1918. A generation later, however, the German and Austrian Jews who fell in battle during the Second World War lie at rest in British war cemeteries. At Ranville War Cemetery in Normandy, Sergeant Eugene Fuller, the *nom de guerre* taken by an Austrian Jew, was Eugen Kagerer-Stein; Private Ernest Norton was Ernst Nathan, and Private Frederick Fletcher was Friedrich Fleischer. Alongside these members of the select No. 10 Commando unit, no. 3 "Jewish" Troop, lies a young German Jew whose personal details outline the choice that he and his fellows made:

FORMERLY HANS ARENSTEIN. BORN 18TH FEBRUARY 1922, ERFURT, GERMANY.
Lance Corporal Harry Andrews, Royal Sussex Regiment, no. 10 Commando,
11.8.44 (age 22)

A commemorative booklet published by the Canadian Jewish Congress in 1948 lists two German-born Jews who died on active service with the RCAF. Flight Sergeant Nat Dlusy, by birth Nathan Dlusniewski, left his native Berlin with his family in 1938 to settle in Montreal. He enlisted in the air force in 1942 and flew on anti-submarine operations until his death off the coast of Scotland in August 1944. *The memory of him who did his full duty shall be forever a blessing* reads the inscription on his headstone in the Glasgow Jewish cemetery. Cowan was the anglicised surname of Flight Lieutenant Henry Cohen who served with distinction in Fighter Command after escaping to Canada in 1939 and enlisting in 1941. Less than three weeks before the end of the war in Europe, he was brought down by anti-aircraft fire over Germany. He lies buried in his native land among the 527 Canadian airmen in the Berlin War Cemetery.

Canadian Jews did not have to wrestle with the painful choice between country and people. Still, as members of a distinct religious minority (170,000 strong according to the 1941 census) they lived in two worlds. The standard details on the headstones of two young artillerymen at Agira record their service as Canadian soldiers, whereas the Hebrew inscriptions supplied by their families gather their memories into the traditions of their ancient faith. They identify the fallen soldier by the Hebrew name he used on religious occasions, and mark his passing by the month and world year of the Jewish calendar:

HERE LIES VELVEL THE SON OF SHIMON ZELIG WHO DIED ON THE TWENTY-SECOND DAY OF TAMMUZ 5703. MAY HIS SOUL BE BOUND UP IN THE BOND OF ETERNAL LIFE.
Gunner William Guy Rosenthal, RCA, *25.7.43 (age 20)*

IN MEMORY OF MY GOOD AND BELOVED SON'S SOUL. YOSEF, SON OF ALTER ATTIS, WHO WAS KILLED ON THE SIXTH DAY OF AV 5703.
Bombardier Joseph Wilfred Attis, RCA, *7.8.43 (age 32)*

Patterns long established in Jewish funerary inscriptions guided the composition of the Hebrew epitaphs engraved on the headstones of Jewish Canadian servicemen. All give the Hebrew name of the deceased and of his father. His place of birth, his years or stage of life, the sorrow of his family, and a brief tribute could be added to the inscription which usually concluded with the Old Testament passage recited at Jewish funerals as part of the ritual prayers for the dead, "May his soul be bound up in the bond of eternal life" (I Samuel 25: 29). Lack of space precluded the longer eulogy or quotations from the Old Testament that might elaborate on the plain details. In their time-honoured simplicity, however, these Hebrew epitaphs show the durability of Jewish traditions over many centuries, in many lands, and hallow the memory of the young men who rallied to the defence of their country and people:

HERE LIES BURIED THE YOUNG LAD ISRAEL ZE'EV, SON OF HAYYIM.
Warrant Officer II Irving Walter Garfin, RCAF, *28.6.42 (age 27)* [SAGE]

HERE LIES BURIED ABRAHAM, SON OF YITZHAK SIRLUCK, FROM CANADA, DEAR TO HIS FATHER, BROTHER AND SISTER. 14TH ADAR 5704. MAY HIS SOUL BE BOUND UP IN THE BOND OF ETERNAL LIFE.
Pilot Officer Robert Sirluck, RCAF, *1.3.44 (age 22)* [HARROGATE]

ZEV, THE SON OF JOSHUA DUBINSKY, WHO DIED ON THE TWENTY-FOURTH DAY OF AV IN THE YEAR 5704. MAY HIS SOUL BE BOUND UP IN THE BOND OF ETERNAL LIFE.
Private William Harvey Dubinsky, CH, *13.8.44 (age 30)* [BRETTEVILLE-SUR-LAIZE]

YOEL, THE SON OF MEYER MENDEL BERLIN, FROM THE CITY OF WINNIPEG, WHO WAS KILLED IN THE WAR ON THE SECOND DAY OF ELUL 5704 AT 29 YEARS OF AGE.
Sergeant Yale Berlin, CRCE, *21.8.44 (age 29)* [ANCONA]

HERE LIES BURIED THE YOUNG MAN HAYYIM, SON OF GEDALYAHU. 1922–1944
Flying Officer Irving Jack Kirschner, RCAF, *26.8.44 (age 21)* [BROOKWOOD]

THE YOUNG MAN GEDALYAHU, THE SON OF SHLOMO VINSKY, FROM THE TOWN OF WINNIPEG, CANADA, WHO DIED ON THE THIRTEENTH DAY OF ELUL 5703. MAY HIS SOUL BE BOUND UP IN THE BOND OF ETERNAL LIFE.
Private Gordon Vinsky, 4th PLDG, *1.9.44 (age 24)* [MONTECCHIO]

HERE LIES BURIED MESHULLAM YOSEF, SON OF MENACHEM DAVID ZAREIKIN,
WHO DIED A CASUALTY IN THE SECOND WORLD WAR, 18TH TISHREI 5705.
Pilot Officer Joseph Zareikin, RCAF, 5.10.44 (age 36) [HARROGATE]

HERE LIES GEDALYAHU, THE SON OF MORDECHAI, WHO DIED ON THE FOURTH DAY OF HOL
HA-MO'ED SUKKOT 5705. MAY HIS SOUL BE BOUND UP IN THE BOND OF ETERNAL LIFE.
Private Gordon Krofchick, 4th PLDG, 5.10.44 [CESENA]

OUR BELOVED SON WHO WAS TAKEN IN HIS YOUTH. MORDECHAI, THE SON OF ISAAC
OLSHANSKY OF BLESSED MEMORY, WHO FELL A CASUALTY ON THE BATTLEFIELD
ON THE TWENTY-FIFTH DAY OF TISHREI 5705. MAY HIS SOUL BE BOUND UP IN THE
BOND OF ETERNAL LIFE.
Leading Aircraftman Maxwell Olshansky, RCAF, 12.10.44 (age 22) [GROESBEEK]

HERE LIES BURIED MORDECHAI, THE SON OF MOSHE BERNSTEIN AND HIS WIFE SARAH
SCHMELTZER BERNSTEIN, WHO DIED ON THE FOURTH DAY OF TEVET IN THE YEAR 5704.
Private Mike Bernstein, IRC, 20.12.44 (age 21) [VILLANOVA]

HERE LIES ONE BELOVED TO HIS PARENTS AND FAMILY. TZVI, THE SON OF ELIAHU. FOR THE
FREEDOM OF THE WORLD HE SACRIFICED HIS LIFE, AT THE BEGINNING OF SHEVAT 5705.
Flying Officer Harry Bloch, RCAF, 2.2.45 (age 33) [REICHSWALD FOREST]

BENTZION, THE SON OF MENASHE HOCKENSTEIN, WHO SACRIFICED HIS LIFE FOR
HIS NATIVE LAND. HIS MEMORY WILL NEVER PASS FROM THE HEARTS OF HIS MOTHER,
HIS BROTHERS AND SISTER WHO MOURN.
Corporal Ben Hockenstein, AR, 8.3.45 (age 28) [GROESBEEK]

Nearly 17,000 Jewish men and women served in Canada's armed forces during the Second World War, the great majority in the army or the RCAF. The scale of their contribution to the war effort becomes clear when this number is rendered in statistical terms demonstrating that a minority representing less than two per cent of the country's population supplied 7.5% of the national enlistment. Four hundred and twenty-one lost their lives on active service. A sample of their epitaphs draws a small portrait of Canada's Jewish population nearly seventy years ago—an already longstanding community with its origins mainly in Eastern Europe, more urban than rural in their patterns of settlement, and more generous in spirit to their country than their country was at times to them:

SON OF HYMAN PAVELOW. BORN IN KIEV, RUSSIA.
Israel Pavelow served as Corporal Ervin Povol, RRR, 9.6.44 (age 31) [BÉNY-SUR-MER]

ВЕЧНАЯ ПАМИТ ВАСИЛЮ Г. МАЛАВЬМУ. РАЖДЕНИН В КАНАДЕ В 1917 Г. ПОМЕР В 1944 Г.
(Eternal memory to Vasily G. Maloff. Born in Canada in 1917. Died in 1944.)
Rifleman William Maloff, QORC, 10.8.44 (age 27) [BRETTEVILLE-SUR-LAIZE]

BORN INVERNESS, N.S., CANADA. BELOVED SON OF FANNIE FEINSTEIN AND
THE LATE ISIDOR FEINSTEIN.
Flight Sergeant Samuel Feinstein, RCAF, 30.9.42 (age 21) [BERGEN]
Private Nathan Feinstein, NNSH, 2.11.44 (age 27) [ADEGEM]

RAYMOND, BELOVED ONLY SON OF I. AND J. LESSER, SUDBURY, CANADA.
WE CHERISH HIS MEMORY.
Flight Sergeant Raymond Lesser, RCAF, 4.9.43 (age 21) [BERLIN]

The castle-crowned peak of Assoro (centre), scaled and captured by the Hastings and Prince Edward Regiment during the night of July 20–21, 1943.

Rows of headstones tapered to the hillside at Agira Canadian War Cemetery.

(top) *The terrace of pebbled mosaic and the stone stairway leading to the burial ground at Agira.*

(bottom) *From defeat to victory—the pride of the Eighth Army sounds forth in this list of battles.*

פ' נ

NATHAN FRANK
WEHRMANN
GEF. 15.5.1915

תנצב'ה

2/548

A *German grave of the First World War* (Matt Symes).

The Jewish section in the Polish cemetery at Monte Cassino.

Graves in Ranville War Cemetery of German and Austrian Jews who died in British service (Matt Symes).

SON OF LOUIS AND DORA ABRAMSON, OTTAWA, ONTARIO, CANADA.
Flying Officer Mark Leslie Abramson, RCAF, 16.5.44 (age 30) [ASSENS]

SON OF THE LATE MR. AND MRS. MAX RABKIN, PORTAGE LA PRAIRIE, CANADA.
Flying Officer Hyman Rabkin, RCAF, 2.11.44 (age 23) [RHEINBERG]

A GOOD SON.
Flight Lieutenant Max Samuels, RCAF, 20.6.43 (age 24) [BRETTEVILLE]

SON, BROTHER, FRIEND, YOUR LIGHT WILL EVER SHINE IN OUR LIVES. REST IN PEACE.
Flying Officer George Lyon Gilbert, RCAF, 15.10.44 (age 30) [SAGE]

SOFTLY HE WHISPERS, "SMILE, MY DEAR ONES, NOTHING CAN OUR LOVE DESTROY."
NINNY AND MOTHER
Lieutenant Simeon Ira Besen, CGG, 23.10.44 (age 26) [BERGEN-OP-ZOOM]

"IN YOUR HEART AND MIND I WILL EXIST AS YOU ARE EVER IN MINE."
Lieutenant Lawrence Cohen, RCIC, 8.7.44 (age 22) [BRETTEVILLE-SUR-LAIZE]

TO OUR BELOVED HUSBAND, SON AND BROTHER WHO LOVED LIFE DEARLY.
Rifleman Harry Segal, RWR, 8.6.44 (age 25) [BÉNY-SUR-MER]

HE DIED FOR WHAT HE BELIEVED IN.
Flight Officer John Henry Vanular, RCAF, 11.5.45 (age 28) [EINDHOVEN (WOENSEL)]

NO GREATER LOVE THAN THIS.
Pilot Officer Allan Bernard Miller, RCAF, 16.1.45 (age 34) [DURNBACH]

HERE LIES A MAN WHO DIED SO THAT YOU MAY LIVE.
Private Louis Paul, RCASC, 9.8.44 (age 29) [BAYEUX]

HE GAVE HIS LIFE IN A FOREIGN LAND FOR THE FREEDOM OF HIS COUNTRY.
Flying Officer Benjamin Sidney Sussmann, RCAF, 24.3.44 (age 24) [BROOKWOOD]

FOR THE LIFE HE GAVE HIS COUNTRY HE WILL EVER BE REMEMBERED BY HIS LOVED
AND DEAR ONES.
Private Arthur Osher Lewis, LWR, 2.8.44 (age 23) [BRETTEVILLE-SUR-LAIZE]

IN MEMORY OF A BELOVED SON WHO DIED SERVING THE CAUSE. ALWAYS IN OUR HEARTS.
Flying Officer Harry Knobovitch DFC, RCAF, 2.11.44 (age 21) [RHEINBERG]

A YOUTH OF GREAT MERIT, RESPECTED AND LOVED BY ALL, WHO DIED FOR HUMANITY.
Private Samuel Norman Nichols, RCOC, 14.10.44 (age 25) [SCHOONSELHOF]

"O LOVE THAT WILL NOT LET ME GO, I GIVE THEE BACK THE LIFE I OWE."
Private Michael Stanislaus de Vries DCM, IRC, 26.5.44 (age 41) [CASSINO]
[GEORGE MATHESON, 1842–1906, HYMN, O LOVE THAT WILT NOT LET ME GO, 1882]

HE LABOURED LONG INTO THE NIGHT, HE SAW THE DAWN BUT WAS DENIED ITS LIGHT.
Flying Officer Morley Bernard Stock, RCAF, 18.2.45 (age 21) [HARROGATE]

The epitaphs provide a coda to the obituaries gathered by the Canadian Jewish Congress. The notices describe young men of various backgrounds who left jobs, trades, or school to sign up, as did most of their fellow Canadians. They were active in their communities as members of synagogues, Hebrew schools, cultural societes, the Young Mens Hebrew Association, and organisations dedicated to the as yet unrealised Zionist cause. Many came from the same neighbourhoods and had attended the same schools:

ISSIE OF 463 HUTCHISON STREET, MONTREAL, QUEBEC. MAY YOUR SOUL REST IN PEACE.
Private Issie Elias, SDGH, 13.8.44 (age 25) [BRETTEVILLE-SUR-LAIZE]

BELOVED SON OF L. AND H. COHEN. ALWAYS REMEMBERED AND LOVED FOR LOYALTY AND DEVOTION TO FAMILY, KING AND COUNTRY.
Private Hyman Cohen, LER, 18.9.44 (age 23) [CORIANO RIDGE]

Issie Elias was one of nine Jewish boys who did not return to their homes on Hutchison Street; Hyman Cohen, killed a month later, was one of his neighbours. They count among a larger group of thirty-five young men lost to families living on streets nearby—Esplanade, Clark, St. Urbain, Park, Jeanne Mance, Prince Arthur—once the heart of Jewish Montreal, familiar as the setting for many of Mordecai Richler's stories. The impact of the war on this and other neighbourhoods fell more heavily on families which had lost one son and stood to lose another. The obituaries of seventy-four Jewish servicemen note that a brother, or brothers, also served overseas. One of the seven Jewish Canadian families to lose two sons, the Goldbergs of Montreal, suffered the loss of one son early in the war, and lived with the possibility of losing two more. The second of their sons was killed just twelve days before VE Day. Both had enlisted in 1940; the third son in arms survived the war.

MAY HIS SOUL BE BOUND UP IN THE BOND OF ETERNAL LIFE. GOLDBERG, JACOB ARYEH, SON OF YOSEF, 12TH DAY OF TAMMUZ 5701.
Sergeant Louis Curly Goldberg, RCAF, 7.7.41 (age 27) [MERTHYR TYDFIL]
BROTHER OF SGT. PILOT CURLY GOLDBERG, KILLED IN ACTION 7TH JULY 1941, AGE 27.
Corporal Harry Goldberg, 17th DY, 26.4.45 (age 26) [HOLTEN]

Among the lives cut off in their prime were some especially rich in promise. Lou Somers excelled in track, rugby, and football at high school and subsequently at the University of Toronto where he won a series of academic awards. So distinguished was his university career that a scholarship was dedicated in his name. Flying Officer Titleman's epitaph alludes to his athletic prowess which led his branch of the YMHA in Montreal to establish a trophy in his memory. The depth of respect and affection that Captain Sheps inspired in his comrades make the pledge of remembrance in his epitaph more than rote repetition of an oft cited verse. One of the several letters of condolence sent to his family in Winnipeg stated that "his sincerity and reliability combined with the high standard of knowledge assured the young barrister of the high esteem of his colleagues as well as of those who sought him for advice and help. His keen interest in politics . . . led his friends to hope that he would be enabled to take an active part in the post-war world."

BELOVED SON OF BETTY AND JOSEPH SOMERS. OUTSTANDING SCHOLAR AND ATHLETE.
Flying Officer Lou Warren Somers, RCAF, 25.6.43 (age 24) [GROESBEEK]

HE ALWAYS PLAYED THE GAME.
Flying Officer Daniel Titleman, RCAF, 16.6.44 (age 26) [CHESTER (BLACON)]

AT THE GOING DOWN OF THE SUN AND IN THE MORNING WE WILL REMEMBER YOU, DEAR SON.
Captain Sam Barry Sheps, RCA, 16.9.44 (age 31) [GRADARA]

The impressive tally of decorations and citations won by Jewish Canadian servicemen speaks for their courage in battle; but many brave acts, like Private Besserman's furious rush at Valguarnera, were swallowed up in the vortex of the war. So were the efforts of young men killed in the scattered actions of a larger battle. Nine epitaphs in the Moro River Canadian War Cemetery at Ortona commemorate soldiers whose stories profile the background, beliefs, and experiences of their fellow Jewish Canadians. Three were from Winnipeg, three from Montreal, and two from Toronto. Two went overseas with the 1st Division in December 1939, having signed up shortly after the outbreak of the war; one had joined the army before the war and went overseas in June 1940; Wolinsky enrolled in September 1940 and got to England fourteen months later. All nine were employed or in university before enlistment.

The epitaphs show some of them to have been pious Jews. A verse from the Psalms, commonly cited in Jewish funerary inscriptions, honours Private Shanas, a graduate of the Hebrew Free School; Private Yuffe, commemorated in Hebrew, had attended the same school. The other soldier with an epitaph in Hebrew, Private Wolinsky, had combined Talmud Torah with his secular education. In turn, the idealistic declaration (in his own words) on Lieutenant Bindman's grave is consistent with his gallant conduct in what proved to be a brief career on active service. On his first day in action, Bindman made a singlehanded rush on a German position and captured nine prisoners; the following morning he flushed out another enemy position before returning to his own lines to deploy his men against an impending counterattack. Disdaining cover, he was struck by shell fragments and died of his wounds the next day. Private Ofner's epitaph speaks for itself:

HIS GLORY IS GREAT THROUGH THY SALVATION; HONOUR DOST THOU LAY UPON HIM.
Private Ben-Zion Bert Shanas, PPCLI, 7.12.43 (age 25) [PSALM 21: 5]

HERE LIES THE YOUNG MAN CHAIM YUFFE. PEACE BE UPON HIM. THE SON OF AARON WHO FELL IN BATTLE ON THE TWELFTH DAY OF KISLEV 5705 AT TWENTY YEARS OF AGE. MAY HIS SOUL BE BOUND UP IN THE BOND OF ETERNAL LIFE.
Private Hyman Yuffe, RCR, 9.12.43 (age 20)

HERE LIES BURIED THE YOUNG MAN LEIB WOLINSKY, SON OF SHIMON WOLINSKY, 25 YEARS OF AGE, WHO DIED ON THE 14TH OF TEVET 5704. MAY HIS SOUL BE BOUND UP IN THE BOND OF ETERNAL LIFE.
Private Lone Wolinsky, HPER, 10.1.44 (age 25)

"I AM GLAD . . . TO HAVE THE OPPORTUNITY OF SERVING IN A CAUSE SO RIGHT AND JUST."
Lieutenant David Harold Bindman, RCR, 10.12.43 (age 24)

HE COUNTED NOT HIS LIFE. IN THE FRONT RANKS OF THE FIGHT AGAINST FASCISM.
Private Sidney Ofner, RCR, 15.1.44 (age 27)

The Latin inscription on Captain Charles Krakauer's headstone cites the motto of the Order of St. John. It makes an apt tribute to a dedicated medical officer who, in Farley Mowat's words, "laboured in a welter of confusion and turmoil, and fretted because he could not move his Post across the river, closer to the places where the wounded lay." A stray shell descended on the Regimental Aid Post where Captain Krakauer and half a dozen orderlies were working; none survived.

PRO UTILITATE HOMINUM.
(For the service of humanity.)
Captain Charles Krakauer, RCAMC, 22.12.43 (age 29)

Ortona was the watershed of the war for the 1st Division battalions ravaged by the high losses of the December battles. The little remembered prolongation of the fighting along the Arielli River proved to be a rough initiation for the green soldiers of the 5th Division as they were sent to learn their trade against the seasoned enemy awaiting them. These two soldiers died in their regiments' baptisms of fire:

DUTY ASKS A HEAVY PRICE; WE PRAY GOD WILL REMEMBER A DEAR ONE'S SACRIFICE.
Corporal Arthur Gold, 4th PLDG, 14.1.44 (age 28)

IN MEMORY OF MY BELOVED SON MOSES KILLED ON ACTIVE SERVICE.
Private Moses Shacter, PR, 20.1.44 (age 22)

There is one headstone at Ortona connected to a famous episode in the battle. Not far from the cemetery entrance a road with two pronounced bends connects the hamlets of San Donato and San Leonardo. These bends marked stages in an assault along the plateau carried out by the Royal Canadian Regiment whose soldiers ever afterwards referred to the road as Royal Canadian Avenue. At the first bend stands a house, identified by a plaque as "Sterlin Castle." It was the site of a gallant defence made by an isolated band of Royal Canadians, under the command of Lieutenant Mitchell Sterlin, who clung to their little fortress against repeated attacks by a German force far superior in numbers. Their brave stand helped to save the fragile Canadian bridgeheads over the Moro, and made "Sterlin Castle," as the house was ever afterwards known, into one of the most celebrated Canadian monuments of the Italian campaign.

Lieutenant Mitchell Sterlin was killed in action ten days after his platoon's gallant stand. His friends remembered him as the antithesis of the soldierly type—stocky, ungainly, informal—yet his composure and conduct on that one day proved that courage comes in many guises. The words on his headstone, chosen from the Talmud, honour the heritage and the memory of a brave Jewish Canadian soldier: *"Some gain eternity in a lifetime, others gain it in one brief hour."*

THOUGH SILENT, THEY CRY ALOUD.
Trooper Arthur Coldoff, 4th PLDG, 21.5.44 (age 31) [CASSINO]

HE THAT HATH CLEAN HANDS AND A PURE HEART SHALL RECEIVE GOD'S BLESSING.
Rifleman Ernest Charlet, QORC, 20.10.44 (age 21) [ADEGEM] [CF. PSALM 24: 4–5]

GRANT ME ONE PRAYER. DOOM NOT THE HEREAFTER OF MANKIND TO WAR AS THOUGH I HAD DIED NOT.
Private Henry Badleck, PPCLI, 27.10.44 (age 27) [CORIANO RIDGE]
[JOHN GALSWORTHY, VALLEY OF THE SHADOW]

WHEN THE RIGHTEOUS DIE THEY LIVE: FOR THEIR EXAMPLE LIVES.
Warrant Officer II Julius Spiegel, RCAF, 28.10.44 (age 24) [GROESBEEK]

Visitors to the war cemeteries will often notice a pebble laid on top of a headstone marked by a Star of David. It has been left as a token to show that a fellow Jew has visited the grave in an act of remembrance which, one suspects, embraces not only the memory of the fallen soldier but the cause for which he gave his life. There can be few more powerful symbols of resistance to the ghastly ends of Nazism than the Star of David on the grave of an Allied soldier, of any nationality. Over one and a half million Jews served in the Allied coalition, in which the part played by Canadian Jews is apparent in every Canadian war cemetery. The graves and epitaphs of the young men who died for their country and people have a significance beyond the confines of the Second World War, for the shadow of the Holocaust will never recede. Anyone who has read Primo Levi's heartrending description of the Jewish mothers tending lovingly to their children even as they awaited deportation to Auschwitz and certain death will recognise the courage of people who refused to be stripped of their humanity by inhuman oppressors; and anyone who reads the epitaphs will see in them a message of lasting significance in Jewish history. The Holocaust destroyed a third of the Jewish people, leaving a poisonous legacy to the survivors and all subsequent generations. As one historian tracing the impact of the Holocaust on Canadian Jews has written,

> ... for an ethnic community to wrap its identity around its own victimization is counterproductive to its vitality ... To reduce Jewish identity to martyrdom would, in the words of Peter Novich and Emil Fackenheim, provide Hitler with a "posthumous victory" ... by making the Holocaust the emblematic Jewish experience. Instead, by adopting the Holocaust as a pillar of ethnic identity, the Canadian Jewish community must utilize the universal lessons of the event to press for all-embracing human rights. Not to do so would be the ultimate injustice to the memory of the victims and to the community's determination to commemorate and learn about the destroyed Jewish civilization.

In light of these words, the last selection of epitaphs provides a moral bulwark against the corrosive evil of the Holocaust and the posthumous victory of its architects. The courage and sacrifice of these young Jewish Canadians, at Dieppe, on D-Day, in the advance along the Channel coast, in the air war, in Italy, and in the liberation of the Netherlands, encapsulate the contribution of their fellow Jewish comrades to Canada's war effort. In broader terms, and more importantly, their example combines with others to demolish the heartless myth that the Jews went like lambs to the slaughter, as though defenceless women and children, the elderly and the infirm, were somehow complicit in their own destruction. Those in a position to resist did so. What is most striking, however, and admirable, in their families' farewells is the extension of the struggle for freedom and justice to all humanity:

HE DIED A HERO'S DEATH THAT WE MIGHT LIVE IN PEACE.
Lance Corporal Meyer Bubis, RRC, 19.8.42 (age 27) [DUNKIRK]

THAT JUSTICE AND DECENCY MAY PREVAIL.
Flight Sergeant Jacob Jensky, RCAF, 31.8.43 (age 32) [RHEINBERG]

THE MEMORY LIVES OF ONE WHO GAVE HIS LIFE TO MAKE THE WORLD A BETTER PLACE.
Sergeant Frederick Bernard Harris, QORC, 6.6.44 (age 23) [BÉNY-SUR-MER]

HERE LIES ONE OF THE JEWISH FAITH. HE GAVE HIS LIFE FOR GOD,
HIS PEOPLE AND COUNTRY.
Lieutenant Morris Marvin Soronow, RWR, 28.8.44 (age 33) [CALAIS]

A LOVING HUSBAND AND SON. YOU'VE GIVEN YOUR YOUNG LIFE FOR LIBERTY AND JUSTICE.
WE PRAY IT WAS NOT IN VAIN.
Private David Rodness, IRC, 2.1.45 (age 23) [CORIANO RIDGE]

A SON OF ISRAEL WHO GAVE HIS LIFE THAT OTHERS MIGHT CHERISH FREEDOM.
Flight Lieutenant Hector Bernard Rubin DFC, RCAF, 21.3.45 (age 29) [HAMBURG]

YOU BRAVELY FOUGHT AND GAVE YOUR ALL. WE PLEDGE TO KEEP YOUR IDEALS ALOFT.
Corporal Abraham Rochlin, PR, 29.4.45 (age 20) [HOLTEN]

The trail that began in Sicily ends near Ravenna where I Canadian Corps fought its last battles in Italy before being transferred to northwestern Europe. One of the formations that replaced the Canadians in the Eighth Army's order of battle was the Palestine Regiment, made up of Jewish volunteers from British-controlled Palestine (as well as fifty-three different countries) and commanded by Brigadier Ernest Frank Benjamin, a Canadian-born career soldier of the Jewish faith. A monument outside the entrance to the Ravenna War Cemetery honours their service in the concluding battles of the Italian campaign during the spring of 1945, and a separate plot contains thirty-three headstones incised with the trilingual regimental badge and a Star of David. It is moving and appropriate to see British and Canadian soldiers of the Jewish faith laid to rest among them. Linguistic hurdles and the dislocations of the post-war world prevented the families of the fallen from contributing epitaphs, but an apposite passage from the Old Testament on the grave of a young Jewish soldier from Tel Aviv, killed in Sicily and buried in Syracuse, sanctifies the memory of the Jews who died for their brethren, a sacrifice redeemed by the rebirth of the Jewish people:

"BEHOLD, I WILL OPEN YOUR GRAVES AND I WILL BRING YOU INTO THE LAND OF ISRAEL."
Driver Eliezer Isaac Freund, Royal Army Service Corps, 17.7.43 (age 20) [SYRACUSE]
[EZEKIEL 37: 12]

FURTHER READING:

Bialystok, Franklin. *Delayed Impact. The Holocaust and the Canadian Jewish Community.* Montreal-Kingston-London-Ithaca: McGill-Queen's University Press, 2000.

Beckman, Morris. *The Jewish Brigade. An Army with Two Masters, 1944–1945.* Staplehurst: Spellmount Limited, 1998.

Brocke, Michael, and Müller, Christiane E. *Haus des Lebens. Jüdische Friedhöfe in Deutschland.* Leipzig: Reclam Verlag, 2001.

Dear, Ian. *Ten Commando 1942–1945.* London: Cooper, 1987.

Dunkelman, Ben. *Dual Allegiance. An Autobiography of Ben Dunkelman.* Toronto: MacMillan, 1976.

Krajewska, Monika. A *Tribute of Stones. Jewish Cemeteries in Poland.* Warsaw: Polish Scientific Publishers Ltd., 1993

Masters, Peter. *Striking Back. A Jewish Commando's War Against the Nazis.* Novato, California: Presidio Press, 1998

McGeer, Eric. "'*Asleep beneath Sicilian skies.* . .' The Canadian War Cemetery at Agira," *Scripta Mediterranea* 24 (2003), 49–66.

Shapiro, Lionel. *They Left the Back Door Open. A Chronicle of the Allied Campaign in Sicily and Italy.* Jarrolds: London, 1944.

van der Horst, Pieter W. *Ancient Jewish Epitaphs. An Introductory Survey of a Millennium of Jewish Funerary Epigraphy (300 BCE–700 CE).* Kampen: Kok Pharos Publishing House, 1991.

CHAPTER ELEVEN

Parta quies
Bretteville-sur-Laize Canadian War Cemetery,
Normandy

ECHOES STEAL BACK TO THE LISTENING HEART.
Corporal Paul Urbanski, RRC, 29.8.44 (age 28)

In the plain south of Caen, beneath the vast canopy of the sky, lies the largest Canadian war cemetery of the Second World War and the second largest of the twenty-two Commonwealth war cemeteries in Normandy. With 2,872 Canadian burials, Bretteville-sur-Laize contains nearly a third again as many graves as its better known and more frequented counterpart at Bény-sur-Mer. The cemetery does not command the dramatic setting and associations germane to Bény-sur-Mer, nor are the architectural effects as grand. It is a more austere place of remembrance that reveals the cost of victory not just in the loss of life but in the thrift of the postwar years. Hedgerow, rather than brick or stone, lines the precincts. The masonry is confined to the colonnade and flanking shelters forming the main gate, centred within the hedge-bordered rectangle of open lawn that spans the front of the cemetery. The original design called for long reflecting pools to be laid out on either side of the entrance; but with the exhaustion of the victors evident in the shortages and rationing that persisted in Britain into the 1950s, budgets were tight, and so the area where the architect had envisioned an elegant forecourt inviting pause and contemplation had to be left vacant. Although the maple trees planted along the borders provide shade and protection, much of the burial ground lies exposed to the elements, to the sun which scorches the lawn during the summer and to the wind which coats the headstones with dust when the surrounding farmlands are busy with cultivation. Yet the modesty of the site magnifies its effect. There is nothing to distract the visitor from the rigid geometry of the headstones and the farewells to young volunteers who forsook their homes and families to enter the alien, lethal world of war:

HE LEFT HOME AND ALL. KILLED IN BATTLE. SLEEPS HERE WITH THE BRAVE. DAD
Private Angus MacDonald, BWC, 23.7.44 (age 30)

A YOUTH NOBLE AND TRUE, WHO LEFT HOME & FRIENDS THAT RIGHT
AND FREEDOM MIGHT NOT DIE.
Gunner Gordon Albert Dewar, RCA, 8.8.44 (age 21)

DEAR GOD, MAKE UP TO HIM FOR THE THINGS HE LOVED HERE ON EARTH. MUM
Private Gordon William Bunn, NS(NB)R, 8.8.44 (age 28)

SOUS LA RAFALE AMÈRE IL TOMBA EN CE LIEU EN PENSANT À SA MÈRE ET À DIEU.
(In the bitter hail of gunfire he fell in this place, thinking of his mother and God)
Rifleman Gaetan Vézina, QORC, 10.8.44 (age 23)

MY DEAR SON WHOSE AFFECTIONATE NATURE ENDEARED HIM TO HIS FRIENDS AND FAMILY.
Gunner Gerald Charles Garceau, RCA, 12.8.44 (age 46)

REST IN PEACE. A LOVING JESUS GAVE YOU AND MAN DENIED YOU.
Lieutenant Maurice Arthur Trudeau, RCIC, 12.8.44 (age 23)

GOD BLESS MY LOVING SON.
Rifleman Roland Joseph Choquette, RWR, 15.8.44 (age 22)

WE LOVED HIM.
Private Louis G. Paul, RRC, 24.8.44 (age 21)

Bény-sur-Mer enshrines the memory of the 3rd Canadian Division which carried the fight from the D-Day landings to the capture of Caen. Bretteville-sur-Laize takes up the sequel. The men buried there belonged to every unit in II Canadian Corps, created when the 2nd Division returned to the continent to lend its weight to the Anglo-Canadian thrust across the Orne river into the green fields beyond. Instead of the decisive armoured breakout sought by the commanders, however, the fighting stayed true to form as an attritional struggle imposing rates of loss approaching Great War ratios of casualties to ground gained. The Germans regarded the plateau between Caen and Falaise as the sector vital to their hold on Normandy, and so they packed their defences in depth along the rises and ridgelines dominating the routes they knew the British and Canadians must take. They set their gunlines to give themselves full observation and fields of fire, and they converted the sturdy Norman hamlets and farms into local strongholds. The battleweary veterans of the 3rd Division and their largely untested comrades of the 2nd Division, supported by their accompanying armoured and artillery units, mounted four major attacks to bore through the German defenders, who resisted just as stubbornly to prevent the Falaise sector from collapsing. The fury of these battles and the toll in lives, disproportionately high among the rifle companies, bulk ever larger in the mind of the visitor walking through the rank and file arrayed in long, silent rows at Bretteville-sur-Laize. The headstones stand over the men killed in the places whose names haunt the story of the road to Falaise—Vaucelles, Louvigny, and Giberville; Tilly-la-Campagne, Rocquancourt, and Fontenay-le-Marmion; Bretteville-le-Rabet, Langannerie, and Quesnay Wood; Barbéry, the Laison River, Clair Tison, and Soulangy; and the hamlet of Cintheaux where a green CWGC sign points the way to the Canadian war cemetery named for the larger village three kilometres away:

IN MEMORY OF A LIFE IN TUNE WITH THE MELODIES OF HEAVEN.
Gunner Albert Elbridge Sargent, RCA, 21.7.44 (age 21)

LIKE A STAR HE HAS CLIMBED TO HIS APPOINTED PLACE IN ETERNITY.
Private Thomas Henry Casey Jones, CH, 25.7.44 (age 28)

SLEEP, BELOVED, 'NEATH HALLOWED GROUND. STRANGE WINDS SWEEP THY CROSS-MARKED MOUND.
Private Frederick Ann Noftall, BWC, 26.7.44 (age 20)

A LA DOUCE MÉMOIRE D'UN PÈRE QUI A SACRIFIÉ SA VIE POUR SA FAMILLE.
(In tender memory of a father who sacrificed his life for his family.)
Sapper Saul Alphie Arsenault, CRCE, 26.7.44 (age 36)

OUR SON. QUIETLY, A HERO. TOO DEARLY LOVED TO BE FORGOTTEN. R.I.P.
Private Joseph Louis Kenneth McCann, BWC, 28.7.44

AND THERE SHALL BE NO NIGHT THERE FOR THE LORD GOD GIVETH HIM LIGHT.
Lance Corporal Gordon William Manels, BWC, 28.7.44 (age 21) [REVELATION 22: 5]

EACH DAY A CHAPTER IN HIS BOOK OF LIFE BEAUTIFULLY WRITTEN AND LIVED. MOTHER, EDITH AND PAUL
Private Jack Ronald Winthers, CH, 1.8.44 (age 20)

YOURS NOT TO REASON WHY, YOURS BUT TO DO AND DIE.
Private Richard Maxwell Dibsor Love, BWC, 5.8.44 (age 32)

BORN IN CANADA. VOLUNTARILY GAVE HIS LIFE FOR WORLD PEACE.
Lance Corporal Allan Edwin Perryman, TSR, 5.8.44 (age 22)

THE FITTEST PLACE WHERE MAN CAN DIE IS WHERE HE DIES FOR MAN.
Gunner Craig Thomas, RCA, 8.8.44 (age 21)

NOT PASSED AWAY, THE LOVE SO RICH, SO TRUE, SO PURE, ONLY A STEP AWAY.
Private Nelson Thomas Boyce, ASHC, 9.8.44 (age 20)

ONE OF CANADA'S BEST. LIKE OTHERS HE DIED THAT WE MIGHT LIVE WITH FREEDOM.
Private Donald Arthur McKellar, AR, 9.8.44

FRANCE, WHERE HEROES LIE, A DEAR LAND THROUGH LOVE'S SWEETEST TIE AND GOD'S UNFAILING GRACE.
Private Allen Norman Gordon, AR, 10.8.44 (age 22)

YOU DID ALL YOU COULD FOR PEACE ON EARTH, GOOD WILL TOWARDS MEN. SADLY MISSED.
Private Glen Howard Fishbach, AR, 10.8.44 (age 24)

DAVE KNEW AND DIED BECAUSE "THE LOVE OF MONEY IS THE ROOT OF ALL EVIL." I. TIM. VI. 10
Private David Ronald Hardy, RHLI, 12.8.44 (age 21)

TO HIM WHO DIED A SOLDIER. "THY NAME IS IN THE GOLDEN BOOK AND ON THE ROLL OF HONOR."
Private Gerald Robert Rafelton, RHLI, 12.8.44 (age 23)

HE WAS LOYAL TO HIS COUNTRY AND GAVE FREELY OF THAT WHICH HE SO RICHLY INHERITED.
Sergeant Paul Albert Roeder, CSR, 12.8.44 (age 25)

HE GAVE THE GREATEST GIFT OF ALL, THE GIFT OF HIS UNFINISHED LIFE.
Private Frank Kenneth Pattinson, RRC, 12.8.44 (age 20)

THAT LOVE SO GREAT BE JUSTIFIED AND THAT THY NAME BE MAGNIFIED.
Lieutenant John Roper Henderson, RCA, 13.8.44 (age 23)

"I AM THE LORD YOUR GOD, AND NONE ELSE: AND MY PEOPLE SHALL NEVER BE ASHAMED"
JOEL II. 27
Gunner Frank James Cornish, RCA, 13.8.44 (age 25)

HE ONLY LIVED BUT TILL HE WAS A MAN, BUT LIKE A MAN HE DIED.
Gunner René Joseph Spooner, RCA, 13.8.44

IL EST NÉ À MONTRÉAL. IL EST DÉCÉDÉ À L'INVASION DE FRANCE. QU'IL REPOSE EN PAIX.
(He was born in Montreal. He died in the invasion of France. May he rest in peace.)
Private Joseph Roland Héroux, FMR, 14.8.44 (age 20)

"THE BOUNDARY STONE OF LIFE BUT NOT OF LOVE."
Captain Charles Graham Sanderson, RCAMC, 14.8.44 (age 27)

FREEDOM WAS ALL. HIS WAS A PART OF IT. HALLOWED HIS MEMORY THROUGH THE YEARS.
Lieutenant Curtis McLam Cole, 1st Hussars, 15.8.44 (age 29)

SOMEWHERE BACK OF THE SUNSET HE LIVES IN GLORY MID THE GOLD AND
BLUE OF THE SKIES.
Rifleman George James Leathwood, RWR, 15.8.44 (age 21)

SLEEP, SOLDIER, SLEEP IN HONORED REST, YOUR TRUTH AND VALOUR WEARING.
Sergeant William Harvey Calmain, RWR, 16.8.44 (age 25)

A TRIBUTE TO A GALLANT CREW WHO DIED THAT WE MIGHT LIVE.
MOTHER, FATHER, AND FAMILY
Lance Corporal Henry Knisley Allinott, RRR, 17.8.44 (age 23)

As the suburbs of Caen creep slowly over the places where the long second act of the Normandy campaign began, the scenes familiar to the veterans who fought there change out of recognition. Beyond the ring road and the urban sprawl it is still possible to enter a world very much as it was in the high summer of 1944, or for that matter, much as it had been for centuries. Turn the paved roads back into tracks, subtract the mechanised transport and farm equipment, and the setting would seem more mediaeval than modern in its rhythms and appearance, with tall church steeples fixing the location of each village like pins in a map. Strangely, it is here, in the places where the passage of time and the hand of man have wrought the least change, where it taxes the imagination to the utmost to picture the tide of battle that surged through these quiet, lonely fields, and the terrible trail strewn in its wake. Save for a scattering of monuments it would be easy to miss the significance of the villages and features where the memories of sorrow felt far away cling to their names:

TOMBÉ À ETAVAUX, À LA TÊTE DE SA COMPAGNIE.
(Fell at Etavaux, at the head of his company)
Major Gérard Vallières, RM, 22.7.44 (age 26)

Half the headstones at Bretteville-sur-Laize bear dates from August of 1944. The fatalities assigned to the first week resulted from the subsidiary attacks carried out by tired battalions to maintain pressure on the eastern side of the Allied front as the Americans exploited their hard-won breakthrough in western Normandy and Brittany. Overshadowed by the dramatic shift in the Normandy campaign are costly minor actions, such as the attacks at Tilly-la-Campagne that account for the headstones of the Calgary Highlanders and the Lincoln and Wellands killed on the first two days of August 1944. Also lost in the swirl of larger events are the actions at the end of the month that took the lustre off the pursuit to the Seine and the liberation of Rouen. These soldiers died in the nasty, forgotten scuffles in the Forêt de la Londe that culled the already depleted ranks of the regiments ordered to persist in attacks memorable only for their needlessness:

PARTED ON EARTH TO MEET IN HEAVEN.
Private Malcolm John Bowern, LWR, 26.8.44 (age 21)
Private Jerry Milton Bowern, LWR, 28.8.44 (age 21)

IN MEMORY OF ANTHONY. KILLED ON ACTIVE SERVICE.
Private Anthony George Surette, RHLI, 28.8.44 (age 31)

IN MEMORY OF RAYMOND WHO SERVED AND STRUGGLED FOR HIS COUNTRY.
HIS LOVING PARENTS
Private Raymond Parisian, SSR, 28.8.44 (age 24)

BENEATH THIS STONE A BRAVE CANADIAN LIES: HE GAVE HIS LIFE THAT WE MIGHT LIVE.
Private Raymond Robert Alexander Speers, ASHC, 28.8.44 (age 24)

AND SO HE PASSED TO LIFE AND LOVE AND PEACE.
Sapper William Wilbert Edge, CRCE, 28.8.44 (age 44)

IN LOVING MEMORY OF "SONNY". A GALLANT FIGHTER.
Corporal Jordan Gordon Clifford Jones, RRC, 28.8.44

HE GAVE HIS ALL. "THE JUDGE OF ALL THE EARTH DOES RIGHT AND HIS NAME IS LOVE."
Private Ole Wyatt Swanson, RRC, 29.8.44 (age 19) [GENESIS 18: 25]

The August fatalities cluster around the two set-piece attacks, Operations Totalize (8 August) and Tractable (14 August), that carried the Canadians to Falaise and beyond in an effort to close the Germans' escape routes out of Normandy. The innovations that distinguish these operations—the use of armoured troop carriers, the staggered barrages and aerial bombardments, night attacks guided forward by tracers and radio beams—were contrived to free the Canadians from the extortionate terms set by the German occupants of a topographical feature synonymous with the worst days in the Norman summer:

> *Three miles or so south of Caen the present-day tourist, driving down the arrow-straight road that leads to Falaise, sees immediately to his right a rounded hill crowned by farm buildings. If the traveller be Canadian, he would do well to stay the wheels at this point and cast his mind back to the events of 1944; for this apparently insignificant eminence is the Verrières ridge. Well may the wheat and sugar-beets grow green and lush upon its gentle slopes, for in that now half-forgotten summer the best blood of Canada was freely poured out upon them.*

Charles Stacey's oft-quoted preface to his account of the battles south of Caen evinces a compassion for the nameless many who did the fighting and the dying seldom expressed in the clinical prose of official histories. To Stacey, as to historians ever since, the punishing contests in the fields and villages along the approaches to the ridge represented the crucible of the Canadian battle in Normandy. Those who follow in their countrymen's footsteps down the road to Falaise today will realise the import of his words if they stand on the crest of the Verrières ridge and gaze back towards Caen. This "apparently insignificant eminence" provided the Germans with a natural rampart overlooking the Anglo-Canadian armour and infantry as they advanced through the fields to the coverless slopes below. In the arena framed by the Orne river valley to the west and the highway to the east, between the crest of the ridge and the southern edges of Caen, nearly a thousand Canadian soldiers died in a week that commenced with Operation Atlantic (18–21 July) and ended with Operation Spring (25 July), one of the country's bravest, and saddest, days of the war.

REPOSE EN PAIX SUR LA TERRE DES AÏEUX. AU REVOIR DANS LA CÉLESTE PATRIE.
*(Rest in peace in the earth of your forefathers. We will see you again
in the heavenly home.)*
Private Robert Mark Quenneville, RC, 18.7.44 (age 19)

FOR KING AND COUNTRY HE DID HIS DUTY WITH A LOYAL HEART. ALWAYS IN OUR THOUGHTS.
Private Alexander Sheriff, BWC, 19.7.44 (age 21)

"THE DAY THOU GAVEST, LORD, IS ENDED."
Major Robert Sladden Wells, SSR, 20.7.44 (age 32)

"THESE ARE THEY WHICH CAME OUT OF GREAT TRIBULATION." REVELATION VII. 14
Private Edward George McCorry, ESR, 21.7.44 (age 21)

WENT THE DAY WELL? WE DIED AND NEVER KNEW, BUT WELL OR ILL, FREEDOM,
WE DIED FOR YOU.
Lieutenant William James Robert Fogerty, ESR, 22.7.44 (age 33)

THOUGH DARK MY ROAD TODAY, SOME DAY I KNOW I'LL TURN A BEND AND FIND YOU THERE.
Gunner Cameron Craib, RCA, 23.7.44 (age 22)

UN CANADIEN FRANÇAIS MORT LOIN DE SON PAYS ET DE SES PARENTS À OTTAWA.
(A French Canadian who died far from his country and his parents in Ottawa)
Private Robert Joseph Gravelle, FMR, 24.7.44 (age 25)

PERHAPS A FRAIL MEMORIAL BUT SINCERE.
Private Innes Ewen, BWC, 25.7.44 (age 20)

The details on the headstones plot the course of the battles for Verrières ridge. The epitaphs quicken the emotional response to a set of events easily retraced today. The best vantage point stands just south of Fleury-sur-Orne where the ground rises like a cresting wave. In 1944 this spur of the Verrières ridge appeared on maps as Point 67, a tactically important piece of ground that served as the Canadian bastion in the fighting that swept back and forth over the approaches to the ridge. Now the site of a battlefield monument bedecked with regimental memorials and a viewing platform, it presides over the scenes of the 2nd Division's first test of arms since Dieppe. Directly ahead the Verrières ridge lines the horizon; to the right is the D562, dipping slightly where it bisects the villages of St. André-sur-Orne and St. Martin-de-Fontenay before rising up to May-sur-Orne. To the west, the village of Etavaux nestles into a bend of the Orne; and beyond, across the river, sits the low mass of Hill 112, the key to Normandy, which gave the Germans full surveillance over the Canadians' right flank. Even to the layman, the task confronting the attackers assumes a menacing clarity: an uphill advance over open ground, one flank exposed, into craftily sited defences manned by an enemy whose positions and weapons tipped the scales in his favour.

THERE IS SOME CORNER OF A FOREIGN FIELD THAT IS FOREVER CANADA.
Private Glyn Walters, SSR, 20.7.44 (age 22)

The Canadian part in the Allied breakout from the Caen bridgehead began well enough. Hard fighting cleared the industrial suburbs on the southern bank of the Orne and brought the necklace of villages along the river into Canadian hands. Once the Calgary Highlanders had struck south from Fleury-sur-Orne to seize Point 67 on 19 July, the final objective in Operation Atlantic, capturing the "Verrières feature", seemed well within reach. A Calgary patrol set off towards St-André, but the fierce German riposte portended the reception in store for the battalions preparing to take up the advance. Two brothers were among the Calgaries killed in the first foray into the villages clustered along the western edge of the ridge:

A FAITHFUL SOLDIER'S NOBLE END. SADLY MISSED.
Private Robert Louis Brown, CH, 19.7.44 (age 29)
Private Theodore Brown, CH, 19.7.44 (age 33)

WE WILL ALWAYS BE TOGETHER ALTHOUGH WE ARE NOT NEAR.
Sergeant Russell Deforest Hudson, CH, 19.7.44 (age 25)

HIS TOILS ARE PASSED, HIS WORK IS DONE. HE FOUGHT THE FIGHT, THE VICTORY WON.
Lance Corporal Menno Wheeler, CH, 19.7.44 (age 28)

Spread before Point 67 are the scenes of Canadian attacks the next day that saw the fortunes of each battalion alternate by the hour. Back, to the east, the ground between Fleury-sur-Orne and Ifs was the assembly area for the South Saskatchewans. They began their advance through fields teeming with waist-high grain that must have reminded so many of them of home. The track leading south from Ifs doubled as the battalion's centre line as it followed timed barrages towards the objectives on the forward slope; today, the gaunt frames of pylons guide the viewer's eye along their route. The forward companies grappled with German infantry lying in wait by the lateral road from St. Martin, but the reserve companies pushed through to the assigned positions on the slope. They were the first to feel the wrath of the enemy counterattacks that came hurtling over the ridge in a blinding rainstorm that disabled the radio sets and deprived the riflemen of air or artillery support. Half who rest beneath the headstones at Bretteville-sur-Laize dated 20th July 1944 perished in the maelstrom that descended on the South Saskatchewans in the fields between the hamlet of Verrières and St. Martin:

HE LIVES ON IN THE REFLECTION OF HIS LIFE WHICH HE SHARED WITH US.
Captain John Lothian Gates, SSR, 20.7.44

"SONNY" THINE WAS THE COURAGE, LAUGHING SOLDIER, BE MINE THE FORTITUDE.
Lieutenant Charles Douglas Grayson, SSR, 20.7.44 (age 24)

IN THE HEARTS OF THOSE WHO LOVE HIM HE DOES NOT DIE.
Lance Sergeant Donald Everett Purvis, SSR, 20.7.44 (age 28)

NO LOVED ONE STOOD NEAR TO SAY GOOD-BYE BUT SAFE IN GOD'S KEEPING NOW YOU LIE.
Private Jerome Albert Malbranck, SSR, 20.7.44 (age 23)

MORT POUR DIEU ET SON PAYS, ET LA LIBÉRATION DES OPPRIMÉS. PRIEZ POUR LUI.
(Died for God and his country, and for the liberation of the oppressed. Pray for him.)
Corporal Maximin Perpete, SSR, 20.7.44 (age 26)

"ANDY" A DEAR HUSBAND AND FATHER. LOVINGLY REMEMBERED BY YOUR WIFE AND SON RUSSELL.
Private Andrew Ross Hunt, SSR, 20.7.44 (age 21)

ALWAYS REMEMBERED THO' YOU REST FAR OUT OF REACH OF THOSE YOU LOVED THE BEST.
Private Robert Reid, SSR, 20.7.44 (age 26)

ELHERVADT VIRÀGOM NYILÓ IDEJÉBEN KIALUDT ÉLETEM MOSOLYGÓ FÉNYÉBEN.
(My flower wilted while still blossoming, my life ended with a smiling light.)
Private Bertrum Sabados, SSR, 20.7.44 (age 21)

GOD LOOKED AND SAW THE STRUGGLE AND WHISPERED, "PEACE BE THINE." LOVE, KATE
Private Harold Kvam, SSR, 20.7.44 (age 37)

The German tanks that prowled like iron predators among the dispersed riflemen also wrought havoc upon the anti-tank guns sent forward to bolster the battalion fortress the Saskatchewans intended to establish on the northern slope of the ridge. Before they could engage the German armour the guns and their crews were intercepted on the move and destroyed. The losses included a French Canadian gunner from Montreal and two brothers from Sault Ste Marie who died within minutes of one another:

IN MEMORY OF MY DEAR SON WHO DIED FOR HIS COUNTRY AND KING. LOVING MOTHER
Gunner Marcel Maisonneuve, RCA, 20.7.44 (age 27)

HIS GLORIOUS YOUTH HE GAVE AND NOW HE LIES, WHERE POPPIES YIELD, IN A SOLDIER'S GRAVE.
Gunner Robert Tasse, RCA, 20.7.44 (age 34)

"SPLENDID YOU PASSED, THE GREAT SURRENDER MADE, INTO THE LIGHT. . ."
Gunner George Tasse, RCA, 20.7.44 (age 29)

The fate of the forward units remained unconfirmed until early August when the Totalize offensive put the ridge in Canadian hands for good. The parties sent to collect the dead found, contrary to the allegations of senior commanders and some historians, that the Saskatchewans had not broken and run, flinging away their weapons in panic, but had offered what opposition they could against the tanks and superior firepower that inevitably overwhelmed them. The epitaphs on these Essex Scottish graves commemorate soldiers who parried the German counterthrust towards Ifs. Left isolated in their flooded slit trenches in the fields east of Point 67, two companies of the Essex held on until they too, for lack of support, were compelled to give way after putting up resistance more tenacious than some have recognised:

THRO' AN OPEN GATE AT THE END OF THE ROAD EACH MUST GO ALONE:
THERE GOD CLAIMS HIS OWN.
Sergeant Joseph Henry Ivison, ESR, 21.7.44 (age 37)

"IN CHRIST SHALL ALL BE MADE ALIVE." "HE IS OUR PEACE." "ABIDE WITH ME."
Corporal Matthew Alexander Brash, ESR, 21.7.44 (age 24)
[I CORINTHIANS 15: 22; EPHESIANS 2: 14]

WAS HE NOT ALSO ENGLAND'S SON. SHE HAD THE FIRST AND GREATER CLAIM.
Lance Corporal Herbert Lawrence Godfrey, ESR, 21.7.44 (age 28)

OUR LOVED ONE.
Private Lloyd Kenneth MacDonald, ESR, 21.7.44 (age 20)

HE GAVE HIS BEST.
Private Raymond John Frizell, ESR, 21.7.44 (age 29)

FOR KING AND COUNTRY. MEMBER OF THE HOUSE OF CROY. 'N'
Private George Eugene Leopold Neyrinck de Croy, ESR, 21.7.44 (age 23)

HERE LIES OUR ONLY SON. GOD CALLED HIM HOME, HIS WORK WAS DONE.
Private Eldon Francis Brox, ESR, 22.7.44 (age 23)

SURVIVED BY HIS WIFE BARBARA LOUDON AND BABY SON THOMAS EDMOND.
TORONTO, CANADA
Lieutenant Thomas Edmond Martin, ESR, 22.7.44

The crisis in the Canadian centre, though serious, was soon stabilised. On either side, the advance turned into protracted duels for possession of the settlements bracketing the lower slope of the ridge. On the left, two farm complexes, Beauvoir and Troteval, straddle the lateral road from St. Martin. They form the base of a triangle whose apex is the hamlet of Verrières about a kilometre south along a track from Troteval farm. Like the Saskatchewans, the Fusiliers Mont-Royal quickly secured their initial objectives on the lateral road, only to see events take a very different turn once they crossed this line. The company that proceeded towards Verrières was engulfed in the same counterattack that soon swirled around the two farms. The ferocity of these actions stares back from the aerial photos taken a few days later showing the fields pockmarked by shells and lacerated by tank treads. For four days the Fusiliers held off repeated attacks until Beauvoir was finally reported lost and the men who had held, lost, and retaken Troteval were withdrawn:

"CURSUM CONSUMMAVI." S. PAUL. DANS LA PAIX ET LA GLOIRE DE DIEU
JE VOUS ATTENDS.
("I have finished my course." St. Paul. In the peace and glory of God I await you.)
Corporal Joseph Alfred René Gaulin, FMR, 21.7.44 (age 21)

MORT DE SES BLESSURES, LAISSANT SON PÈRE, SA MÈRE, TROIS FRÈRES, CINQ SŒURS.
(Died of his wounds, leaving his father, mother, three brothers, five sisters.)
Private André Daoust, FMR, 22.7.44 (age 21)

ICI REPOSE EN PAIX GÉRARD, MORT EN FRANCE POUR SA PATRIE. UNE PRIÈRE S.V.P.
(Here resting in peace is Gerard who died in France for his country. A prayer, please.)
Private Gérard Millaire, FMR, 22.7.44 *(age 22)*

"THE LOVE THAT PAYS THE PRICE, THE LOVE THAT MAKES UNDAUNTED THE FINAL SACRIFICE."
Corporal Maurice Dionne, FMR, 22.7.44 *(age 25)*

ETERNEL SOUVENIR, CHER ENFANT, QUI A PAYÉ DE TA VIE LA RANÇON DE NOTRE PAIX.
(Eternal remembrance, dear child, who paid with your life the ransom of our peace.)
Private Gabriel Bonneau, FMR, 23.7.44 *(age 20)*

IL ÉTAIT ICI-BAS NOTRE CONSOLATION, MAINTENANT, NOTRE ANGE GARDIEN.
(On this earth he was our consolation; now, our guardian angel.)
Sergeant Gérald Michaud, FMR, 25.7.44 *(age 24)*

FILS DE J.A. NOEL, MONTRÉAL, CANADA. MORT EN DEFENDANT LE PAYS DE SES ANCÊTRES.
(Son of J.A. Noel, Montreal, Canada. Died defending the land of his ancestors.)
Private Joseph Noel, FMR, 26.7.44 *(age 34)*

FILS DE M. ET MDE. ROCHETTE, PONT DE QUÉBEC. MORT POUR SA PATRIE.
(Son of Mr. and Mrs. Rochette, Pont de Québec. Died for his country.)
Private Georges Forgues, FMR, 26.7.44 *(age 25)*

Only on the right did the Cameron Highlanders gain a tenuous grip on the objective. Their war diary describes a different kind of battle than the one their comrades were fighting in the fields to their left. The Camerons got into St-André, a typical Norman village composed of stone houses, orchards, and walled enclosures, where neither attackers nor defenders could dislodge the other. Of the many toilsome obstacles blocking the way over the Verrières ridge, the villages and the notorious factory zone with its subterranean dens of mineshafts and tunnels, proved the most intractable. Like the hydra, the seemingly vanquished enemy kept resurfacing to strike at the battalions working their way along the road to May-sur-Orne. It would take three weeks and hundreds of casualties before the Canadians controlled the area between the Point 67 memorial and the church steeple crowning the western side of the ridge. The Camerons' travails in St-André went on for days:

HOWARD, BELOVED HUSBAND, FATHER AND ONLY SON. FOREVER WITH THE LORD.
Captain Howard Grundy, QOCHC, 20.7.44 *(age 26)*

ONE, OF MANY, WHO FOUGHT FOR THOSE HE LOVED. DAVID WILL EVER BE REMEMBERED WITH PRIDE.
Private John David McKay, QOCHC, 20.7.44 *(age 28)*

HE RESTS IN THE SWEET AND BLESSED COUNTRY, THE HOME OF GOD'S ELECT.
Lance Corporal Nels David Johnson, QOCHC, 21.7.44 *(age 26)*

I HAVE LAID DOWN MY LIFE THAT YOU MAY LIVE. BE EVER GRATEFUL AND PRAY FOR ME.
Private Edward Stanley Eyahpaise, QOCHC, 21.7.44 *(age 25)*

HE IS OUR HERO WHO DIED FOR FREEDOM'S SAKE.
Private John Peter Saleski, QOCHC, 21.7.44 *(age 19)*

DEAR SON, IN MY LONELY HOURS THOUGHTS OF YOU ARE EVER NEAR. MOTHER
Private John Albert McKay, QOCHC, 21.7.44 *(age 28)*

HE DID HIS BEST. HE GAVE HIS ALL THAT WE MIGHT BE FREE.
Corporal Thomas James Vernon Grundy, QOCHC, 24.7.44 (age 27)

"BUT MEMORY IS THE ONLY FRIEND THAT GRIEF CAN CALL ITS OWN."
Corporal Robert Percival Peters, QOCHC, 29.7.44 (age 35)

The advantages of terrain and position that accrued to the defenders in Normandy forced the attackers into a series of laborious frontal assaults. Some of these operations aimed at achieving breakthroughs, others at keeping the Germans committed to one sector so as to allow the Allies to strike in another. Operation Spring fits into the latter category. That it fulfilled its purpose in holding the German armoured units on the eastern end of the Allied front while the Americans punched their way through in the west only underlines the thanklessness of the task set the regiments ordered to make the second try for the Verrières ridge:

TITLES OF HONOUR ADD NOT TO HIS WORTH WHO HIMSELF IS AN HONOUR TO HIS TITLE.
Lieutenant Hubert Frederick Pedlar, BWC, 25.7.44 (age 24)

FOR HONOR AND GLORY WE DIE.
Gunner Edward Charles Kidston, RCA, 25.7.44 (age 38)

A LIFE LINKED WITH MY OWN. DAY BY DAY I MISS HIM MORE AS I WALK THROUGH LIFE ALONE.
Private James Palmer, NNSH, 25.7.44 (age 25)

IN SACRED AND LOVING MEMORY OF MY DEAR SON. HIS SUN HAS GONE DOWN
WHILE IT WAS YET DAY.
Private James O'Neill, RRC, 25.7.44 (age 23)

TO ALL HONOUR AND GLORY.
Major George Henry Basil Stinson, RHLI, 25.7.44 (age 29)

It is hard not to surmise that when Stacey penned his tribute to the best blood of Canada, he was thinking above all of the Black Watch going open-eyed into an attack which promised to be "a dicey proposition" at best. The Black Watch was not the only regiment that bled half to death in Operation Spring, but in bare outline their attack would pass for an account of the first day on the Somme. A young, courageous officer, new to battle, decided to proceed as the plan called for, despite a tactical picture gone awry, and led his men unflinchingly, under continuous fire, into the teeth of the German defences. For all the attempts to reconstruct the train of events that led to the annihilation of the attacking companies (fifteen men returned unscathed), the story of the Black Watch at Verrières ridge retains the stark simplicity of a Greek tragedy moving to a terrible, ineluctable ending:

"THAT THEY MIGHT HAVE LIFE." "AND ALL THE TRUMPETS SOUNDED FOR HIM
ON THE OTHER SIDE."
Major Frederick Philip Griffin, BWC, 25.7.44 (age 26)

Visible above the crest of Verrières ridge, directly opposite Point 67, is a tall white water tower. This incongruous but useful marker indicates the location on the reverse slope of Fontenay-le-Marmion. On the forward slope, to the right, the ground descends in an easy gradient towards St-Martin. The diagonal line between the two villages was the route taken by the Black Watch of Canada on the morning of July 25. A farm track just outside St-Martin that marked their start line is still used, and despite the housing developments edging out from the village you can walk through the same fields up towards the trees along the crest. This approach across open ground to the objective at Fontenay-le-Marmion exposed them to crossfire from the German machine guns, mortars, and tanks dug in along the ridge ahead of them and in May-sur-Orne to their right. With their ranks thinning by the minute they pressed on to the crest of the ridge where their commander ordered the remaining few to go back. Over three hundred headstones in Bretteville-sur-Laize bear the date 25th July 1944. One in three identifies a soldier of The Black Watch (Royal Highland Regiment) of Canada:

"THERE IS MUSIC IN THE MIDST OF DESOLATION AND A GLORY THAT SHINES UPON OUR TEARS."
Lieutenant Alan Reginald Wynne Robinson, BWC, 25.7.44 (age 25)

MIZPAH. FOR EVER REMEMBERED BY ALL.
Sergeant Victor Leonard Foam, BWC, 25.7.44 (age 26)

HE, HAVING LIVED A SHORT TIME, FULFILLED A LONG TIME.
Sergeant Fred Plewes Janes, BWC, 25.7.44 (age 33)

THE LORD REDEEMETH THE SOUL OF HIS SERVANTS. PSALM XXXIV. 22
Sergeant John Gordon Anderson, BWC, 25.7.44 (age 24)

GOD MADE HIM A LITTLE LOWER THAN ANGELS, CROWNED HIM WITH GLORY AND HONOUR.
Corporal William Steel, BWC, 25.7.44 (age 27)

WE WERE BLESSED WITH JOYS DENIED TO SOME; IN EACH OTHER'S HEART WE HAD A HOME.
Corporal Daniel Sheehan, BWC, 25.7.44 (age 30)

YOU ARE AT REST NOW.
Corporal George Mervyn Gale, BWC, 25.7.44 (age 33)

IN THE PRIDE OF HIS DAYS HIS LIFE WAS SHORTENED BY FATE'S MYSTERIOUS WAYS.
LOVING FAMILY
Lance Corporal Joseph Chomyshyn, BWC, 25.7.44 (age 23)

THE GIFT OF GOD IS ETERNAL LIFE THROUGH JESUS CHRIST OUR LORD. ROMANS VI. 23
Private Richard Harold Dawson, BWC, 25.7.44 (age 22)

FOREVER WITH THE LORD. AMEN, SO LET IT BE
Private Findlay Buchanan, BWC, 25.7.44 (age 19)

DEAD HE IS NOT BUT DEPARTED FOR THE CHRISTIAN NEVER DIES.
Private Milton Thomas Hannah, BWC, 25.7.44 (age 19)

"WHILE THE BATTLE RAGED AND WILD WINDS BLEW, I HEARD HIS VOICE
AND PERFECT PEACE I KNEW"
Private James William Cockburn, BWC, 25.7.44 (age 22)

"WHEN OTHER HELPERS FAIL AND COMFORTS FLEE, HELP OF THE HELPLESS,
O ABIDE WITH ME."
Private Robert John Barrie, BWC, 25.7.44 (age 30)

EVER REMEMBERED BY HELEN, KATY AND FAMILIES.
Private Cornelius Peter Buhler, BWC, 25.7.44 (age 34)

**REST IN PEACE, OUR BELOVED YOUNG SON. THO' IN A STRANGE LAND
YOU ARE NOT ALONE.**
Private Harvey Frank Booth, BWC, 25.7.44 (age 19)

Normandy holds pride of place in Canadian memories of the Second World War. It was here that the eventual defeat of Nazi Germany and liberation of Europe were assured, and it is in Normandy that Canada's effort and sacrifice are most dramatically displayed. But the summer that was already half-forgotten by 1960 when Stacey published *The Victory Campaign* is now in the twilight of living memory. The events and effects of the Second World War will never pass from memory; rather, what we are losing is direct contact with those events and effects as the people who went through the war, felt its impact, and lived with its consequences fade from our midst. With their parting go their habits of thinking, their realms of experience, and the idioms of their popular culture, as the epitaphs reveal in small but telling ways. Melodies once familiar and emotive now pass us by like the utterances of a foreign language. How many today would recognise the words, or feel the reflex of emotion, of songs from the 1930s and 1940s—for instance, Gene Autry's 1935 hit that for this husband and wife may have been "their song"?

YOU'RE THE ONLY STAR IN MY BLUE HEAVEN AND YOU'RE SHINING FOR ME. DEVOTED WIFE
Gunner Charles William Bunnell, RCA, 9.6.44 (age 26)

Reminiscences of romance, and the yearning for a lost husband linger in the song lyrics chosen as epitaphs by the wives of these two soldiers. The first quotes the title and refrain of a number one hit recorded by Bing Crosby in 1940, a song that kindles hopes of lasting love and the accumulation of memories over the years:

"ONLY FOREVER."
Major Thomas Spencer Baron, BCD, 9.8.44 (age 38)

> *Do I want to be with you*
> *As the years come and go?*
> *Only forever. . .*
> *Do you think I'll remember*
> *How you look when you smile?*
> *Only forever. . .*

Noel Coward's *I'll See You Again* turns on the refrain quoted in this epitaph. The lyrics dwell wistfully on the parting of love, the passage of time, and the promise to remember past happiness—*"All my life I shall remember knowing you, all the pleasure I have had in showing you the different ways. . ."*

WHAT HAS BEEN IS PAST FORGETTING.
Private Gordon Louis Thompson, RCASC, 14.10.44 (age 36)

> *I'll see you again*
> *When spring breaks through again*
> *Time may lie heavy between*
> *But what has been*
> *Is past forgetting. . .*

Another echoes the final words of Charles Dickens's A Tale of Two Cities. The novel was once standard fare in high-school English courses, but it might not raise an eyebrow in recognition quite so quickly today. Passersby familiar with the book, however, would connect the words on this soldier's headstone with the story of a man who gives his life to save another man and his family during the French Revolution:

THIS IS A FAR GREATER PEACE I GO TO THAN I HAVE EVER KNOWN.
Private William Lester Fish, ESR, 27.8.44 (age 34)

As he goes to the guillotine, Sidney Carton looks out over the Paris streets and foresees a happier world emerging one day from the chaotic present. He imagines the family he has rescued living safely and contentedly, cherishing the memory of his selfless act for the rest of their lives and passing his name down through the generations. This consoling vision enables him to face death bravely, as perhaps the self-sacrifice and acceptance portrayed in this famous story comforted the parents who framed the loss of their son in its image.

GOD GAVE ME COURAGE BUT WHAT IT MEANT TO LOSE HIM NONE WILL EVER KNOW. ELSIE
Private Roy Edgar Sager, HLIC, 1.8.44 (age 23)

WE MISS HIM MORE EACH DAY. FRIENDS KNOW NOT THE SORROW WITHIN OUR HEARTS CONCEALED.
Gunner Valentine Solomon Crawford, RCA, 20.7.44 (age 44)

IN MEMORY OF OUR HERO. WIFE AND CHILDREN, MOTHER, FATHER, BROTHER AND SISTERS
Gunner Gerrard Joseph Roy, RCA, 8.8.44 (age 21)

SON OF W.A. AND E.M. TEMPLETON AND BELOVED HUSBAND OF GEORGIE D. SCOTT.
Gunner William Templeton, RCA, 21.7.44 (age 31)

SON OF W.A. AND E.M. TEMPLETON AND BELOVED HUSBAND OF CYNTHIA I.M. SPINK.
Lieutenant Robert Keith Templeton, TSR, 14.8.44 (age 25)

IN LOVING MEMORY OF MY BELOVED HUSBAND. YOUR LOVING WIFE, GAIL AND STAN
Corporal Stanley Seivewright, CSR, 15.8.44 (age 23)

VICTORY WON, YOUR DUTY DONE, NOW WITH THY BROTHER WHO LIES IN FRANCE. JUST SLEEP IN PEACE, DEAR SON.
Private John Seivewright, PPCLI, 1.9.44 (age 25) [MONTECCHIO]

Canadians will never again know firsthand the experience of war so widespread among their forebears during the first half of the twentieth century. Nor will we ever know to the same degree the anxiety and tension felt across the country in 1944 as thousands of telegrams, opening with the ominous formula *"Regret to inform you. . ."*, streamed forth from the Ministry of National Defence. The penultimate year of the war began with the last shots at Ortona and carried on through the battles in the Liri Valley before the long anticipated Normandy invasion claimed centre stage. The second half of 1944 saw Canada's war effort reach its peak, with the army fighting on two fronts, the RCAF heavily engaged in the air war, and the RCN assuming an ever greater role at sea. The closer victory came, however, the higher the price in lives. The families of seven soldiers buried in Bretteville had already lost a son; six were to lose two sons in Normandy, and a second loss awaited nine families as the Canadians advanced through the Low Countries and on into Germany. These losses came years, months, or just a few weeks apart:

TO THE GLORY OF GOD AND IN MEMORY OF OUR BELOVED SON BRUCE.
"THY WILL BE DONE"
Lieutenant Bruce Wilson, BCR, 13.8.44 (age 25)

TO THE GLORY OF GOD AND IN MEMORY OF OUR BELOVED SON CAYLEY.
"THY WILL BE DONE"
Pilot Officer John Cayley Wilson, RCAF, 9.11.41 (age 27)
[WESTKERKE CHURCHYARD]

ASLEEP IN JESUS. EVER MISSED BY PARENTS AND FAMILY.
Private Gilbert McWilliams, LER, 5.8.43 (age 22) [AGIRA]

ASLEEP IN JESUS. SADLY MISSED BY PARENTS AND FAMILY.
Private Ira McWilliams, CSR, 15.8.44 (age 19)

IN LIFE, LOVED AND HONORED. IN DEATH, REMEMBERED.
Sergeant Jack MacIver, SSTCA, 23.5.44 (age 20) [BEACH HEAD]
Private Donald MacIver, ASHC, 5.8.44 (age 20)

"THE CAPTAIN SPEAKS. HIS WORD OBEY, SO SHALL THY STRENGTH BE AS THY DAY"
Private Douglas Albert Henry Boutilier, RHLI, 29.8.44 (age 23)

SOLDIERS WHO ARE CHRIST'S BELOW, STRONG IN FAITH RESIST THE FOE.
Corporal William Charles Boutilier, LWR, 10.9.44 (age 22) [ADEGEM]

"THY DEAD MEN SHALL LIVE, TOGETHER WITH MY DEAD BODY SHALL THEY ARISE."
ISAIAH XXVI. 19
Lance Bombardier Henry George Dyke, RCA, 10.8.44 (age 25)

"LET ME DIE THE DEATH OF THE RIGHTEOUS AND LET MY LAST END BE LIKE HIS."
Private Victor Edward Dyke, SSR, 13.10.44 (age 22) [BERGEN-OP-ZOOM] [NUMBERS 23: 10]

HE LIVES NOT IN HEAVEN ALONE BUT IN HEARTS TO WHICH HIS MEMORY IS A PRESENCE.
Gunner Walter Carlyle Little, RCA, 22.7.44 (age 39)

"THERE IS NO DEATH! WHAT SEEMS SO IS TRANSITION."
Lieutenant Kenneth Wayne Little, SAR, 28.1.45 (age 35) [GROESBEEK]

Valedictions from three generations juxtapose the distance and the links between the Second World War and the present. What is to us just a name spoke for a whole life in the memory of bereaved parents:

THERE IS NOT A DAY, DEAR MALCOLM, THAT WE DO NOT THINK OF YOU.
Private Malcolm James Cook, NS(NB)R, 8.8.44 (age 20)

OUR BELOVED BERT.
Lance Corporal Frederick Adelbert Skinner, RRC, 29.8.44 (age 20)

WE, WHO ARE LEFT BEHIND, SHALL NEVER BREAK FAITH WITH YOU, EMMETT.
Lieutenant Emmett Joseph Dillon, ASH, 5.8.44 (age 24)

Pledges of lasting love and memory from parents become more affecting when we remember that they come from people born over a hundred years ago, most before the turn of the twentieth century, who have long since served their day. Their farewells are weighted with the pathos of latter years darkened by loss and loneliness, and the awareness, more keenly felt in the second half of life, that human memory, no matter how faithful and true, is finite:

MEMORIES OF YOU SHALL LINGER ON LONG AFTER THE DAYS ARE ALL GONE. FAMILY
Lance Sergeant Stanley Bernard Leszczynski, QORC, 10.8.44 (age 23)

A SILENT THOUGHT IN MEMORY'S CHORD IS GENTLY TOUCHED EVERY DAY. MOTHER & DAD
Corporal Victor Ernest Maynard, BCR, 23.8.44 (age 23)

WE WILL ALWAYS REMEMBER OUR SON THOUGH THE REST OF THE WORLD MAY FORGET.
Lance Corporal Pete Trakalo, QOCHC, 16.8.44 (age 27)

WE SHALL REMEMBER HIM AS HE WAS, A DEAR SON AND A GOOD BRAVE LAD.
Flying Officer William Harold Morrison, RCAF, 15.8.44 (age 23)

HIS BEST MEMORIES ARE IN THE HEARTS OF THOSE WHO KNEW AND LOVED HIM.
Private Winston Irvine Doherty, RHLI, 12.8.44 (age 19)

MAY YOU REST IN PEACE, OUR BELOVED SON, YOUR LOVE NEVER TO BE FORGOTTEN.
Private Leslie Albert Yates, LWR, 11.8.44 (age 22)

MOST DEAR TO US, MOST BRAVE AND GLORIOUS. LOVING FATHER, MOTHER AND SISTER
Trooper Everett Eugene Borgald, BCR, 23.8.44 (age 23)

YOU WERE THE KIND OF SON YOUR LOVED ONES NEVER FORGET.
Private Edward Floyd Crosson, RHLI, 25.8.44 (age 23)

WE ARE PROUD OF OUR BOY WHO DID A MAN'S JOB. HE WILL NEVER BE FORGOTTEN.
Private Robert John Stansbury, BWC, 5.8.44 (age 20)

OUR ONLY SON. HIS MEMORY LIVETH.
Lieutenant Bernard Perry Jennings, CRCE, 14.8.44 (age 21)

GONE TO JOIN HIS MOTHER.
Lieutenant Edward Drew Glass, RCIC, 15.8.44 (age 20)

The years of loneliness and regret stretched longer before young wives, widowed in their twenties and thirties. Doubtless some went on to remarry and to make new lives, but these epitaphs speak for all who retained memories of a life broken off from their own:

I LEAVE HIM SLEEPING, LIFE'S RACE WELL WON. A TRUST MY HEART IS KEEPING
TILL LIFE IS DONE.
Corporal Hugh George Paterson, BCR, 9.8.44 (age 28)

MY BELOVED HUSBAND WHO GAVE HIS LIFE THAT I MIGHT LIVE.
MAY HIS NAME LIVE ON. R.I.P.
Signalman George Gadsdon, RCCS, 14.8.44 (age 24)

TILL THE END OF LIFE'S STORY I'LL CHERISH THEE BECAUSE GOD MADE THEE MINE.
Lance Sergeant Harold Edward Spaetzel, HLIC, 12.8.44 (age 23)

WHEREVER I AM, WHATEVER I DO, ALWAYS, DEAR HAROLD, I'M THINKING OF YOU. WIFE EVELYN
Private Harold Stephen Odrowski, RHLI, 8.8.44 (age 27)

IN MEMORY OF DAVID. BELOVED HUSBAND OF FERN. THE FRUIT OF THE SPIRIT
IS LOVE, JOY, PEACE. . .
Trooper David Andres, SFR, 13.8.44 (age 24) [GALATIANS 5: 22]

R.I.P. ICI REPOSE SUR LE SOL DE FRANCE L'ÉPOUX BIEN-AIMÉ DE
EMERENTIENNE NOEL.
(R.I.P. Here in the earth of France lies the beloved husband of Emerentienne Noel.)
Private Arthur Paquin, RM, 6.8.44 (age 32)

"HIS ARMOUR LAID DOWN, HIS BATTLE WON." ALWAYS REMEMBERED
BY HIS WIFE MURIEL.
Private Henry Evers, RCASC, 14.8.44 (age 29)

KEEPING YOU IN MEMORY AS I SAW YOU LAST. I, WHO LOVED YOU, NEVER FORGET.
LOVING WIFE, EDITH.
Sergeant James Elliott Main, SSR, 14.8.44 (age 24)

TODAY AS EVERY DAY I REMEMBER. SADLY MISSED. WIFE VELMA
Private Thomas Bernard Vincent, QOCHC, 22.8.44 (age 32)

A MEMORY, DEAR HUBBY, I WILL TREASURE MY WHOLE LIFE THROUGH.
LOVING WIFE EDITH
Corporal John Lewis Slade, RHLI, 29.8.44 (age 33)

Scattered throughout Bretteville-sur-Laize are reminders that many of these young soldiers were also young fathers, whose images still flicker in fragments of childhood recollections, or whose deaths left a void in the lives of the children who never knew them. These inscriptions serve notice that the effects of a war fought over sixty years ago will be felt for some time to come:

IN OUR MEMORY YOU WILL REMAIN EVER DEAR. WIFE ANNA AND BABY SHARON ROSE
Private Thomas Duncan, CSR, 8.6.44 (age 26)

PROUDLY WE SALUTE YOU, SOLDIER. WIFE AND LITTLE SON RONNIE.
Lance Corporal Herbert Emery Ripley, 14th CH, 14.7.44 (age 24)

EVERLOVING MEMORY OF JIM. WITH HIM I SPENT MY HAPPIEST DAYS.
WIFE HELEN & DAUGHTER ENID.
Private Wilfred James Collier, CH, 20.7.44 (age 26)

HUSBAND OF EVELYN E. FORSTER. FATHER OF LORNA, WAYNE AND VINCENT.
Sapper Arthur William McFarlane, CRCE, 21.7.44 (age 26)

TON SOUVENIR SERA TOUJOURS VIVACE DANS MON CŒUR ET CELUI DE TA FILLE.
(Your memory will always be alive in my heart and in your daughter's.)
Sergeant John Joseph McCann, BWC, 28.7.44 (age 32)

ALWAYS REMEMBERED BY HIS WIFE AND SON IN ENGLAND AND HIS FAMILY IN CANADA.
Flying Officer Douglas Keith Moores, RCAF, 3.8.44 (age 22)

EN MÉMOIRE DE MON ÉPOUX QUI LAISSE SON ÉPOUSE ET SON FILS INCONSOLABLE.
(In memory of my husband who leaves his wife and his inconsolable son.)
Corporal Laurent Loranger, RM, 8.8.44 (age 29)

HE GAVE HIS LIFE SO THAT HIS WIFE GLADYS AND SON DOUGLAS MIGHT LIVE IN PEACE.
Private Norman George Ellis, ESR, 8.8.44 (age 23)

ALWAYS LOVED AND REMEMBERED BY HIS WIFE NORA AND LITTLE DAUGHTER PEGGIE.
Private Kenneth Hendren, RCASC, 8.8.44 (age 30)

IN LOVING MEMORY OF OUR SOLDIER DADDY. SADLY MISSED BY THREE HOLMES.
Gunner Wilfred Murray Holmes, RCA, 10.8.44 (age 28)

LOVED IN LIFE, IN DEATH JUST THE SAME. FOR EVER MISSED BY HIS
LOVING WIFE AND BABIES.
Sergeant Jack Grimmer, SSR, 14.8.44 (age 30)

"HYIE" ALWAYS LOVED BY YOUR WIFE KATE AND SON GRANT.
Private Henry Gilbert, CSR, 15.8.44 (age 21)

SURVIVORS ARE HIS WIFE ESTELLE AND TWO CHILDREN, ROGER AND LORRAINE.
Private Ernest Tourville, ASHC, 15.8.44 (age 26)

BELOVED DADDY OF KAYE.
Corporal James Marvan Dougherty, GGFG, 20.8.44 (age 26)

IN MEMORY OF DADDY. NOT JUST TODAY BUT EVERY DAY IN SILENCE WE REMEMBER.
Gunner Stanley Parker, RCA, 23.8.44 (age 25)

YOU FOUGHT AND DIED BRAVELY. WE ARE PROUD. YOUR WIFE, SON AND DAUGHTER.
Private William Hugh Cameron, SSR, 28.8.44 (age 25)

SURVIVING BESIDES HIS WIDOW ANNIE IS ONE SON, D. ROY WHO NEVER SAW HIS DADDY.
Private Roy Burnett Clarke, CH, 25.7.44 (age 23)

As the memory of the Second World War becomes more historical than personal, more objective than subjective, the war cemeteries acquire a different kind of significance. They keep a remnant of the vanishing past for the living present to reflect upon, whether the causes and consequences of a war that pitted civilization against barbarism, or its imprint on the lives of the ordinary human beings who walked the earth with the great names of the time, Churchill, Roosevelt, Eisenhower, Montgomery. They will endure as tributes to the fallen and the victory they helped to achieve while stating, headstone by headstone, the cost in human lives. They will preserve a register of the debt owed to a generation that, no matter the evils to come, prevented an incomparable evil from destroying the foundations on which democratic, civilized countries rest. The tens of thousands who died to stop this deserve better than anonymity.

ALWAYS WILL YOUR NAME, HONOUR AND GLORY REMAIN. WE MISS YOU, SON.
LOVE, MOTHER AND DAD
Lance Corporal Robert Stanley Louis Cline, NS(NB)R, 8.8.44 (age 20)

Among the thousands of personal inscriptions inscribed on Canadian headstones, there happen to be five similarly worded valedictions found in Normandy and nowhere else. All are taken from the same passage in the *Aeneid* of Virgil, the epic poem which tells of the wanderings and struggles of the Trojan hero Aeneas as he leads his people to a new land:

ALWAYS WILL YOUR HONOUR AND YOUR NAME AND YOUR GLORY REMAIN. VIRGIL
Lieutenant David Gordon Hilborn, RCIC, 29.6.44 (age 23) [HOTTOT-LES-BAGUES]

ALWAYS WILL YOUR HONOUR AND YOUR NAME AND YOUR GLORY REMAIN.
Lieutenant James Gordon Sloane, ASHC, 5.8.44 (age 24)

ALWAYS WILL YOUR HONOUR, YOUR NAME AND YOUR GLORY REMAIN. EXETER, CANADA
Flight Lieutenant Clifford Waldron Hicks, RCAF, 8.8.44 (age 22)

WHILE RIVERS RUN TO THE OCEAN ALWAYS WILL YOUR HONOUR AND GLORY REMAIN.
Bombardier Robert Spring, RCA, 23.8.44 (age 24)

In the course of their wanderings, Aeneas and his fellow refugees are shipwrecked near the city of Carthage. They beseech the city's queen, Dido, to offer them shelter and help. This she readily agrees to do. Her magnanimous, humane reply, *"no stranger to misfortune myself, I have learned to come to the aid of others in distress,"* underlies her decision. In gratitude, Aeneas assures her that *"as long as the rivers run to the ocean, the shadows glide over the mountain vales, and the heavens nourish the stars,"* in other words, as long as the natural world shall last, *"always will your name, your honour, and your glory remain."* Within the larger compass of the poem, however, this promise has a sad ring, since it foreshadows the end in store for Dido—*"a death neither deserved nor fated, but miserable and before her time,"* set in motion, ironically, by the noble gesture which will earn her everlasting remembrance.

This exchange between Aeneas and Dido follows closely upon the most famous passage in the *Aeneid*, where the hero's encounter with the past elicits reactions which must in some way parallel those felt by visitors to the war cemeteries today. On his way through Carthage Aeneas comes upon a temple decorated with friezes depicting scenes from the Trojan War. The setting of the temple, secluded within a grove, and the skill of the artisans who built it fill him with admiration; but the friezes confront him with memories of strife and suffering that reduce him to tears. They illustrate episodes universal in war—the ebb and flow of combat, the slaughter of whole contingents, and the death of mere boys:

FERVENT CHRÉTIEN, FIER ET BRAVE SOLDAT, REPOSE DANS LA PAIX DU SEIGNEUR.
(Devout Christian, soldier proud and brave, rest in the peace of the Lord.)
Private Gérard Doré, FMR, 23.7.44 (age 16)

HE LEFT HIS HOME TO GO TO WAR AND LOST HIS LIFE ON A DISTANT SHORE.
Private Roy Taylor, CH, 1.8.44 (age 16)

TO LIVE IN THE HEARTS OF THOSE THAT LOVED ME IS NOT TO DIE.
Rifleman Roger Stewart, RRR, 16.8.44 (age 17)

"HIS GLORY IS ABOVE THE EARTH." GLORY FOR EVERMORE.
Trooper Harvey Walton, SAR, 21.8.44 (age 17)

MY ONLY SON GAVE HIS LIFE FOR HIS COUNTRY.
Private Anford Joseph Magoon, CH, 26.8.44 (age 18)

OUR DARLING LIES HERE. ALL YOU WHO PASS BY, PRAY FOR HIM.
Private Robert Waugh, RRC, 29.8.44 (age 18)

The depictions of war go beyond the battlefield to record the duress of the womenfolk whose prayers for deliverance are fated to go unheeded. Central in these portrayals of the suffering war inflicts on all is the powerful scene in which Priam ransoms the body of his son Hector. The sight summons from Aeneas the greatest lines in the poem: *"Here, too, honour receives its due; here are the tears of the world, and the sorrows of human beings touch the heart"* . . . *So he spoke, feeding his soul on a picture that had no life.*

Father Owen Lee, the most perceptive commentator on this passage, has seen in these words Virgil's admission of the limits of his poem, and by extension, of all works of art that address human suffering in war. They can honour the memory of those who died, give meaning to their sacrifice, and offer the solace of dignified remembrance to the mourners. Yet, like Aeneas gazing at pictures that had no life, the visitor beholding the graves in a war cemetery is aware that no commemoration can restore to the fallen what they have lost. Nothing can give them their lives back.

BE STRONG AND OF GOOD COURAGE, FEAR NOT, FOR THE LORD WILL BE WITH THEE.
Trooper Ralph Kenneth Goode, 1st Hussars, 14.8.44 (age 23)

HIS SPIRIT LIVES WHILE GOOD MEN WALK THE EARTH. MOTHER, JUNE, ISOBEL AND MARG.
Lieutenant Ross Charles Fawthrop, SDGH, 22.8.44 (age 25)

The sorrows of human beings that wring tears from Aeneas, however, have another effect on him. He has come upon these saddening memories at the nadir of his fortunes, shipwrecked, lost, his fate in the hands of strangers, and yet his grief is tempered by pride. Upon seeing the renown of his comrades who fought at Troy he feels his courage and sense of purpose come trickling back: *"Here, for the first time, he dared to hope that he had found safety, and to have greater faith even though his fortunes were in ruins."* The good name that his countrymen have left upon the earth reminds him that the past, although painful to recall, also bequeaths a record of bravery, fortitude, and right conduct, that can brace the survivors left to carry on, and inspire their descendants:

WHO THROUGH FAITH WAXED VALIANT IN FIGHT. HE LED HIS MEN ALL THE WAY.
Corporal John James Watson, BWC, 22.7.44 (age 27)

HE GAVE HIS LIFE WHOLLY AND FREELY, NOT CARELESSLY, BUT THOUGHTFUL OF US ALL.
Lieutenant Laird Weldon Blakney, CH, 1.8.44 (age 23)

HE GAVE ALL THAT CHILDREN EVERYWHERE COULD GROW IN PEACE, TRUST AND FAITH.
Sergeant William Louis Flath, CH, 1.8.44 (age 28)

IL LAISSE DEUX SOUVENIRS: CELUI DE CE QU'IL ÉTAIT, CELUI DE CE QU'IL A FAIT.
(He leaves two memories: what he was, and what he did.)
Private Roger Bourdages, NS(NB)R, 8.8.44 (age 22)

PREPARED AS A SCOUT TO SERVE HIS GOD AND KING.
LOVINGLY REMEMBERED AT HOME.
Sergeant Arthur Frederick Moore, 1st Hussars, 8.8.44 (age 37)

LORD, HAVE MERCY ON THIS GOOD SOLDIER: IN OUR HEARTS LIVES HIS BRAVE SPIRIT.
Lance Corporal Thomas Ryan, CGG, 8.8.44 (age 21)

THE FIRE OF YOUR SPIRIT CANNOT DIE. THE VALUE OF YOUR GIFT CAN NEVER FADE.
Private Hughie Munro, SDGH, 12.8.44 (age 25)

MAY YOUR GALLANT SPIRIT EVER BE NEAR US.
Captain Harry Edward Dickson, RRR, 13.8.44 (age 26)

DEARLY LOVED. A MAN OF STERLING CHARACTER GONE HOME TO BE WITH THE LORD.
Gunner Charles Clarence Frederick Mattie, RCA, 13.8.44 (age 31)

A GALLANT SOLDIER RESTS. HE LOVED HIS COUNTRY WELL AND SERVED IT TRULY.
Captain Henry Maxwell Inglis, SSR, 14.8.44 (age 20)

ALWAYS MAY THERE BE PEACE. FOR THAT A BRAVE HONEST MAN DIED.
Corporal Wilbert Russell Airhart, RCAC, 14.8.44 (age 35)

HIS LIFE WAS OUR LIGHT AND INSPIRATION.
Trooper Earle Cameron Daubney, 12th MD, 15.8.44 (age 20)

"FREEDOM IS THE POSSESSION OF THOSE ALONE WHO HAVE THE COURAGE TO DEFEND IT."
Sergeant John Angus MacDonald, SDGH, 21.8.44 (age 24)

AWARDED THE BELGIAN CROIX DE GUERRE 1940 WITH PALM. "O VALIANT HEARTS."
Lieutenant Ward Campbell Hughson, CRCE, 26.8.44 (age 23)

HIS COURAGE AND DEVOTION TO DUTY WILL EVER LINGER IN OUR MEMORY OF HIM.
Private Everett Filmore Oakes, CH, 26.8.44 (age 22)

YOU UNTO DEATH WERE FAITHFUL. YOURS IS THE VICTOR'S CROWN.
Private Charles Wallace Bowen, HLIC, 24.9.44 (age 28)

The *Aeneid* is a monument of European literature that has not received the unqualified acclaim accorded to the Homeric poems. Virgil's Roman epic has always drawn the charge of being a triumphalist piece of propaganda commissioned by an emperor, but in the second half of the troubled twentieth century the majestic sadness of the poem and the sympathy it projects for the victims of history have made a deeper impression on readers. The great questions posed by the *Aeneid*—Why do the innocent suffer? Why to achieve necessary and worthy ends must so many lives be lost?—and the story it tells of men and women who do not deserve the cruel fates meted out to them, who press on towards a destination ever receding from view, and who neither control nor fully comprehend the forces driving them, speak to the predicament of the people caught up in the tumult of the 1930s and 1940s. In a poem brimming with memorable, strangely prophetic lines, Juno's avowal as she sows Aeneas's path with the seeds of a long and destructive war, *"If I cannot bend the heavens to my will, I shall unleash the powers of hell,"* anticipates the irrational, hideous ambitions of the dictators who twenty years after one mass slaughter saw fit to launch another with nary a qualm for the misery and death it would bring. To defeat their aims it was necessary for decent human beings to act against the norms of conscience and morality—to fight, to kill, to destroy—in the belief that some greater good required that they do so. The only response that Aeneas can make in the face of inexplicable hardship and suffering, perhaps the only thing that most soldiers could tell themselves, was to endure, to go on, until that greater good was reached. And, as in the *Aeneid*, many never got there.

"FOR HE THAT IS ENTERED INTO HIS REST, HE ALSO HATH CEASED FROM HIS OWN WORKS."
HEB. IV. 10
Private Jacob Enns, CH, 21.7.44 (age 20)

MAY YOU BE AT PEACE NOW, DARLING.
Corporal John Snider, RCCS, 8.8.44 (age 20)

HE HATH DELIVERED MY SOUL IN PEACE FROM THE BATTLE. PSALM LV. 18
Lance Corporal Percy Robert Scott, NS(NB)R, 8.8.44 (age 22)

LET HIS SOUL BE AT EVERLASTING PEACE. HE SERVED HIS COUNTRY AND FULFILLED HIS DUTY.
Private Robert Byers, RCASC, 8.8.44 (age 24)

LOVED IN LIFE, LOVED IN DEATH. SLEEP THE SLEEP OF PEACE. "BE MINDFUL,
O LORD, OF THY SERVANT."
Corporal Philip Peter Biernaskie, CHO, 11.8.44 (age 35)

"LORD, LEAD US IN THE PATHS OF PEACE." HE LIES IN PEACEFUL SLEEP.
HIS MEMORY WE WILL KEEP.
Private Michael Howanyk, CSR, 12.8.44 (age 20)

REST IN PEACE, MY SON. WAR WITH ITS BLOOD AND TEARS WILL NOT TOUCH YOU AGAIN.
Lance Corporal George Edward Spraggett, BCR, 14.8.44 (age 33)

ASLEEP IN ETERNAL PEACE. THE REWARD OF THE VALIANT.
Private Morris George Herbert, CSR, 15.8.44 (age 22)

O GOD, GRANT US SUCH PEACE AS OUR SON WHO SLEEPS WITHIN THIS HALLOWED PLACE.
Bombardier Horace William Knight, RCA, 25.8.44 (age 23)

TRANSLATED FROM THE WARFARE OF THE WORLD INTO THE PEACE OF GOD.
Private Gordon Henry Joseph Burrows, BWC, 26.8.44 (age 21)

THE CONFLICT IS OVER, YOUR DUTY IS DONE. REST IN PEACE, MY SON, MY SON.
Lance Corporal Frederick John Pawsey, RHLI, 29.8.44 (age 21)

Recurrent in the epitaphs is the hope, often the assurance, of untroubled rest. It confers peace upon the fallen, released from the toils of war, and comfort to the survivors in the knowledge that a loved one need suffer no more. It is at once ironic and apt to find the longing for peace, and for an end to suffering, expressed in so many ways in the war cemeteries, themselves some of the most peaceful places on earth. A simple epitaph in Bretteville-sur-Laize echoes a Virgilian passage that bestows peace upon the fallen and those who mourned them:

HIS REST IS WON.
Private Alfred Earl Killins, LSR, 5.8.44 (age 22)

At several stages in the *Aeneid*, Aeneas must come to terms with the past before he can go on to fulfill his destiny. His final, necessary parting from the past comes when he takes his leave of Hector's widow Andromache, who after years of suffering has at last found sanctuary. Married to a former Trojan prince, she still conducts rituals of

Monument to Private Gérard Doré of the Fusiliers Mont-Royal, a young French Canadian soldier who died in the land of his ancestors.

Typical Normandy church spire, near the village of Cully.

The church at Estrées-la-Campagne, in the open fields south of Caen.

The road to Falaise where it runs past the Verrières ridge.

Point 67, the Canadian bastion facing the Verrières ridge.

Graves of the Black Watch soldiers killed in the assault on Verrières ridge.

mourning for her dead husband, and in one of the most affecting moments in the poem she cannot compose her words when she sees in Aeneas's son the likeness of her own child, killed years before when her city was destroyed. *"Vobis parta quies,"* begins Aeneas as he bids farewell to Andromache and her husband, the last living links to the world of his past, *"your rest is won."* It is my duty to forge on, he says, leaving you whose struggles are over to honour the memory of those you have lost, to live the rest of your lives in peace, and to find respite from your sorrows.

WE, WHO LIE HERE, WERE YOUNG: WE TOO LOVED LIFE AND HOME. REMEMBER US.
Trooper Colin Earl Wood, SFR, 12.8.44 (age 22)

JUST IN THE MORNING OF HIS DAY, IN YOUTH AND LOVE, HE DIED.
Private Garfield Ernest Boyce, RRC, 28.8.44 (age 22)

BLOW SOFTLY, BUGLES, FOR OUR BELOVED DEAD WHO DID NOT DIE IN VAIN.
Sergeant William Owen Cartwright, BWC, 21.8.44 (age 20)

HE GAVE HIS LIFE THAT WE MIGHT LIVE FREE FROM WANT AND FEAR.
REMEMBERED BY MOM & DAD
Private William Maurice Duncan, NNSH, 8.7.44 (age 20)

HE GAVE HIS LIFE FOR FREEDOM, THAT OTHERS, AS WELL AS US, MAY LIVE IN PEACE. R.I.P.
Rifleman Benjamin Wilson, RRR, 17.8.44 (age 38)

HE DIED DEFENDING HIS COUNTRY AND FOR THE FREEDOM OF THE WORLD.
Lieutenant Henry Harrison Bennett, CHO, 14.8.44 (age 24)

WILLINGLY HE GAVE HIS ALL THAT PEACE BE RESTORED FOR THOSE HE LOVED.
Lieutenant Milton Howard Boyd, ASHC, 10.8.44 (age 27)

"THINK I, THE ROUND WORLD OVER, WHAT GOLDEN LADS ARE LOW."
Lieutenant Angus George Steel Brown, RCCS, 8.8.44 (age 23)
[A.E. HOUSMAN, LAST POEMS]

As for the fallen, honoured remembrance and peaceful repose are the last gifts that the living can offer to them. The words spoken by Aeneas to Andromache were taken up by the poet and classical scholar A.E. Housman (1859–1936) whose poem *Parta quies* is quoted on the headstone of a Canadian airman buried in Holland. The lines come from a poet famous for his lyrics evoking the love of the countryside, the yearning for home and the familiar, the brevity of youth and of life, and the intensity of youthful emotions and passions. Although Housman does not spring to mind as a war poet, many of his poems meditate on war and the death of young soldiers. The pain of loss was personal, if sublimated, in his poetry. He had lost a brother in the South African War and a nephew on the Somme, and in several of his poems published after the Great War he lamented the nameless soldiers who died in nameless battles. They were the *"fellows that were good and brave and died because they were"*, the ones who had done their duty without a lot of lofty talk and sentiments. There was nothing intrinsically heroic in their deaths, which had not contributed to a glorious feat of arms or won them everlasting renown. A mournful irony pervades these poems, tinged with a grateful respect for the fallen. Housman rued the fact that in a flawed universe the peace and welfare of his country had come from the deaths of these young men, and that the peace of death had been their only release from the torments and madness of war. *Parta quies*, a work of Housman's youth, does not relate to war, but its gentle, dignified words of valediction, chosen by the family of Flight Sergeant John Daniel Williams, embrace all the young soldiers, sailors, and airmen not destined to share in the blessings of peace and the life unmenaced by tyranny which their sacrifice won for others:

> *Good night. Ensured release,*
> *Imperishable peace,*
> *Have these for yours,*
> *While sea abides, and land,*
> *And earth's foundations stand,*
> *And heaven endures.*

FURTHER READING:

Copp, Terry. "Operation 'Spring': An historian's view," *Canadian Military History* 12/1–2 (2003), 63–70.

Durflinger, Serge. "'I regret to inform you. . .' Next-of-kin notification and official condolences—The case of Flight Lieutenant George J. Chequer, RCAF," *Canadian Military History* 9/4 (2000) , 44–56.

Edmondson, John S., and Edmondson, R.D. "The Pawns of War: A personal account of the attack on Verrières Ridge by The South Saskatchewan Regiment, 20 July 1944," *Canadian Military History* 14/4 (2005), 49–66.

Efrati, Carole. "Housman's military epitaphs," *Housman Society Journal* 27 (2001), 79–90.

————. "Housman, Hardy, and the Boer War elegy," *Housman Society Journal* 25 (1999), 73–78.

————. "Housman's price of empire," *Housman Society Journal* 24 (1998), 69–73.

————. "Housman's own Tommy Atkinses," *Housman Society Journal* 21 (1995), 37–39.

Lee, M. Owen. *Fathers and Sons in Virgil's* Aeneid: Tum genitor natum. Albany: State University of New York Press, 1979.

McAndrew, Bill. "The Canadians on Verrières Ridge: A historiographical survey," in: *The Valour and the Horror Revisited*, ed. David J. Bercuson and S.F. Wise. Montreal & Kingston: McGill-Queen's University Press, 1994, pp. 128–152.

Parry, Adam. "The two voices of Virgil's *Aeneid*," in: *Virgil. A Collection of Critical Essays*. Ed. Steele Commager. Englewood Cliffs, N.J.: Prentice-Hall Inc., 1966, pp. 107–123.

Smith, A. Britton. "A FOO at Troteval Farm, 20–21 July 1944," *Canadian Military History* 14/4 (2005), 67–74.

Ziolkowski, Theodore. *Virgil and the Moderns*. Princeton: Princeton University Press, 1993.

List of Abbreviations

UNITS

1st CPB	1st Canadian Parachute Battalion
1st Hussars	—
4th PLDG	4th Princess Louise Dragoon Guards
8th PL(NB)H	8th Princess Louise's (New Brunswick) Hussars
12th MD	12th Manitoba Dragoons
14th CH	14th Canadian Hussars
17th DY	17th Duke of York's Royal Canadian Hussars
48th HC	48th Highlanders of Canada
166th (Nfld.) FA/RA	166th (Newfoundland) Field Artillery, Royal Artillery
AR	Algonquin Regiment
ASHC	Argyll and Sutherland Highlanders of Canada (Princess Louise's)
BCD	British Columbia Dragoons
BCI	Battalion Canadian Infantry
BCR	British Columbia Regiment
BWC	Black Watch (Royal Highland Regiment) of Canada
CAAB	Canadian Anti-Aircraft Battery
CADC	Canadian Army Dental Corps
CAMC	Canadian Army Medical Corps
CBH	Cape Breton Highlanders
CCS	Canadian Chaplain Service
CE	Canadian Engineers
CFA	Canadian Field Artillery
CFC	Canadian Forestry Corps
CGA	Canadian Garrison Artillery
CGG	Canadian Grenadier Guards
CH	Calgary Highlanders
CHO	Cameron Highlanders of Ottawa
CMGC	Canadian Machine Gun Corps
CMR	Canadian Mounted Rifles
CMSC	Corps of Military Staff Clerks
CPB	Canadian Parachute Battalion
CPC	Canadian Provost Corps
CR	Calgary Regiment
CRCE	Corps of Royal Canadian Engineers
CRCEME	Corps of Royal Canadian Electrical and Mechanical Engineers
CSR	Canadian Scottish Regiment
CYR	Carleton and York Regiment
ESR	Essex Scottish Regiment
(FC)B	(French Canadian) Battalion
FGH	Fort Garry Horse
FMR	Fusiliers Mont-Royal
GGFG	Governor General's Foot Guards
GGHG	Governor General's Horse Guards
GLCA	General List Canadian Army
HLIC	Highland Light Infantry of Canada
HPER	Hastings and Prince Edward Regiment
IRC	Irish Regiment of Canada
LER	Loyal Edmonton Regiment
LRSR	Lanark and Renfrew Scottish Regiment
LSH(RC)	Lord Strathcona's Horse (Royal Canadians)
LSR	Lake Superior Regiment
LWR	Lincoln and Welland Regiment
MN	Merchant Navy
NBR	New Brunswick Rangers
NNSH	North Nova Scotia Highlanders
NS(NB)R	North Shore (New Brunswick) Regiment
OR	Ontario Regiment
PPCLI	Princess Patricia's Canadian Light Infantry
PR	Perth Regiment
QOCHC	Queen's Own Cameron Highlanders of Canada
QORC	Queen's Own Rifles of Canada
RA	Royal Artillery
RAF	Royal Air Force
RC	Régiment de la Chaudière
RCA	Royal Canadian Artillery
RCAC	Royal Canadian Armoured Corps
RCAF	Royal Canadian Air Force
RCAMC	Royal Canadian Army Medical Corps
RCAPC	Royal Canadian Army Pay Corps
RCASC	Royal Canadian Army Service Corps
RCCS	Royal Canadian Corps of Signals
RCD	Royal Canadian Dragoons
RCIC	Royal Canadian Infantry Corps
RCNVR	Royal Canadian Naval Volunteer Reserve
RCOC	Royal Canadian Ordnance Corps
RCR	Royal Canadian Regiment
RFC	Royal Flying Corps
RGA	Royal Garrison Artillery
RHLI	Royal Hamilton Light Infantry
RM	Régiment de Maisonneuve
RNR	Royal Newfoundland Regiment
RRC	Royal Regiment of Canada
RRfC	Royal Rifles of Canada
RRR	Regina Rifle Regiment
R22R	Royal 22ème Régiment
RWR	Royal Winnipeg Regiment
SAR	South Alberta Regiment
SDGH	Stormont, Dundas and Glengarry Highlanders
SFR	Sherbrooke Fusiliers Regiment
SHC	Seaforth Highlanders of Canada
SLI	Saskatoon Light Infantry
SSR	South Saskatchewan Regiment
SSTCA	Special Service Troops Canadian Army
TRR	Three Rivers Regiment
TSR	Toronto Scottish Regiment
WG	Winnipeg Grenadiers
WNSR	West Nova Scotia Highlanders
WR	Westminster Regiment
WRCNS	Women's Royal Canadian Naval Service

DECORATIONS:

DCM	Distinguished Conduct Medal
DFC	Distinguished Flying Cross
DFM	Distinguished Flying Medal
DSO	Distinguished Service Order
MBE	Member of the British Empire
MC	Military Cross
MM	Military Medal
VC	Victoria Cross

Index of names

McCorry, Pte Edward George, 278
McCoy, F/S Alfred Ernest, 156
McCulloch, F/O William Donald, 157
McCutcheon, F/O Ernest Borden, 136
McDermott, Lt George Alfred, 166
McDonald, Pte Alexander Falconer, 67
McDonald, Pte Donald Roderick, 162
McElhoes, LCpl Spencer Kay, 256
McEwen, Pte Raymond, 16
McFarlane, Spr Arthur William, 289
McFarlane, Pte John Charles, 21
McGarrity, Cpl Joseph Jerome, 171
McGill, F/O Jack Lawrie, 87
McGill, Wren Margaret Airlie, 186
McGinn, Gnr Francis, 229
McGolrick, F/O George Gordon, 130
McGreer, Pte William Gilbert Raymond, 64
McGuigan, Sgt William Henry, 118
McGuire, F/L Michael Kidston, 169
McHaffie-Gow, Cpl James, 158
McIntee, Cpl Douglas Haig, 69
McIntosh, Pte Lionel Arthur, 142
McIvor, Pte Thomas, 37
McKague, Capt James McLean, 101
McKay, Pte John Albert, 282
McKay, Pte John David, 282
McKay, Gnr Murray Charles, 99
McKee, Tpr Francis Ross, 144
McKee, F/O Terrence Velleau, 85
McKellar, Pte Donald Arthur, 275
McKenna, Pte Patrick Joseph, 253
McKillop, Pte Charles, 67
McKinlay, Tpr George Nugent, 16
McKinley, Pte Albert George, 157
McKinnon, Gnr Donald Lachlan, 54
McLean, Pte Alexander John, 176
McLean, F/S Ernest Caldwell, 117
McLean, Pte George Irvine, 161
McLean, Spr Keith Mabin, 176
McLean, Pte Malcolm, 66
McLean, Pte Norman, 37
McLean, Sgt William James, 19
McLeod, S/L Henry Wallace, 172
McLintock, F/O William Stewart, 105
McMillan, Pte Allan Robert, 186
McMillan, F/O Donald James, 89
McMillan, W/O Glen Allen, 125
McMillan, Pte Robert Stephens, 184
McNabb, Cpl Alexander, 175
McNaughton, S/L Ian George Armour, 69, 134
McNeil, Pte Fred Gordon, 68
McNeily, Lt James Rogerson, 110
McPherson, F/O Coran Cyman, 129
McQuillan, Pte Cyril, 31
McQuitty, Pte Lewis Neil, 164
McRae, Spr Donald Lloyd, 87
McRae, Rfn Jarvis Alloun, 174
McRitchie, Rfn Fred William, 172
McRoberts, Lt Bruce Herbert, 13
McWhirter, Sgt Robert Edward, 173
McWilliams, Pte Gilbert, 287
McWilliams, Pte Ira, 287
Meers, Pte Norman Francis, 159

Melanson, Cpl Fernand Joseph Hector, 101
Melanson, Pte Wilfred, 183
Melling, Pte Gordon, 76
Melling, Pte Samuel, 76
Melnyk, Pte John, 155
Meltz, Bdr George, 14-15
Menzies, Pte James Kitchener, 83
Mercer, Cpl Albert George, 19
Merchant, Pte Vernon Keith, 63
Merritt, Pte Neale Warren, 177
Messing, Rfn Earl James Elliot, 183
Messum, F/O Stanley Ernest, 185
Michaeud, Pte Gérard, 282
Michaud, Pte Joseph, 66
Milburn, Pte Robert Cameron, 13
Millaire, Pte Gérard, 282
Millard, LCpl Hugh Maitland, 178
Miller, P/O Allan Bernard, 265
Miller, Sgt Glen, 185
Miller, F/S Ronald William, 124
Miller, Pte Stanley John, 254
Mills, Pte Clive Austin, 59
Mills, Pte Thomas, 140
Mills, Pte William Stanley, 53
Millson, F/S Harold Roy, 158
Milne, F/O Douglas Stewart, 159
Minion, LBdr Donald Laverne, 174
Misiurka, Gnr Paul John, 235
Miskow, Sgt Wesley Williams, 24
Mitchell, Lt Eric Lawson, 156
Mitchell, Pte Ernest Vernon, 76
Mitchell, Pte John David, 175
Mitchell, Sgt John McKenzie, 86
Mogalki, W/O Roy Edwards, 120
Mohlman, LCpl Douglas Earl, 89
Mohlman, Pte Robert Edward, 89
Molesworth, Pte Harry Oliver, 224
Monaco, Pte Ernest Guiseppe, 243
Monson, Pte Harold Roscoe, 229
Montgomery, Pte Donald, 183
Mooney, Rev Thomas Edmund, 149
Moor, F/O Maurice Gordon, 126
Moore, Sgt Arthur Frederick, 292
Moore, Pte Charles Douglas, 63
Moore, Pte Eric Herbert, 227
Moore, Sgt William John, 160
Moore, Pte William Joseph, 110
Moores, F/O Douglas Keith, 289
Moran, F/O Walter Franklin, 174
Morehouse, Gnr Winston Hart, 184
Morey, F/S Wesley, 111
Morgan, Rfn James Brisbane, 19
Morgan, Lt John Lawrence, 59
Morgan, W/O Rhys Hallam, 157
Morgan, Pte William Thomas, 94
Morley, F/S George Allen, 127
Morris, Tpr Willard James, 106
Morris, W/O William Penri, 163
Morrison, P/O Alfred Hector, 177
Morrison, Cpl Benjamin, 51
Morrison, Pte Donald Rhyburn, 23
Morrison, Pte John Gilbert, 162
Morrison, Sgt John Murray, 124
Morrison, P/O Martin, 166
Morrison, Pte Murdoch Ian Leslie, 174
Morrison, F/O William Harold, 288
Morrissette, Lt Joseph Raymond Yves, 203

Morrow, Lt William Waddell, 163
Mortimer, F/O George Alexander, 88
Morton, Cpl Alfred Thomas, 16
Morton, Pte Arthur, 255
Morton, Tpr Robert Lawrence, 16
Mosher, Cpl Sydney Guy, 86
Moss, Pte Charles Edward, 102
Mossop, Sgt Matthew Hudson, 36
Mount, Sgmn Phillip James, 168
Mountford, Lt Kenneth William, 97
Moyer, LCpl Abraham Alexander, 183
Muir, Sgt John, 61
Muir, Pte Roy James, 86
Mulholland, Pte James, 38
Muller, Lt Kenneth George, 144
Mullen, Pte John William, 227
Mullins, Lt Frederick Ernest, 153
Mullis, Pte James Robert, 31
Munn, Rfn James Hector, 144
Munn, P/O William Forsythe, 156
Munro, Pte Hughie, 293
Munroe, Cpl Hugh Archibald, 15
Murcell, Pte William Baines, 44
Murdock, P/O Billie Herman, 164
Murphy, W/O Edward Warren, 123
Murphy, LCpl John Ralph, 155
Murphy, Pte Robert Davidson, 44
Murray, Sgt Christopher Desmond, 142
Murray, Pte Daniel James, 253
Murray, Sgt John James, 82
Murray, CSM Joseph Henry O'Leary Louis, 166
Murray, LCpl Joseph Irwin, 150
Murray, Sgt William George, 13
Mydaski, W/O Stanley, 239
Myers, Tpr Edward, 252
Mylles, Rfn Allan Robert Lawson, 114
Myrick, P/O John Frederick, 125
Nahornyk, Pte William, 237
Nash, Pte Ferdinand Leonard, 85
Naylor, F/L Ralph Edward, 80
Neale, Cpl Charles, 77
Neault, Pte Romeo, 19
Needham, LSgt James Gerard, 248
Neff, Tpr Howard Wilson, 81
Neilly, Pte Roy Wilmert, 88
Nelson, Pte Leonard, 229
Nelson, Rfn Raymond Morse, 19
Nenonen, Pte Olavi, 244
Newcombe, W/O Jack Dunbar, 120
Newman, F/S Davey William, 85
Newman, Pte Walter, 140
Neyrinck de Croy, Pte George Eugene Leopold, 281
Nichols, Pte Leroy Charles, 58
Nichols, Pte Samuel Norman, 265
Nicholson, Pte Basil, 77
Nickerson, P/O Roland Otis, 85
Nilsson, Gnr Ivan Rayburn, 235
Nilsson, Spr Ture Adolph, 240
Noah, Pte Alphonsus Francis, 172
Noakes, W/O Daniel Harmer, 79
Noble, Cpl James Edward, 63
Noel, Pte Joseph, 282
Noftall, Pte Frederick Ann, 275
Norman, Pte Franklin Crosby, 184
Normandin, Capt Jean Pierre, 212